T0330050

EDUCATION AND DEVELOPMENT IN CENTRAL AMERICA AND THE LATIN CARIBBEAN

Bristol Studies in Comparative and International Education

Series Editors: **Michael Crossley**, Emeritus Professor of Comparative and International Education, University of Bristol, UK, **Leon Tikly**, UNESCO Chair in Inclusive, Good Quality Education, University of Bristol, UK, **Angeline M. Barrett**, Reader in Education, University of Bristol, UK, and **Julia Paulson**, Reader in Education, Peace and Conflict, University of Bristol, UK

The series critically engages with education and international development from a comparative and interdisciplinary perspective. It emphasises work that bridges theory, policy and practice, supporting early career researchers and the publication of studies led by researchers in and from the Global South.

Also available in the series

Transitioning Vocational Education and Training in Africa
A Social Skills Ecosystem Perspective
By **VET AFRICA 4.0 COLLECTIVE**

Decolonizing Education for Sustainable Futures
Edited by **Yvette Hutchinson, Artemio Arturo Cortez Ochoa, Julia Paulson** and **Leon Tikly**

Assembling Comparison
Understanding Education Policy Through Mobilities and Assemblage
By **Steven Lewis** and **Rebecca Spratt**

Find out more at

bristoluniversitypress.co.uk/
bristol-studies-in-comparative-and-international-education

Forthcoming in the series

Find out more at

bristoluniversitypress.co.uk/
bristol-studies-in-comparative-and-international-education

Find out more at
bristoluniversitypress.co.uk/
bristol-studies-in-comparative-and-international-education

EDUCATION AND DEVELOPMENT IN CENTRAL AMERICA AND THE LATIN CARIBBEAN

Global Forces and Local Responses

Edited by
D. Brent Edwards Jr., Mauro C. Moschetti,
Pauline Martin, and Ricardo Morales-Ulloa

BRISTOL
UNIVERSITY
PRESS

First published in Great Britain in 2024 by

Bristol University Press
University of Bristol
1–9 Old Park Hill
Bristol
BS2 8BB
UK
t: +44 (0)117 374 6645
e: bup-info@bristol.ac.uk

Details of international sales and distribution partners are available at bristoluniversitypress.co.uk

© Bristol University Press 2024

British Library Cataloguing in Publication Data
A catalogue record for this book is available from the British Library

ISBN 978-1-5292-3171-7 hardcover
ISBN 978-1-5292-3173-1 ePub
ISBN 978-1-5292-3174-8 ePdf

The right of D. Brent Edwards Jr., Mauro C. Moschetti, Pauline Martin, and Ricardo Morales-Ulloa
to be identified as editors of this work has been asserted by them in accordance with the Copyright,
Designs and Patents Act 1988.

Cover design: Blu Inc
Front cover art: Fredy Granillo
Bristol University Press uses environmentally responsible print partners.
Printed and bound in Great Britain by CPI Group (UK) Ltd, Croydon, CR0 4YY

FSC
www.fsc.org
MIX
Paper | Supporting
responsible forestry
FSC® C013604

Contents

Series Editor Preface

This book brings together a combination of local and international scholars who have long been engaged in educational research, policy and practice in Central America and the Latin Caribbean (CALC). This is a region characterized by precarity and insecurity, stemming from social, economic, and political structures that are seen to 'deeply entrench patterns of inequality'. We are pleased to support this work in a region where there is scant English language literature on the challenges faced by education, the dynamics of global forces and the 'local efforts that seek to address, mitigate and even counteract these forces'.

Chapters in Education and Development in Central America and the Latin Caribbean cover all of the Spanish speaking countries of the region: Guatemala, Honduras, El Salvador, Nicaragua, Costa Rica, Panama, Cuba, the Dominican Republic, and Puerto Rico. This, when combined with a common and challenging theoretical framework rooted in international political economy, provides a unique focus and distinctive analytical strengths. Collectively, the authors critically examine how education is both challenging and contributing to inequalities and exclusion in the face of global and local pressures. This is informed by original empirical research, the shared theoretical frame, decolonial influences and insights derived from deep local engagement with educational policy and practice.

We hope that this timely contribution to the Bristol Studies in Comparative and International Education series will stimulate further transformative research within the CALC region, contribute to pertinent theoretical advances and make helpful and informed contributions to ongoing policy and practice.

Michael Crossley
Emeritus Professor of Comparative and International Education
University of Bristol

List of Figures and Tables

Figures

Tables

Notes on Contributors

Felix Alvarado has a PhD in Public Administration (SUNY Albany) and an MD (Universidad de San Carlos de Guatemala). For 9 years president of Vitruvian Consulting LLC. He was previously with FHI 360 and the Academy for International Development managing international education projects in Guatemala and El Salvador, as well as designing projects in countries in Latin America, Africa, and Asia. In 2015 he was the founder of the Online Learning Initiative.

Matthew Aruch, PhD, is the Director of Indigenous Conservation Programs with the International Conservation Fund of Canada, in addition to being an at-large board member of the Online Learning Initiative (OLI). Previously, he was the Director of Global Education at EARTHDAY.ORG and former Assistant Director of the Science, Technology, and Society Program at the University of Maryland. He also coordinates the OLI research team.

Carolina Bodewig studied social communication at the Central American University 'José Simeón Cañas' (UCA) in El Salvador and holds a master's in research and education development from the Ibero-American University in Mexico City. She is based in El Salvador and works in educational research, advocacy on educational policy, and teacher professional development. She works at ConTextos designing teacher training programmes and as a monitoring and evaluation coordinator. She also works with the UCA in the master's in educational policy and evaluation programme.

Xavier Bonal is Professor of Sociology at the Universitat Autònoma de Barcelona (UAB) and Special Professor of Education and International Development at the University of Amsterdam (UvA). He is the director of the Globalization, Education and Social Policies (GEPS) research group at the UAB and is coordinator of the GLOBED Project, an Erasmus Mundus Master on Education Policies for Global Development. He has been member of the EU Network of Experts in Social Sciences and Education (NESSE) and is a member of the Editorial Board of several international journals of education policies and educational development. He has written articles in national and international journals, and is the author of several books on sociology of education, education policy and globalization, education and development. He has worked as a consultant for international organizations such as UNESCO, UNICEF, the European Commission, and the Council of Europe.

Alejandro Caravaca is a PhD candidate in education at the Autonomous University of Barcelona and holds an MSc in social policy, work, and welfare from the same university. He teaches undergraduate courses on educational policy and inequalities, and is a member of the Education and Gender–UAB research and innovation group. He has worked in several research projects on: (a) education policy in Central America and the Caribbean; (b) the historical role of the World Bank in education policy-making processes; (c) gender and sexuality studies in education in Spanish academia; and (d) the configuration of multicultural identities in Catalonia. He has produced reports for international organizations such as Education International and the UNESCO Institute for Higher Education in Latin America and the Caribbean (UNESCO-IESALC), where he worked as a junior policy analyst. His main research interests are located at the intersection between higher education, education policy, comparative and international education, and gender studies.

Rachel Dyl is a Master of Arts candidate in International Development Studies with a concentration in International Education at the George Washington University Elliott School of International Affairs. Her research interests include democracy and governance, intercultural/bilingual education, rural education, and human rights issues in the Latin America region. She currently works at Freedom House as an intern on the Latin America and Caribbean team, and is a part-time communications specialist for the Education Development Center.

D. Brent Edwards Jr. is Graduate Chair of the Department of Educational Foundations and Professor of Theory and Methodology in the Study of Education at the University of Hawaii. His work focuses on: (a) the global governance of education; and (b) education policy, politics, and political economy, with a focus on low-income countries. Within these two research lines, he has focused on investigating the rise of global education policies and the influence of international organizations in education reform. Geographically, these areas of focus have led to research primarily in Latin America (Mexico, Colombia, El Salvador, Honduras, and the Dominican Republic), Southeast Asia (Cambodia, Indonesia, and the Philippines), and Africa (Zambia). In addition to publishing regularly in journals in the fields of education policy and comparative and international education, he is on the advisory board for the *Comparative Education Review*. His recent books include *The Trajectory of Global Education Policy: Community-Based Management in El Salvador and the Global Reform Agenda* and *Global Education Policy, Impact Evaluations, and Alternatives: The Political Economy of Knowledge Production*, both with Palgrave Macmillan. He also has two forthcoming books, both with Routledge: *Globalization, Privatization, and the State: Contemporary Education Reform in Post-colonial Contexts* and Rethinking World Bank Influence: *Governance Reforms and the Ritual Aid Dance in Indonesia*. He is currently the Principal Investigator for a three-year, $900,000 grant-funded project entitled 'Crisis Management for Disaster Risk Reduction in Education Systems: Learning from the Elaboration and Integration of Technology-Focused Strategies in El Salvador, Honduras, and Colombia'. Previously, he was awarded Fulbright Funding for his work in El Salvador. He has produced reports for international organizations such as USAID, UNESCO, and Education International, and was a consultant for the World Bank. He received his PhD in international education policy from the University of Maryland.

Changha Lee is an educator and researcher. She is an expert on the effect of changes in the economy for education systems and has extensive experience with teacher policies in Cuba, Bangladesh, Indonesia, and Paraguay. In 2016–2017 she was a research fellow for Save the Children US. She is the recipient of multiple merit-based awards, including the KOICA Scholarship for Graduate Studies (2012–2013) and the Korean Government Scholarship Program for Study Overseas (2014–2016). She holds a PhD in international education policy from the University of Maryland.

Mariana León serves as Academic Vice President and member of the Board of Directors at Quality Leadership University (QLU), a private university in Panama City, Panama. She holds a Doctorate in Education from Johns Hopkins University and an MBA from Florida International University. She has published on transformational leadership in private higher education in Panama and on multicultural identity perceptions of high school students in Panama. She is a member of Global Shapers, a youth leadership initiative of the World Economic Forum, and of the Asociación Panameña de Ejecutivos de Empresa (APEDE), where she has served as President of the Free Enterprise Commission.

Michael C. Lisman, EdD, is a former board member of the Online Learning Initiative. He is currently Education Team Leader for the Bureau of Latin American and the Caribbean (LAC) at USAID.

Kate Maloney Williams is a doctoral student in international education policy at the University of Maryland. She holds an MSc in Media, Communication and Development from the London School of Economics and Political Science. She is passionate about helping transform 21st century education across global communities, particularly for better technology integration, critical consciousness, and online learning. She investigates how digital technologies change literacies and lived experiences – and how classrooms can adapt accordingly. Her work has been dedicated to supporting evidence-based policy making, implementation, and sustainable technology and media literacy interventions. She has worked in several countries, supporting various stages of business development, proposal management, award compliance, technical assistance, professional editing, and mixed methods evaluation.

Pauline Martin worked with the Central American University (UCA) in El Salvador for 23 years as a professor and researcher. For eight years, she was the director of the master's program in education policy and evaluation. She has extensive experience with pre-service and in-service teacher training, graduate-level teaching, research, and project coordination. She is the coordinator for the Education in Risk and Conflict Situations programme at the UCA, a multiphase, multifunded research project on the influence of gangs in schools. In addition to numerous publications in Spanish and English, and participation in education projects with GIZ, USAID, Catholic Relief Services, and the Salvadoran Ministry of Education, she is presently an independent consultant on topics of policy analysis, nonstate education, evaluation, curriculum development, and gender in education.

Loida M. Martínez Ramos is Full Professor at the Department of Graduate Studies of the University of Puerto Rico, Río Piedras campus (UPRRP), where she teaches foundation of education courses. She obtained an undergraduate degree in philosophy from the UPRRP and a master's degree in Education from Boston University. She also obtained a doctoral degree in cultural diversity and curriculum reform from the University of Massachusetts at Amherst. As director of the research unit of the Commission of Women's Affairs Governor's Office, she was director of the Collaborative Project on Gender Educational Equity at the beginning of the 1990s. From 1994 to 2000 she was co-founder and first coordinator of the Interdisciplinary Center for Research on Gender at the Inter American University, Metro Campus. She has collaborated with the women and gender studies programme of the UPRRP, as well as in the creation of the first master's degree in women and gender studies at the Inter American University. She was director of the Department of Graduate Studies at the College of Education of UPRRP

(2006–2010) and Dean of Academic Affairs of the same College (2015–2018). She has taught a course entitled 'Knowledge and Gender: Implications for Education' at the graduate level since 2003 and a course entitled 'Gender, Knowledge and School' at the undergraduate level since 2015. She has served as director and committee member of several dissertations related to gender, sexuality and public policy.

Shue-kei Joanna Mok is a PhD student in international education policy at the University of Maryland. Her research interests and experience centre on curriculum development, authentic arts integration, and global citizenship education. She is currently a network facilitator who provides online teaching and learning support to public school teachers in Prince George's County, Maryland.

Ricardo Morales-Ulloa holds a doctorate in educational sciences from the Universidad de Oporto, Portugal and a master's in public policy from the German University of Administrative Sciences Speyer, Germany, in addition to completing doctoral coursework in education and society at the Universidad Autónoma de Barcelona. He is also a professor, researcher and director of the Cooperation and Development Institute at the Universidad Pedagógica Nacional Francisco Morazán in Honduras. From a critical perspective, he has studied education policy developments in Honduras for the last 30 years, in particular considering the global forces and the national and local interpretations that give them meaning, and their impact on social inequality. His latest publication in the *RASE Journal* in Spain is an article with his colleagues from the Universidad de Barcelona about life and study conditions of students from indigenous backgrounds.

Celia Morán holds a master's in education from the Universidad Internacional Iberoaméricana de México. She has led or supported human development activities, including competency-based learning, training in intercultural education, communication, gender, human rights and civic education, and violence prevention. Since 2012, she has been El Salvador's Education Officer at the Pestalozzi Children Foundation, where she has had experience of project design and oversight, monitoring, evaluation, and stakeholder management. She has 25 years of experience combining teaching, research, management, and consulting. Her professional work has been primarily in Central America, but also includes programme implementation in Equatorial Guinea, where she helped to reform the national curriculum. She has worked with international nongovernmental organizations, educational institutions, governments, the private sector, and civil society organizations.

Mauro C. Moschetti is Assistant Professor at the Department of Theories of Education and Social Pedagogy of the Autonomous University of Barcelona and Senior Researcher at the Department of Sociology in the context of the ERC-funded project 'ReformED' (GA-680172). His research is located at the intersection of policy sociology, sociology of education, education policy, and comparative and international education. His work has focused on education privatization, public-private partnerships, market policies in education, and the political economy of education policy in low- and middle-income countries (particularly in Latin America). He is currently one of the coordinators of a three-year $900,000 grant-funded project entitled 'Crisis Management for Disaster Risk Reduction in Education Systems: Learning from the Elaboration and Integration of Technology-Focused Strategies in El Salvador, Honduras, and Colombia'. Previously, he has worked in R+D+I competitive research projects funded by different European and Latin American research agencies that have allowed him to analyse processes of education reform in different national and subnational contexts. Over the years, he has collaborated with various educational and research organizations, including Education International, UNESCO, the Global Partnership for Education, and the Open Societies Foundation, and has held permanent, research, and visiting positions at the University of San Andrés (Argentina), the University of the North (Colombia), Torcuato Di Tella University (Argentina), the University of Buenos Aires (Argentina), and the University of Girona (Spain).

Vanessa Pietras is an instructor and educational consultant in Pennsylvania. She holds three master's degrees: an MEd in international education from Columbia University, New York; an MA in foreign languages and literatures from North Carolina State University; and an MSS in international relations from the National University of Costa Rica. Having previously worked at the United Nations, she now focuses her research on Costa Rica and the implications of its socialist/capitalist cosmovision on education. Her recent work is published in the *Anuario de Estudios Centroamericanos*.

Tobias Roberts has lived in El Salvador and Guatemala for the past 15 years. For the first ten of those years, he worked with the Mennonite Central Committee (MCC), supporting different local organizations in grassroots development projects in rural areas. While living in the Maya Ixil region of Guatemala (northern Quiché department), he had the opportunity to work with the Ixil University during its early years. This unique educational project has created an alternative university in an effort to reclaim ancestral knowledge of the Maya Ixil people and reject the imposition of Western educational norms and epistemologies. During the past five years, he and his family have lived and worked as farmers on a small, agro-ecological farm in the mountains of northern El Salvador, where they have worked with their neighbors developing a community ecotourism and organic agriculture project. With regard to institutional affiliation, he belongs only to the land that is shared with his community, though in the past he has worked with the Ixil University and the Mennonite Central Committee. He is also a founding member of the "Colectivo Utz´ K´aslimaal", an educational organization in Guatemala that engages in diverse efforts to promote and make visible Mayan expressions and articulations of The Good Life (Buen Vivir).

Kristin Rosekrans, PhD, is an education researcher and evaluator who has worked in international education development globally for over 20 years with governments, universities, civil society organizations, donor agencies, and international nongovernmental organizations. Her work weaves together policy decision making and improving access to quality education for underserved populations in the US, Central America, and Africa. She also examines how instructional policy and teaching practices can create supportive environments for students to foment agency and social incorporation. Her work and publications focus on bilingual/ multilingual education, teacher preparation, action research, and instructional policy implementation.

Wim Savenije is the lead researcher at the 'Education in Risk and Conflict Situations' research programme at the Central American University (UCA) in El Salvador. His other research interests are student and street gangs or 'maras' in Central America, social violence prevention, and community policing. He is author of *Maras y Barras: Pandillas y violencia juvenil en los barrios marginales de Centroamérica* (FLACSO El Salvador, 2009), *Persiguiendo Seguridad. Acercamiento de la Policía a las Comunidades con Problemas de Inseguridad en Centroamérica* (FLACSO El Salvador, 2010), and various articles in the *Journal of Latin American Studies* and the *ECA Estudios Centroamericano*s.

Katharine Summers is a master of arts candidate in international development studies at the George Washington University Elliott School of International Affairs. Her research interests and professional experience have focused on the intersection of migration and education challenges in Latin America, particularly for transnational students. She currently works as a development practitioner for a small, woman-owned consulting firm.

Nanette Archer Svenson is a scholar and consultant with over 25 years of experience in education and global development. She is based in Panama and currently serves as Executive Director of the Centro de Investigación Educativa, the country's first think tank dedicated to education research. For the past two decades, she has worked and consulted for the United

Nations, as well as other international organizations, governments and various universities. From 2011 to 2017, she directed the Panama programming for Tulane University's Global Development Master's. Prior to this, she worked to establish the UNDP Regional Centre for Latin America and the Caribbean in Panama City, and headed its research and knowledge management efforts. She holds a PhD in international development from Tulane, an MBA from the Instituto de Estudios Superiores de la Empresa in Barcelona, and a BA from Stanford University. Her publications on global development and education in emerging regions include two books, numerous chapters and articles, and a recent documentary.

Preface

This book has emerged from the long-term engagement of the editors in research on Central America and the Latin Caribbean (CALC). There are other books about education in this region, but they are relatively few in number, and they tend not to address the issues of central concern here – namely, the way that education policy and its enactment is the result of the interaction of global forces, national actors, and local responses. Put differently, research on education in the CALC region has tended to shy away from looking explicitly at the way that education is shaped by larger political-economic forces. And, moreover, the extant scholarship has shied away from taking the additional step of interpreting global-local dynamics in relation to the dialectic of the state and capitalism. What we have in mind here is how education reform is central to resolving tensions that emerge as states and other actors seek to manage threats (for example, relating to the legitimacy of prevailing political and economic systems) that result from states' embeddedness in the global capitalist economy.

The questions that guide this volume derive from the above observations. The chapter authors examine a variety of education policy themes, ranging from community-based management to decentralization, privatization, digital technologies, gender inequities, gang influence, peer bullying, and sexual violence, among others. In all cases, however, the chapters are concerned with rooting their analysis in a consideration of how the case of interest is influenced by larger political-economic forces. This is then followed, in the cross-case analyses (presented in the final two chapters), by an explicit interest in explaining whether, how, and to what extent the development and implementation of education policy in the CALC region connects with the dialectic between the state and capitalism.

Thus, to restate, in addition to making visible what is often left out of view – that is, the multilevel politics behind education policies – a primary goal of this volume is to make obvious that which is typically unacknowledged or insufficiently addressed in research on education in CALC: the extent to which education, in its reform and implementation (or lack thereof), is inextricably linked to and constrained by tensions and incentives produced as a result of the relationship between the state and the global capitalist economy. A key insight of the volume is that education not only helps to resolve or reduce tensions between the state and capitalism, but also that the ways in which these tensions are resolved create new opportunities for a range of international actors to insert themselves into education reform dynamics in the region. As shown in this volume, involvement by these actors, together with counterparts from state agencies and (less frequently) local organizations, then proceeds − typically while ignoring or without input from teachers, students, and families − until a new crisis emerges, at which point the cycle repeats itself. Destiny in the region seems to take pleasure in repetition.

An additional, and perhaps larger, purpose of this volume is to encourage readers to feel unsatisfied with the depths of the insights described above. On the one hand, the kinds of critical insights mentioned above are essential for understanding the difficult position in which education policy in the CALC region finds itself, nested as it is at the intersection of agendas, actors, and activism from multiple levels, ranging from the global to the local. On the other hand, these insights, while crucial, are primarily concerned with *how* prevailing political, economic, social, and cultural systems work and reinforce one another as they respond to the incentives at the heart of the state-capital dialectic. The next step that needs to be taken, and the proposition with which this book concludes, is that building a more just and equitable world (including through education and 'development') requires an understanding of the systems and logics upon which modern states and capitalism are, in turn, constructed. The point here is that future scholarship on the region should go beyond a critique of the current political-economic order to examine the broader foundations of thought that have guided the development of − and the belief in − the systems of Western rationality, modern states, neoclassical economics, global governance, and education. In other words, what should be explored is a decolonial approach to unpacking the foundations of modernity, for it is these foundations of thought out of which those discriminatory and destructive practices and traditions (relating, for example, to racism, sexism, patriarchy, Christianity, environmental degradation, and epistemicide) have grown that continue to affect the peoples of the CALC region, both generally and through education. We see the present volume as one step in this direction.

PART I

Introduction, Context, and Framework

Neglect of Central America and the Latin Caribbean

*D. Brent Edwards Jr., Mauro C. Moschetti, Pauline Martin,
and Ricardo Morales-Ulloa*

Thomas Skidmore and Peter Smith, well-known historians of Latin America, characterized the minimal attention that Central America has received from scholars. From their perspective, neglect of Central America:

> is partly due to the relative paucity of archives, libraries, and research centers in the nations of the isthmus. It is partly due to the smallness of the individual countries, which makes them appear less significant than Argentina, Brazil, or Mexico. And it is also due to the common assumption that the countries of Central America are backward: the least developed area in a developing world. Dominated by dictators, the 'banana republics' of the isthmus were viewed as sleepy relics of the past. (Skidmore and Smith, 2001, p 316)

Though their comments were directed at the lack of attention from US scholars, this argument is at least (if not more) relevant for scholars from other regions that are even farther removed (geographically, economically, etc.) than North America. And though these comments do not name the countries and colonial territories of the Latin Caribbean, they are no less applicable there. Indeed, as Allahar argues with regard to the Spanish-speaking Caribbean, not only is this region neglected by academics, but this neglect 'is synonymous with erasure and constitutes a major obstacle for anyone wishing to develop a truly comprehensive understanding of the entire region' (2005, p 126). As will be further explained later on, the present volume seeks to make a contribution to the scholarship on these regions – Central America and the

Latin Caribbean (CALC) – by drawing attention to the global and local forces that influence the relationship between education and development.

First, however, it is important to underscore the fact that, despite relative academic neglect, the region has been, and continues to be, important in numerous ways. In other words, while 'Central America was [historically] not a source of great wealth' and while it 'received correspondingly little attention from the Spanish crown', its perception as a source of wealth changed in the 19th century, as further explained in Chapter 2 of this volume (Skidmore and Smith, 2001, p 319). In the post-independence period (after the mid-1800s), international banana and mining corporations, for example, began to enrich themselves (Coatsworth, 1994), a trend which would continue to the present day. In the post-Second World War period, the CALC region was also central to Cold War politics, to countering the tide of communism, and to 'promoting democracy' (Diamond, 1992). The last years of the Cold War also coincided with – and helped to propel – the integration of CALC into the global economy in the 1980s and 1990s (Robinson, 2003). The last decades of the 20th century also witnessed an explosion of development aid, the intervention of international financial institutions, and the growth of nongovernmental organizations during and after the revolutionary conflicts that wracked the region in the 1980s (Sollis, 1995).

More contemporary examples of interest in the CALC region and its relevance more broadly can also be offered. There has been, for example, a consistent focus by the US government on the 'Northern Triangle' of Central America (Guatemala, Honduras, and El Salvador) in an attempt to create jobs, develop workplace skills, increase entrepreneurship, and mitigate the effects of climate crises – all in order to stem the migration that flows from the region towards the US (Kitroeff and Shear, 2021; USAID, n.d.). On this later point, the contribution of migrant workers to the US economy should arguably also be included in the discussion of CALC's centrality to international political-economic dynamics. Workers from this region have been incentivized to leave their home countries in search of higher wages, due in no small part to the history of foreign influence in economic and political terms (Gonzalez, 2001). Indeed, this transnational phenomenon is, in many ways, a legacy of Cold War intervention by the US (see Chapter 2). In a cruel twist, the reverse trend of deportation back to Central America and its consequences for both the emergence of gangs and the increase in US funding for 'mano dura' (strong hand) public security measures should not be overlooked (Wolf, 2017; see also Savenije, this volume Chapter 7).

Investment from another major world power has also been evident since 2000, namely from China (Wise, 2020). To give one example, in 2014, Chinese banks loaned $22.1 billion to Latin American governments, a figure which exceeds the total lending of the World Bank and the Inter-American Development Bank combined (Dollar, 2017). The attention from China is unlikely to wane any time soon as it seeks to secure new markets for its products, to obtain key energy, mining, and agricultural resources, and to strengthen and tighten lasting diplomatic ties (that displace Taiwan; Bland and Fredrick, 2017; Wintgens, 2017).

Additionally, the tense relationship between Cuba and the US since Fidel Castro's successful socialist revolution in 1959 has been central to the region's political dynamics (see Lee, this volume Chapter 12). Also in the Latin Caribbean, the centrality of international tourism and an export-oriented economy (the latter of which is also relevant for Central America) can be underscored in relation to the Dominican Republic. Finally, the neocolonial relationship between the US and the territory of Puerto Rico should not be overlooked (see Martínez Ramos, this volume Chapter 14). These are just a few of the many examples that could be invoked.

Above all, the foregoing discussion demonstrates the importance of being attentive to international political-economic forces when considering the position and politics in which Central America is embedded. Crucially for the present volume, this assertion also extends to the realm of education, which is one of the primary areas of state responsibility. Indeed, it is out of the recognition of the dynamics briefly sketched earlier (and their implications for education) that the genesis for this book has emerged. Each of the editors of this volume has 15+ years of experience with the research and literature on education in CALC. Over this time, our perspective has come to mirror that of Allahar (2005) and Skidmore and Smith (2001), as noted earlier. We have observed a dearth of scholarship that approaches education and education policy as nested between the global and the local, as affecting and affected by the larger political-economic trends and forces shape the development experience of the region. This gap in research and scholarly attention leads to two consequences: first, a lack of (or a simplistic) understanding of the dynamics that confront the region generally and its education systems specifically; and, second, a lack of insight into the contextualized solutions to educational problems that are being pursued by a variety of actors.

The present volume responds by bringing together scholars who are either from the region or have long-term engagement there. The chapters that follow look explicitly at a range of education policies (described further below) that have emerged in the CALC region, with the analyses presented being the result of research that has been guided by an explicit concern with the relationship between international influence, national politics, and local agency (see Chapter 2 for the analytic framework that guides the book). In all, this volume contains 11 case studies that include all the Spanish-speaking countries of CALC. However, before transitioning to the case studies themselves, the remainder of this chapter further situates the need for, and the contributions of, a volume of this nature. The following section discusses the gap in research on CALC that focuses specifically on the global-national-local dynamics mentioned in this paragraph. The second section further characterizes the focus and approach of the volume, while the third and final section provides a brief overview of the remaining chapters.

Global-local research on education in Central America and the Latin Caribbean: a gap

There are at least three ways to characterize the gap in literature to which this volume responds. First, it can be pointed out that literature on 'Latin America' frequently fails to include any focus on the CALC countries. Analysis typically attends to Mexico and then the countries of South America, particularly Argentina, Brazil, Chile, and Colombia. A case in point is the otherwise excellent book by Rivas (2022), *Examining Educational Policy in Latin America*. Another example is the recent volume by Ornelas (2019), *Politics of Education in Latin America*, which includes only one chapter on a CALC country. And while the region has received attention recently, for example, through the publication of an edited volume entitled *Education in Mexico, Central America and the Latin Caribbean*, the chapters of this volume are more focused on describing the organization and operation of the region's education systems than they are with analysing the interaction of the global and local forces that impinge on them (Posner et al, 2017). Furthermore, though there is a long history – since at least the early 20th century – of criticism from the region focused on international intervention and influence, especially as relates to the US,[1] this literature has tended not to focus on the connection with education (Deves-Valdes, 2016). Although promising collaborations by scholars in the region have led to recent publications that do zero in on education and international influence, these publications are, to date, only available in Spanish (see, for example, Alemán et al, 2016; Cruz, 2022).

A second way to grasp the extent to which international influence has been a focus of education research in the region is the scoping review conducted by Edwards (2018a). This review examined the countries of El Salvador, Guatemala, Honduras, and Nicaragua. It retained studies that were explicitly attentive to the international political economy of education policy. Based on a review of results in English and Spanish from Web of Science, Google Scholar,[2] and university holdings,[3] a total of 34 publications were identified as relevant. Given that this search was done without restriction of time period and with very broad search terms (for example, the searches in Web of Science were conducted for each country with the country's name and then the term 'education'),[4] one might be surprised that there were not more studies of relevance. What also stands out is that an additional 27 publications were included after the personal archives of Edwards were reviewed, with this personal library having been amassed while working on and in the region over many years (that is, by collecting studies available through university libraries in the region, network contacts, and local organizations).[5] Table 1.1 shows the publications retained according to source, while Table 1.2 shows the geographical and temporal focus of the publications retained. Table 1.3 indicates the type and language of the publications.

Table 1.1: IPE literature on education in Central America by source

Focus	Web of Science	One Search	Google Scholar	Personal collection	Total
El Salvador	8	0	1	15	24
Guatemala	2	0	0	1	3
Honduras	1*	0	1	3	5
Nicaragua	9	1	0	1**	11
Regionally focused	0	6	5	7	18
Grand total	20	7	7	27	59***

Notes: IPE = international political economy. * Same as one of the articles for Guatemala (Altschuler, 2013). ** Same as those of publications listed for El Salvador (Gillies, 2010). *** This figure represents the number of distinct publications, as it has been reduced from 61 to 59 to reflect the fact that one result each for Web of Science and personal collection pertained to more than one country.

Source: Edwards (2018)

Table 1.2: IPE literature on education in Central America by geographical focus and publication date

Focus	1970s	1980s	1990s	2000s	2010s	Total
El Salvador	1	1	6	4	12*	24
Guatemala	0	0	1	1	1	3
Honduras	0	0	0	1	4	5
Nicaragua	0	1	4	4	2	11
Regionally focused	2	3	5	7	1	18
Grand total	3	5	16	17	20	59*

Notes: IPE = international political economy. * This figure represents the number of distinct publications, as it has been reduced from 61 to 59 to reflect the fact that two results pertain to more than one country and are not listed in the regionally focused row. See note to Table 1.1 for more information.

Source: Edwards (2018)

Table 1.3: Type and language of IPE literature on education and Central America

Publication type	Number of publications	Percentage of total publications
Articles	34 (12)	57.63 (20.34)
Books	12 (2)	20.34 (3.40)
Chapters	7 (3)	11.86 (5.10)
Reports	3 (2)	5.01 (3.40)
Dissertations	2 (1)	3.39 (1.70)
Other	1 (1)	1.70 (1.70)
Total	59 (21)	100.00 (35.60)

Note: Figures in brackets refer to publications produced in Spanish.

Source: Edwards (2018)

There are at least two observations that can be gleaned from these figures. The first is that, beyond the low overall total for publications in Table 1.1, it is clear that some countries are more under-researched than others. Guatemala and Honduras, across all time periods, only had three and five publications, respectively, while Nicaragua and El Salvador had significantly more – 11 and 24, respectively. To be sure, the higher number of publications retained on El Salvador is at least in part due to the fact that Edwards' previous research had focused on El Salvador, with the implication that he was able to locate and collect more literature on this country while doing fieldwork. This comment leads to a second observation: that one must not assume that all research of relevance will appear in international publication databases and foreign university library database networks. Scholars in/from the region are undoubtedly aware of – and are writing on – the ways that education is affected by international political economy, but these publications may not be known beyond local organizational and professional networks. One challenge for international (and often even local) researchers interested in the region is to locate these studies. The present book seeks to make a contribution in this direction by making available studies that otherwise would have not been published or would have remained available only as grey literature, theses, or studies in Spanish-language outlets (see, for example, the chapters by Edwards [Chapter 2], Martin [Chapter 6], Morales-Ulloa and Moschetti [Chapter 4], Savenije [Chapter 7], Martínez Ramos [Chapter 14], and Pietras [Chapter 9]).

Further observations speak to the content of the studies retained by Edwards (2018a). Across the region, the available studies have certainly been attentive to issues that are of central importance for education from an international political economy perspective. Scholarship has addressed, for example, the following interrelated points:

a) the work of the United Nations Educational, Scientific and Cultural Organization (UNESCO) in the 1950s and the promotion of education as a human right (Reimers, 2000);

b) the relationship between education planning, international organizations, and international development (for example, Waggoner and Waggoner, 1971; Cummings and Lemke, 1973; McGinn et al, 1979; Bernède, 1980; Puiggrós, 1999; McGinn and Warwick, 2006; Gomez, 2011; Lindo-Fuentes and Ching, 2012);

c) the international spread of fundamentalist Christianity and its effects on education (Rose and Brouwer, 1990);

d) the politics of higher education reform during the Cold War (Feldman, 1989; Mason et al, 2001; Harrington, 2009);

e) the political–institutional dynamics of Central American ministries of education (Lourié, 1989);

f) the role of international organizations during the 1980s (Archer, 1994; Bujazán et al, 1987), with a focus on the effect of the armed conflicts (Graham-Brown, 1991) and the economic reforms required by international financial institutions (Reimers, 1991, 2000; Arnove et al, 1996);

g) the difficulty of adapting, implementing, and supporting international conventions in national contexts (Maclure, 2003, 2004; Cassimon et al, 2011; Edwards et al, 2015);

h) the projects and reform agenda promoted by and implemented with support from international development organizations, including the politics around whether or not they were successful (Moncada-Davidson, 1995; Quesada, 2001; Chapman and Quijada, 2008; Poppema, 2009; Gillies, 2010; Ruckert, 2010; Tinoco, 2010; Edwards, 2013, 2018b; Morales-Ulloa and Magalhaes, 2013; Edwards et al, 2015); and

i) the production of knowledge relating to education policy and how knowledge products can affect the direction of education reform (Reimers and McGinn, 1997; Dijkstra, 2004; Moncada et al, 2004; Rosekrans, 2006; Edwards, 2013; Edwards and Loucel, 2016).

For one thing, these points highlight the various topics of relevance when looking at education in terms of the range of international forces that affect it. They also highlight the long-term nature of the phenomenon of international influence. Publications have been attentive to this issue since at least the 1950s (see Chapter 2 of this volume for more on the international political economy of the region since the 1800s).

The numerous studies cited previously also underscore the fact that there is, indeed, a foundation of research on the region that makes the connection between education and international political-economic dynamics. However, what the points in the previous list do not immediately reveal is that these studies tend to be limited in the sense that they focus on short time periods, individual international organizations, local-level implementation of international trends, or the internal politics of national ministries of education. The present volume represents a significant contribution from a perspective that encompasses all Spanish-speaking countries of the CALC region, draws attention to the long-term and macro-trends in international development (see, for example, Chapters 2 and 3), and is guided by a focus that includes the relationship between the global and the local as well as the central role of national ministries of education and other governmental entities. The present volume thus spans the region while also spanning multiple levels (global, national, and local), and doing so in a way that is dynamic and dialectical in nature (for more, see the guiding analytic framework in Chapter 2). In these ways, the volume builds on but goes beyond previous research.

A third way to draw attention to the relative paucity of research on CALC countries is to look at the frequency with which they are the subject of presentations at the conferences of the Comparative and International Education Society (CIES).[6] Given that this society is explicitly concerned with education from comparative and international perspectives, it represents a good indicator of the extent to which these countries are receiving attention in international academic circles. Of course, one could also look to the meetings of academic societies that are based in the CALC region, but one of the guiding concerns of the present volume is the relative difficulty – for those located within *and* beyond the region – of understanding the position and politics of education in CALC countries.

The results of a search of the CIES conference programmes during the period from 2015 to 2022 can be seen in Table 1.4.[7] This table contains results for all Spanish-speaking countries of CALC, plus Puerto Rica – a Spanish-speaking territory of the US that has been (and continues to be) subject to many of the same political-economic dynamics as the countries in the region. A number of things stand out from these figures. First, the overall number of presentations during this time period has ranged from a low of 11 in 2020 (with this figure likely affected by the outbreak of the COVID-19 pandemic) to a high of 43 in 2021. Second, the number of presentations at the CIES on CALC far outnumbers the quantity of publications located in the literature review discussed earlier, a fact which reveals that there is more research being conducted on CALC than is widely known (or locatable). However, third, it is important to put these figures into context. According to the 2020 CIES conference report, a total of 1,017 formal paper presentations were accepted (Silova et al, 2020), of which only 11 (or 1.08 per cent) were about CALC countries.[8]

Table 1.4: Presentations focused on Spanish-speaking countries of Central America and the Latin Caribbean at the Conferences of the Comparative and International Education Society, 2015–2023

Country	2015	2016	2017	2018	2019	2020	2021	2022	2023	Total
Costa Rica	5	2	1	1	0	0	1	1	1	12
Cuba	4	2	4	0	3	1	3	1	1	19
Dominican Republic	3	1	1	1	1	0	3	3	1	14
El Salvador	3	0	5	2	1	3	7	1	3	25
Guatemala	8	1	1	6	2	4	11	13	7	53
Honduras	2	2	2	1	4	2	14	4	3	34
Nicaragua	1	5	1	1	1	0	4	0	1	14
Panama	0	1	0	1	0	0	0	0	0	2
Puerto Rico	1	0	0	1	0	1	0	1	0	3
Grand total	27	14	15	14	12	11	43	24	17	176

Note: Although Puerto Rico is not a country, it is included here because it is a focus of the present volume.

Source: Author

If we take the overall 2020 figure for CIES presentations as a reference point, even in the year with the most presentations (2021), only 4.2 per cent of the presentations had anything to do with CALC. Fourth, there is disparity across the region in terms of the number of presentations, as can be seen in Figure 1.1. While Guatemala has been the focus of the greatest number of presentations (n=53), Puerto Rico and Panama have only been the focus of three and two, respectively. It can thus be argued that, overall, the CALC region receives very little attention at CIES and that, across the region, there are some countries that are more marginalized than others.

But what about the nature of the presentations? Table 1.4 includes all presentations focused on education in a CALC country. In contrast, Table 1.5 indicates the number of presentations for each country/year that could be expected (based on their titles) to address international political economy issues, just as the present volume is concerned to do (see Chapter 2 for more on what is meant by international political economy issues). While perhaps the numbers should be higher in Table 1.5 (given the difficulty of judging solely based on presentation titles), the figures provided there provide a rough estimate. Combined, Tables 1.4 and 1.5 indicate that only approximately 18 out of 176 presentations (or 10.2 per cent) during the period from 2015 to 2023 explicitly addressed or framed

Figure 1.1: Number of presentations focused on Spanish-speaking countries of Central America and the Latin Caribbean at the Conferences of the Comparative and International Education Society, 2015–2023

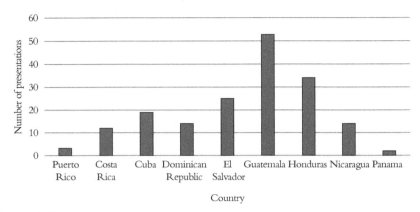

Source: Author

Table 1.5: Presentations focused on Spanish-speaking countries of Central America and the Latin Caribbean at the Conferences of the Comparative and International Education Society with an international political economy focus or local author affiliation, 2015–2023

Country	International political economy focus	Local author affiliation
Costa Rica	4	2
Cuba	2	7
Dominican Republic	3	1
El Salvador	3	7
Guatemala	2	8
Honduras	3	3
Nicaragua	1	5
Panama	0	0
Puerto Rico	0	1
Total	18	34

Notes: See Chapter 2 of this volume for more on what is meant by international political economy focus. Presentations were considered to have a local author affiliation if at least one of the authors was affiliated with an organization located in the country in question that was not a local office of an organization with headquarters elsewhere (for example, a local office of an international organization). The number of presentations with a local author does not reflect the number of different authors because a number of authors have multiple presentations in the same year or participate across years. Although Puerto Rico is not a country, it is included here because it is a focus of the present volume.

Source: Author

their studies with reference to the international forces that influence the realities in which education and education policy evolve in the region. Of course, it should be noted that this is 10 per cent of an already very small percentage of presentations (1–4 per cent depending on the year) concerned with CALC countries. Moreover, the country which ranks highest here still only had a total of four, while some countries did not have any presentations perceived to have an international political economy focus. This discussion thus highlights that the present volume addresses a crucial gap in research on the CALC region. A few examples of presentations which, based on their titles, appear to have an international political economy lens include:

- South-south migration and the educational impact of globalized racism in Costa Rica (Locke and Ovando, 2015)
- The effectiveness of aid-based adolescent reproductive health education in Nicaragua (Morita, 2018)
- Regionalization of higher education in the Northern Triangle: a qualitative meta-analysis of higher education systems in El Salvador, Guatemala, and Honduras (Griffin and Gall, 2018)
- Globalization, privatization, and the state: education reform in postcolonial contexts – the case of Honduras (Edwards et al, 2022)
- Economic and Media War against Socialist Societies: The Case of U.S.-Cuban Relations (Ginsburg, 2022)

A review of paper titles from CIES conference programs also indicates that a large percentage of presentations are focused not on international political economy issues, but rather, one might say, on their opposite. For example, and particularly in recent years, there seems to be an increase in the number of presentations that share the results of impact evaluations and donor-funded projects in the region, that is, presentations which typically focus on the outcomes of a project, but not on the potential role of international donors and other international organizations in influencing the direction of policy or perhaps even in creating or contributing to the challenges which now affect education in the region. A few examples of presentations of this type include:

- Adapting and scaling teacher professional development in Honduras 2020–2022 (Castillo, 2021)
- Integrating life/soft skills into technical training curricula for youth in El Salvador: A manual for instructors (Kaplan-Nunes, 2018)
- The power of observation: Using classroom observation to measure the impacts of teacher professional development in Guatemala (Moore et al, 2020).

While such presentations may offer valuable insights, the point here is that they do not bring to bear the kind of long-term, multiple-level, and dialectical lens which the present volume argues is essential.

As a final point, it should be noted that research authors are not typically based in the region. Since the fact of whether someone is 'from' the region is hard to determine from the limited information available in the conference programme, Table 1.5 includes information on the number presentations which have at least one author affiliated with a locally based organization that *is not* the local office of an international organization. For the period from 2015 to 2023, Guatemala has had a total of eight presentations by locally affiliated authors, while Panama had zero. The present volume makes a contribution in that eight of the 12 case study chapters are authored by individuals who are from the country being researched or who are affiliated with organizations based there (all except Chapters 12 and 13). Put differently, nine of the 21 authors in this volume fall into this category. In the case of all chapters, they have been written by authors with long-term engagement in the country of focus.

Having characterized the lack of scholarly attention to the CALC region in various ways, the next section turns to further describe the focus and structure of this volume.

The focus and structure of this volume

The gaps identified earlier have a number of related consequences. One consequence is a lack of understanding of the dynamics that confront the region generally and its education systems specifically. A second consequence is that interested individuals – and particularly those without the luxury of attending CIES conferences – are unable to understand the ways that the global affects the local and vice versa. Third, such gaps make it all the more difficult to conceptualize, develop, or revise educational strategies such that they are likely to have their intended effects. If politicians, reformers, education professionals, and others do not have an understanding of the multilevel and dialectical systems in which education is embedded, there is little hope that reforms will reflect in practice the intentions with which they were designed. Indeed, without an understanding of the international political economic dimensions of context, it is all the more likely that those involved in education will remain oblivious to the reasons for which traditional approaches to education in the region will not only fail to produce a 'quality education' (as judged, problematically, by test scores), but will also reproduce historical inequalities and will not produce the kinds of critical consciousness necessary to address injustices of both a socioeconomic and cognitive nature, where the latter refers, for example, to the way that Indigenous and non-Western worldviews have been marginalized if not erased.

As a whole, this volume addresses each of the consequences highlighted earlier. It does so, as noted previously, by bringing a long-term, multilevel, dialectical, and region-wide focus to the relationship between global forces and local responses. At the same time, individual chapters dig into the details and enactment of specific policies. In this way, a sensitivity to larger and deeper contextual constraints is paired with attention to local realities, initiatives, and forms of agency that often go undetected in studies that draw on an international political economy lens. This volume is thus unique in terms of the extent to which it captures and brings into conversation insights that are both macro and micro in nature.

In order to bring its contributions to fruition, the present volume has a particular structure. In addition to this introductory chapter, Part I contains a chapter that places into historical context the political-economic dynamics that have affected the region since the 1800s. This chapter also presents the theoretical framework (rooted in international political economy) that orients the volume. Part I is then complemented by Parts II and III, which focus, respectively, on Central America (nine chapters) and the Latin Caribbean (three chapters). The chapters in these parts present individual and comparative case studies of education reform in the region. The final part of the book discusses comparative findings, their implications (for theory, policy, and practice), and ways forward (again for theory, policy, and practice). It should also be noted that the chapters in Part IV serve to draw out and to emphasize the insights which stem from an international political economy perspective. While the case studies presented across the chapters do situate themselves in relation to global-national-local dynamics, they are concerned primarily with presenting and analysing the details of the policies being examined. The final two chapters thus take the extra step of exploring the individual and collective findings and implications from the perspective of the international political economy.

Empirically, the chapters take a variety of contemporary and historical policies and practices as their focus. To summarize, the chapters examine the following areas:

- The political economy of education reform in the 1990s and 2000s (multicountry comparison of Guatemala, El Salvador, Honduras, and Nicaragua).
- New Public Management strategies such as administrative decentralization (Honduras).
- Trends in educational privatization (Honduras and the Dominican Republic).
- The impact of market liberalization on education and teachers (Cuba).

- Locally driven innovations in teacher education (El Salvador).
- 'Convivencia' policies, that is, policies related to learning to get along/ live harmoniously together (El Salvador).
- Education in gang-controlled territory (El Salvador).
- Open education resources and digitization of education (Guatemala).
- Educational technology and implications for equity (Costa Rica and Panama).
- Gender equity and education (Puerto Rico).
- Education as a counterforce to epistemicide (Guatemala).

In all cases, the chapters make explicit connections to the international forces that affect education. Examples of the global forces to which chapters in this volume are attentive include macro-economic pressures, geopolitical intervention, neocolonial relationships, global pandemics, international policy trends, transnational gang networks, international development cooperation, and the influence of international organizations. In making connections to these forces, the chapters first consider how such forces encourage or discourage certain kinds of reforms over others. Second, and importantly, they also consider the implications of national policies and political dynamics as well as local realities for international trends and forces. Overall, then, this volume brings together researchers of – and research on – the CALC region to explore the dynamics of global forces that challenge education systems therein and to highlight the local efforts that seek to enact, mitigate, and even counteract these forces. While, as discussed, there exists literature on the global forces that have historically and generally affected CALC, and while some literature documents the challenges that face the education systems of this region, there are few publications that bring these two sets of issues into conversation with each other. This is an important gap that warrants critical attention, for both sets of issues are intricately related.

Notes

[1] Of course, this is to say nothing of the history of resistance and anti-imperialist thought directed, for example, towards the Spanish monarchy and the settler colonialists who created the modern-day states of the region.

[2] The first 100 Google Scholar results in Spanish were reviewed. The search terms were: [educación]- AND [política OR reforma] AND [El Salvador OR Guatemala OR Honduras OR Nicaragua]. The search terms were selected to target any Spanish-language studies that were missed by Web of Science, since the results there were predominantly in English.

[3] The university holdings of the University of Hawaii were explored using the 'One Search' function. This function goes beyond the holdings of the host library to also access 'a mega-aggregation of hundreds of millions of scholarly e-resources of global and regional importance' (Ex Libris Group, as cited in Hooper, 2012, p 119).

[4] The individual results were assessed and retained if they were attentive to the ways in which education is affected by international political economic conditions.

5   Fifteen of the 27 publications were focused on El Salvador, a consequence of the fact that Edwards' work had, through 2018, focused more on El Salvador than the other countries in the study.

6   There are many such societies. Here we refer to the one based in the US.

7   The table was created by searching the conference programmes for the names of the countries in the region. Thanks go to Yanilis Romero and Patricia Grillet for their help with this.

8   Note that the papers submitted to CIES 2020 were reviewed and accepted before the outbreak of the COVID-19 pandemic, meaning that the pandemic did not affect these numbers. It should also be noted that the figure of 1 per cent reported here may actually be an overestimate. The conference programmes were searched for presentations with the names of CALC countries in their titles. The totals reported in Table 1.4 are not differentiated according to whether the presentations were an individual paper presentation, a poster presentation, or part of a roundtable or panel submission. If all kinds of presentations were used for estimating the percentage of presentations focused on CALC country, the denominator would jump from 1,107 (the figure only for individual paper presentations) to 2,187 (Silova et al, 2020). This would mean that the percentage focused on CALC countries for 2020 would drop to 0.5 per cent.

References

Alemán, N., Cruz, M. T., Daz, L., Flores, H., and Salazar, M. (2016). *Reescrituras de la educación pública desde Centroamérica*. Cara Parens.

Allahar, A. (2005). Identity and erasure: finding the elusive Caribbean [Review of *Caribbean Autobiography: Cultural Identity and Self-Representation; Decolonising the Caribbean: Dutch Policies in a Comparative Perspective; Ah Come Back Home: Perspectives on the Trinidad and Tobago Carnival*, by S. P. Paquet, G. Oostindie, I. Klinkers, I. I. Smart, and K. S. K. Nehusi]. *Revista Europea de Estudios Latinoamericanos y Del Caribe/European Review of Latin American and Caribbean Studies*, 79, 125–134. http://www.jstor.org/stable/25676189

Altschuler, D. (2013). How patronage politics undermines parental participation and accountability: community-managed schools in Honduras and Guatemala. *Comparative Education Review*, 57(1), 117–144. https://doi.org/10.1086/667963

Archer, D. (1994). The changing roles of non-governmental organizations in the field of education (in the context of changing relationships with the state). *International Journal of Educational Development*, 14(3), 223–232. https://doi.org/10.1016/0738-0593(94)90036-1

Arnove, R., Torres, C., Franz, S., and Morse, K. (1996). A political sociology of education and development in Latin America. *International Journal of Comparative Sociology*, 37(1–2), 140–158. https://doi.org/10.1177/002071529603700108

Bernède, J. F. (1980). *El Proyecto 'Red de Sistemas Educativos para el Desarrollo en Centroamérica y Panamá': una experiencia de cooperación técnica entre países*. UNESCO.

Bland, B., and Fredrick, J. (2017). Taiwan tries to keep Central American allies away from China. *Financial Times*, 6 January https://www.ft.com/content/1318e4fc-d3e1-11e6-9341-7393bb2e1b51

Buzajan, M., Hare, S., La Belle, T., and Stafford, L. (1987). International agency assistance to education in Latin America and the Caribbean, 1970–1984. *Comparative Education*, 23(2), 161–171. https://doi.org/10.1080/0305006870230204

Cassimon, D., Essers, D., and Renard, R. (2011). An assessment of debt-for-education swaps: case studies on swap initiatives between Germany and Indonesia and between Spain and El Salvador. *Comparative Education*, 47(2), 139–156. https://doi.org/10.1080/00263206.2011.553931

Castillo, D. (2021). Adapting and scaling teacher professional development in Honduras 2020–2022. Paper presentation, Conference of the Comparative and International Education Society 2021, Seattle, 25 April–2 May. https://cies2021.org/wp-content/uploads/CIES2021Program-April26.pdf

Chapman, D., and Quijada, J. (2008*). An Analysis of USAID Assistance to Basic Educantion in the Developing World, 1990–2005* (USAID Working Paper). https://www.epdc.org/sites/default/files/documents/An%20Analysis%20of%20USAID%20Assistance%20to%20Basic%20Education.pdf

Coatsworth, J. (1994). *Central America and the United States: The Clients and the Colossus.* Twayne.

Cruz Bustamante, M. T. (ed.). (2022). *Quality of Education in Central America: Dynamics and Tensions between the Model of Education and the Model of Development.* Publicaciones Académicas UCA.

Cummings, R. L., and Lemke, D. A. (1973). *Educational Innovations in Latin America.* Scarecrow Press.

Devés-Valdés, E. (2016). International topics in Central America's thought and agenda, 1900–2010: a framework in five moments. *Universum. Revista de Humanidades y Ciencias Sociales*, 31(1), 81–104.

Diamond, L. (1992). Promoting democracy. *Foreign Policy*, 87 (Summer), 25–46.

Dijkstra, A. G. (2004). Governance for sustainable poverty reduction: the social fund in Nicaragua. *Public Administration and Development*, 24(3), 197–211. https://doi.org/10.1002/pad.297

Dollar. (2017, January). China's investment in Latin America. *Brookings.*

Edwards Jr., D. B. (2013). International processes of education policy formation: an analytic framework and the case of Plan 2021 in El Salvador. *Comparative Education Review*, 57(1), 22–53.

Edwards Jr., D. B. (2018). Education in Central America: trends, tensions, and trade-offs. Paper presented on a 'presidential session' at the conference of the Comparative and International Education Society, Mexico City, Mexico, 25–29 March.

Edwards Jr., D. B. (2018). *The Trajectory of Global Education Policy: Community-Based Management in El Salvador and the Global Reform Agenda.* Palgrave Macmillan.

Edwards Jr., D. B., and Loucel, C. (2016). The EDUCO program, impact evaluations, and the political economy of global education reform. *Education Policy Analysis Archives*, 24(49), 1–50.

Edwards Jr., D. B., Victoria, J.A., and Martin, P. (2015). The geometry of policy implementation: lessons from the political economy of three education reforms in El Salvador during 1990–2005. *International Journal of Educational Development*, 44, 28–41.

Edwards, D. B., Moschetti, M. C., and Caravaca. C. (2022). Globalization, privatization, and the state: education reform in post-colonial contexts – the case of Honduras. Paper presentation, Conference of the Comparative and International Education Society 2022, Minneapolis, 18–22 April. https://cies.lasaweb.org/cmsb/uploads/CIES2022_Program.pdf

Feldman, M. S. (1989). *Order without Design: Information Production and Policy Making.* Stanford University Press.

Gillies, J. (2010). *Education System Reform and Aid Effectiveness: The Power of Persistence.* Washington, DC: United States Agency for International Development and Equip 2.

Ginsburg, M. (2022). Economic and media war against socialist societies: the case of U.S.-Cuban relations. Paper presentation, Conference of the Comparative and International Education Society 2022, Minneapolis, 18–22 April. https://cies.lasaweb.org/cmsb/uploads/CIES2022_Program.pdf

Gonzalez, J. (2001). *Harvest of Empire: A History of Latinos in America.* Penguin.

Gómez Arévalo, A. P. (2011). Una genealogía de la educación en El Salvador. *Revista Latinoamericana de Estudios Educativos (México)*, XLI(3–4), 73–117.

Graham-Brown, S. (1991). *Education in the Developing World: Conflict and Crisis.* Longman.

Griffin, J. and Gall, L. (2018). Regionalization of higher education in the Northern Triangle: a qualitative meta-analysis of higher education systems in El Salvador, Guatemala, and Honduras. Paper presentation, Conference of the Comparative and International Education Society 2018, Mexico, 25–29 March. https://cies2018.org/

Harrington, J. (2009). Private higher education in a Cold War world: Central America. *American Educational History Journal*, 36(1), 133–150.

Hooper, L. (2012). ExLibris's primo and musical research. *Music Reference Services Quarterly*, 15(2), 119–124. https://doi.org/10.1080/10588167.2012.672088

Kaplan-Nunes, L. (2018). Integrating life/soft skills into technical training curricula for youth in El Salvador: a manual for instructors. Paper presentation, Conference of the Comparative and International Education Society 2018, Mexico, 25–29 March. https://cies2018.org/

Kitroeff, N., and Shear, M. D. (2021). U.S. aid to Central America hasn't slowed migration: can Kamala Harris? *New York Times*, 6 June. https://www.nytimes.com/2021/06/06/world/americas/central-america-migration-kamala-harris.html

Lindo-Fuentes, H., and Ching, E. (2012). *Modernizing Minds in El Salvador: Education Reform and the Cold War, 1960–1980.* UNM Press.

Locke, S. and Ovando, C. (2015). South-south migration and the educational impact of globalized racism in Costa Rica. Paper presentation, Conference of the Comparative and International Education Society 2015, Washington DC, 8–13 March. https://convention2.allacademic.com/one/cies/cies15/

Lourié, S. (1989). *Education and Development: Strategies and Decisions in Central America.* Trentham Books.

Maclure, R., and Sotelo, M. (2003). Children's rights as residual social policy in Nicaragua: state priorities and the Code of Childhood and Adolescence. *Third World Quarterly*, 24(4), 671–689. https://doi.org/10.1080/0143659032000105812

Maclure, R., and Sotelo, M. (2004). Children's rights and the tenuousness of local coalitions: a case Study in Nicaragua. *Journal of Latin American Studies*, 36(1), 85–108. http://www.jstor.org/stable/3875425

Mason, T. C., Arnove, R. F., and Sutton, M. (2001). Credits, curriculum, and control in higher education: cross-national perspectives. *Higher Education*, 42(1), 107–137. http://www.jstor.org/stable/3448085

McGinn, N., and Reimers, F. (1997). *Informed Dialogue: Using Research to Shape Education Policy around the World.* Praeger.

McGinn, N., and Warwick, D. P. (2006). La planeación educativa ¿Ciencia o política? [Education planning: science or politics?]. *Revista Latinoamericana de Estudios Educativos*, 36(1–2), 153–182.

McGinn, N., Schiefelbein, E., and Warwick, D. P. (1979). Educational planning as political process: two case studies from Latin America. *Comparative Education Review*, 23(2), 218–239. http://www.jstor.org/stable/1187691

Moncada, G., Hernandez Rodríguez, R., Chávez de Aguilar, M., Orellana, D., Alas Solís, M., and Hernández, B. D. (2004). *Uso e Impacto de la Información Empírica en la Formulación y Ejecución de Políticas de Educación Básica en Honduras en el Período 1990–2002* [*Use and Impact of Empirical Information on the Formulation and Execution of Basic Education Policies in Honduras in the Period 1990–2002*]. PREAL, GDN, and UPNFM.

Moncada-Davidson, L. (1995). Education and its limitations in the maintenance of peace in El Salvador. *Comparative Education Review*, 39(1), 54–75.

Moore, A., Torrente, C., Liuzzi, S., Morgan, S., Lapadatova, G., and Claxton, J. (2020). The power of observation: using classroom observation to measure the impacts of teacher professional development in Guatemala. Paper presentation, Conference of the Comparative and International Education Society 2020, Miami, 22–26 March. https://convention2.alla cademic.com/one/cies/cies20/#selected_tag

Morales Ulloa, R., and Magalhães, A. M. (2013). Visiones, tensiones y resultados. La nueva gobernanza de la educación en Honduras. *Education Policy Analysis Archives*, 21(3), 1–23. https://doi.org/10.14507/epaa. v21n3.2013

Morita, M. (2018). The effectiveness of aid-based adolescent reproductive health education in Nicaragua. Paper presentation, Conference of the Comparative and International Education Society 2018, Mexico, 25–29 March. https://cies2018.org/

Ornelas, C. (2019). *Politics of Education in Latin America: Reforms, Resistance and Persistence*. Brill Sense.

Poppema, M. (2009). Guatemala, the Peace Accords and education: a post-conflict struggle for equal opportunities, cultural recognition and participation in education. *Globalisation, Societies and Education*, 7(4), 383–408.

Posner, C. M., Martin, C., Elvir, A. P., and Brock, C. (2017). *Education in Mexico, Central America and the Latin Caribbean*. Bloomsbury Academic.

Puiggrós, A. (1999). *Imperialism and Education in Latin America*. Westview.

Quesada Ugalde, M. (2001). Proyección de organismos internacionales y formulación de políticas educativas: Costa Rica y El Salvador 1995. *Anuario de Estudios Centroamericanos*, 27(1), 7–29. http://www.jstor.org/ stable/25661338

Reimers, F. (1991). The impact of economic stabilization and adjustment on education in Latin America. *Comparative Education Review*, 35(2), 319–353. http://www.jstor.org/stable/1188166

Reimers, F. (2000). Educación, desigualdad y opciones de política en América Latina en el siglo XXI. *Revista Latinoamericana de Estudios Educativos (México)*, XXX(2), 11–42.

Rivas, A. (2022). *Examining Educational Policy in Latin America: Comprehensive Insights into Contemporary Reform*. Routledge.

Robinson, W. I. (2003). *Transnational Conflicts: Central America, Social Change, and Globalization*. Verso.

Rose, S. D., and Brouwer, S. (1990). The export of fundamentalist Americanism: US evangelical education in Guatemala. *Latin American Perspectives*, 17(4), 42–56. http://www.jstor.org/stable/2633571

Rosekrans, K. (2006). Using participatory research and informed dialogue to influence education policy: lessons from El Salvador. *Journal of Education in International Development*, 2(2), 1–14.

Ruckert, A. (2010). The forgotten dimension of social reproduction: the World Bank and the poverty reduction strategy paradigm. *Review of International Political Economy*, 17(5), 816–839. https://doi.org/10.1080/09692291003712113

Silova, I., Goebel, J., Chachkhiani, K., Gong, B., Palandjian, G., Jiang, J., and Tsotniashvili, K. (2020). Education beyond the Human: toward sympoiesis. In *vCIES 2020 Conference Report*. Arizona State University.

Skidmore, T. E., and Smith, P. H. (2001). *Modern Latin America*. Oxford University Press.

Sollis, P. (1995). Partners in development? The state, nongovernmental organisations and the UN in Central America. *Third World Quarterly*, 16(3), 525–542. http://www.jstor.org/stable/3992891

Tinoco, M. A. (2010). *Política educativa y Banco Mundial: La educación comunitaria en Honduras* [*Education Policy and the World Bank: Community education in Honduras*]. Guaymuras.

USAID (n.d.). Generating hope: USAID in El Salvador, Guatemala, and Honduras. https://www.usaid.gov/where-we-work/latin-america-and-the-caribbean/generating-hope-usaid-el-salvador-guatemala-and-honduras

Waggoner, G., and Waggoner, B. (1971). *Education in Central America*. University Press of Kansas.

Wintgens, S. (2017). China's new relations with Panama and Costa Rica are another step towards a Beijing Consensus in Central America. *London School of Economics and Political Science*, 8 November. https://blogs.lse.ac.uk/latamcaribbean/2017/11/08/chinas-new-relations-with-panama-and-costa-rica-are-another-step-towards-a-beijing-consensus-in-central-america/

Wise, C. (2020). *Dragonomics: How Latin America Is Maximizing (or Missing out on) China's International Development Strategy*. Yale University Press.

Wolf, S. (2017). *Mano Dura: The Politics of Gang Control in El Salvador*. University of Texas Press.

2

The Political Economy
of Education and Development
in Central America and the Latin
Caribbean: Regional Dynamics and
a Framework for Analysis

D. Brent Edwards Jr.

Introduction

This chapter concerns itself with three tasks: first, to depict some key historical and regional dynamics in Central America from a political economy perspective; second, to contextualize *education reform* in relation to international political-economic forces affecting the region; and, third, to outline the framework that informs the analysis and commentary presented in subsequent chapters. In attending to these tasks, the purpose is not only to provide essential background context relevant to all the chapters in this volume, but also to make explicit the dimensions and tensions to which the chapters in this volume speak.

The outline sketched here of historical and regional dynamics grew out of a multiyear collaboration with a network of colleagues from Central America. Teams of scholars from El Salvador, Honduras, Guatemala, and Nicaragua carried out case studies of education policy making in these countries, with a focus on the 1990s and 2000s. At the invitation of this network of scholars, my contribution to this collaboration was, first, to situate the aforementioned case studies in a long-term perspective. I did so by engaging literature from the fields of international development studies, international relations, sociology, history, and political economy. Second, my contribution was to engage in a cross-case analysis of those case studies in order to examine commonalities and differences in terms of the factors that influence education policy making, as well as how education serves to resolve the political and economic tensions that characterize the region. Both the individual case studies and my contributions are contained in a book published by the Central American University, entitled *Quality of Education in Central America: Dynamics and Tensions between the ~Model of Education and the Model of Development* (Cruz, 2022). However, to date, the results of this multicountry and multiyear research collaboration are only available in Spanish.

Chapters 2 and 3 of the present volume thus seek to share the fruits of the aforementioned collaboration with a wider audience by making them available in English. This chapter does this by presenting the historical and regional panorama, while Chapter 3 then presents the insights generated through comparative analysis of the individual case studies. While sharing these insights is intrinsically valuable in the sense of making research more broadly available, it is argued that the historical, regional, and cross-country findings documented in Chapters 2 and 3 are particularly valuable in the context of the present volume. This is so in the sense that these two chapters will help readers to situate the other chapters of this book in a broad and long-term perspective. That is, even though these two chapters focus empirically on a subset of countries (El Salvador, Honduras, Guatemala, and Nicaragua), the argument is that the content of this and the next chapter is helpful in informing the reader when it comes to dynamics and trends that have affected the region more generally.

In order to address the purposes set out earlier, the chapter proceeds as follows. First, it characterizes regional political-economic dynamics in a historical perspective. This section is divided into three subsections. It begins in the 1800s and covers the time up to the Second World War. This is then followed by an examination of the post-Second World War period up to approximately 1970. The final subsection takes as its object dynamics during the 1970s and 1980s. Chronologically, Chapter 3 picks up where Chapter 2 leaves off in terms of the discussion of regional political-economic dynamics.

The chapter then turns to contextualizing education reform in relation to international political-economic forces affecting the region. This section is likewise historically and regionally focused. It attends to the pressures facing the education systems of Central America from the 1950s to the 1980s, the period in which education systems began to expand dramatically – and often with assistance from international organizations. As with the previous section, this section primarily discusses examples from El Salvador, Honduras, Guatemala, and Honduras, though, again, the tendencies portrayed are, it is argued, reflective of the experiences of other countries in Central America and the Latin Caribbean.

The third and final section of the chapter pivots to present the framework that serves as the overarching analytic lens for the present volume. It is important to acknowledge (again) that this framework has grown out of – that is, has been adapted from – the framework that guided the regional collaboration described earlier. As will be seen, this framework is a natural extension of the discussion offered in the first two sections of this chapter. This is so in the sense that the framework maintains a focus on the political-economic constraints and enablers, while at the same time providing additional detail and discussion. Importantly, this framework is employed directly by the authors in this volume to guide their study and to inform the summative analysis and commentary included at the end of their chapters as they reflect on the contributions of their research for understanding the global-local tensions that manifest in and through education reform in Central America and the Latin Caribbean.

Regional international political–economic dynamics in historical perspective

Dynamics up to the Second World War

Although Central America's history has been affected by international intervention since the 1600s (Patch, 2013), the roots of current dynamics can be clearly traced back to the 1800s. During this time, the relevant development occurred in 1823 when, shortly after Central America[1] declared independence from Spain in 1821 and formed the Central American Federation (a single country that lasted until 1838), the US put forth the Monroe Doctrine. The Doctrine warned European powers not to interfere in the affairs of the Western Hemisphere and would serve as the basis for US foreign policy in Latin America for over 100 years. However, beyond justifying a protective function, the Monroe Doctrine also helped the development of US business interests in Central America (Langley and Schoonover, 1995). To that end, Coatsworth (1994) notes that from 1898 to 1933, Central American countries became 'client states' of the US, thanks to economic opportunities related especially to coffee and bananas, and the willingness of the US to advocate for, and to intervene on behalf of, US business investments.

Political dynamics shifted in the years between the First World War and the Second World War, though the US was not genuinely threatened in terms of its dominance in the region. This was because, after the First World War, European countries were focused inward on reconstruction.[2] The major change came in the form of the Good Neighbor Policy of US President Franklin D. Roosevelt, starting in 1933. After some pushback from Mexico, Argentina, and other Latin American governments in the 1920s and early 1930s to US invasion, occupation, and control in the region,

Roosevelt pledged nonintervention. However, while the new policy meant that 'Central American governments were no longer required to seek the approval of the U.S. ambassador on every major question of policy and personnel', the downside was that the Good Neighbor Policy left a power vacuum that allowed for the rise of military regimes that focused on imposing order in the context of economic depression and social unrest in the 1930s (Coatsworth, 1994, p 43).

The Second World War reversed the trend of the Good Neighbor Policy and set the stage for US involvement during the Cold War. Economically, in the early 1940s, the US took a more hands-on approach by signing price stabilization agreements with Latin American countries and by setting high quotas for Central American imports in order to ease pressure from the loss of European markets. Politically, the Second World War also prompted the US to work with Central American military governments on security issues. Cooperation focused on military equipment, training programmes, the production of war material, and the provision of military bases (Bulmer-Thomas, 1987; Coatsworth, 1994). Collaboration between the US and Central America would only strengthen after the Second World War.

Dynamics in the post-Second World War period

In the post-Second World War period, while Europe was again reconstructing, the US enjoyed a period of 'unchallenged power' for 25 years (Coatsworth, 1994, p 49). Rather than offering foreign aid, the US began this period by continuing with the tradition of promoting US economic interests, while also encouraging Central American nations to move away from economic nationalism and to improve their attractiveness to international (that is, US) business. According to Coatsworth, 'US diplomats, technical aid officers, and State Department officials pressured constantly for these changes' (1994, p 53). Anyone who did not go along with these priorities was labelled a communist (many parties for which had been founded in the 1930s and during the Second World War; McClellan, 1963). The overthrow of President Jacobo Arbenz in 1954 in Guatemala by the US was the prime example of the extent to which the latter country was willing to go in order to fight the real or perceived threat of communism in the region. Unsurprisingly, after the deposing of Arbenz in Guatemala, 'visible or public opposition to U.S. political and economic dominance in Central America virtually disappeared' (Coatsworth, 1994, p 74).[3]

However, heading into the 1960s, the US shifted to focus more on creating the conditions for economic and social stability within Central American countries, as opposed to focusing on support for military regimes that would maintain order. This shift came about as a result of the experience in the 1950s of officials who worked in the administration of US President

Dwight D. Eisenhower and who would subsequently go on to work in the administration of President John F. Kennedy. It also came about as a result of criticism from Latin Americans who: (a) felt ignored after Second World War (when Europe was benefitting from the Marshal Plan); (b) observed that military aid only served to keep authoritarian regimes in power; and (c) wanted to 'construct self-sufficient economic systems and to reconstruct outmoded social systems' (McClellan, 1963, p 211).

Thus, in 1961, after the election of President Kennedy, a new policy towards Latin America was initiated, known as the Alliance for Progress (AFP). The purpose (at least officially) was to counter the effects of poverty and injustice, no doubt as one prong of the US approach to maintaining stability and to undermining the appeal of communism. It was thought that this was 'a task for a decade' (Kennedy, 1962, p 217). While it may not surprise us now, it should be noted that such a task was conceived as appropriate in the first place. The idea of 'international development' was born only a few years prior, in the 1940s, in the post-Second World War context of European reconstruction and the founding of both the World Bank (1944) and the United Nations (1945).

As for the AFP, although Kennedy did not get the immense funding he wanted from the US Congress to support this initiative (McCall, 1989), US aid to Latin America increased dramatically. For example, from 1960 to 1963, total annual US assistance to Latin America jumped from $380 to $972 million (Gambone, 2001). The economic assistance figures for select countries in Central America for this and surrounding time periods are presented in Table 2.1, which shows a jump in funding starting in the late 1950s. Much of the assistance was approved on the basis of detailed development plans for how countries would address economic, social, and educational issues. However, a number of factors hampered the AFP from functioning as envisioned. These issues included: (a) the fact that the US officials who approved the loans were, in the end, more concerned with how the underlying plans would affect US imports and exports (McCall, 1989); (b) the lack or absence of governmental capacity and processes in Central America (and elsewhere in Latin America) for creating development plans; and (c) the extensive requirements of the United States Agency for International Development (USAID) in terms of data and detail (Gambone, 2001). As one example of the consequences of these dynamics, between 1958 and 1962, 80 per cent of the development loans made to Central America were undisbursed (Gambone, 2001).[4]

The AFP was further impeded by its theory of action. Leaders in Central America (as elsewhere in Latin America) were not welcoming of either major social reform or the creation of better opportunities and economic conditions for the poor (and especially the agrarian workforce) that could be brought about through politically democratic processes (McCall, 1989).

Table 2.1: US economic assistance to Central America, 1953–1988

Years	El Salvador	Guatemala	Honduras	Nicaragua	Total
1953–1957	3.1	41.9	10.3	9.2	64.5
1958–1961	6.9	52.9	16.8	23.1	99.7
1962–1964	58.7	36.0	25.6	27.9	148.2
1965–1969	30.7	33.4	25.9	47.5	137.5
1970–1977	14.7	29.4	29.3	31.1	104.5
1978–1981	56.3	26.6	40.0	27.3	150.2
1982–1988	343.6	82.5	137.7	0.0	563.8
Total	514.0	302.7	285.6	166.1	1,268.4

Note: Amounts are for annual averages in 1982 dollars. Only those Central American countries that are the subject of this chapter are included in the table. Figures (given in millions of dollars) include both loans and grants.

Source: Adapted from Coatsworth (1994, p 107)

Prioritizing security concerns over the idealism of the AFP's origins, by the mid-1960s, both the US Department of State and USAID shifted back to the traditional approach of fostering economic development, protecting US business investments, opposing communism, and working with nondemocratic regimes if necessary (McCall, 1989).

Given the focus of this chapter on international involvement in Central America, it is important to note that international assistance to Latin America during the 1960s did not only come from the US government. Of the estimated $18 billion to Latin America that was provided between 1961 and 1969, $4.8 billion was provided by US government sources, with the remainder coming from international financial institutions, the United Nations, the European Common Market, and the Organisation for Economic Co-operation and Development (McCall, 1989).[5] As for US economic assistance, Table 2.1, as noted earlier, shows its growth in select Central American countries during the 1960s and places this growth into a long-term context.

Dynamics during the 1970s and 1980s

The political and economic dynamics of Central America from the 1970s to the 1980s provide the immediate backdrop for the chapters in this book. To begin, it should be noted that the export-led growth of the 1960s (and prior to that) had left many in Central America not only landless (as land was taken for beef and agricultural production), but also exposed the world to economy shocks that would come in the 1970s, especially since much of the business activity on which this growth relied was, in turn, dependent on international inputs and loans from North American banks, which were likewise affected by the rise in oil prices (Williams, 1986; Cox, 1994) (see the next section for more on this) The economic crises of the 1970s – combined with the reduction in international aid during the 1970s from the US, which was also experiencing economic recession (Gambone, 2001) – thus served to exacerbate the simmering economic tensions internal to Central American countries that have always affected them.

As a result, during the late 1970s (and the 1960s in Guatemala), peasants in Central America (with the exception of Honduras) began to arm themselves in reaction to their economic conditions and the 'authoritarian civilian-military regimes' that governed the countries of the isthmus (Robinson, 2003, p 151).[6] These dynamics led to a successful socialist revolution in Nicaragua in 1979 (that would conclude in 1990 with the election of an opposition candidate) and a civil war beginning in 1980 in El Salvador between the repressive government and a coalition of socialist rebels (with the war ending in 1992), while the military in Guatemala continued with the persecution that had begun in 1962 (and which would not formally end with Peace Accords until 1996). In Honduras, after experiencing several military governments in the 1970s, democratic elections were reintroduced in 1980, though the civilian governments had to negotiate with both the military and with the US, the latter of which used Honduras as a staging ground for military operations in the region, where it was dedicated not only to fighting socialism but also to preserving and extending its interests (Bull, 2005).

In order to contain and respond to the crises mentioned earlier, the US spent an enormous sum of money. According to Barry (1991), *economic* aid in the 1980s to the four countries of interest here ranged from a low of $729 million for Nicaragua to a high of $2.9 billion for El Salvador, while *military* aid ranged from a low of $0 for Nicaragua (given that the government was controlled by socialists) to a high of $1 billion in El Salvador. Total economic and military aid for El Salvador, Guatemala, Honduras, and Nicaragua during this time totalled approximately $7.5 billion (Barry, 1991). Table 2.2 portrays the levels of economic and military aid for these countries individually during the 1980s. While the United Nations, international nongovernmental organizations (NGOs), and some European countries provided aid to affected populations in Central America during and after the conflict (Archer, 1994; Robinson, 2003; Biekart, 2013), the larger point here is the outsized influence of the US when it came to containing socialism and economically propping up impoverished Central American governments. Another major issue, to which the next section will return in more detail (in order to make the connection with education) is the fact that the conflicts in this region also created an opportunity for the neoliberal

Table 2.2: US economic and military aid to Central America, 1980–1990

Aid focus	El Salvador	Guatemala	Honduras	Nicaragua	Total
Economic	2,885.90	902.6	1,286.40	729.7	5,804.60
Military	1,014.80	33.5	463.1	0	1,511.40
Total	3,900.70	936.10	1,749.50	729.70	7,316.00

Note: Figures are in millions of dollars.

Source: Adapted from Barry (1991, Table 7)

reorientation of Central American elites such that they were more open to economic liberalization (Robinson, 2003).

Keeping in mind the long-term perspective presented earlier on the general structures and dynamics that have affected international involvement in Central America, the next section turns to characterizing the ways in which international influence has affected the development of education policy specifically.

Situating education in relation to international political-economic forces

The focus here is on summarizing the pressures facing the education systems of Central America from the 1950s to the 1980s in order to contextualize both the comparative findings discussed in the next chapter and to provide background for other chapters in this volume. Due to space constraints, this section does not provide a review of the literature on each of the four countries of interest, but rather comments on regional dynamics. Moreover, the focus here is on insights that have been produced from – or are sensitive to – an international political economy perspective. While more will be said about the characteristics of the international political economy perspective (that is, the framework) in the next section, here, it can be mentioned that, on one level, such a perspective is attentive to the involvement of international organizations in formal and informal processes related to policy change that involve local, national, and international actors. What research exists in this area reveals that international organizations have a long history of coordinating and guiding reform in Central America. On a second level, an international political economy perspective is concerned with the way in which education fits into the tensions generated by global capitalist development.

One example of international involvement is the regional cooperation that began in the 1950s with the creation of the Organization of Central American States (ODECA). Although this organization suffered from problems of administration, finances, and legal issues, it was intended to be an 'indispensable organism for the progressive development of Central America in all its relations' (Waggoner and Waggoner, 1971, p 20). As such, one of its areas of emphasis was education. Accordingly, ODECA created the Cultural and Educational Council, made up of the ministers of education of the member countries (initially, Costa Rica, Nicaragua, El Salvador, Honduras, and Guatemala; Panama joined in 1968). The first meeting in December 1956 was followed by a series of seminars in the late 1950s with assistance from the United Nations Education, Science and Culture Organization (UNESCO), the Organization of American States, and the International Cooperation Administration of the United States (the forerunner to USAID). The goal of these meetings, which focused on urban primary schooling, teacher training for rural primary schools, vocational–technical education, and academic secondary education, was 'an agreement concerning common purposes and organizational patterns of education in Central America' (Waggoner and Waggoner, 1971, p 140). These seminars produced high numbers of recommendations for how each area of education should be organized and why. They also espoused the objective of 'educational and cultural unity as a basis for future economic and political unity' (Waggoner and Waggoner, 1971, p 140). However, while in 1962 the ministers of education of the region agreed on the 'development of parallel programs, similar structures, and equivalent standards among the six ministries of education', overall ODECA 'moved slowly in the area of education', and by 1969 it sought a new secretary-general in order to help stimulate 'fruitful activity' (Waggoner and Waggoner, 1971, p 141). A major limitation of ODECA's activity was that it depended on financial support from member countries. A further limitation was that this supranational approach to regional cooperation, driven as it was by external actors, did not have buy-in from the governments of the region.

At the same time that regional cooperation struggled to advance, international organizations operating in Latin America focused on the introduction of scientific management practices in the education sector as part of wider efforts towards modernization of government. In the early 1960s, with funding from UNESCO, the World Bank and private foundations, 25 missions composed of educators and economists were sent to countries throughout the region to 'advise the countries on comprehensive educational planning' (Puiggrós, 1999, p 35). The intention of technical support during this time was to 'put education at the service of socioeconomic planning being undertaken by the capitalist interests in each country' (Puiggrós, 1999, p 36). However, it was thought that the region lacked the scientific and technical knowledge necessary for capitalist progress (Puiggrós, 1999). As such, multilateral and bilateral organizations and private foundations directed resources not only at creating education planning offices in Central

American countries that could guide efforts to create national education systems, but also to the establishment of private universities that could be expected to produce the knowledge that would serve the development of private industry (McGinn and Warwick, 2006; Harrington, 2009).

As with the 1950s, planning in the 1960s and 1970s also had a regional character. The Regional Office for Central America and Panama of USAID, for example, sponsored a Regional Textbook Center, set up under the supervision of ODECA (Waggoner and Waggoner, 1971). With the help of USAID, 10.1 million textbooks were printed between 1963 and 1969. Given that funding from the US government for this regional centre was set to expire in 1970, ODECA created the Central American Office for Educational Planning in 1967. Nevertheless, the budget was extremely limited (only $42,000 in 1969), with the implication that this office, like other efforts before it, continued to rely on the assistance of international organizations.

In this context, in the 1970s and 1980s – while the case countries analysed in the next chapter experienced repression, revolution, military governments, and social conflict – international assistance continued to play a major role, with each organization approaching education according to its priorities. One example from the 1970s is the support of USAID for TV-based education in El Salvador, as part of the efforts to increase the (cost-effective) coverage and modernization of the system (Lindo-Fuentes and Ching, 2012). These efforts went along with others during the same time in El Salvador related to support for the collection and publication of educational statistics as well as the development of five-year plans (for example, McGinn and Warwick, 2006). Generally, however, there is extremely scant literature that looks at the politics of international cooperation around education in Central America during the 1970s and 1980s.[7] While future research should seek to fill this gap in knowledge, it should be remembered that governments and international organizations during this period were preoccupied with the social unrest that characterized the region (described in the previous section), which led to a decreased emphasis on educational development.

Recalling this regional unrest prompts us to place international involvement related to education within the larger political-economic forces that were transforming Central America. Despite the gains that had been made since the 1950s as Central American governments and international organizations worked together to build up and to modernize education systems, these developments could not contain – and, through heightened expectations of social mobility, perhaps contributed to – social upheaval in the region. For some international organizations, education had been approached from humanist and human rights conceptions; however, from the 1970s onwards, the conception of education put forth by the most influential organizations saw education as an input to the economy (Buzajan et al, 1987). However, the problem was that education did not determine the structure of the economy, meaning that higher levels of education did not lead to better economic opportunities for the majority of the population. In other words, while greater portions of the Central American population were being brought into the formal schooling system (Newland, 1995), it was also the case that the economies of the region were changing, as countries shifted to agro-export and industrial capitalist development, but with the important caveat that the benefits of this development were not distributed in such a way as to prevent social conflict. Robinson (2002) summarizes the dynamic of the time period succinctly:

> From the 1960s onwards the post-Second World War social structure in Central America could no longer be reproduced and began to unravel ... This was a period of very rapid and successful capitalist development in the isthmus. The massive dislocations brought about by capitalist development and the new sets of social contradictions, rather than the lack of changes and development, spawned social crisis and political, and later military, conflict. (Robinson, 2002, pp 228–229)

Importantly, as is often the case, this crisis was also an opportunity for structural transformation, though, as will be described later on, this transformation did not take the form that the revolutionaries would have liked.

The relevant dynamic to which the cases analysed in the next chapter respond would emerge in the 1980s as a result of the dialectic of the global economy. The point here is that the discontent that characterized Nicaragua, El Salvador, Guatemala, and, to a lesser extent, Honduras was not only between peasants and the landed elite who benefited from the traditional agricultural production of such crops as bananas and coffee together with newer agro-exports like sugar, cotton, and beef that had surged in importance from 1945 to the 1970s; rather, there had also emerged other economic elites who benefited from industrialization in the post-Second World War period and who, in the 1980s, would further benefit from nontraditional agricultural exports (for example, specialized fruits and vegetables, canned juices, and boxed beef), the development of maquiladoras, and financial services. Interestingly, while these elites were trapped between traditional oligarchic structures and peasant revolutions, it was only because of the combination of the latter (revolutions) together with macro-economic shifts (explained shortly) that these new elites were able to push for (or at least to benefit from) a new model of development (Robinson, 2002).

Of course, the restructuring of Central America's economies did not occur in a vacuum. This restructuring was prompted by the augmentation and integration of the global economy during the 1960s and 1970s. It was also prompted by changes that were a consequence of the debt crisis of the late 1970s and early 1980s. Contractions in oil production from the Middle East caused global oil prices to rise, which, in turn, directly and indirectly affected the countries of Central America. Directly, oil imports were more expensive. Indirectly, higher oil prices affected these countries because a decrease in oil production in the Middle East meant a drop in investment from oil-producing countries in those same international banks that had lent large sums of money to Central American countries to fund industrialization and development in the 1960s and 1970s. International banks thus contracted their lending while also raising interest rates, which had the effect of making borrowing more expensive and raised the cost of debt service payments (since the loans were denominated in dollars). At the same time, the global recession of the early 1980s meant that Central American exports took a hit. To prevent economic collapse in the region, international financial institutions offered new loans that came along with strict conditions related to restructuring their economies so that they would be more open to the world economy. The efforts of these financial institutions were further supported by both USAID (following the foreign policy priorities of the Reagan Administration) and the local elite who would benefit from the proposed restructuring. Robinson describes the economic transformation of the 1980s well:

> Between 1980 and 1983 all the countries of the isthmus entered into negotiation with the [international financial institutions], particularly with the [International Monetary Fund], and embarked on adjustment programmes. Precursors to full-blown neo-liberalism, these programmes were at first limited and not subject to conditionality, but, as the decade progressed and adjustment increasingly involved conditionality, it became clear that major economic restructuring was in the works. The [International Monetary Fund], the World Bank, the Inter-American Development Bank, and [USAID] and other institutions of a transnational state apparatus began to press the dominant groups in Central America to turn towards 'outward-looking' strategies. Using the region's escalating external debt and balance of payments crisis as leverage, they emphasised liberalisation and non-traditional export-promotion, including export tax exemptions, credits and the use of Export Processing … Zones. (Robinson, 2002, pp 230–232)

From a long-term perspective, then, we can see that: 'The debt crisis of the 1970s and subsequent neoliberal project institutionalized the new definition of development as participation in the world market and the transition from managed national economic growth to managed global economic growth'

(Robinson, 2002, pp 233–234). The implication here is that the logic guiding education reform would also have to change. Education could no longer be seen as an input to a domestically controlled economy, but rather would have to respond more explicitly to the pressures of the global economy, just as other sectors would have to do. This is the key overarching condition that faced the four countries of interest here and in the next chapter in the late 1980s and early 1990s. It is important to keep this in mind because, if the next chapter (and other chapters in this volume) seek to understand the common dynamics of education reform in Central America from 1990 to 2010, then it is necessary to be clear about the larger political-economic pressures that faced the region and that would have ripple effects in terms of how the purpose and nature of education reform was conceptualized.

Thus, to restate, the period of interest began with agreement among (new) national economic elites (and their technocrats), international financial institutions, transnational corporations, and the US government that development should seek to further bring these countries' economies into line with the interests of the global economy. However, each of the actors previously mentioned saw that this kind of development could not be fully successful in the context of socialist revolution (Nicaragua), civil conflict (El Salvador and Guatemala), or inward-looking civilian government (Honduras). Thus, while future research should seek to provide a detailed discussion of the forms of international support for education in these countries in the 1970s and 1980s, the larger and more relevant question at this point relates to how the macro-context of the late 1980s and early 1990s has affected education reform in the countries of Central America as they transitioned out of conflict, continued to open up to the world economy, were subject to geopolitical pressure from the US, and experienced a new wave of intense engagement from international organizations. Before offering an answer to that question in the next chapter, the next section first describes the framework that has guided the analysis.

Framework of analysis

The analytic framework that orients this volume responds directly to the purpose of the present book.[8] As noted in the introductory chapter, the purpose is to draw attention to the global and local forces – and their interaction – that affect education reform in Central America and the Latin Caribbean. Following on from this purpose, the analytic framework contains three interrelated dimensions (Salazar et al, 2018). These dimensions and the dynamics of focus are summarized in Table 2.3.

The first dimension analyses the political economy of education reform. The goal is to unpack the ways in which political and economic forces at the national and international levels structure and constrain periods and processes

Table 2.3: International political economy analytic framework: dimensions and dynamics of focus

Dimension	Dynamics of focus
1. Political economic *drivers* of education reform	The ways in which political and economic forces at the national and international levels structure and constrain periods and processes of education reform. The processes through which policies are produced, the ways in which these processes are affected by political and economic globalization, and how, in turn, they are characterized by interaction (and different forms of influence) among global, national, and local actors.
2. Vested interests and embedded *perspectives* in policy making and enactment	The ways in which different agendas and interests are advanced or brought into tension through the reform in question. How reforms are experienced and perceived by affected or interested parties. The ways in which positions and preferences of different actors are improved or weakened through the enactment of a given reform.
3. Resolution of tensions within the state-capital-education dialectic through ongoing reform	How struggle among interests from different political and economic groups is resolved through the making and enactment of education reform.

Source: Adapted from Salazar et al (2018)

of education reform (Dale, 1999; Edwards, 2018; Verger et al, 2018). Taking these forces into account means being attentive to the ways in which global, national, and local actors engage with one another, which is necessary because, in Central America as elsewhere, education policy is created in ways that are affected by the interplay of influence from each of these levels. At the same time, the economic side of this dimension requires attention to be paid to the tensions engendered by the contradictions that are inherent in education reform within the context of capitalist development (Dale, 1989). Here, the fundamental contradiction is that states are simultaneously driven to pursue policies that advance (global) capitalist interests (in order to grow the economy) while they are also pushed to attend to the needs of the majority of citizens (in order to retain their legitimacy). These tensions have led to pressures to enact governance reforms that enhance access to education, while, in parallel, finding ways not only to reduce the size of the state but also to make it more efficient, more effective, and more accountable (Dale, 1997, 2000; Bonal, 2003; Tarabini and Bonal, 2011).

Of course, there is complementarity between the political and economic sides of this first dimension, since (global) political actors such as the World

Bank and other international organizations as well as corporations use their (material and symbolic) resources to advance policy reforms and rhetoric that align with the economic visions and interests they prefer (Verger, 2012, 2014). In other words, there is also a cultural or semiotic side to this first dimension, in that prominent actors from within and outside government can advance different ideas about what is deemed to be 'good' or 'proper' education, development, or ways of living – and the reform that should lead to it. As these ideas circulate, they have the ability to affect the discursive context within which policy debates occur in complex ways (Campbell, 2002; Béland and Cox, 2010). A central idea here is that policy problems are constructed and not pre-given, with the implication being that one must pay attention to how (and by whom) discourses around education reform are produced and disseminated (Zapp, 2017; Edwards et al, 2020), and how they legitimate certain assumptions or worldviews and not others, thus differentially positioning or characterizing those who are affected by reform (Vavrus and Seghers, 2010).

While the first dimension is more focused on the prevailing structures and relationships within which reforms are developed, the second dimension is directed at understanding the ways in which different agendas and interests are advanced or brought into tension in the development and enactment of the reform in question. Similarly, while the first dimension is concerned, in part, with the sources and production of different discourses, the second dimension turns to assess to those outlooks that are held by a diversity of key actors. The questions of interest, then, are: how and why the reforms being pursued align with the interests of different actors, the ways in which they are advanced in practice, how they are experienced and perceived by affected or interested parties, and the manner in which these different perspectives may reveal tensions across different interest groups. In the sense that this dimension has an underlying focus on the ways in which the interests of individuals, groups, government, and international organizations, among others, are furthered and may create conflict, this dimension can be characterized as political in nature (Malen and Knapp, 1997). However, the emphasis is not only on the making of reform; it is also on the ways in which positions and preferences of different actors are improved or weakened through the enactment of a given reform, where enactment refers to the ways in which policies are interpreted and translated into practice (Braun et al, 2010).

The third dimension – based on (neo)Marxist insights – is an extension of the second, in that it is preoccupied with the ways in which the tensions highlighted earlier are resolved (Apple, 2001; Au, 2018). Whereas the first dimension drew our attention to the structures within which reform occurs, this dimension shifts the analysis to the ways in which conflicts and tensions evolve over the course of a reform and through the pursuit of subsequent reforms (Au, 2018).[9] More specifically, the third dimension zeroes in on the *dialectic* between the economic (capital), the political (state), and the cultural (education) factors that drive education reform (Salazar et al, 2018). Although at times there is a clearer relationship or tension among a pair of these factors, it is important to consider the wider implications of a reform for all three. For example, while the analysis of a given case may focus explicitly on the relationship between political actors and the pursuit of a particular reform, the indirect implications should also be incorporated into the analysis in terms of how the pursuit of a particular policy may benefit the economic interests of certain actors or of the larger global capitalist system (see Chapter 15, this volume).

As with the first dimension, this third one connects with the cultural or semiotic nature of reform. This is so in the sense that the struggle for subsequent reform is inherently about, or guided by, ideas – and, as Farahmandpur writes, 'ideological and discursive struggles must be linked to "material-practical" struggles' (2004, p 12). The implication, then, is that we should be attentive to the way in which discursive production accompanies the alteration or maintenance of the reform context, and to the way in which this discourse may benefit certain (political-economic) interests and not others.

The framework employed here is not only appropriate for the purpose of the kinds of analysis presented in this volume, but also makes a contribution to the literature on how global forces affect education reform. It does so by going beyond a concern with the process of policy formation and the influence of international organizations to also consider the ways in which reform and its inherent tensions are experienced, driven by, and resolved through the perspectives of national and local actors – all while being attentive to the macro-structural developments of a political-economic nature that have both conditioned governments in the region and have facilitated the advance of global capitalism. Ultimately, the goal is to understand the dynamics that produce policies, but also the way in which underlying political and economic tensions, within a capitalist system, are advanced and reconciled through the making and enactment of education reform. The next chapter moves in this direction by applying this framework to a cross-country analysis of El Salvador, Guatemala, Honduras, and Nicaragua.

Notes

[1] Until 1821, much of what is now called Central America was the Captaincy General of Guatemala, a territory of New Spain.

[2] For more on German involvement in Central American trade during the 1930s, see Coatsworth (1994).

[3] This is not to say that there were not internal political dynamics that were unfavourable to the US and its business interests, including worker strikes and the influence of the labour movement (Bulmer-Thomas, 1987).

[4]   Gambone (2001) provides an insightful quote from Aaron Brown, the US ambassador to Nicaragua, on the difficulty of gaining USAID approval for new development projects. In a letter to USAID, Brown wrote: 'We cannot avoid the suspicion that a request at this late date for additional information of such enormously demanding scope, and largely of such questionable relevance to a serious consideration of the loan application, can only have been concocted with the deliberate intent of delaying indefinitely any real action on this loan, or even burying it once and for all under the weight of a hostile bureaucracy' (2001, p 75).

[5]   However, having noted this, it is surprisingly difficult to find information on the nature or details of support to Central America before the 2000s that is not related to US bilateral support or to multilateral support from the World Bank and to the Inter-American Development Bank (Baumann, 2008; Krakowski, 2008).

[6]   It should be noted that peasants in these countries also had the backing of the urban middle class.

[7]   Buzajan et al (1987) address international organization rhetoric and involvement in Latin America during the period from 1970 to 1984, but the commentary and examples included are not specific to Central America.

[8]   It should be noted that this framework orients the book project as a whole. Although not explicitly discussed in some of the cases, all chapters, first, situate themselves in relation to the interaction of global, national, and local dynamics, and, second, offer commentary that speaks to the way in which forces from these three levels interact, and with implications for the political-economic drivers of reform, the vested interests and embedded perspectives in policy making and policy enactment, and, finally, the way in which ongoing reforms help to resolve tensions within the state-capital-education dialectic (this will be explained later on). The implications of each chapter are then further drawn out and analysed in the cross-case analysis chapter (Chapter 15).

[9]   Rather than, as is often the case in neo-Marxist scholarship, in the content of the curriculum.

References

Apple, M. (2001). *Educating the Right Way Book*. Routledge.

Archer, D. (1994). The changing roles of non-governmental organizations in the field of education (in the context of changing relationships with the state). *International Journal of Educational Development*, 14(3), 223–232.

Au, W. (2018). *A Marxist Education: Learning to Change the World*. Haymarket Books.

Barry, T. (1991). *Central America Inside out: The Essential Guide to Its Societies, Politics, and Economics*. Grove Weidenfeld.

Baumann, R. (2008). Integration in Latin America: trends and challenges. Economic Commission for Latin America and the Caribbean. LC/BRS/R.190. https://www.cepal.org/en/publications/37936-integration-latin-america-trends-and-challenges

Béland, D., and Cox, R. H. (eds.). (2010). *Ideas and Politics in Social Science Research*. Oxford University Press.

Biekart, K. (2013). European NGOs and democratisation in Central America: assessing performance in the light of changing priorities. In M. Edwards and D. Hulme (eds.), *Non-governmental Organizations: Performance and Accountability beyond the Magic Bullet* (pp 63–72). Earthscan.

Bonal, X. (2003). The neoliberal educational agenda and the legitimation crisis: old and new state strategies. *British Journal of Sociology of Education*, 24(2), 159–175.

Braun, A., Maguire, M., and Ball, S. (2010). Policy enactments in the UK secondary school: examining policy, practice and school positioning. *Journal of Education Policy*, 24(4), 547–560.

Bull, B. (2005). *Aid, Power and Privatization: The Politics of Telecommunication Reform in Central America*. Edward Elgar.

Bulmer-Thomas, V. (1987). *The Political Economy of Central America since 1920*. Cambridge University Press.

Buzajan, M., Hare, S., La Belle, T., and Stafford, L. (1987). International agency assistance to education in Latin America and the Caribbean, 1970–1984. *Comparative Education*, 23(2), 161–171.

Campbell, J. L. (2002). Ideas, politics, and public policy. *Annual Review of Sociology*, 28, 21–38.

Coatsworth, J. (1994). *Central America and the United States: The Clients and the Colossus*. Twayne.

Cox, R. (1994). *Power and Profits: US policy in Central America*. University Press of Kentucky.

Cruz Bustamante, M. T. (ed.) (2022). *Quality of Education in Central America: Dynamics and Tensions between the Model of Education and the Model of Development*. Publicaciones Académicas UCA.

Dale, R. (1989). *The State and Education Policy*. Open University Press.

Dale, R. (1997). The state and the governance of education: an analysis of the restructuring of the state-education relationship. In A. H. Halsey, H. Lauder, P. Brown, and A. S. Wells (eds.), *Education: Culture, Economy, Society* (pp 273–282). Oxford University Press.

Dale, R. (1999). Specifying globalization effects on national policy: focus on the mechanisms. *Journal of Education Policy*, 14(1), 1–17.

Dale, R. (2000). Globalization and education: demonstrating a 'common world educational culture' or locating a 'globally structured educational agenda'? *Educational Theory*, 50(4), 427–448.

Edwards Jr., D. B. (2018). *The Trajectory of Global Education Policy: Community-Based Management in El Salvador and the Global Reform Agenda*. Palgrave Macmillan.

Edwards Jr., D. B, Morrison, J., and Hall, S. (2020). The suspect statistics of best practices: a triple critique of knowledge production and mobilization in the global education policy field. *Globalsation, Societies and Education*, 18(2), 125–148.

Farahmandpur, R. (2004). Essay review: a Marxist critique of Michael Apple's neo-Marxist approach to educational reform. *Journal for Critical Education Policy Studies*, 2(1), 1–30. http://www.jceps.com/wp-content/uploads/PDFs/02-1-4.pdf

Gambone, M. (2001). *Capturing the Revolution: The US, Central America, and Nicaragua, 1961–1972*. Praeger.

Harrington, J. (2009). Private higher education in a Cold War world: Central America. *American Educational History Journal*, 36(1), 133–150.

Kennedy, J. (1962). *Public Papers of the Presidents of the United States: January 1 to December 31, 1962*. US Government Printing Office.

Krakowski, M. (2008). The relations between the European Union and Latin America and the Caribbean: current state and perspectives, *Intereconomics* (March/April), 112–120.

Langley, L., and Schoonover, T. (1995). *The Banana Men: American Mercenaries and Entrepreneurs in Central America, 1880–1930*. University Press of Kentucky.

Lindo-Fuentes, H., and Ching, E. (2012). *Modernizing Minds in El Salvador: Education Reform and the Cold War, 1960–1980*. University of New Mexico Press.

Malen, B., and Knapp, M. (1997). Rethinking the multiple perspectives approach to education policy analysis: implications for policy-practice connections. *Journal of Education Policy*, 12(5), 419–445.

McCall, R. (1989). The Alliance for Progress: an appraisal. In W. Ascher and A. Hubbard (eds.), *Central American Recovery and Development: Task Force Report to the International Commission* (pp 343–356). Duke University Press.

McClellan, G. (1963). *US Policy in Latin America*. H. W. Wilson Company.

McGinn, N., and Warwick, D. (2006). La planeación educativa: ¿Ciencia o política? *Revista Latinoamericana de Estudios Educativos*, XXXVI(1–2), 153–182.

Newland, C. (1995). Spanish American elementary education 1950–1992: bureaucracy, growth and decentralization. *International Journal of Educational Development*, 15(2), 103–114.

Patch, R. (2013). *Indians and the Political Economy of Colonial Central America, 1670–1810*. University of Oklahoma Press.

Puiggrós, A. (1999). *Imperialism and Education in Latin America*. Westview.

Robinson, W. (2002). Globalisation as a macro-structural-historical framework of analysis: the case of Central America. *New Political Economy*, 7(2), 221–250.

Robinson, W. (2003). *Transnational Conflicts: Central America, Social Change, and Globalization*. Verso.

Salazar, M., Cruz, M., Vasquéz, L., Delgado, B., and Paz, L. (2018). Calidad de la educación en Centroamérica: Dinámicas y tensiones entre los modelos de educación y de desarrollo. Universidad Centroaméricana, José Simeón Cañas.

Tarabini, A., & Bonal, X. (2011). Globalización y política educativa: los mecanismos como método. Revista de Educación, 235–255.

Waggoner, G., and Waggoner, B. (1971). *Education in Central America*. University Press of Kansas.

Vavrus, F., and Seghers, M. (2010). Critical discourse analysis in comparative education: a discursive study of 'partnership' in Tanzania's poverty reduction policies. *Comparative Education Review*, 54(1), 77–103.

Verger, A. (2012). Framing and selling global education policy: the promotion of public–private partnerships for education in low-income contexts. *Journal of Education Policy*, 27(1), 109–130.

Verger, A. (2014). Why do policy-makers adopt global education policies? Toward a research framework on the varying role of ideas in education reform. *Current Issues in Comparative Education*, 16(2), 14–29.

Verger, A., Novelli, M., and Kosar-Altinyelken, H. (eds.). (2018). *Global Education Policy and International Development: New Agendas, Issues and Policies*. Bloomsbury.

Williams, R. (1986). *Export Agriculture and the Crisis in Central America*. University of North Carolina Press.

World Bank. (1994). *El Salvador: Community Education Strategy: Decentralized School Management*. World Bank.

Zapp, M. (2017) The World Bank and education: governing (through) knowledge. *International Journal of Educational Development*, 53(1), 1–11.

PART II

Central America

3

Comparative Analysis of Education Reform in Central America: El Salvador, Guatemala, Honduras, and Nicaragua, 1990–2010

D. Brent Edwards Jr.

Introduction

As noted in the introductory chapter to this volume, Central America is a region about which comparatively little academic literature is produced that focuses on the political-economic dynamics that constrain education reform. However, one research project stands out as an exception. This research project, carried out from 2018 to 2022 by a network of researchers from the region,[1] was entitled 'Quality Education in Central America: Dynamics and Tensions among Models of Education and Development'. It brought together scholars from four Central American countries to produce case studies on El Salvador, Guatemala, Honduras, and Nicaragua. These case studies – published in Cruz (2022) and summarized in Table 3.1 – offer nuanced insights into the national- and local-level tensions that have surrounded the development and implementation of education reform in these countries, while also being attentive to the influence of geopolitical dynamics, macro-economic pressures, global policy trends, and the role of international organizations. In other words, the value of these studies stems from the multilevel and international political-economic perspective that guides them. These studies are also unique in terms of the level of complexity and depth by which they are characterized, not to mention the extended time period (from around 1990 to 2010) that served as the focus of their investigations.

Table 3.1: Summary of case studies compared

Country	Title of case study	Author (affiliation)	Policy focus
El Salvador	Education reform 1995–2005: a social and political pact between the model of education and the model of development	María Teresa Cruz, Knut Walter, Luis Calero, Rolando Flores (Central American University, San Salvador)	Ten Year Plan, community-based management of education
Guatemala	A superficial model of education quality: between seduction, privatization and continuity with the past	Mónica Salazar Vides (Rafael Lándivar University)	Community-based management of education
Honduras	Evaluation policy in Honduras: characterizing the structural limitations, evolution, and perspectives of key actors	Carla Leticia Paz, Ricardo Morales (National Pedagogic University)	Evaluation policy in education
Nicaragua	School autonomy: participation, decentralization, and education quality	Byron Antonio Delgado Paz (Central American University, Managua)	Community-based management of education

Source: Author

The present chapter thus makes a contribution by presenting insights that derive from a cross-case analysis of these studies, each of which was based on document analysis, literature review, and interviews.[2] In so doing, it seeks to add breadth to the depth provided by each individual case. This is achieved by analysing the chapters jointly in order to present cross-cutting themes. The themes included here are organized according to the framework discussed in Chapter 2 – rooted in international political economy – which, it should be noted, also served as the analytic guide in the process of producing the individual studies.[3] To summarize the discussion of the framework from Chapter 2, the three levels, or dimensions, of the framework highlight: (a) processes of policy making and how these are affected by such considerations as geopolitical constraints, capitalist pressures, and international organizations; (b) the ways in which different reform visions are communicated, interpreted, and experienced; and (c) the manner in which tensions across political-economic forces and interest groups are resolved. Specifically, this last dimension refers to the way in which education helps to mediate and resolve tensions that arise between the state and capital in the context of capitalist development.

Cross-case analysis is facilitated by a number of characteristics. These include the close geographical proximity of the case study countries and, along with this, the interrelated geopolitical pressures experienced by them (as will be further discussed). Other characteristics that enable cross-case analysis are: the examination of a common time period from around 1990 to 2010), similar domestic political struggles, and related kinds of policies being analysed. On this last point, two of the four case studies focus squarely on community involvement in the management of education. One of these cases is Guatemala, which examines the life and death of the programme known as the National Community-Managed Program for Educational Development (or PRONADE, for its name in Spanish). The second of these cases is Nicaragua, where the Autonomous Schools Program was created. While the case study of El Salvador focuses primarily on the development and experience of the Ten Year Plan during the 1990s, it also situates its analysis in relation to that country's experience with community management of education, which enhances its comparability with Guatemala and Nicaragua.[4] The final case, Honduras, took as its unit of analysis the policy of evaluation in schools, with a focus specifically on the development and enactment of standardized tests. However, most important is that in all four cases there are not only similar principles (efficiency, effectiveness, and accountability) which underlie the policies being analysed, but also similar political-economic dynamics driving the reform processes, with the implication being that all four policies are apt for comparison. This is particularly true when, in being guided by the framework in Chapter 2, the focus of analysis is not so much on the outcomes of reform (as in student learning), but rather the structural, perspectival, and dialectical nature of the reforms being studied.

A core concept for each of the case studies is the idea of education quality. As will be discussed, in Guatemala and Nicaragua, the approach of community-based management was supposed to lead to improved education quality, while in Honduras, a focus on evaluation and standardized testing was supposed to do the same. In El Salvador, the idea of education quality meant different things to different actors, though some actors' voices were more influential than others in terms of steering the direction of policy. However, what is most salient, and what will be highlighted in this chapter, is that across the region, the idea of education quality has varied along with changes to the thinking that has guided the dominant approach to development. In other words, the definition of education quality is flexible and can be seen as a function of the paradigm of international development within which the countries of Central America have operated at different times. Since the 1980s, the most influential approach to governance has been known as New Public Management. The details of this approach will be discussed in a later section.

For now, it is important to underscore that this chapter, in providing a comparative analysis, responds to the questions that guided the production of each underlying case study. These questions were as follows:

> How were the educational quality models configured in the education reform processes in Central America, considering the dynamics and tensions between educational models and development models? To solve this great question, it will be important to understand: How is the relationship between development models and educational models in the region configured? And, how is the relationship between the educational model and the models of educational quality in the region configured? To have clarity on the relationship between the economic and the educational, and then between the educational model and the quality models in the region, it is necessary to know: Which actors participated – and how – in the formation of the educational quality model included in the educational reform process? (Salazar et al, 2018, p 231)

To answer these questions, the chapter is structured in the following way. The first section discusses the political economy of processes of education policy formation. This section addresses five themes: (a) structural constraints; (b) education within the Washington Consensus and the emergence of New Public Management; (c) pilot programmes as the entry point for international influence; (d) implications for equity; (e) the way in which New Public Management reforms become the centre of gravity in education reform dynamics; and (f) the role of knowledge production and mobilization.

The second section of the chapter then shifts away from larger political-economic considerations to focus instead on the perspectives, agendas, and interests of key actors in education reform. This section has four subsections, which focus on: (a) the role of international agendas; (b) the way in which education reform has been used to undermine political opposition in these countries; (c) tensions between governments and teachers' unions; and (d) the perspectives of teachers related to the examined reforms.

The third section of the chapter then brings the dynamics of the first two sections into conversation by focusing on how education can serve to resolve the tensions between state and capital identified in Chapter 2. This section discusses Honduras on its own, given that the kind of reform of interest in that case was different from the other three. Here, the relationship between capital, the approach of New Public Management, and the dysfunctional state in Honduras is addressed. Then, the cases of El Salvador, Honduras, and Nicaragua are discussed together, given their common focus on community involvement policies. This section highlights the structural limitations of the post-community-based management period in Central America.

The concluding section then offers brief comments on the benefits of employing a political economy lens for analysing education reform in Central America.

Political economy of education policy processes

Structural constraints

A cross-case analysis of the political economy of education reform must draw attention to the structural relationships that constrained certain kinds of policy and enabled others. The studies being compared here highlighted three structural features: first, geopolitical intervention from the US; second, economic dependency on the world economy; and, third, economic reforms associated with the 'Washington Consensus'. On the first point, while the US government sought to undermine the Sandinista revolution in Nicaragua and to defeat the guerrilla groups in El Salvador, it also secretly supported the Guatemalan government in its genocidal campaign against indigenous populations who were in conflict with the government. Of course, this conflict had grown out of the destabilization that resulted from the US-backed coup in 1954 against President Jacobo Árbenz, who favoured land reform. And in Honduras, although the military was no longer formally in control in the 1980s, those civilians in power were still loyal to it. Moreover, Honduras was, for the US, a centre of coordination for intervention in other countries, and thus received immense sums of military aid (see Chapter 2). The backdrop of the Cold War and the desire of the US to maintain its economic interests in the region drove these interventions.

The second and third structural features were extensively addressed in Chapter 2. What can be added here are examples of the nature of the Washington Consensus. As noted in the study on Honduras, agreements with the International Monetary Fund (IMF) starting in 1990 required, among other things, that the government remove price controls (including on basic needs), allow interest rates to be set by the market, reduce income taxes, eliminate taxes on exports, decrease the government budget, and privatize public services (see also Morales–Ulloa and Moschetti, this volume Chapter 4). While such reforms have a clear impact on education, for example, in that the government's ability to generate revenue (for example, through taxes) is limited, what is also important to remember here is that these economic policies were part of a larger reorientation of Central American economies towards the global marketplace (see Chapter 2). Thus, at the same time that countries in the region were making efforts to shift from conflict and authoritarianism to peace and democracy, a simultaneous economic transition was occurring that, in effect, would undermine the ability of these states to address the root causes of conflict. Incorporation into the global economy transformed the nature of the government's relationship to the economy – going from being director of it to serving as a facilitator for global capital – and further eschewed the question of structural transformation of the economy in favour of those who had been historically dispossessed and disadvantaged by capitalist accumulation.

Worryingly, these reforms combined with and reinforced colonial tendencies, where the economic and political elite saw the state as a vehicle for its own advancement. Not only were the economic and the education systems of the region to be put in the service of the global economy, but these same systems would be used to enrich members of the upper classes, just as they always had been. Perhaps nowhere is this more clear than in Honduras. With political parties themselves having been founded by banana companies in the late 1800s, the state has historically operated as a vehicle for the benefit of those in power together with their networks. This point will be further addressed later.

Education within the Washington Consensus: towards New Public Management

If the Washington Consensus was a tool by which the economies of the region were liberalized, then education was seen as a means by which the countries of Central America could prepare themselves to benefit from this liberalization. This way of thinking about education was consistent with human capital theory, which had gained traction since the 1960s. However, this perspective – with its emphasis on producing the skills that would be necessary inputs for the economy – was not new to the region in the 1980s and 1990s; rather, the logic of human capital theory had guided education planning since the 1960s. In this respect, we can see continuity in the pronouncements in high-profile reports from governments and international organizations in the postwar period about the importance of education for contributing to economic growth.

What was new was the added emphasis on reducing the size and increasing the efficiency of government. The latter goal was to be achieved through a focus on governance, that is, a focus on the way that education systems were managed. The focus on management grew out of the frustration that resulted from perceptions of unsuccessful development in the 1960s and 1970s, where success was thought of in terms of countries advancing on the path to modernization, 'catching up' and joining the ranks of consumerist societies (Leys, 1996). Whereas state-led development had been typical during the 1970s, development organizations began to see the state itself as a problem. As one example, the World Bank, in its World Development Report, indicated that it now considered the organization and operation of central governments to be fundamental obstacles to progress (World Bank, 1980). This document pointed to both 'inappropriate administrative structures' and an 'undue emphasis on central control' as 'institutional problems' impeding development (World Bank, 1980, p 76).

Over the course of the 1980s, the argument developed that the challenges of the state should be addressed through the incorporation of principles from New Public Management. As Anderson and Cohen write, 'public organizations have always been *managed*, but in the last four decades there has been a shift from a rule-governed, administrative, bureaucratic management to an outcomes-based, entrepreneurial, corporate model of management' (2015, p 3, emphasis in original). In education, this has meant, among other things:

- the introduction of markets and quasi-markets to create competition among public organizations and private entities;
- an emphasis on explicit standards and measures of performance;
- greater emphasis on outcomes and their measurement using quantitative data;
- contracting-out of public services to vendors in the private sector and the increased use of consulting companies;
- a trend towards temporary and short-term workers and against unionization;
- administrative decentralization and bounded autonomy;
- greater discipline and parsimony in resource use (Anderson and Cohen, 2015, p 3).

These tendencies have been adapted to education reforms throughout Latin America (Straubhaar, 2017). In Central America, the most prominent examples of New Public Management have been related to evaluation, accountability, and decentralization. Perhaps unsurprisingly, the four studies being comparatively analysed here focus on these kinds of reforms.

There is a direct connection between New Public Management and the idea of quality, which is relevant to point out, given the centrality of the concept of quality to the reforms analysed in each of the case studies. For New Public Management, quality is measured by outcomes (usually test score data), and better outcomes should result from the implementation of the practices described earlier. Thus, if systems achieve 'good governance' through New Public Management, then quality will be improved, with the underlying assumption that test scores are a proxy for learning, and learning is, in turn, a proxy for the calibre of a country's human capital, which itself is assumed to be a key ingredient in achieving positive economic growth.

New Public Management in Central America's education reform

The case studies of El Salvador, Guatemala, Honduras, and Nicaragua look at high-profile education reforms. In each case, the logic of New Public Management is clearly visible. In Honduras, since the late 1980s, there has been, and continues to be, a focus on standardized testing, particularly in maths and Spanish. This emphasis has consistently been supported by projects from international organizations. Notably, the focus is not only on the development of standardized tests but also on the creation of curriculum objectives and information systems. This is important to note because it is not possible to use test scores as part of an accountability mechanism for schools and teachers without some means of recording and disseminating those test scores and then judging them against what students should learn. In 2007, with support from United States Agency for International Development (USAID), Honduras began to test students in grades 1–9 in maths and Spanish. This has been complemented with participation in a range of international standardized tests in 2011, 2013, and 2018.[5] More will be said later on about how standardized tests in Honduras have been perceived and contested.

The other three case studies looked at different models of community-based management (CBM). (Although it is not the focus of the Honduras case study, this country also adopted CBM.) The thinking behind these models is that school management councils at the local level can do a better job of managing schools than can functionaries located at other levels of government (see later on for details of council composition). CBM, in its logic, can thus be seen as a response to frustrations with ineffective state management of the education system. More explicitly, the logic of CBM is that councils at the school level will lead to greater: (a) *accountability* through their ability to hire/fire and monitor teachers (or, in Nicaragua, the principal); (b) *efficiency* through their ability to make decisions (or to provide input) on how the school budget is spent, with the assumption being that schools will only purchase those materials that they most need; (c) *cost savings* since community members contribute to the construction and maintenance of schools and/or contribute financially through paying school fees; and (d) *effectiveness* in the sense of producing better outcomes, a result of the fact that teachers will be absent less often and will try harder (so as not to lose their job) and students will have those resources that they need. Table 3.2 summarizes the functions that were decentralized in each country.

An additional consideration (except in Nicaragua) was that this model would help to rapidly extend educational access in those areas where communities did not have schools. This dimension of the CBM experience reveals – from the perspective of its proponents – the compatibility of New Public Management approaches with the simultaneous push during the 1990s to achieve the goals of the Education for All campaign. Although New Public Management strategies frequently led to greater inequity (as will be discussed later on), there is no inherent tension in the logic of New Public Management with the political priority of enrolling more children in school. New Public Management advocates are not against the massification of education; rather, they focus on how schools and the system should be governed once children are enrolled.

Table 3.2: Functions decentralized to school councils

Council functions	El Salvador	Guatemala	Honduras	Nicaragua
Personnel management				
Paying staff salaries	★	★	★	★
Establishing incentives for teaching staff				★
Hiring/firing teaching staff	★	★	★	★
Supervising and evaluating teachers	★	★	★	★
Hiring/firing administrative staff				★
Pedagogy				
Setting classroom hours by subject				★
Selecting some textbooks				★
School calendar		★		★
Maintenance and infrastructure				
Building/maintaining school	★	★	★	★
Buying school material	★	★	★	★
Budget				
Budget oversight	★	★	★	★
Budget allocation				★
Establishing school fees				★

Source: Di Gropello (2006)

With regard to key characteristics, in Nicaragua, the school councils were made up of teachers together with the school principal, who retained formal decision-making power.[6] In El Salvador, the councils were composed of five parents elected from the community; these parents then had the legal responsibility of contracting teachers and spending the school budget, in addition to carrying out the other tasks described earlier and in Table 4.1. The situation in Guatemala was similar in that school councils were only composed of parents, who assumed the same responsibilities as in El Salvador. Interestingly, Guatemala represented the furthest step towards privatization in that the government's implementing unit subcontracted 'educational supervision institutions' (ISEs) to provide support to communities as they joined the CBM programme and implemented the model. These subcontracted institutions could be private companies, nongovernmental organizations (NGOs), foundations, international cooperation organizations, investment funds, mayor's offices, or civil society organizations. In El Salvador and Nicaragua, support (where it was offered) came from the departmental and municipal levels of government, respectively.

Following on from this point, it is necessary to signal that the pursuit of New Public Management policies in Central America did not represent the abdication of government responsibility, for, in each country, the Ministry of Education retained key roles. For example, the case of Guatemala highlights the financial contributions of the government. Although financial and technical support from the World Bank was instrumental in the trajectory of Guatemala's CBM programme, it is also the case that external funding represented no more than 10 per cent of the total investment. In Nicaragua and El Salvador, the central Ministry of Education maintained control over the curriculum, auditing of administrative processes, development of standards, evaluation of quality, and the creation of new teacher positions. And in the case of standardized testing in Honduras, despite the persistent interest in this topic from international organizations, it is the government that decided the extent of testing and that formally implements it. In all cases, what we can see is that the enactment of New Public Management reforms did not lead to the elimination of the state, but rather to a transformation in its role, where it is expected to govern according to the principles of accountability, efficiency, and effectiveness.

Pilot programmes as the entry point for education reform

Pilot programmes, not formal policy-making processes, have often been the key entry point for education reform in Central America. This is true in the case of the four case studies. In Guatemala, for example, the CBM programme was first introduced as a pilot programme in early 1992, though it would not be until late 1996 that the government institutionalized it as its principal focus for education reform. The timing of these actions is conspicuous because it shows that PRONADE was already de facto government policy before the Peace Accords had been signed (at the end of 1996) and before the official and participatory process of generating policy recommendations could conclude (in 1998). Moreover, the pilot programme itself was designed by the United Nations Development Programme together with the government. This technical support, together with financial support from the World Bank starting in 1994 in the form of a $20 million loan, was key, first, in creating the opportunity to experiment with the CBM model and, second, in helping to generate momentum for it among those in power (though it should be noted that officials from Guatemala had since the early days of El Salvador's CBM experiment been interested in learning from and adapting the latter's model;

Edwards, 2018). The fact that public consultation and transparent processes were bypassed indicates the extent to which the government wanted to move forward without pushback. More will be said later on about the government's perspective.

Guatemala was not alone. El Salvador and Nicaragua had similar experiences. In El Salvador's case, the Education with Community Participation programme (EDUCO) was created as a pilot project in late 1990 with technical assistance from the United Nations Children's Fund and was further supported financially and technically in 1991 (and beyond) by the World Bank, once the government agreed to pursue this model. Again, the key decisions were made prior to the Peace Accords and outside of public processes for consultation and setting priorities, which would culminate with the Ten Year Plan. In Nicaragua, the CBM model was piloted with support from both USAID and the World Bank, though in this case programme experimentation began in 1993, three years after the peace agreement was signed in 1990. Honduras, for its part, began to experiment with standardized testing in the late 1980s through one of USAID's programmes, a trend that has continued as governmental support for standardized testing waxes and wanes.

But in all cases, what is clear is the connection between these policy reforms, on the one hand, and what has been labelled 'disaster capitalism' (Klein, 2007) and 'privatization by way of catastrophe' (Verger et al, 2016). These terms refer to the way in which crises are used to advance capitalism and privatization. It is true that only El Salvador and Guatemala were still in contexts of conflict, but it is also the case that Nicaragua and Honduras (like El Salvador and Guatemala) were not only in economic crisis but were also in the midst of structural adjustment reforms. They were thus dependent on both financial infusions from international institutions like the IMF and the World Bank, and the technical support provided by other international organizations that were guiding reform in the context of low administrative and planning capacity. It is in this way that the logic of private sector managerialism has made inroads in the education systems of Central America.

Implications for equity

All of the reforms examined here had negative implications for equity. The next section addresses why reforms of a different nature were not pursued. For now, comments are offered to explain the equity dimension.

In the case of Honduras, the preoccupation with standardized tests equated to a focus on outcomes rather than a consideration of the unequal conditions that are found across schools and that characterize different families. As the authors of the case study note: 'Assessment

… becomes a political instrument, aimed at avoiding the discourse of educational inequalities, since what is intended is the standardization of basic competencies' (Paz and Morales, 2022, p 219). Standardization and evaluation become part of a self-reinforcing cycle that leads to greater inequality since, in the words of these authors, 'these data are used to discredit public education and thus to justify the reduction of the education sector budget, as well as the opening of the education system to private companies and non-governmental organizations who, through alternative approaches, cover those sectors that the State fails to reach' (Paz and Morales, 2022, p 221).

The CBM models show similar tendencies. In Nicaragua, schools working under this model were found to charge significant fees equivalent to at least 20 per cent of the annual Ministry of Education budget. While traditional public schools also charged fees, students in CBM schools paid 40 per cent more on average. The ability to raise funds was central to the Nicaraguan model of CBM, since these funds were used to supplement teacher salaries (more on this later). Over time, the effect of this practice was the creation of a two-tier system of CBM schools divided along lines of location (urban vs. peri-urban/rural), class (higher vs. lower socioeconomic status), and size (more vs. fewer students to serve, and from whom to collect fees). In addition to the fact that the CBM programme in El Salvador charged fees slightly higher than the level collected by traditional public schools (Cuéllar-Marchelli, 2003), the EDUCO model was associated with inequity for two additional reasons. The first of these was because the councils depended on the labour of (primarily rural) parents in marginalized communities. Cuéllar-Marchelli estimated that the value of these parents' contributions was equivalent to '28% of the work done by all [of the Ministry of Education's] administrative and support staff assisting all public schools' (2003, p 159). Second, EDUCO, like the CBM models in Guatemala and Honduras, offered undignified working conditions for teachers in that they were only given one-year contracts and were not allowed to join the teachers' unions. An additional characteristic of these CBM models noted by the case study of Guatemala (but true of the other countries as well) is that teachers were younger, had less experience, and were working in schools that were in poor condition in terms of infrastructure and didactic materials. Thus, even though the CBM model in Guatemala was, in part, supposed to enable indigenous teachers to teach in their own community schools, the programme was not equipped to set them up for success. For all the rhetoric of accountability, these programmes were not designed with the aim of holding the government accountable for the equitable provision of resources; rather, they were designed in a way that allowed the state to reduce its costs and to shift the burden on to other (marginalized) actors.

New Public Management reforms as centre of gravity

Given the implications for equity, it might seem curious that these models were adopted and continued for so long (the demise of the CBM programmes is discussed later). In order to explain their longevity, it must be recalled that these reforms were the centre of gravity in that they diverted attention away from other programmes and were a focal point for national and international actors alike. On this point, while the education systems in these (and all) countries do many things, the question here is where the attention, energy, and excitement are directed when it comes to education reform. When there are budget constraints, change to the status quo often come about through resource infusions that fall outside the recurrent expenses that consume the majority (typically 90 per cent or more) of the budget. Starting from such a position, the authors of the study on Honduras note that 'the Honduran government is not in a position to reject any proposal from the World Bank and international cooperating partners' (Paz and Morales, 2022, p 251). But what is not typically acknowledged is the fact that government investment in education is inadequate. Rather, as noted by Delgado (2022) in the case of Nicaragua, donor organizations focus on the inefficiency of the system and, in line with New Public Management thinking, the need to introduce managerial principles and practices adapted from or inspired by the business sector.

At the same time, because of the clout and resources of such organizations as the World Bank and USAID, the initiatives of other organizations may lack the political support necessary to be successful. In contexts where ministers of education have many demands on their time and many urgent matters that need attention (as in the 1990s, when transitioning out of conflict and crisis), those organizations that are better able to advance their own agendas and to align them with the priorities of the government are going to have more success. These dynamics contribute to explaining the lack of either prominence or longevity of the projects initiated by UNESCO in Honduras and El Salvador which focused on education for peace and democracy (Edwards, Victoria, and Martin, 2015; Delgado, 2022). In the words of Delgado, 'it was not possible for [UNESCO's] efforts to take root due to the State's emphasis on promoting curricular transformation and educational decentralization', the latter of which was supported by USAID and the World Bank (Delgado, 2022, p 252).

As a final point here, the study of El Salvador highlights the need to look beyond official policy texts in order to understand the real priorities of government, that is, the need to look at which programmes are being supported. These programmes may align with the language of official policy texts without being named explicitly in them. And, indeed, it may be the case that policy texts are constructed to reflect the priorities embedded in those programmes supported by international organizations rather than the other way around. The Ten Year Plan in El Salvador was presented in 1995 and included four general areas of emphasis: educational access ('coverage'); institutional modernization; quality improvement; and education for human, ethical, and civic values. This language was broad enough to encompass any programmes that the government or international donors might want to pursue, or, indeed, were already pursuing – and this is exactly what happened. As one example, the EDUCO programme had begun in 1991 and was the focal point of the Ministry of Education and international partners in the postwar period, with the implication being that the multiyear process of consultation, dialogue, and commissions that preceded the production of the Ten Year Plan can be seen as an exercise in compensatory legitimation (Weiler, 1983), that is, as an effort to legitimate the decisions that, in practical terms, had already been made, such as institutional commitment to achieving modernization and efficiency through the EDUCO programme (Edwards, 2018).

Knowledge production and mobilization

Part of the reason why the reforms highlighted in these case studies were able to maintain momentum, or were able to take precedence over other reforms, is because of the discourse and knowledge production abilities of international organizations. In Honduras, for example, the idea that education quality should be linked to processes of evaluation and standardization was promoted by USAID's Education Modernization Program (Programa de Modernización de la Educación, 1990–1994). Paz and Morales write that this programme 'was clear in stating that the educational system needed to introduce assessment as a mechanism of control and standardization for the improvement of learning outcomes' (2022, p 252). Or, when not sending out messages themselves in an attempt to influence reform priorities, international organizations can create the research infrastructure necessary at the country level so that surrogate entities will advance their perspectives. Again, the words of Paz and Morales are revelatory in the case of Honduras:

> Following this policy line, in 1996, the Honduran government initiated the first major project for the modernization of education financed by the World Bank and the German Development Bank (KFW) and with which the External Unit for the Measurement of Education Quality (*Unidad Externa de Medición de la Calidad de la Educación,* UMCE) was created. This entity would be outside the Ministry of Education, would implement standardized tests, would carry out research on factors associated with learning, and would lay the foundations of evaluation for accountability purposes. (Paz and Morales, 2022, p 203)

Of course, the point here is not only the fact of knowledge production, but the connection between research capacity, the policy priorities that are advanced through that capacity, and the way in which the discursive context around a given reform context can be driven by the ideological interests of international organizations. Samoff refers to this constellation of factors as the 'financial–intellectual complex' within which research for development is produced (1993, p 213).

To be sure, the dynamics mentioned previously have played out in the other country studies as well. For example, in Nicaragua, Delgado writes that 'the international organizations sponsored research processes on the effectiveness of School Autonomy. In the resulting studies, the model was presented as a bold route to decentralization throughout the Central American region' (2022), p 163). The same experience occurred in El Salvador, where the World Bank not only produced six impact evaluations of the EDUCO programme but also extensively promoted the results within and beyond Latin America (Edwards and Loucel, 2016). Moreover, the positive results claimed by these studies were widely disseminated, despite the limitations of the underlying data and methods, and the fact that these programmes did not unequivocally produce desirable outcomes; indeed, quite the opposite has been argued (Kaester and Gershberg, 2002; Edwards, 2019). And at the national level, even though, as Delgado (2022) notes, some researchers critiqued the CBM programme in Nicaragua, only those with favourable results were able, with government support, to participate in processes of policy making and implementation. In this last statement, the part about government support is key, for while that knowledge regarded as legitimate frequently reflects the interests of international organizations, it is also the case that the national government plays a key role as a gatekeeper, with the implication being that we must also understand the perspectives of these actors. It is to this task that the discussion will now turn.

Key actor perspectives: agendas and interests in tension

Part of the reason for the dominance of international models in Central America is that they aligned with the preferences and priorities of national actors – though the manner in which each reform evolved was accompanied by new tensions, with the point being that not all actors were aligned in their interests or satisfied with the new policy. These dynamics are explained with examples from the case studies in this section.

Access and international goals

Adopting the CBM model of education governance was not only attractive from the perspective of making education more efficient and accountable;

CBM was also strategic because, through community participation, it would allow governments in the region to rapidly address insufficient access to education in the postwar context. As the case of El Salvador notes: 'One of the priorities of the [Ministry of Education] after 1990, when the end of the war was already in sight, aimed to address the most obvious deficit areas, that is, the coverage and reconstruction of schools destroyed or neglected during the conflict' (Cruz and Walter, 2022, p 126). Throughout El Salvador, Guatemala, and Nicaragua, enrolment rates were low, either because schools had been destroyed during wartime or because the government had not been able to provide or maintain educational services to all regions during the conflict. By transferring responsibility for school management to parent councils, they were motivated to hire teachers, but were also incentivized to construct and maintain community schools, or to find a place where classes could be offered on an interim basis until a suitable school building could be built.

At the same time, CBM models aligned with the language and principles embedded in the Declaration that came from the World Conference on Education for All in 1990. On the one hand, and most obviously, Education for All focused on universalizing access to education. As was noted earlier, CBM contributed to this, not least because, in the case of El Salvador, EDUCO was the only programme through which the government would allow (rural) communities to receive assistance once this programme was initiated. On the other hand, Education for All connected with CBM through its focus on participation. Here, it was asserted that 'partnerships at the community level ... should be encouraged' because 'they can help harmonize activities, utilize resources more effectively, and mobilize additional financial and human resources' (WCEFA Secretariat, 1990, p 58, as cited in Bray, 2003, p 32). Thus, the World Conference on Education for All elevated the necessity of enrolling all children in school, but did so in a way that reinforced the notion that this should be accomplished by incorporating community-level partnerships as a primary strategy.

The reason for mentioning the connections among CBM, access, and participation is to emphasize the multiple strategic interests that CBM served. Up to this point, the present chapter has primarily underscored CBM as a form of New Public Management. But it is also important to acknowledge that CBM helped the governments of Central America to make progress towards other, more tangible goals (like expanding access), while simultaneously being able to claim that they were acting in alignment with the global education agenda. Salazar (2022), in the case of Guatemala, brings these different motivations together when she writes:

the funding of [PRONADE] with public funds was welcomed by most members of the [National Advancement Party (Partido de

Avanzada Nacional)] and the allied business sector since doing so was faithful to the strategy of reducing the state, and because it benefited economically part of the business sector through the [Educational Supervision Institutions]. But even more so, because the country managed to increase educational coverage with the scarce public funds available and with the 'contribution' of [(that is, fees paid by)] poor communities, without raising the tax burden. This improved the image of the country at the international level as they were on the way to fulfilling a millennium goal: the universalization of the primary level (or the first three years of education); at the same time, cheap labor was produced (people with basic levels of education). (Salazar, 2022, p 89)

It is little surprise, then, that CBM was seen by state actors themselves – and not only by international organizations – as a viable way forward for education reform in the 1990s.

Undermining the opposition

Another consideration that is less obvious and has received less attention is how the governments of Nicaragua, El Salvador, and Guatemala used CBM programmes to eliminate the opposition. The case study of Nicaragua notes that 'the first task of the National Salvation Government (*Gobierno de Salvación Nacional*) in educational matters was the elimination of all vestiges of Sandinista education' (Delgado, 2022, p 154). More specifically, the goal was to purge the education system of the socialist rhetoric and principles, and to change the nature of the relationship between the governments and its citizens:

the period of 1990–1991 was one of elimination and purification of what had been inherited. The idea was to create the conditions for a restructuring of the educational system under the new model of economic and social development, where the market and neoliberal theories were the parameters, even in education. It began with curriculum reform, including the introduction of new school textbooks and many school administrators, and then focused on reinventing the relationship between the Nicaraguan state and the citizenry in the area of education. (Delgado, 2022, p 155)

Of course, the new relationship between the government and citizens was to be strongly influenced by the principles of New Public Management, not least through CBM, meaning that citizens would function as part of an accountability mechanism rather than seeing themselves in solidarity with each other.

A parallel phenomenon played out in El Salvador. Here, the government saw its CBM programme as an opportunity to extend educational access into those areas controlled by rebel groups in the context of civil war (see Chapter 2), while simultaneously undermining their efforts at autonomy and bringing them into the formal school system. In 1992, the government rejected requests from popular educators to remain independent and to have the parallel system of schools (with approximately 1,000 teachers and 13,500 students) recognized that they had developed during the war. The response was that the Ministry of Education would offer recognition and funding only to those communities that agreed to join the EDUCO programme. In addition to bringing these schools under government control and introducing a different logic to how the schools were managed, this incorporation also had the effect of undermining the connections and solidarity that had developed between schools and the broader social movement that the resistance represented. This effect was a consequence of the fact that teachers hired in EDUCO schools had to have their teaching certificates. Popular educators did not have this qualification, which meant that parents would have to hire teachers from outside their communities (Edwards, 2018).

In Guatemala, the primary tensions to which CBM responded were tensions between the government and areas controlled by indigenous peoples. As Salazar (2022) writes, in the mid-1990s, a commission composed of indigenous and governmental representatives had the task of designing reforms that would:

> Acknowledge Mayan identity, values, and educational systems; improve the socio-economic conditions of communities; increase the country's education budget; and promote the recruitment and training of 'bilingual teachers and indigenous technical administrative personnel' (AIDPI, 1995, pp 74–75). Likewise, [the reforms] should conceive of communities as the source of education and as key players in the definition of the curriculum, the school calendar, and in 'the appointment and removal of their teachers in order to respond to the interests of cultural educational communities'. (AIDPI, 1995, p 74)

And, beyond this, indigenous communities sought to 'regionalize' education services through the creation of their own institutional apparatus so that they would have more control. However, far from achieving this vision, the government of Guatemala pursued the PRONADE programme, which, in theory (if not in practice), would allow indigenous communities to attain some of the outcomes they desired, such as community control of schools and the ability to hire teachers who spoke the local language. Like Nicaragua and El Salvador, then, CBM was used as a tool to meet the political objectives of the national government, while also avoiding making concessions to the demands of oppositional groups that did not align with the government's priorities.

The government and teachers' unions

Given the neoliberal orientation of governments in Central America in the 1990s, it is no shock that they were looking for ways to attack teachers' unions, since unions represented an obstacle to reducing the state budget by preventing layoffs and salary cuts. Beyond this, the Nicaraguan government, as part of its campaign to eliminate the remnants of socialism, set out to create 'new unions to break ... the National Association of Educators of Nicaragua, which was a political operator of the Sandinista National Liberation Front in schools', as Delgado (2022, p 256) writes. Likewise, in El Salvador, previous research has quoted a UNESCO representative as saying, in the early 1990s: 'Yes, the government in that moment, and the [Ministry of Education] as a subsystem, aimed to decouple and dismantle the teachers' unions. The teaching syndicate was a great force and it applied great pressure, pressure that made [the] government very uncomfortable' (Edwards, 2018, p 182). Moreover, as in Nicaragua, the teachers' unions were closely aligned with the opposition, who fought the government during the civil war and who the government sought to crush. The EDUCO model in El Salvador helped the government to achieve this aim because teachers working in these schools could not belong to the teachers' unions. However, in Nicaragua, CBM was not a threat to the unions because the school councils could not hire and fire teachers, and the teachers did not work on one-year contracts; rather, the school councils could contract or dismiss the principal, who, in turn had the responsibility of managing the teachers.

In Guatemala, the representatives of the government and the United Nations Development Programme who started the pilot programme that would become PRONADE intentionally ensured that the programme kept a low profile so as not to attract the attention and opposition of teachers' unions. But even as the programme grew, although teachers spoke out against it, the unions did not initially mobilize to try to end it. This was because they did not see it as a threat, given that the PRONADE programme was targeted to rural communities where 'few of their members wanted to work' (Ganimian, 2016, p 42). And teachers without teaching certificates could not belong to the unions, which meant that PRONADE would not siphon off members (Ganimian, 2016). It was only later, when the government began to threaten that all schools would be converted to the PRONADE programme, that unions began to focus more on its termination. This multiyear process culminated in 2007, when a congressional decree was signed by the president which began the process of undoing PRONADE.

In El Salvador, the unions had the same reasons (as in Guatemala) for not initially opposing the EDUCO programme – because it would operate in rural areas and because the existing membership would not be affected by it. School councils had to hire teachers who could not belong to the unions, but teachers in traditional schools did not want to work in EDUCO schools in any case, due to the lack of job security, rural locations, and the poor quality of the schools where EDUCO operated.[7] However, another similarity with Guatemala was that, after years of slowly building opposition to the programme (in this case, through the creation of a new union for EDUCO teachers), 2009 marked the beginning of the end for this programme. In that year, a new president (Mauricio Funes, from the opposition party that grew out of the former revolutionary groups) was elected who had come to power in part through his promise to the unions that he would eliminate the EDUCO programme. This process took a few years, but eventually culminated in teachers being converted to permanent status and receiving all the benefits to which traditional teachers were entitled.

Interestingly, in Honduras, Paz and Morales report that there has not been much resistance to the trend of standardized tests. As they write:

> In Honduras, a counter-hegemonic discourse has never been constructed to question evaluation; on the contrary, universities have been used as a means to legitimize it, with examples being: the installation of the External Unit for the Measurement of Education Quality (*Unidad Externa de Medición de la Calidad de la Educación*) at the National Pedagogical University, Francisco Morazán [and] the master's program in educational evaluation that the USAID Project, Improving the Impact of Educational Performance in Honduras (*Mejorando el Impacto al Desempeño Educativo de Honduras*), created at the National Autonomous University of Honduras. (Paz and Morales, 2022, p 208)

While these authors go on to say that teachers' unions have resisted evaluation somewhat, they have actually been more active in combating Honduras' CBM model (which is just like EDUCO and PRONADE). They explain this differential resistance, first, as a function of a lack of understanding of standardized tests (and thus a lack of counter-arguments) and, second, as a function of the more direct threat posed by a CBM model where communities have the ability to hire and fire teachers.

In El Salvador and Guatemala, then, the governments saw value in pursuing CBM, while the only actor who could oppose it – the unions – did not see sufficient value in mobilizing against it, or at least not at first. These same tensions in favour and against have been witnessed at the school level in the experience of individual teachers, particularly in Nicaragua.

Teacher perspectives

In El Salvador and Guatemala, CBM was undesirable from the perspective of teachers because it meant job instability. It also frequently meant that teachers would have to teach in the countryside, far from their families. The two-tier system – divided between the traditional system and the CBM schools – also made teachers in the latter group feel undignified. In a similar way, standardized tests have been used in Honduras to advance the notion that teachers are poor quality and that they should be held accountable. Of course, teachers in Honduras oppose this manner of using standardized tests (this will be more discussion on this later on).

However, in Nicaragua, teacher perspectives were more divided on the issue of CBM. On the one hand, the union affiliated with the Sandinista National Liberation Front (the opposition party that evolved from the socialist revolution of the 1980s) did what it could to obstruct the advancement of CBM. As Delgado explains:

> In essence, the National Association of Nicaraguan Educators (*Asociación Nacional de Educadores de Nicaragua*), with a clear affiliation with the then-opposition Sandinista National Liberation Front, employed the same mechanisms of autonomy to curb it. For a school to enter the School Autonomy regime, a simple majority of the votes in the teaching staff was necessary. Therefore, at first, the members of this union, due to ideological opposition, did not provide decisive support to the reform process. (Delgado 2022, p 258)

On the other hand, individual teachers were caught in a set of uncomfortable dynamics that pulled them in different directions. Here, it should be remembered that CBM was used as a way to increase the salaries of teachers, which were no more than $70–100 a month, compared to $160 a month for the price of basic needs. However, rather than salary increases being provided by the state, it was the state that encouraged schools to pass the cost on to families. This was done by school councils approving fees (*cuotas*) that had to be paid by families. Even in the 2000s, when this practice was discouraged, Delgado (2022) reports that the majority of schools continued to charge fees for teacher salary supplements precisely because the teachers were in favour of it.

At the same time, teachers felt that it was ethically inappropriate to impose fees on families because it meant that the ability of students to acquire education – to which they had a right – was based on their ability to pay. This preoccupation was all the more pronounced because CBM schools tended to serve disadvantaged students. An additional complication was the fact that the payment of fees not only came to be used as a barometer for families' commitment to education, but also came to be seen as a substitute for meaningful participation (for example, in the school council). This way of thinking created tensions between schools and families, especially in rural and poor communities, where families were less able to contribute financially.

Nicaraguan teachers, too, were frustrated with certain aspects of the CBM model. Teachers may have benefited financially, but they lacked power within the decision-making structure of the school. Moreover, as Delgado explains, while 'teachers perceived a decrease in their influence on decision-making', it was also the case that principals retained power: 'The principal and parents turned out to be the majority in the School Councils, and although they could ... request dismissal of the principal, having the approval of the Ministry of Education at headquarters or at the departmental or municipal level, the principal had considerable room for "arbitrary" management' (2022, p 167). Thus, as with the other reforms analysed in this chapter, teachers in Nicaragua were structurally disadvantaged and thus demotivated. There is no doubt that teachers took advantage of families through fee requirements; however, this fee-paying dynamic brought with it the creation of a client-provider relationship, one that offered inconsistent compensation based on families' ability to afford the fees. Delgado summarizes this situation nicely and connects it back to the issue of teacher motivation: 'By creating a client-server system, with unstable reward mechanisms due to inconsistency in the collection of fees, and with a crisis of both authority and participation, the commitment of teachers to pedagogical improvement was subverted' (2022, p 259).

Think tanks, New Public Management reforms, and golden eggs

Despite all the internal contradictions highlighted earlier, it is important to note that the political-economic transformation of Central America in the 1980s and 1990s could not have produced anything else, that is, a situation in which New Public Management would not have been dominant. Following the crises of the 1980s and early 1990s, the governments of all four countries being analysed here were neoliberal in nature. This orientation to economic and social policy, which, as noted earlier, was brought about by macrostructural shifts, then combined with the agendas of international organizations and national think tanks to advance both New Public Management reforms and the careers of those who promoted them. The cases of Nicaragua and El Salvador make this clear.

In these two countries, a precursor to the end of conflict was the election of political parties that were in favour of transforming their country's economy in order to more fully join the global market. These elections themselves were the outcome of years of organizing among the new business elite, a process which was extensively supported by USAID, who helped to create organizations and associations that would not only help to bring together the new elite but would also facilitate policy dialogue, reform proposals, and agenda setting (Robinson, 2003; Edwards, 2018). These efforts were further complemented by the founding of think tanks – by USAID, by the new economic elite, or by a collaboration of the two – that would provide the technical legitimacy needed to put forward credible proposals. In El Salvador, the key organizations were the Salvadoran Foundation for Economic and Social Development and the Business Foundation for Educational Development, while in Nicaragua, these were the Association for Research and Social Studies (ASIES) and the National Economic Research Center.

Interestingly, in both countries, these think tanks played key roles in facilitating political developments that would have an effect on the trajectory of CBM reform. They served as spaces of incubation and preparation for policy reforms, and, in some cases, the reformers who would move into the government bureaucracy and who would advance the New Public Management agenda in the area of education. Because of the number of individuals who made the transition into government from the aforementioned think tanks in El Salvador, a USAID consultant from the early 1990s characterized them as 'ministries in waiting' and as a 'parallel ministry of planning [and] ministry of finance' (Edwards, 2018, pp 165–166). In the case of Guatemala, the individual who would become Minister of Education in 1996, as part of the right-wing Party for National Advancement, was advised during the preceding six to eight months by specialists from both the Association for Research and Social Studies and the Center for National Economic Research. Then, as soon as the Minister – Arabella Castro – assumed her post, she began to promote the intensive expansion of PRONADE.

Moreover, these CBM reforms also served as launchpads for careers for Salvadorans and Guatemalans with high aspirations and with the right background and positioning in the political landscape. In both cases, those functionaries who played key roles in extending the reach of these reforms and in ensuring their success would experience great personal benefit and political influence. For example, in Guatemala, the first director of the PRONADE office in the administration of the Party for National Advancement, who was previously a prominent economist with the Center for National Economic Research, would herself go on to become Minister of Education in 2004. Likewise, a key champion of EDUCO from the programme's early days would become Minister of Education in El Salvador in that same year. These are only two examples among many individuals who capitalized on the cachet and experience of working with these prominent education reforms. Many individuals who passed through these programmes would later serve in diplomatic positions, as high-level administrators and leaders within the government, and as consultants with international organizations. It was for this reason that a former Ministry of Education employee from El Salvador characterized EDUCO as 'the goose that laid the golden egg' (Edwards et al, 2015, p 34). Ministry of Education personnel had the sense, due to the extensive support and significant excitement that these programmes received from national political actors and international organizations, that CBM reforms were not only going to make their countries exemplars for others to follow, but would also bring success to those individuals associated with its development.

Accounts of education reform often leave out those factors that motivate key individuals operating within and through the government; it is important to take their perspectives into consideration as well in order to better understand how the personal and the political are interrelated. That said, personal trajectories are constrained by larger political and economic constraints. It is to this issue that the next section turns.

Resolving tensions in the state-capital-education dialectic

Having looked, first, at the drivers of reform and, second, at the perspectives of key actors in the making and implementation of reform, the question now is how the underlying political and economic tensions inherent in these reforms and the contexts in which they operate have been resolved. More specifically, the core concern here has to do with the way in which (the logic of) economic capital functions through the state with the help of education and the dominant rhetoric that surrounds it. While these dynamics are always in play, the case study of Honduras makes them explicit.

Capital, New Public Management, and the dysfunctional state in Honduras

To start with, it should be noted that in Honduras standardized tests have been used by the state to delegitimize teachers and public education. In the words of Paz and Morales, 'the results of the assessment have been utilized symbolically, specifically to accredit or discredit teaching performance and to strengthen or damage the institutional image of schools' (2022, p 220). The flipside of this statement is that test results have been used punitively – to hold teachers accountable – rather than for monitoring to guide the provision of support. In the words of a teacher quoted by Paz and Morales:

> Measurements are taken with the desire to persecute the teacher and, moreover, when they find deficiencies, they don't tell them 'Well, we are going to include this in a training plan, we are going to help you in this, we are going to help your school improve.' They simply expose

him or her, like an unskilled professional, who cannot do their job, who knows nothing, and that devalues them in the eyes of society; then, only one sector is blamed, and that is the tone with which the evaluation processes are developed. (Paz and Morales, 2022, p 220)

Zooming out, the importance of this statement is not just that it leads to a loss of prestige for teachers and public education, but also that low test scores can be used as pretext for reducing education funding and for pursuing 'privatization processes, masked in the models of community participation and school autonomy, that place their trust in private actors who have become educational agents attempting to substitute and assume the responsibilities that constitutionally correspond to the State' (Paz and Morales, 2022, p 262).

One way in which states in budget crisis, like Honduras, would like to cut funding to education is by reducing teacher salaries. Standardized testing in a context of inequality and inadequate support can only lead to poor test results. However, rather than addressing the causes of inequality, test results can be used to claim that teachers work too little and earn too much. Where it is not possible to cut salaries, withholding salary increases has the same effect. Paz and Morales connect these points:

In the Honduran case, the evaluation of student performance has led to conflicts between the teacher's unions and the government, perhaps also motivated by a government propaganda campaign, which has led to an apparent rejection of teachers and with this, a loss of social prestige of their profession. The idea has spread that teachers work little and have high salaries; the evidence says otherwise, teaching work has become precarious, salaries have been frozen since 2010. (Paz and Morales, 2022, p 261)

But how does this relate back to the dialectic between capital and the state? When, as noted in the discussion of the historical context in Chapter 2, states are situated within a global economic system that requires them to compete based on exports and cheap labour and that makes it very difficult to generate or spend resources for public services, one of the only strategies states can pursue is to make the provision of those services more efficient and less expensive. Of course, this tendency can be reinforced by private actors who would like to open additional space for the privatization of education, allowing them to benefit from government subcontracts, vouchers, or tuition payments from families. These larger dynamics thus propel the ideology of New Public Management. In this way, policy reform is one component of the dialectic between capital, the state, and education.

However, we must emphasize that the nuances in how this dialectic evolve are themselves responsive to historical dynamics between the state and capital. Consider, for example, that in the late 1890s the initial formation of the Honduran state was intimately intertwined with the involvement of foreign capital. As described in Chapter 2, between 1898 and 1933, Central American countries became 'client states' of the US, thanks to economic opportunities related to coffee and bananas and the willingness of the US to advocate for, and to intervene on behalf of, US business investments (Coatsworth, 1994). In the context of Honduras, the presence and influence of transnational companies inhibited the emergence of a strong local elite and, relatedly, an autonomous state (World Bank, 2009). Moreover, not only were the two main political parties (who continue to dominate politics today) founded with support from competing banana companies, but – and this is crucial – these companies served as the primary source of finance for the government. These companies 'ensured the loyalty of lower-level governmental officials through generous payment [of salaries] … that [was] twice what the government paid' (Bull, 2005, p 132).

The implications of this cannot be understated. The combination of factors described previously created the foundation for the way in which the Honduran state continues to operate today, where clientelism and dependence on foreign actors and international markets is taken for granted. Honduras has continued to operate as an economy that is dependent on both foreign aid and foreign markets – and these sources of financial capital are then used to the benefit of the party in power, which uses its political biases to regulate access to the state apparatus based on party loyalty (for example, in the distribution of teaching positions, school buildings, etc.). It has thus become accepted and expected that the function of the state is to distribute privileges to those who form part of it or are somehow connected to it, to such an extent that Honduran researchers have concluded that 'the political class resists the institutional strengthening of the State as a distributor of social well-being, because the political game operates according to the logic of personal and private benefit' (Morales, 2013, p 315; see also Caravaca et al, this volume Chapter 13).

Extending the previous point to education, while the Honduran state serves the interests of capital, it does so without fully implementing the education policies suggested by it. Standardized testing is one example. Here, interest from the government has waxed and waned. While the government and the media have taken an interest in using test results to criticize teachers as part of a broader strategy to reduce pressure to invest in education, there has not been consistent interest in developing and applying systems that would integrate standardized tests into decision making within the education sector. Ultimately, this is because there is a political advantage to a dysfunctional state that does not work well or in the interests of its citizens. Rather than striving to develop well-functioning and modern systems and processes, public sector leaders prefer to retain some degree of flexibility within the state so that politicians and their networks can benefit (Edwards et al, 2023). Furthermore, as a perpetual work in progress, the state remains a candidate for international assistance, from which key actors derive value (by bringing in funding, giving the appearance of doing something to address deficiencies, financing pet projects, providing contracts to contacts in their personal networks, etc.). In this way, the aid dance continues, played out on the cultural battlefield of education policy, where the dialectic between the political and economic is facilitated (Edwards, 2023).

The structural limitations of education reform in Central America

A previous section described the way in which teachers fought against CBM reforms. These tensions were resolved (or transformed) when the CBM reforms were undone. In Nicaragua, this occurred in 2007, when the Sandinista National Liberation Front once again came to power (for the first time since the end of the Sandinsta revolution); similarly, in El Salvador, this happened in 2009, when, for the first time since the end of the civil war, the left-wing political party of the former rebels (the Farabundo Martí National Liberation Front) took power; and in Guatemala, the CBM programme was cancelled in 2007 by congressional decree thanks to teacher mobilization and just before a new president took office who had pledged to the unions that he would eliminate it. (The single country not to overturn their CBM programme is Honduras. Here, the only president who might have done away with it, Manuel Zelaya, was ousted in a coup in 2009.) A few observations follow from these changes.

First, these examples show that changes in political constraints have consequences for education reform. This is so in the sense that, following these political transitions, school governance was no longer conceptualized in terms of New Public Management principles. In El Salvador, for example, the government's vision for education was to create integrated systems of full-time inclusive schools (Edwards et al, 2021). Participation was still a key concept, but rather than focus on efficiency and accountability, the idea was that schools, organized into clusters, would work together to support one another and to share resources, all with the goal of making schools more inclusive and more prepared to meet students' needs. But even if the rhetoric around education has changed, so what? This leads to the next point.

Second, while the logic of New Public Management no longer featured prominently in the discourse around school governance due to the discontinuation of these programmes, there are other considerations which highlight the subordinate role that education plays in the dialectic with the state and capital. One consideration is the fact that most schools did not participate in the CBM programmes, the implication being that their removal failed to change the dynamic between traditional public schools and the state. A second consideration is that the structure of the economy and the state's relationship to it has not changed drastically. The countries being compared remain primarily dependent on agricultural and textile (that is, maquiladora) exports. The middle and upper classes are small, as is the proportion of well-paying jobs. A report of the IMF from 2008 stated that 50 per cent of the families in this region (with the exception of Costa Rica) live in poverty (Desuelle and Schipke, 2008). Many families thus rely on remittances from relatives who have left the country in search of better opportunities.

One consequence of this is that the education system does not lead to upward mobility for the majority of the population. Another consequence is that international organizations themselves are encouraging the countries of the region to improve their social policies and to increase social spending in order to improve the quality of life for the average citizen – and in order to preserve the stability of the system (Desuelle and Schipke, 2008). However, these reforms depend on the political dynamics found within each country. The concentration of wealth at the top of the income pyramid does not bode well for the passage of redistributive economic policies, or for the collection of additional tax revenue to fund social programmes. Inaction or inconsequential action are more likely to prevail.

In this context of stalemate and restricted options, international organizations continue to support education in accordance with their own development theories and preferences. Governments, for their part, continue to collaborate with these organizations where agreement can be reached on overlapping priorities. Though many international development organizations have been involved within and beyond the education sector in Central America during the 1990s and 2000s, those that have remained the most involved and influential are USAID, the World Bank, and the Inter-American Development Bank. Additionally, while each of these actors is focused on economic issues, USAID is also concerned with social stability, the connection between education and employment, and providing opportunities apart from gang membership (the presence of which has grown significantly in Central America since the 2000s) (USAID, 2011; Bruneau, 2014; see also Savenije, this volume Chapter 7).

Culturally, then, while education cannot – due to structural constraints – offer the majority of students the promise of meaningful employment or economic advancement, it is still the case that the rhetoric and reform of education play key roles in the dialectic between the state and capital. Here, by rhetoric and reform, we refer to the policies and programmes promoted by the government and international organizations. These entities are aware of the structural constraints within which education operates. But, in order to manage expectations and to preserve social stability, these policies and programmes extend the promise of a better future by focusing on such things the acquisition of 21st-century skills, technological competencies, job preparation, and entrepreneurship. Policies and programmes thus circulate a certain discourse about how education is central both to better opportunities at the individual level and to the engine of national economic growth. To the extent that education is successful in advancing this belief, it helps to maintain the legitimacy of a system that tends towards inequality and concentration of power.

Education can lead to structural change, but this is a slow process at best. One example is the radical education provided by Catholic priests, who were inspired by liberation theology, in rural areas of El Salvador through base communities in the 1970s (Hammond, 1998). But even here, education was one of many factors. It was only when these teachings coincided with an organic popular movement that resistance to the government and the prevailing economic system materialized. Moreover, this kind of radical and transformative education cannot be provided by the state itself, for the state will not explicitly teach students its limitations and the reasons for challenging either it or the economic system in which it is embedded. The implication is that education is trapped within the current nature of the state, which, in turn, is trapped within the constraints of the global capitalist economy.

Pointing towards a conclusion

There is a great deal that can and should be said about the implications of the comparative analysis presented in this chapter. However, given that these countries are not alone in their experiences, an extensive discussion will be withheld for now and will, instead, be presented in the concluding chapter to this volume. There, the implications of the experiences of these four countries, as synthesized here, will be further discussed and brought into conversation with the insights presented in the remaining chapters of this volume.

For now, what can be underscored is the value of applying a political economy lens. In doing so, the factors and logics that constrain and facilitate reform come into the picture. The paradigms upon which education reform is based become more clear. At the same time, the fuzzy and abstract way in which 'quality education' is discussed becomes more obvious. The notion of education quality, like development more generally, only has meaning within the set of assumptions and worldview that guide it. It may be politically wise for reformers to remain vague in terms of their ideological commitments, as doing so increases the likelihood that their proposals will engender less resistance. The more that a reform can be sold as beneficial to all or as accommodating multiple agendas, the greater the chances that it will be approved and perhaps even put into action. This dynamic has certainly been evident in Central America, as has been discussed in this chapter.

However, clarifying the guiding interests and principles as well as structural factors that shape reform is a necessary step to more fully grasping – that is, more fully than is typical in the literature on education policy in the region – why certain reforms are advanced over others. And this kind of clarity is, in turn, an opportunity for individuals and different groups to question whether the direction of reform is the one in which the countries of the region ought to be moving. While there is no single answer to this issue, the concluding chapter of this volume offers some additional thoughts beyond those presented here.

Notes

[1] See the introduction to Chapter 2 for more information on this project.

[2] As with the case studies themselves, a previous version of the analysis presented in this chapter was also published as a chapter in Cruz (2022). See Edwards and Martin (2022).

[3] For more on the methodological approach taken by the case studies being compared, see the chapter on methods in Cruz et al (2022).

[4] El Salvador's programme for community involvement in school management was known as Education with Community Participation (EDUCO). When it comes to the experience of community participation and education reform, the work of the present author is drawn upon where helpful to make connections between the experience of El Salvador, on the one hand, and Nicaragua and Guatemala, on the other hand (Edwards, Victoria, and Martin, 2015; Edwards and Loucel, 2016; Edwards, 2018, 2019).

[5] These were, in 2011, the Trends in International Mathematics and Science Study (TIMSS) and the Progress in International Reading Literacy Study (PIRLS); in 2013, the Third Regional Comparative and Explicative Study (TERCE); and, in 2018, the version of the Program for International Student Assessment that was designed for middle- and low-income countries (PISA-D).

[6] Gershberg notes that 'teachers have half or one-third the number of representatives on the councils as parents' (1999, p 24). For more details on the size and composition of the school councils, see Gershberg (1999, p 17).

[7] Edwards notes that school councils had to 'hire teachers who were not members of the official [Ministry of Education] career system … If a teacher was not a member of that system, they were not eligible to join a teachers' union' (2018, p 62).

References

AIDPI (1995). Acuerdo sobre identidad y derechos de los pueblos indígenas, Diario Centroamérica: 31 de marzo de 1995. http://www.lacult.unesco.org/docc/oralidad_08_70-79-anales.pdf

Anderson, G. and Cohen, M. (2015). Redesigning the identities of teachers and leaders: a framework for studying new professionalism and educator resistance. *Education Policy Analysis Archives*, 23, 85. https://doi.org/10.14507/epaa.v23.2086

Bray, M. (2003). Community initiatives in education: goals, dimensions and linkages with governments. *Compare: A Journal of Comparative and International Education*, 33(1), 31–45.

Bruneau, T. (2014). Pandillas and security in Central America. *Latin American Research Review*, 49(2), 152–172.

Bull, B. (2005). *Aid, Power and Privatization: The Politics of Telecommunication Reform in Central America*. Edward Elgar.

Coatsworth, J. (1994). *Central America and the United States: The Clients and the Colossus*. Twayne.

Cruz Bustamante, M. T. and Walter, K. (2022). La reforma educativa 1995–2005: Pacto social y político entre el modelo de educación y el modelo de desarrollo en El Salvador. In M. T. Cruz Bustamante (ed.), *Quality of education in Central America: Dynamics and tensions between the model of education and the model of development* (pp 107–146). Publicaciones Académicas UCA.

Cruz Bustamante, M. T. (ed.) (2022). *Quality of Education in Central America: Dynamics and Tensions between the Model of Education and the Model of Development*. Publicaciones Académicas UCA.

Cuéllar-Marchelli, H. (2003). Decentralization and privatization of education in El Salvador: assessing the experience. *International Journal of Educational Development*, 23(2), 45–166.

Delgado, A. (2022). Autonomía Escolar: participación, descentralización y calidad educativa. In M. T. Cruz Bustamanre (ed.), *Quality of Education in Central America: Dynamics and Tensions between the Model of Education and the Model of Development* (pp 147–188). Publicaciones Académicas UCA.

Desuelle, D. and Schipke, A. (eds.) (2008). *Central America: Economic Progress and Reforms*. International Monetary Fund.

Di Gropello, E. (2006). A comparative analysis of school-based management in Central America. World Bank Working Paper 72. World Bank.

Edwards Jr., D. B. (2018). *The Trajectory of Global Education Policy: Community-Based Management in El Salvador and the Global Reform Agenda*. Palgrave Macmillan.

Edwards Jr., D. B. (2019). Shifting the perspective on community-based management of education: from systems theory to social capital and community empowerment. *International Journal of Educational Development*, 64, 17–26.

Edwards Jr., D. B. (2023). *Rethinking World Bank Influence: Governance Reforms and the Ritual aid Dance in Indonesia*. Routledge.

Edwards Jr., D. B., and Loucel, C. (2016). The EDUCO program, impact evaluations, and the political economy of global education reform. *Education Policy Analysis Archives*, 24(49), 1–50.

Edwards Jr., D. B., and Martin, P. (2022). La Economía Política Internacional de las Reformas Educativas en Centroamérica: un análisis comparativo y rumbos futuros. In M. T. Cruz Bustamanre (ed.), *Quality of Education in Central America: Dynamics and Tensions between the Model of Education and the Model of Development* (pp 227–268). Publicaciones Académicas UCA.

Edwards Jr., D. B., Erazo, M., and Martin, P. (2021). Islas en el mar: participación y descentralización en 'sistemas integrados' en educación. *Educacao & Sociedade*, 42, 1–18. https://www.scielo.br/j/es/a/vKGt3Jwq tLcNCG4BcLYhwYw/?lang=es&andformat=pdf

Edwards Jr., D.B., Moschetti, M., and Caravaca, A. (2023). *Globalization, Privatization, and the State: Contemporary Education Reform in Post-colonial Contexts*. Routledge.

Edwards Jr., D. B., Victoria, J.A., and Martin, P. (2015). The geometry of policy implementation: lessons from the political economy of three education reforms in El Salvador during 1990–2005. *International Journal of Educational Development*, 44, 28–41.

Ganimian, A. (2016). Why do some school-based management reforms survive while others are reversed? The cases of Honduras and Guatemala. *International Journal of Educational Development*, 47, 33–46.

Gershberg, A. (1999). Decentralization, citizen participation, and the role of the state: the Autonomous School Program in Nicaragua. *Latin American Perspectives*, 26(4), 8–38.

Hammond, J. (1998). *Fighting to Learn: Popular Education and Guerrilla War in El Salvador*. Rutgers University Press.

Kaestner, R., and Gershberg, A. (2002). Lessons learned from Nicaragua's School Autonomy reform: a review of research by the Nicaragua reform evaluation team of the World Bank. Paper written for the 'Empowering parents while making them pay: Autonomous Schools in Nicaragua' project, New School University.

Klein, N. (2007). *The Shock Doctrine: The Rise of Disaster Capitalism*. Picadur.

Leys, C. (1996). *The Rise and Fall of Development Theory*. Indiana University Press.

Morales, R. (2013). *Los cambios en la gobernanza del sistema educativo en Honduras: la política de desconcentración de la educación pre-básica, básica y media (1990–2010)*. Universidade do Porto.

Paz, C. L., and Morales, C. (2022). La política de evaluación en Honduras: caracterizando las limitaciones estructurales, la evolución y las perspectivas de los actores clave. In M. T. Cruz Bustamanre (ed.), *Quality of Education in Central America: Dynamics and Tensions between the Model of Education and the Model of Development* (pp 189–226). Publicaciones Académicas UCA.

Robinson, W. (2003). *Transnational Conflicts: Central America, Social Change, and Globalization*. Verso.

Salazar, M. (2022). Modelo de calidad educativa 'superficial': entre la sesucción, la privatización y la continuidad del pasado. In M. T. Cruz Bustamanre (ed.), *Quality of Education in Central America: Dynamics and Tensions between the Model of Education and the Model of Development* (pp 21–63). Publicaciones Académicas UCA.

Salazar, M., Cruz, M., Vasquéz, L., Delgado, B., and Paz, L. (2018). Calidad de la educación en Centroamérica: dinámicas y tensiones entre los modelos de educación y de desarrollo. Universidad Centroaméricana, José Simeón Cañas.

Samoff, J. (1993). The reconstruction of schooling in Africa. *Comparative Education Review*, 37, 181–222.

Straubhaar, R. (2017). Educational excellence versus educational justice: how Latin American policymakers respond to these competing demands with the evaluative state. In T. Jules (ed.), *The Global Educational Policy Environment in the Fourth Industrial Revolution: Gated, Regulated and Governed* (pp 265–281). Emerald.

USAID (2011). *Opportunity through Learning: USAID Education Strategy*. USAID.

Verger, A., Fontdevila, C., and Zancajo, A. (2016). *The Privatization of Education: A Political Economy of Global Education Reform*. Teachers College Press.

Weiler, H. (1983). Legalization, expertise, and participation: strategies of compensatory legitimation in education policy. *Comparative Education Review*, 27(2), 259–277.

World Bank (1980). *World Development Report, 1980*. World Bank.

World Bank (1994). *El Salvador: Community Education Strategy: Decentralized School Management*. World Bank.

World Bank (2009). *Strengthening Performance Accountability in Honduras*. World Bank.

World Conference on Education for All [WCEFA] Secretariat (1990) WCEFA Framework for Action (New York, WCEFA Inter-Agency Commission). https://unesdoc.unesco.org/ark:/48223/pf0000097551

4

Deconcentration of Education in Honduras: Restriction and Ritualization of a Chimeric Reform

Ricardo Morales-Ulloa and Mauro C. Moschetti

Introduction

The formation of the liberal state has been linked from its inception to the creation of national education systems. Education has been the means par excellence for the transmission of bourgeois liberal values, and, in the course of its development, the state consolidated its educational role and education's character as a public good. However, this conception has changed considerably in recent decades: nation-states are no longer the only space of production of education policy and, on a global scale, they are ceding space to other actors, other agendas, and other interests. The state's central role in education policy making has been substantially modified; government decisions are influenced and even altered by a range of other actors and powers that challenge the idea of state sovereignty.

There is now a 'global education policy field' involving multiple and diverse actors – for example, state, private, and civil society organizations as well as international agencies – which operate at different scales (that is, locally, nationally, internationally, and transnationally) simultaneously (Lingard and Rawolle, 2011). Yet, in this context, states retain a central role as coordinators and activators of educational policy options, but are simultaneously pressured and 'coordinated' by local and external actors in a framework of heterarchical relationships, typical of network governance (Ball and Junemann, 2012; Shiroma, 2014). In this sense, for example, in relation to the reforms inspired by the paradigm of New Public Management that spread globally since the 1990s (see Chapter 3), the state continues to be a key actor in terms of regulating the system – for example, in limiting the power and presence of private agents or in the creation of opportunities for the private sector as a 'market-maker, commissioner of services and performance monitor' (Avelar and Ball, 2019, p 66).

However, states' room for manoeuvre is limited by factors that are largely beyond their control. When trying to understand changes in educational policy, it is not enough to understand the motivations of individual state actors or the conditions of the micro-institutional context in which these changes occur. In line with the conceptual and analytical approach of this book (see Chapter 2), we concur with the fundamental need to understand the structural constraints that affect and shape the educational policy choices and decisions of policy makers, as well as their discourses, interests, and justifications. Among these factors, economic, political, and macro-institutional contingencies stand out, which, in a more or less dynamic way, play a fundamental role in fostering or inhibiting the selection and viability of certain policies (Verger et al, 2016; Edwards, 2018; Edwards et al, 2023a). Added to this is the role played by the ideas or frames of reference promoted by different actors with varying power to influence policy makers. With structural constraints as a background, it is understood that power is exercised based on ideas that define which policy paradigms are acceptable or even desirable to address educational challenges and problems whose definition, in turn, rarely responds to purely technical considerations (Jessop, 2010; Verger, 2014).

With these premises as a frame of reference, this chapter analyses the changes that occurred in the governance of the Honduran education system during the 1990s, focusing on the global discourses that defined the contents and agendas of the main educational reforms in this historical period. Based on the analysis of educational policy documents, a review of the academic literature, and information gathered from interviews with key actors – government officials, union representatives, former ministers of education, departmental officials, representatives of the private sector, advisors, and education specialists (n=31) – the chapter addresses the complexity of the global–local when it comes to the making and enactment of education policy. Based on the triangulation of data, the chapter describes and analyses, on the one hand, the economic conditions under which educational reforms were promoted during the period and, on the other hand, the translation and recontextualization of the global educational policy prescriptions. As will be shown, these processes gave rise to the implementation of highly idiosyncratic interpretations of such policies.

The chapter is structured as follows. The first section describes the economic circumstances promoted by the 1990 economic Structural Adjustment Program which constituted the starting point of the reform process. An analysis is made of the role of external actors, particularly the International Monetary Fund and the World Bank, and of the global discourses that shaped the neoliberal economic reforms of the Honduran state. The discussion then addresses the economic content (that is, market-based logic) of the resulting educational reforms, paying particular attention to the rationale behind the World Bank's recommendations. Next, the case of educational decentralization is considered a flagship policy that would characterize the core of the reforms promoted in Honduras during the period. The subsequent section offers an analysis that identifies the recontextualization in the implementation of the reform and seeks to explain the underlying logic of the 'deviation' from the recommendations promoted by international organizations. Finally, the chapter ends with a discussion on how local inertia and the particular dynamics of the national political fabric have translated the external discourse.

The economic underpinning of educational reforms

The educational reforms promoted in Honduras in the 1990s are part of a broader reform process called the 'modernization of the State'. Chronologically, this process began in 1990, after the transition from a military to a civilian government, coinciding with the first term of the National Party of Honduras (Partido Nacional de Honduras or PNH),[1] a political party historically recognized for its authoritarian, pro-military, and conservative tendencies. By then, seeking solutions to the debt crisis and having negotiated agreements with the International Monetary Fund, most Latin American countries had already implemented similar economic and political reforms, the definitions of which were mainly based on the so-called Washington Consensus, a formula that included the shared visions of international credit institutions and related to the policies of fiscal austerity, privatization, and market liberalization (Bonal, 2002; Morales-Ulloa and Magalhães, 2013). In Honduras, such reforms aimed not only at transforming the more bureaucratic aspects of public administration and provision of services, but also, and more fundamentally, the entire productive matrix and institutional architecture of the country (Morales-Ulloa and Magalhães, 2013). In essence, these reforms were the starting point for institutionalizing a neoliberal project that would seek to promote a 'new definition for development as participation in the world market and the transition from managed national economic growth to managed global economic growth' (Robinson, 2002, pp 233–234; for more on this, see Chapter 2, this volume).

There are two important milestones that set the pace for this process. The first, in 1990, was known as the Structural Adjustment Program. This was supervised by the International Monetary Fund and would include macro-economic stabilization measures and a commitment to transforming the role of the state such that it would be compatible with an open economy, in which the market would tend to gain access to spaces previously firmly within state control. This Program constituted, on the one hand, the breaking point of the Honduran developmentalist state – or what was left of it – which was considered at this point obsolete and inefficient. On the other hand, it would lay the foundations for an economic programme that would (ideally) define a new profile for the state as well as new conceptions of social and economic development for the current and subsequent governments, for whom it would be very difficult to depart from the basic precepts of this adjustment programme.

The second milestone of the reform process is the State Modernization Act of 1991 (Decree 190/91), another legal instrument that complements the package of economic measures and outlines the model of a 'minimum State' and a 'modern' public administration. The main characteristics of this modernizing paradigm in the country derive from the globally circulated principles of the reform approach known as New Public Management (Polidano, 1999). In Honduras, this approach inspired an attempt to decentralize public administration (Morales-Ulloa, 2013).

The implications of these two macro-reforms were fundamental for the direction that education policy would take. On the one hand, the economic reforms guided by the Structural Adjustment Program required changes that derived mainly from the trade openness expressed in free trade agreements aimed at increasing the flow of foreign investment. Consequently, the logic that would guide educational reform from the 1990s onwards would also change: education could no longer be seen as an input for an internally controlled economy, but would have to respond more explicitly to the pressures of the global economy (see Chapter 2, this volume). In Honduras, as in most countries of the region, the production of educational policies would thus lose autonomy, now constrained by economic policy and, in general, by macro-economic decisions ultimately conditioned by international agencies and multilateral banks (Tinoco, 2010). Ball (2001) describes this phenomenon as a growing colonization of educational policies by the demands of economic policies. When we talk about educational reforms in this context, they must therefore be understood as part of an integral set of policies that, in the first instance, are of an economic, political, and macro-institutional nature.

In line with the structural adjustment of the economy, the 'modernizing' mandate, for its part, introduced in the field of education what we could call a supervised path dependence: the successive educational reforms from 1990 onwards were, to a greater or lesser extent, always in the direction of the general framework of the principles of New Public Management, and their advances and setbacks would be subject to constant scrutiny by external actors and, in particular during the period analysed, by the

World Bank. In this sense, for example, the government that took office in 1994 inherited the execution of the modernization programme under the supervision of the World Bank as a pending task of the previous government and without too much room for manoeuvre, while the resources of the loans negotiated with the previous government began to flow (Salazar Vides, 2018). Additionally, given that Honduras was still undergoing a process of transition from military authoritarianism to civilian government in the 1990s, the idea of modernization was closely linked to the concept of 'good governance', an important element of the World Bank's agenda since the 1990s that was not by chance explicitly included in the state Modernization Act.

The consolidation of the World Bank as the main funding agency for educational development in the region from the 1990s is, as one might anticipate, the piece that completes the context. In the case of Honduras, several studies show the marked dependence of education funding on international cooperation resources since the 1960s (Secretaría de Educación/GTZ, 1997; Tinoco, 2010; Edwards et al, 2023a). However, they also show that since the mid-1990s there has been a drastic reduction in the contributions of traditional bilateral partners – for example, the United States Agency for Development (USAID), an entity with a large presence in the country during the previous decades. These reductions positioned the World Bank as the leading external contributor in the education sector in the country. The dominance of the World Bank was characterized by an asymmetrical relationship between this entity and the Honduran state that implied a clear prioritization of certain policies over others in the educational field. The virtual monopoly of financing for educational development – that is, beyond the financing of current expenditures – gave the World Bank a privileged position not only to mobilize knowledge and produce legitimacy around a limited set of policies, but also to impose a reformist course of action centred on these policies and to make financial support conditional on the implementation of these reforms. As will be presented in the following sections, in the case of Honduras, these dynamics would give a boost to decentralization and accountability policies, typically discussed in relation to a series of policy instruments inspired by the paradigm of New Public Management.

Education reform according to the World Bank

The educational reforms implemented in Honduras since the early 1990s cannot be understood outside the context of the influential international educational reform agenda promoted by the World Bank and, to a lesser extent, by other multilateral credit and development agencies. Inspired in an orthodox way by the premises of public choice theory, this reform agenda has traditionally focused on the momentum given to three fundamental axes: privatization, decentralization, and accountability.

Often presented as complementary, these three axes shape a programme of reforms whose theory of change maintains that public services are provided more efficiently and with higher quality if: (a) provision is made by private entities – or public entities operating similarly to the private sector; (b) the governance structure of the system is 'debureaucratized' and, through a decentralized structure, manages to get closer to the needs of the end users; and (c) 'clients' (that is, citizens) can hold suppliers directly accountable for results. This logic would reach its highest level of conceptual concreteness in a series of policy ideas – that is, decentralization, school-based management, the 'short route' of accountability, and public-private partnerships – widely disseminated by the World Bank during the 2000s through very influential knowledge products (see, for example, World Bank, 2003; Patrinos et al, 2009). It is worth mentioning that these ideas are based on the experiments that the World Bank itself promoted in the 1980s and 1990s in different countries of the Global South (Edwards, 2018).

In the Honduran education context, the World Bank's reform agenda from the 1990s onwards would be characterized primarily by a push for decentralization as a strategy to debureaucratize the education administration and to foster more direct accountability mechanisms. What follows is an analysis of these reform axes furthered in a context in which, although the influence of the World Bank and the economic background of the educational policy decisions were decisive, the characteristics and inertia of the Honduran political system and the role of the teachers' unions ultimately gave these reforms unique characteristics. The following sections explore these two sides of the reform.

Decentralization as a one-size-fits-all chimera

While the Structural Adjustment Program launched in 1990 at the behest of the International Monetary Fund had provoked widespread popular rejection, the positive framing advocated by the World Bank for the ideas of modernization contained in the State Modernization Act (1991), on the contrary, stirred the sympathy of some sectors, especially among civil society organizations. This happened mainly because the modernizing mandate sought, in addition to optimizing the functioning of public administration, to strengthen democracy, citizen participation, and the rule of law, which were understandable social demands as the country emerged from the 1980s with the recent wounds of the armed conflict in Central America. (Honduras was the staging ground for US military operations, and the Honduran military was extremely influential – and beyond reproach – in domestic politics; see Chapter 2.)

In this context, in line with the discourse of 'good governance' disseminated by the World Bank, political-administrative decentralization appears as the cornerstone of the Program for the Modernization of the State (1991), which was conceived as a road map for the implementation of reforms. As early as the 1980s, decentralization had become the World Bank's reform strategy par excellence, recommended not only for the education sector, but also as a widespread transformation of the structure, organization, and management of the public sector as a whole (Winkler, 1989; Edwards and DeMatthews, 2014). In the agency's approach, decentralization was aimed at strengthening the political model of liberal democracy which it was hoped could be used to build the stability base required for the development of an open economy model. Moreover, decentralization was also conceived as a way to establish a political counterweight to the monopoly of the state and trade unions, as it created spaces for more direct participation and validated the right of civil society to demand accountability (World Bank, 1997). As Rhodes pointed out, in summary, '"good governance" marries the new public management to the advocacy of liberal democracy' (2000, p 57).

In the field of education, decentralization began with the adoption of the Plan for the Modernization of Education (PME) in 1993. Although education in Honduras had experienced some timid forms of decentralization since the 1970s, such as 'school hubs',[2] the centralized nature of education administration had never been so directly questioned. On the contrary, in the mid-1950s, the centralization of education had been interpreted as a strategic and genuine interest of the state in fulfilling its essential educational function as a public good. In the context of the approval of the PME and in the years following it, the main source of resistance came from the teachers' unions, which saw in the withdrawal of power from the central state associated with decentralization a clear approach to a form of regulation and educational provision related to the neoliberal logic of the market: 'This is the neoliberal current, this is the current that aims to reduce the State, reduce the size of the State, and thus give more importance and leadership to private enterprise and to transfer to it everything from which private enterprise can benefit. They see education as a commodity' (trade union representative).

From this point of view, decentralization in the field of education was perceived as a way – rather than an end in itself – for education to become a service regulated by the market, as a fundamental part of the new neoliberal configuration of the state.

Despite the opposition that it generated in these sectors, the discourse that prevailed during the 1990s around decentralization is the one that the World Bank developed and mobilized. In this discourse, three interrelated logics converge that were very persuasive, even when they lacked empirical support. The first is a logic of quality from which it is understood that decentralization would improve learning outcomes. In this sense, it is no coincidence that, in parallel with the decentralization policies, emphasis was also placed on the measurement of educational achievements. Within the framework of this logic, the World Bank promoted and financed, for example, the creation of the Education Quality Measurement Unit (UMCE [Unidad de Medición de la Calidad Educativa]) in 1996. The second logic corresponds to citizen participation. The idea here is that a decentralized education system is necessarily more democratic than one with a centralized structure. This idea connects to the paradigm of good governance within which much of the modernization plans are conceived. The World Bank considered that the International Monetary Fund had not given sufficient attention to the political viability of adjustment programmes and that it was necessary to prioritize strategies centred on good governance with a focus on increasing citizen participation and transparency (Borges, 2003). Central America had already had a bitter experience of how poverty and exclusion could seriously compromise political stability.[3] For this reason, incorporating social actors to legitimize decisions and the implementation of policies, in a context in which electoral democracy was not enough to guarantee the representation of all interests and to hold elected representatives accountable, seemed a reasonable measure – even though it was not clear that decentralization alone would be able to produce this increase in democratic quality. However, decentralization as a way to contribute to the democratization of education systems introduced, as reflected in the words of a Honduran social analyst, the idea that 'civil society' has a role to play, an idea that attracted great support and that would be systematically used as a legitimating element in subsequent educational reforms:

'Beginning in the 1990s I would say that this is when another novel element was incorporated that was not present in previous experiences, and within this is the fact of linking the State with civil society and political parties ... Prior to that time, the focus was on the State and tangentially the relationship with the various social groups, but the center remained the State. In this case, since the 1990s, although it is true that the concern is still the State, now comes how society should relate to the State and the role that political parties can play in the intermediation between society and the State. This seems to me extremely interesting because it is when the concept of civil society is introduced.' (Social analyst)

Finally, the World Bank's third logic is that of efficiency. It is assumed that decentralization will be able to generate more resources for the education sector, in addition to using them more efficiently (Hevia Rivas, 1991). It is interesting to note that the logic of efficiency is associated with citizen participation because the latter does not constitute simply a process of democratization of the system, but also a financial strategy: it is expected that communities, social groups, and institutions, when participating in the management of educational centres, will also be more committed to providing the necessary resources (that is, paying the fees) to finance their operation (World Bank, 1995). Efficiency also implies the most appropriate use of resources, in the sense that decentralized management, by being closer to local needs, is able to meet them at a lower cost and with greater relevance in terms of targeting situations that are considered a priority.

Educational quality, citizen participation, and administrative and financial efficiency constituted the main objectives – and legitimizing elements – of decentralization, and this, in turn, became the common thread that bound together all the reforms promoted during the period. While each government promoted its own reform programme – the 'Education Modernization' project (1990–1994), the 'Escuela Morazánica' project (1994–1998), 'The New Agenda' (1998–2002), and the 'Proposal for the Transformation of the Education System' (1999–2006) – this succession should not be understood as discontinuity. Remarkably, consistency over time was ensured by the influential guidelines disseminated by international organizations and which, during the period, revolved around the mandate of educational decentralization. According to Posas, the 'continuity and complementarity of the Honduran educational reform was guaranteed by the hegemonic educational agenda at the international level and by international organizations, such as the World Bank, which have played a stellar role in financing and deciding on the direction of the educational reforms ultimately adopted' (2010, p 31). A specialist in education – and former principal adviser to the Ministry of Education – explains it very eloquently:

'If you see public policy in Honduras, usually the State makes a statement of principles in line with the proposals that the World Bank or any other agency will bring. The State creates the framework of legitimacy and then you can see that it seems that each government makes a new proposal in many areas, but it is a proposal that has already been negotiated with international agencies such as the World Bank, and the State creates all the legal rhetoric so that this type of projects go through, because, in fact, the funds of the Honduran State are earmarked for the payment of teachers, the payment of personnel, they are not funds that are used to finance projects; in fact, if you see the list of educational projects you can verify that they are financed with external funds. These are the problems of a poor country that enacts public policy to meet the projects that have already been previously negotiated with the World Bank.' (Former adviser to the Ministry of Education)

Thus, if the orientation of education policy was determined by international agencies, the World Bank exercised a de facto leadership role among all organizations and agencies with a presence in the country. Proof of this is the project created in 1996 with the aim of promoting the reform of the Ministry of Education called the Project to Improve the Quality of Basic Education (Proyecto de Mejoramiento de la Calidad de la Educación Básica or PROMEB). Beyond its rhetoric, which is in perfect accord with the three logics mentioned earlier,[4] through this project, the World Bank managed to mobilize German financial and technical cooperation represented in its two agencies, the German Development Bank (KfW) and the German Agency for Technical Cooperation (GTZ), and to raise $43 million, an amount that exceeded the management capacity of the Ministry of Education. The PROMEB Initial Assessment Report describes this 'feat' of fundraising as follows:

> IDA's[5] assistance to the proposed project will also help mobilize support from other donors for the improvement of basic education. Likewise, the German government will allocate 20 million (Deutschmarks) of parallel financing through the Reconstruction Credit Institute (KfW) and approximately one million (Deutschmarks) for technical assistance through the German Cooperation Agency (GTZ). (World Bank, 1995, p 5)

Tropicalizing the external discourse: restriction and ritualization of the reform

While the influence that external discourses have had on the framework of the policies developed in Honduras since 1990 is undeniable, this influence has manifested itself in particular ways, mediated by local inertia and forms of administration of power deeply rooted in the Honduran ruling class. The policy of educational modernization promoted through the flagship policy of decentralization was no exception to this dynamic of recontextualization. According to a Honduran political analyst: 'It is a discourse, and here a translation of that discourse is made; when this discourse is translated, it is no longer translated in the same way as, for example, the World Bank thinks of it, and it acquires very particular, more *tropicalized* characteristics that arise from here.'

The *tropicalization* – or *Honduranization* (Morales-Ulloa, 2013) – of the decentralization policy imagined by the World Bank occurred fundamentally through two logics of action, understood as more or less conscious strategies – although strongly conditioned by institutional inertia and structural determinants – that guided government action. These two strategies emerged sequentially and, as we will see, were guided by the way in which power is wielded. The first of these logics of action implied that the policy of educational decentralization was implemented in a restricted way under the formula of 'deconcentration' (Decree 34/96). Deconcentration, in practice, implied relinquishing power to the minimum extent necessary and was thus far removed from the one-size-fits-all approach to decentralization desired by the World Bank. Far from promoting, for example, a plan for the municipalization of education that would provide municipalities and schools with wide margins of pedagogical and organizational autonomy, the Honduran government promoted a territorial reorganization of the Ministry of Education through the creation of Departmental Offices – and, subsequently, District Offices – that would assume technical, administrative, and pedagogical functions at the subnational level.[6] Decree 34/96 reads as follows: 'A Departmental Office of Education shall be established in each Department of the Republic as a deconcentrated agency responsible for administering, guiding, coordinating, and implementing the programs and services of the Ministry of Public Education in its respective territorial jurisdiction, as part of a program to deepen institutional deconcentration and broaden the basis for social participation.'

While the mandate of decentralization aimed at transforming the system as a whole and, in particular, the link between schools and communities, deconcentration aimed only at altering the bureaucratic structure of the system; it was thus an administrative reform in which 'deepening' is posed only as a future possibility. This restricted – or 'mild' decentralization (Morales-Ulloa, 2013) – embodied in the deconcentration policy – can be understood as the result of the need of the government of Carlos Roberto Reina (1994–1998) to please, on the one hand, the teachers' unions and, on the other hand, the World Bank and the international agencies that were financing the reform. The teachers' unions offered a fierce opposition to the policy of maximum decentralization of education because they saw in it the risk of privatization and atomization of their territorial power (Morales-Ulloa, 2013). The recent experiences of other countries in the region and, in particular, the model of municipalization and demand-side financing implemented and sustained in Chile since the 1980s constituted negative benchmarks that fuelled an unprecedented resistance.[7] As a result, Decree 34/96 was limited to stating that the objectives of the new Departmental Offices of Education would be 'to improve the management and quality of education', but did not include an explicit reference to a 'strong' decentralization which, in principle, was the basis of the recommendations of the World Bank and international agencies. However, in a series of preparatory documents for the reform published during the negotiations with the World Bank, the Ministry of Education argued, on the one hand, that deconcentration was in fact a 'modality of decentralization' and a 'starting point towards higher levels of autonomy' that could be achieved under the necessary conditions (Secretaría de Educación, 1995a, 1995b). On the other hand, the rationalities upon which the deconcentration discourse was based referred to the same logics of quality, participation, and efficiency through which the World Bank sought to build a consensus around decentralization. The Honduran government thus used the World Bank's discourse for its own purposes.

The second logic of action that characterized the recontextualization of educational decentralization in Honduras is represented by the ritualization of the functions attributed to the new subnational agencies. It is a reality that, wrapped in the providential rhetoric borrowed from the World Bank, the deconcentration of the Ministry of Education generated great expectations among some local actors. It was assumed that the departmental agencies – and, subsequently, the district-level ones – would be smaller and less bureaucratized organizational structures in contrast to the centralized administration in the country's capital, which had characterized the Ministry of Education. A district director put it this way:

> 'I liked that reform; I think it is good when it creates the district offices and the new functions of the departmental ones. It was said that we would not go to Tegucigalpa (the capital city) and that the problems would be solved in the Departmental office; even the signing of an agreement, now the agreements and the appointments would be made right there.' (District director)

This expectation is understandable since, by then, and just to cite one example, the recruitment of teachers involved a 105-step administrative process (Secretaría de Educación/GTZ, 1997), most of which was carried out at the central level of the Ministry of Education. Frequent administrative errors by the central bureaucracy required traveling to the capital city, and newly recruited teachers generally received no salary until at least six months after the start of the procedure. The 'debureaucratization' that deconcentration would presumably bring was presented as a way to break with 'the problem of centralism of the governing of education' (specialist in education), but, above all, it offered an alternative – naive, perhaps – capable of disrupting a network of clientelist relations and influence peddling that, according to several interviewees, had found fertile ground in the centralized structure.

However, despite the fact that the deconcentration embodied in Decree 34/96 was presented as a solution to these problems, and despite the expectations generated, the departmental offices were not able (or properly empowered) to 'administer, guide, coordinate and execute the programs and services [of the Ministry] of Education' (PREAL, 2010; Morales-Ulloa and Magalhães, 2013, p 10). In practice, the decisions continued to be centralized at the national level and the entire deconcentrated structure has so far been unable to carry out more than 'rituals' of deconcentrated management with no real effects – either pedagogical or material – on the functioning of the system in its territorial areas. The deconcentrated offices have no initiatives of their own and exclusively execute the dictates of the central authorities without taking into consideration their suitability to their particular contexts. The following quotes reflect this gap in the functions of the deconcentrated agencies from three perspectives:

'These departmental directors were never trained. A structure was made, a decree was made, but its implementation was never planned. It was, I would say, without any direction, without any compass, that is, there was no plan, there was no program.' (Trade union leader)

'[T]he District Director is also alone, he does not have a secretary, he does not have an assistant, he does not have a vehicle for transportation, he travels with his own resources, so how can he distribute educational materials from community to community if he does not have resources and does not have a vehicle, he does not have fuel, nor does he have money to get around?' (Former departmental officer)

'The idea that the government should not be at the central level was promoted … [T]hat was the discourse enunciated, but the culture of the people that led was a very personalistic culture that did not allow them to release power.' (Education specialist)

The *tropicalization* of the educational reform that characterized its restricted and ritualized implementation has been attributed, first, to the government's difficulties in mediating between antagonistic actors – that is, teacher unions and international agencies – and, second, to the lack of technical support, funding and personnel aimed at guaranteeing the functionality of the new deconcentrated entities (PREAL, 2010). However, while these factors are undeniably relevant – and this is argued by several interviewees – such an explanation does not recognize the deeper logic that guides the functioning of the education system and the Honduran state. In the deconcentration of the Ministry of Education, the major conflict was the power dispute – or, rather, a power that does not want disputes – and, in this context, certain interpretations of the policy texts have been imposed in order to restrict and ritualize the implementation of the deconcentration of administrative and pedagogical functions. According to a specialist who participated in the implementation of the reform, the recentralization occurred almost as a reflexive act, shortly after deconcentration was approved:

'The changes have not occurred because there is a certain interest of the government to do so and I will tell you clearly, for example, one of the changes: the Departmental Offices Coordinating Unit [Oficina Coordinadora de Direcciones Departamentales] that had originally been created in Decree 34/96 was eliminated and it was established that these offices would depend directly on the head of the Ministry of Education.' (Education specialist)

The recentralization that took place even before the deconcentration policy could be fully deployed leaves no doubt that the government and the Ministry of Education had no interest in distributing power across 18 subnational autonomous units and, more importantly, that if they had been able to restrict the World Bank's original decentralization project, they could also make sure that their apparently deconcentrated functioning was ritualized to maintain central control of the system. It was then a question of modifying the government, but without modifying the nature of the centralized state. A former departmental official explains it this way:

'We understood it that way when we had the meetings that prepared us for the departmental offices, and they talked to us about deconcentration, we understood that it was very risky to hand over some educational matters to the departmental offices, because it meant handing over power in the first place ... Decentralization was left for a second term in order to evaluate how it went and what benefits deconcentration had, to then unleash it, but it was very difficult because it implied letting go of something politically that they should control, and always in the unconscious of the authorities, they do not want to cede power, they do not want to give it up, they give out tasks, but not the power of deciding over education policy.' (Former departmental officer)

The fact that the Ministry of Education has remained highly centralized, and the fact that there is no definition of the functions that departmental offices are supposed to execute, speaks of the inherently centralized, controlling, and extractive nature of the system (Morales-Ulloa, 2013; Edwards et al, 2023b). As departmental directors describe, in practice, the deconcentration meant that the agencies located at the subnational level would limit themselves to executing the central directives following a logic that reproduces the autocratic and clientelist model that, according to them, has always characterized power relations within the Ministry of Education. These apparently dysfunctional institutional arrangements can be understood as the result of a more or less conscious strategy of concentration of power that sees the development of a modern (that is, rational, technocratic) state bureaucracy as a potential threat to the status quo.[8] In other words, according to Edwards et al in their study on Honduras, decentralization does not occur 'because attempts in that direction contravene both the centripetal and privatizing tendencies that have always guided the state apparatus and the need to avoid the implementation of reforms that reveal the weaknesses of the state and that question its legitimacy' (2023b, p. 10).

Conclusions

Based on the Structural Adjustment Program, the reforms promoted in the field of education since the 1990s in Honduras should be read as economically inspired educational reforms. The key players in this process have been, in addition to the Honduran state, the International Monetary Fund and the World Bank. The International Monetary Fund was the architect of the rules of the macro-economic game, the one in charge of establishing the restrictions – material and symbolic – to the development of a welfare system considered unviable, and the creator of a framework of references and representations of what would subsequently be considered correct and desirable in matters of social policy. The World Bank, for its part, embarked on a task of fine-tuning that ensured, on the one hand, the development of the content of the reforms and, on the other hand, the assurance of their implementation. To this end, it used two well-known tools: framing and conditioning. The pervasive rhetoric of 'modernization' and the granting of conditional loans for the implementation of these reforms illustrate this strategy.

In line with their economic inspiration, the educational reforms promoted globally during the decade by international organizations have a strong administrative component that draws from public choice theory (that is, New Public Management). They focus, in the first place, on the reorganization of the governance of the system – that is, on its 'deconcentration' – and then on the definition of new educational financing schemes and on the development of school-based educational management experiences.[9] The approach to reform relegates the central role of learning in the educational process and assumes that improvements in administrative-financial efficiency are sufficient to cause a positive effect throughout the system.

The transposition of the ideas of the New Public Management to the field of education was installed for the first time in Honduras in the 1990s at the behest of the World Bank and is sustained over time to the present day. In particular, the idea of decentralization has been a perennial theme in successive reform programs, and the logics of efficiency, quality, and participation used to frame the reforms of the 1990s are still present. These economic-administrative ideas have also been promoted by the World Bank through the language of 'good governance' in order to emphasize the notion that such reforms can also contribute to strengthening the political model of liberal democracy, which is seen as a precursor to (or as the foundation for) the development of the open economy model. As with decentralization, 'good governance' is conceived as an antidote, in this case against the monopoly of the state and trade unions, both of which would see their power eroded by a civil society demanding accountability. Finally, the idea of 'modernization' constitutes the umbrella that frames and offers legitimacy to the reform discourse in a constant way.

The modernization of education is seen as a way to meet the objectives of institutional change, decentralization, efficiency, quality and citizen participation, while also resolving problems such as access and equality of educational opportunities. This is an ambitious and eclectic aspiration in a state like the Honduran one, which has not been able to approximate a rational or technocratic bureaucratic administration model, and in which practices such as clientelism and corruption are part of the administrative culture of the public sector. For Braslavsky (1999), this situation is a kind of two-pronged struggle. On the one hand, the aim is to solve the fundamental educational challenges that were solved long ago in industrialized countries and, on the other hand, the aim is to push traditional educational management schemes towards New Public Management approaches. The tensions within these goals can be seen in the fact that the Honduran state is one of the most institutionally precarious states in Latin America and that historically it has been efficient as a repressive apparatus, but not as agent for the common good (Morales-Ulloa, 2013). Consequently, the oligarchic-clientelist logic that mobilizes it is only willing to allow reforms to the point where they do not oppose the interests that the state itself represents. As stated by D'Ans, 'in Honduras, directly or indirectly, the entire social body depends on an oligarchic layer that occupies the top of the social hierarchy' (2007, p 428). A consequence of this is that, beyond union resistance to attempts at decentralization, the very nature of the distribution of power in Honduras blocks any decentralization.

The education sector in Honduras has major technical weaknesses and is highly dependent on external funding. This situation offers international agencies a privileged doorway for the dissemination of ideas. Some domestic actors often offer strong opposition, as in the usual case of trade union organizations. However, if the framing and conditionality designed by international bodies are well defined, peripheral states have few options in terms of rejecting any proposal. Even so, although the influence of these discourses is decisive in defining the reform agenda, the case of Honduras is interesting because it shows how the space of implementation presents a topography – political, cultural, and economic – capable of shifting mandates and political discourses to produce results that ultimately resemble the starting conditions rather than the objectives desired by the unsuspecting reformists. In the case analysed, the restriction and ritualization of the reform in the field of implementation annihilate the expectations generated by the framing and conditioning in the field of the definition of the reform agenda.

Notes

1 The presidents of the period were Rafael Callejas (1990–1994; National Party), Carlos Reina (1994–1998; Liberal Party), and Carlos Flores (1998–2002; Liberal Party).

2 School hubs operated mainly in rural areas. A school considered to be better equipped and more capable coordinated pedagogical support for other schools with smaller capacities and, in this context, had some curricular autonomy.

3 The socioeconomic deterioration resulting from the long civil wars in Guatemala, El Salvador, and Nicaragua, and the virtual occupation of Honduran territory by the UUSarmy in the 1980s had only increased the sources of political instability in the region (Chomsky, 2021).

4 'The main purpose of the institutional strengthening component is to support the government's proposal to restructure and decentralize the Ministry of Public Education, strengthen supervision and develop the necessary administrative capacity in the Ministry, to support the provision of quality basic education to all Hondurans, with higher levels of efficiency and accountability' (World Bank, 1995, p 29).

5 International Development Association (IDA). The World Bank Group consists of five institutions: the IDA provides loans and grants to the governments of the poorest countries.

6 The territory of Honduras is divided into 18 departments, that is, territorial units above the municipalities and below the national state.

7 The municipalization of the Chilean education system and the demand financing system – which included the possibility of schools charging extra fees to families (that is, co-payments) – were conceived as the root causes of the increase in private provision and the socioeconomic segmentation of the system that the country experienced especially during the 1990s.

8 This is a logic similar to that described by William Reno (2000) regarding the functioning of the so-called 'shadow states'.

9 Altschuler and Corrales (2013), Tinoco (2010), and Edwards et al (2023a) report on the development of the Honduran Community Education Project (PROHECO), a school-based management policy implemented since 1998 with funding from the World Bank and the Inter-American Development Bank in the image and likeness of other programmes implemented since the beginning of the decade in other countries of the region (see Chapter 3, this volume).

References

Altschuler, D., and Corrales, J. (2013). Political obstacles: patronage and polarization. In D. Altschuler and J. Corrales (eds.), *The Promise of Participation* (pp 130–146). Palgrave Macmillan. https://doi.org/10.1057/9781137271846_10

Avelar, M., and Ball, S. J. (2019). Mapping new philanthropy and the heterarchical state: the mobilization for the national learning standards in Brazil. *International Journal of Educational Development*, 64, 65–73.

Ball, S. (2001). Diretrizes políticas globais e relações políticas locais em educação [Global political guidelines and local political relations in education]. *Currículo sem Fronteiras*, 1(2), 99–116.

Ball, S., and Junemann, C. (2012). *Networks, New Governance and Education*. Policy Press.

Bonal, X. (2002). Plus ça change ... The World Bank global education policy and the post-Washington Consensus. *International Studies in Sociology of Education*, 12(1), 3–22. https://doi.org/10.1080/09620210200200080

Borges, A. (2003). Gobernança e política educacional: a agenda recente do Banco Mundial [Governance and educational policy: a recent World Bank agenda]. *Revista Brasileira de Ciências Sociais*, 18(52), 125–138. https://doi.org/10.1590/S0102-69092003000200007

Braslavsky, C. (1999). Estudios de caso sobre la reforma de la gestión en América Latina: el caso de Argentina [Case studies on management reform in Latin America: the case of Argentina]. In UNESCO, *La gestión en busca del sujeto. Seminario 'Reformas de la Gestión de los Sistemas Educativos en América Latina* (pp 69–92). UNESCO.

Chomsky, A. (2021). *Central America's Forgotten History: Revolution, Violence, and the Roots of Migration*. Beacon Press.

D'Ans, A.-M. (2007). *Honduras: Difícil emergencia de una nación, de un Estado* [*Honduras: Difficult Emergence of a Nation, of a State*]. Renal Video Production.

Edwards Jr., D. B. (2018). *The Trajectory of Global Education Policy: Community-Based Management in El Salvador and the Global Reform Agenda*. Springer.

Edwards Jr., D. B., and DeMatthews, D. (2014). Historical trends in educational decentralization in the United States and developing countries: a periodization and comparison in the post-WWII context. *Education Policy Analysis Archives*, 22, 40. https://doi.org/10.14507/epaa.v22n40.2014

Edwards Jr., D. B., Moschetti, M. C., and Caravaca, A. (2023a). *Globalization, Privatization, and the State: Contemporary Education Reform in Post-colonial Contexts*. Routledge.

Edwards Jr., D. B., Moschetti, M., and Caravaca, A. (2023b). Estado, política educativa y privatización en contextos postcoloniales. *Cadernos de Pesquisa*, 53, e09662, 1–15.

Hevia, R. (1991). *Política de descentralización de la educación básica y media en América Latina: estado del arte* [*Decentralization Policy of Basic and Secondary Education in Latin America: State of the Art*]. UNESCO/REDUC.

Jessop, B. (2010). Cultural political economy and critical policy studies. *Critical Policy Studies*, 3(3–4), 336–356. https://doi.org/10.1080/19460171003619741

Lingard, B., and Rawolle, S. (2011). New scalar politics: Implications for education policy. *Comparative Education*, 47(4), 489–502.

Morales-Ulloa, R. (2013). Los cambios en la gobernanza del sistema educativo en Honduras: La política de desconcentración de la educación pre-básica, básica y media (1990–2010) [Changes in the governance of the educational system in Honduras: the policy of deconcentration of pre-basic, basic and secondary education (1990–2010)]. Doctoral dissertation, Universidade do Porto.

Morales-Ulloa, R., and Magalhães, A. M. (2013). Visiones, tensiones y resultados. La nueva gobernanza de la educación en Honduras [Visions, tensions and results. the new governance of education in Honduras]. *Education Policy Analysis Archives*, 21(3), 1–24. https://doi.org/10.14507/epaa.v21n3.2013

Patrinos, H. A., Osorio, F. B., and Guáqueta, J. (2009). *The Role and Impact of Public-Private Partnerships in Education*. World Bank.

Polidano, C. (1999). *The New Public Management in Developing Countries*. Institute for Development Policy and Management, University of Manchester.

Posas, M. (2010). Política educativa y reforma educativa en Honduras [Educational policy and educational reform in Honduras]. In M. Posas (ed.), *Estado de la Educación en Honduras* [*The State of Education in Honduras*] (pp 29–58). Universidad Pedagógica Nacional Francisco Morazán.

PREAL (2010). *Un Desafío Impostergable: Informe de Progreso Educativo Honduras* [*An Unpostponable Challenge: Educational Progress Report Honduras*]. FEREMA.

Reno, W. (2000). Clandestine economies, violence and states in Africa. *Journal of International Affairs*, 52(2), 433–459. https://www.jstor.org/stable/24357760

Rhodes, R. (2000). Governance and public administration. In J. Pierre (ed.), *Debating Governance: Authority, Steering, and Democracy* (pp 54–90). Oxford University Press.

Robinson, W. (2002). Globalisation as a macro-structural-historical framework of analysis: the case of Central America. *New Political Economy*, 7(2), 221–250. https://doi. org/10.1080/13563460220138853

Salazar Vides, M. E. (2018). ¿Hasta dónde influyen las agendas internacionales en los sistemas educativos centroamericanos? Un marco teórico para su análisis. *Paradigma: Revista de Investigación Educativa*, 25(40), 69–96.

Secretaría de Educación (1995a). *Directrices para la reorganización de la Secretaría de Educación* [*Guidelines for the Reorganization of the Ministry of Education*]. Secretaría de Educación.

Secretaría de Educación (1995b). *Convergencia hacia la integración de la Planificación a nivel local* [*Convergence towards the Integration of Planning at the Local Level*]. Secretaría de Educación.

Secretaría de Educación/GTZ (1997). *Educación y Desarrollo: Estudio Sectorial /Plan Decenal* [*Education and Development: Sector Study/Ten-Year Plan*]. Secretaría de Educación.

Shiroma, E. O. (2014). Networks in action: new actors and practices in education policy in Brazil. *Journal of Education Policy*, 29(3), 323–348. https://doi.org/10.1080/02680939.2013.831949

Tinoco, M. A. (2010). *Política educativa y Banco Mundial: La educación comunitaria en Honduras* [*Education Policy and the World Bank: Community Education in Honduras*]. Guaymuras.

Verger, A. (2014). Why do policy-makers adopt global education policies? Toward a research framework on the varying role of ideas in education reform. *Current Issues in Comparative Education*, 16(2), 14–29.

Verger, A., Fontdevila, C., and Zancajo, A. (2016). *The Privatization of Education: A Political Economy of Global Education Reform*. Teachers College Press.

Winkler, D. R. (1989). *Decentralization in Education: An Economic Perspective*. World Bank.

World Bank (1995). *Informe de Evaluación Inicial Honduras Proyecto Escuela Morazánica* [*Initial Evaluation Report Honduras Morazánica School Project*]. Report No. 13791-HO. World Bank.

World Bank (1997). *World Development Report: The State in a Changing World*. World Bank.

World Bank (2003). *World Development Report 2004: Making Services Work for Poor People*. World Bank.

5

Locally Driven Innovation Through Teacher Peer Mentoring in Times of COVID-19: A Professional Learning Community in Rural El Salvador

Kristin Rosekrans, Celia Morán, and Carolina Bodewig

Introduction

At the start of 2020, Latin American countries had low levels of learning: 51 per cent of students could not read proficiently by late primary age; in Central American countries such as Guatemala and Honduras, 67 per cent and 75 per cent of students, respectively, could not read proficiently (World Bank, 2021). Educational inequity was exacerbated by the closure of schools due to the COVID-19 pandemic. In El Salvador, where schools were closed between March 2020 and April 2021, the loss in the average number of years of schooling is estimated to be 1.5 years (from 7.6 years of average schooling to 6.1 years) (World Bank, 2021).[1] The global trend in the educational response to the closure of schools due to COVID-19 was, in most countries, to switch to 100 per cent virtual instruction, while others moved to hybrid instruction (UNESCO, 2020). Central American governments followed this trend, trying to mitigate the loss of learning through online instruction and the provision of printed and digital learner guides for students to work on independently at home. Yet this option was unfeasible due to the high percentage of students that lacked access to the internet and/or a digital device and printing options. For most students, schooling was reduced to filling out worksheets and infrequent contact with teachers through the WhatsApp messaging service with a smartphone (of their own or belonging to a family member). The relationship between teachers and their students was weakened, making it difficult to keep track of learning. This lack of interaction led to education delivery that was neither meaningful nor engaging for students.

The recently dominant trend in international donor support has been to fund large-scale early grade literacy programmes globally that prioritize students increasing their reading speed and fluency and measuring for this continually, while de-emphasizing meaningful learning (Dowd and Bartlett, 2019). Many governments, including those in Central America, have adopted such approaches, which leave little room for critical thinking and socioemotional learning. While some reform efforts have emphasized quality through improved curriculum and teacher training, the poorest and most remote public schools remain at a disadvantage due to the already-existing learning gaps and geographical isolation. When teacher training is carried out, it tends to be centralized, large scale, and lacking in ongoing and effective coaching, especially for the most remote schools (Vaillant, 2005; Terigi, 2010; Parra, 2018).

This chapter presents an exception to the downward spiral in learning that poor, rural children across Central America faced in the context of the COVID-19 pandemic. It highlights an innovative approach that has grown out of the commitment of 70 teachers in three rural municipalities (Jocoaitique, San Fernando, and Torola) in the department of Morazán, El Salvador, who dedicated themselves to ensuring that their students continued to learn during the 13 months of school closure. It also presents an exception to the predominant education approaches in national curricula that lack a socioaffective dimension to learning and meaning making, and text production in literacy development. Teachers' efforts were supported by a nonprofit civil society organization, ConTextos, that receives funding and technical support from a Swiss donor, Pestalozzi Children's Foundation (PCF). PCF aims to ensure inclusive, equitable, and quality education, especially to vulnerable and excluded groups, using child-centred pedagogy based on social interaction, communication, and meaningful learning.[2]

El Salvador was PCF's first office in Central America and was established in 1995 to support the peace process after the country's 12-year civil war (1980–1992), specifically through improving education access, retention, and quality for the most vulnerable children and youth in the former conflict zones of the country. El Salvador's civil war had given rise to popular education, which was based on the notion that education is for individual and social transformation and should happen through dialogue, problem solving, and knowledge production (Freire, 2014). With the aim of empowering all persons through literacy and learning, popular education operated by drawing on community members with some level of education to teach children and illiterate adults. During and after the war, donors like

PCF supported these efforts through local nongovernmental organizations (NGOs) and civil society organizations (Dewees et al, 1994).

When schools closed due to the pandemic, the 70 rural teachers in Morazán supported by ConTextos, the majority of whom taught alone or with one other teacher in multigrade classrooms, created their own learning materials and lessons for students instead of waiting for student learner guides to arrive from the Ministry of Education, Science and Technology (MINEDUCYT). During the first three months of school closings, when teachers lacked MINEDUCYT training and support to transition to remote learning, they shared solutions to technological and teaching challenges and created virtual peer-learning, enabling them to build a community for professional and socioemotional support in the face of uncertainty. Using a socioaffective and communicative approach to literacy development, they engaged their students in learning activities that wove self-expression and social interaction into writing and maths. Reading activities, poems, and letters were exchanged through audio and video formats, and were circulated with the support of parents and community leaders so that students could continue learning. Instead of being based on the traditional view of what the teacher lacks, these teachers drew on each other's knowledge and resources to innovate and shape literacy development and text production to the local context. Their engagement in peer-learning and innovative teaching helped foster resilience among teachers, families, and students.

This experience provides insights and lessons to expand the range of strategies that can be offered in future school closures and/or for education policy and interventions in general in light of global trends in education. It encourages governments, donors, and local organizations to: (1) promote literacy development that is rooted in meaningful learning, expression through text, social interaction, and socioemotional learning rather than prioritizing students' reading speed; (2) change the traditional view of professional development through centralized teacher training and turn towards learning communities, study groups, peer observation, mentoring, and accompaniment based on dialogue to build knowledge for transforming teaching and learning practices; and (3) leverage the power of local history and knowledge, whether it be a former conflict context or another context with its particular relevant historical and cultural contextual factors.

This chapter describes the context within which this experience took place, detailing the relevant contextual factors that contributed to this experience despite both the global forces of the pandemic and the centralized delivery of education services in El Salvador. It also describes the methodology used and details the research questions that guided the study, data sources, and analysis. Findings are presented in three parts: (1) the way in which teachers responded to the school closure to ensure continued learning for their students; (2) the innovative teaching practices they implemented; and

(3) how teachers supported each other and collaborated during the pandemic. Finally, the study's implications are discussed, followed by conclusions.

Context

El Salvador, the smallest and most densely populated country in Central America, has high levels of poverty and economic inequality. A total of 22.8 per cent of the population live in poverty, of which 4.5 per cent are in extreme poverty. In rural areas, 24.8 per cent of households are in poverty, of which 5.2 per cent are in extreme poverty (DIGESTYC, 2020). Rural areas face greater deficits in terms of educational access and quality. In 2019, school attendance of seven to 24 year olds was 56.4 per cent in rural areas and 66.6 per cent in urban areas, while the average years of schooling were 5.3 years in rural areas and 8.2 in urban areas (DIGESTYC, 2020).

While teachers can make a difference, many are not equipped to teach effectively. Pre-service training includes minimal content on pedagogical strategies and in-service training is typically done on a large scale and lacks ongoing and effective coaching. The current government centralizes education management in terms of budget allocations, decisions about the type of teacher training it provides, exams for teachers to access a teaching position, and regulation around NGOs entering schools to work with teachers or to donate resources. Thus, in general, local education initiatives are not encouraged or actively supported (Candray, 2021).

Morazán is the second poorest of the 14 departments, with 26 per cent of the population living in poverty (DIGESTYC, 2020) and, according to the Multidimensional Poverty Map, 50.4 per cent of families in Morazán live in extreme poverty (Technical Secretariat of the Presidency (STPP) and MINEDUC-DIGESTYC, 2015). For example, 88.5 per cent of families in the municipality of Torola and 66.7 per cent in the municipality of San Fernando live in extreme poverty. The northern area of the department was ravaged during the civil war in the 1980s and it was home to several of the deadliest and most brutal massacres, such as the one that occurred in El Mozote and caused international shock and condemnation.

Within this already difficult context, face-to-face classes in El Salvador were suspended in March 2020 due to COVID-19 and resumed in a blended mode at the beginning of April 2021. MINEDUCYT trained 56 per cent of teachers nationally in Google Classroom as well as in educational television. This training did not reach teachers in Morazán until August 2020. The MINEDUCYT also produced student learner guides that reached teachers in early May 2020. While well intentioned, they did not reach all children and although they could be downloaded from the official website, this was not possible for students who lacked access to equipment and internet or printing services. In Morazán, three out of ten households do not have a television, only 8 per cent of households have a computer, and while nine out of ten have a smartphone, only one out of ten households have internet access to use it (DIGESTYC, 2020).

Nationally, many teachers struggled due to a lack of technological knowledge and management for designing learning experiences. Yet, in the absence of MINEDUCYT support, many tried to use the resources provided, even though they lacked relevance for poor, rural contexts. The result of this was replicating within the household what happens in the classroom, focusing on content and not on the development of literacy, mathematical reasoning, critical thinking, and social and emotional skills.

In contrast, the 70 teachers in the 24 schools in Morazán in the municipalities of Jocoaitique, San Fernando, and Torola had been receiving support from PCF through ConTextos since 2018.[3] ConTextos is an NGO that was founded in El Salvador in 2011 with the aim of improving students' reading comprehension, writing expression, and mathematical reasoning through resource provision, teacher training, and coaching. In 2016, ConTextos began its work in northern Morazán based on relationships that several of its staff members had developed through establishing a municipal library and supporting a network of teachers in the municipality of Perquín. They also began to build relationships with community members and teachers in neighbouring municipalities.

ConTextos' education model is based on a communicative, sociocultural approach to literacy development (Cassany, 2005; Mar et al, 2006) and socioaffectivity, or socioemotional learning (SEL) (Tri013es and García, 2002; Durlak et al, 2011). Literacy is understood not only as the ability to read and write, but also as a more complex ability that makes it possible to understand how to interact with other people and improve social abilities such as collaboration, teamwork, and respect (Mar et al, 2006). Literacy development must be rooted within real events, people, and social interactions that take place in a social context made up of political, economic, and cultural conflicts. Within this context, literacy skills are developed through the interaction of different coexisting ideas, interests, and beliefs (Sánchez, 2013).

SEL also recognizes the important role that social interaction has in the educational process. Its aim is to develop the personality of the student through cognitive and socioemotional development rather than focusing only on the cognitive, as has traditionally occurred in education (Trianes and Garcia, 2002). It aims to develop students' self-awareness, self-management, social awareness, relationship skills, and responsible decision making (Durlak et al, 2011). Consistent with the sociocultural perspective of literacy, ConTextos' approach to SEL emphasizes the relational dimension of emotions and the importance of social interaction and expression between learners, and between the teacher and students. PCF, unlike the literacy efforts many donors support, embraces the sociocultural and SEL approach that puts students at the centre of their learning, and values local knowledge production.

When faced with the COVID-19 pandemic, from mid-March to April 2020, in the absence of support from MINEDUCYT, these 70 teachers figured out their own ways to ensure that their students continued to learn. In early May 2020, ConTextos carried out an assessment to understand the educational challenges faced by the communities it supports. The assessment revealed that teachers were facing major technological and pedagogical challenges using the online platforms and the worksheets provided by MINEDUCYT. Many teachers felt a lack of clarity about their role, which caused stress, anxiety, and a lack of confidence in their abilities to support their students. This was heightened by physical isolation and loneliness. Thus, ConTextos prioritized the need to attend to the teachers' socioemotional wellbeing based on the premise that teaching performance depends not only on teachers' professionalism or access to technologies, but also on their socioemotional health (INEE, 2020).

Following the assessment, ConTextos held 25 virtual sessions with 200 teachers across the country, including 47 in Morazán. During these sessions, they modelled the use of reading, writing, and dialogue to take care of their own socioemotional health such as using writing prompts to promote emotional expression. Other virtual training was done through Zoom and Google Classroom on developing reading comprehension, writing, and mathematical reasoning that included an emphasis on using new technologies in the educational process. The 70 teachers from the three municipalities in Morazán participated, which was followed up with individual support through Zoom and WhatsApp to provide technical and socioemotional support for each teacher. In mid-August 2020, teachers began incorporating the learned strategies into the practices that they had already begun to develop soon after the pandemic hit.

While ConTextos provided the same training and support to all teachers it coordinated nationally, the teachers of Morazán were unique in terms of how they put it into practice and subsequently assumed ownership and leadership in their educational practices. Through peer mentoring and collaboration to share successes and discuss problems, they developed new ways of supporting their students' learning. They were unique in their explicit commitment to their students and each other. Their experience during the civil war in the 1980s led them to be highly organized, and popular education had left a collective social conscience of solidarity and resourcefulness that likely contributed to their ability and will to respond quickly to the needs of families and students.

Methods

This study was guided by three research questions: (1) how did teachers respond to school closure in the absence of government support?; (2) what types of learning experiences were designed and facilitated to keep students engaged in learning?; and (3) how did teachers support each other and collaborate during the COVID-19 pandemic?

The analysis was based on qualitative data collected in different moments. In December 2020 and January 2021, ConTextos carried out a needs assessment in the communities it supports to understand how to best provide resources during the pandemic. This was done through in-depth interviews and teacher and principal surveys. Additionally, from June to November 2020, ConTextos collected student work and stories, as well as poems produced by teachers to understand what teaching and learning experiences were taking place. For this study, the authors selected three teacher interviews that were carried out for the needs assessment based on the criteria that they: (1) were from one of each of the municipalities examined in this study; (2) contained discussion about how teachers responded immediately after the school closures; and (3) included teachers discussing their experience with their peer circles that were carried out during the pandemic. Additionally, the authors selected 22 writing samples and 15 maths samples of work by students in first to sixth grade, along with the corresponding teacher lesson plans. These were chosen because they were: (1) produced by students from the three municipalities in which this study is situated; (2) the most legible or audible (for videos); and (3) the most expressive. Three teacher stories/poems were also selected based on their expressiveness and clarity. In April 2021, in-person, in-depth interviews were carried out with six teachers, two of whom were also school principals. Two focus groups were held: one with six mothers and one with six children from grades one to six. See Table 5.1 for a summary of all data analysed. Pseudonyms were assigned to all students and teachers who participated in the study.

Table 5.1: Primary data sources

Interviewee	Interviews	Focus groups	Student work samples	Total number of informants
Teachers	9		3	12
Mothers		1 (6 participants)		6
Students		1 (6 participants)	27	33

Source: Author

Analysis was done by extracting data based on codes that corresponded to the research questions. Analytical matrices were used that displayed data by codes across sources. The authors examined patterns and trends, and triangulated across sources and types of data to strengthen validity.

Findings

Teachers' response to COVID-19

When schools closed in El Salvador, teachers had little clarity about what the next steps were for continuing to support their students. The lack of clarity was even more pronounced in the poorest and most remote municipalities of the country like Jocoaitique, San Fernando, and Torola. As a teacher, Mr Escoto, explained: 'COVID-19 brought to light how vulnerable rural areas are – the lack of computers, tablets, smart phones, electricity, poor (internet) signal – and all this contributes to the lack of technological abilities in the community.'

Teachers felt they lacked the knowledge, skills, and resources for remote teaching. They felt frustrated and like they did not have control over the situation. As one teacher, Ana, expressed: 'We could not find a solution, a way. In my case, I felt like I lost control.' Another teacher, Ms Landaverde, explained her frustration: 'It was a challenge, because I had never worked on a virtual education platform before. I cried at first because I could not access the Ministry of Education website.' Some students didn't have phones, and even for those who did, teachers had to figure out what to do to help them learn.

The main actions that teachers took to ensure continued learning were: (1) creating small learner guides and figuring out ways to get them to their students; (2) relocating to the community in which they taught and doing house visits; and (3) recording short videos of themselves teaching content and sending them to students via smartphones.

A teacher, Chamba, explained that they downloaded materials from the internet and adapted the content to the context, including materials for science experiments that students had in their homes, such as crochet yarn:

'We created guides that were downloaded from the internet, but aligned with the content that we were covering [in the national curriculum] ... I would take it (learner guide content) from the official website of the MINEDUCYT, edit it in my own way, and print it. None of it (the material we taught) was from the MINEDUCYT, not even the experiments.'

Another teacher, Ms Lucía, explained how she came up with ways to support younger students by using different materials and activities: 'When they had problems with fine motor skills, I used origami paper so they could make some figures and learn. I bought the materials for them when they didn't have any. Sometimes there were materials at school, but almost always I provided them.'

Another teacher, Guadalupe, explained that she, like other teachers, spent their own money for printing the learner guides and other materials (for example, for science experiments and art projects): 'We spent up to fourteen dollars on printing the guides, and since they were for all subjects, even physics and art, we had to send them all.'

Getting the guides to their students was another challenge that the teachers had to overcome. While teachers could call some parents with phones so that students could pick up the guides at school, those without phones had to be reached in person. In some cases, teachers arranged a local bus to take guides to a police post where parents could pick them up. After students completed their work, the parents had to submit it to the teachers (either physically or by sending photos). This was a challenge for families without internet service and/or a weak phone signal. One father explained that he had to climb a large hill to have enough connectivity to send photos of completed work. Others had to make the journey to the school or teacher's home to hand in their completed work.

WhatsApp was a useful way to communicate because it did not require an internet connection. Some teachers would record themselves teaching a lesson and then send it. They also asked students to record videos of themselves explaining concepts, doing experiments, reading something, or other tasks, as Chamba explained:

'I started creating videos, tutorials from my phone … I bought a whiteboard, but just smaller because it is what I could get. It [the smartphone] didn't allow me to go beyond more than a minute and a half (of video) … sometimes it allowed up to three minutes.'

Some of the parents in the focus groups complained that teachers had abandoned their children; however, these parents tended to live in communities closer to small, urban towns. Parents in the most remote communities expressed that teachers were there when they needed them.

Some teachers who lived away from the communities in which they taught were unable to leave their homes during the first four months of the COVID-19 pandemic due to the strict lockdown. Yet these teachers were present via WhatsApp. Other teachers moved to the community to be near their students. Guadalupe and Lucía explained:

'Sometimes my work was to go to their houses … most of the children don't have phones, well, their parents do not. So, it became difficult.

I had to go and be closer to the community, near the school, and then make some house visits. We walked around the whole village, visiting parents, explaining to the children what they were going to do. We would sit there for a little while at the table with them and explain, because some parents can't read, others don't want to [help their children with schoolwork], and some don't have time.'

However, reaching all the students was a challenge due to the distance of some homes, as one teacher, Ms Landaverde, explained: 'I went and visited only two houses, because there was a lot of distance between them, so at times we only managed to work with three children and for the furthest away, only two.'

The dedication and responsibility that these teachers felt for their students is demonstrated clearly through the case of Mr Escoto. He explained that one month after the pandemic hit, he had managed to communicate with all his students through WhatsApp except for one, Rafael. He gave all his students a message for Rafael, which was to leave a missed call for him so he could call him back without Rafael having to pay for the call. He finally received the call. As he explained:

'It was Rafi! He told me that he had all the guides completed for that month, but that he did not know how to send them. I told him that a classmate of his could send them to me. And from then on, I received his messages from different numbers each time, I think there were 12 or more. 'Hello teacher, I'm Rafael Herrera!' from an unknown number every week and at any time of the day or night. For me, Rafael is an example of resilience, his desire to overcome challenges and turn any difficulty into an opportunity.'

Innovative teaching practices

Teachers focused on combining academic activities with stress management. The tree main strategies developed were: (1) students writing letters and reading them while being video-recorded; (2) the travelling notebook; and (3) mathematics at home. Teachers thought it was important to know how students felt during the pandemic, what they wanted to say, and who they wanted to say it to. Children elaborated letters for their loved ones, such as one student, Juan, who wrote a letter to his teacher, Mr Escoto:

Dear teacher, I hope you are in good health. The reason for this letter is to tell you that I love you very much. Since you left, I felt very sad, but I hope that next year you will also be my teacher to continue learning a lot. I hope next year this has already passed because it separates us from the school. We have been studying at home, and that has helped us a lot to learn a little more because, before this pandemic, we could not even send a text message, but this made us learn a lot more. Well, these are my few words that I wanted to say in this letter that I am sending you. Juan Hernández

One girl wrote to her grandmother to tell her how much she missed her. She read the letter as her mother recorded it with a phone:

Miss, I am going to read you the letter about the person I miss very much. I miss my grandmother very much.

Dear Grandmother, I want to tell you that I miss you very much and that very soon we will be together. This pandemic came to change our lives, it distanced us a lot and I have learned that, despite the distance, I love you much more and I miss the moments we spent together, but very soon we will be able to resume our lives and I hope you are very well, and I love you and miss you a lot.

Teachers also posed questions for their students to write responses to, such as this one: 'What would the parts of your body say if they spoke?' A fourth-grade child wrote:

If my feet could talk, they would say that they miss soccer, going out to play with their friends. If my eyes could talk, they would say that there are many people dead because of this pandemic. If my ears could talk, they would say that there are many children who no longer want to study because they are too tired from so much writing. And if my stomach could talk, it would say that we have not eaten much in this pandemic. And if my hands could talk, they would say that they miss greeting people through shaking hands.

Another student expressed the severity of the loss of people due to the pandemic, also referring to his grandfather:

If my eyes could speak, what would they say? That they are tired of seeing so many people die and so much violence in my country. That I only want to see children playing happily with their parents. If my arms could speak, they would say that I would like to hug my grandfather again, who left when I needed him the most. If my legs could talk, what would they say? That I want to go running with my friends again, to go to the park and play like before.

Another strategy used was the travelling notebook,[4] which had two purposes: (1) to help children express their feelings and share them with each other; and (2) to develop students' reading and writing skills. The teachers asked them to write a letter to someone they missed in the pandemic. One girl wrote a letter to her mother about missing her, as well as her father and sister, all of whom had died. She wrote:

Dear Mom: I miss you so much. I want to tell you that I don't forget the biggest legacy that you and my father left, which is family unity. We always remember you at family reunions and are united through the love of my sister, Lucy, that joined you two in heaven four years ago. This pandemic experience makes me feel that all three of you are with me. I will never forget you. I want you to enjoy God's presence. Rebeca

Additionally, teachers promoted free writing for children to express their feelings and thoughts. Students highly appreciated using the travelling notebook, which they expressed in focus groups: 'When they [the teachers] brought the travelling notebooks, we became very happy, because there was not a single day when we had books from the library (during the pandemic).'

Teachers focused on basic maths facts such as having students solve addition and subtraction problems and explain geometric shapes by using objects they found at home while a family member filmed a video of it. For example, a video showed a third-grade girl explaining geometric shapes made of cardboard. In other cases, students counted chickens or added household items such as trousers and blouses as if they were buying or selling in a store. A sixth-grade boy measured a rectangular box and then calculated its area through multiplication. Even though in some cases the activities were not appropriate to the age level (that is, too easy), the aim was for students to find relevance for maths within common household items and activities and to involve the family in learning.

Among other activities, teachers sent poems and stories written by them. A teacher wrote a story, 'The Flores' Story', and shared it with his students to give them a model and to provide them with reading material and emotional support. The story narrated how the Flores family was facing the pandemic. It described how they milked a cow and sold the milk, and when a family member got sick and how they sold two pigs to pay for the medical expenses. Another teacher sent his students an audio recording of a poem he wrote reminiscing about what Morazán was like a few decades before:

Remembering
How I would like to go back to the times of yesterday, to see a child fly his kite, throw his marbles, and spin his spinning top.

Yesterday's games are forgotten. Where are the children? I don't see them. Will they sleep dreaming of a better tomorrow?

Young people appear with strange marks (tattoos) and with strange advice; they do not want to know anything. Eagerly they want to consume drugs and thus destroy their lives.

Everything has changed. Even the winds are less strong than yesterday. The sky is sad, and the moon is sad and the stars have even lost their brilliance. The fields are no longer green; everyone asks to see the children play, like in the times of yesterday.

Teachers relied on families to help children continue learning by making and sending audio recordings or videos and helping children complete work. As one mother explained: 'I set up a class: what the children used to do at school, they would do here [at home]. We followed a schedule and they always worked in the morning because in the afternoon they got bored or were tired.'

Teacher collaboration and dialogue

Teachers were forced to adapt to what the new context demanded, not only in terms of resources or platforms but also with new ways to organize, share, and dialogue. In a context marked by physical distancing and a strict quarantine, adaptation was key in terms of continuing their work and for the relationships among themselves and with students and families. One of the main responses of teachers was to use technological platforms to meet and talk about how they would continue teaching during the time of suspended classes. As a teacher, Maribel, explained: 'We met virtually to see how we could work better according to our educational and community context. We saw the technological options available to parents and children. They did not have computers, internet, or electricity. As a teaching team, we adapted ourselves to the conditions of each family.'

Support among teachers also arose through helping each other learn the necessary technology, as in the case of Chamba and Mr Escoto. Chamba was younger and had updated technology skills. Mr Escoto had 25 years of teaching experience but few technology skills. They connected through virtual calls in which Chamba explained how to download and use different apps to communicate on a smartphone, how to use a printer, and how to navigate search tools on the internet. As Mr Escoto explained: 'The old teachers can still learn from the young ones. I have relied on Chamba. He supported me with my technological problems; we had a habit of calling each other and he would explain it to me.'

The experiences of these teachers demonstrate the precariousness of their work, yet also show the evolution in their relationships and the need for mutual support. Teachers recognized the virtual meeting spaces as a place for professional sharing of teaching practices and a safe space built on trust and support at a more personal level.

The mandatory confinement measures imposed in El Salvador due to the pandemic deepened the isolation and feeling of loneliness in teachers, which is not a new issue, but rather, as Goodlad (1983, cited in Gaikwad and Brantley, 1992) states, it is a chronic condition that affects teachers' practice and emotional health. The virtual meeting spaces organized by teachers in Morazán were initially led weekly by ConTextos as a response to the need for a sense of community between teachers, yet teachers began assuming more participation and leadership in these learning spaces.

Initially, these spaces were unfamiliar and regarded suspiciously by some teachers. Teachers associated them with feelings of being judged by their peers or by those providing the training and with being heavily theoretical. As Mr Escoto and another teacher, Lucía, commented, the teachers were accustomed to the MINEDUCYT reprimanding them for doing or saying something wrong: 'At the beginning, I felt a lot of mistrust of those spaces – I was afraid to share my experience: I did not know how to do things. I was afraid that anything I said there could leave that space and reach the wrong ears.'

This perception gradually transformed, and teachers began to value these spaces as a safe place to bring teachers together and feel close in difficult moments, as well as to build confidence in themselves and with their peers, stripping them of any desire to put on a performance (Ball, 2003, cited in Luengo and Saura, 2013). As Chamba stated: 'No one felt that they had to put on makeup or that [nice] shirt. Everyone was in their hammock, their dining room, their garden ... we could be who we were on that day.'

Within these spaces, a methodology was used that facilitated trust among teachers. It was centred on practical activities that teachers could try with their students to develop reading comprehension and mathematical reasoning. In subsequent sessions, they would share the results of carrying out these activities. This allowed teachers to share practices that were having positive results with their students and to engage in dialogue about practical problems. Another element they valued was the recognition of each other's socioemotional needs. As Maribel put it: 'I did not have that space (in other training during the pandemic) to express the way I felt. It was the (peer) circles that helped me to cope with the whole situation, the confinement.'

These teachers in the most remote and underserved communities faced high degrees of uncertainty with the sudden onslaught of the global COVID-19 pandemic, especially in terms of continuing to serve their students in the face of school closure and no government support. Yet their specific local dynamic and commitment to their students led to self-initiated peer learning and innovative teaching practices based on the SEL approach and meaningful, context-specific learning that teachers, parents, and students appreciated during social isolation and a lack of resources.

Discussion and implications

There are three main implications from this experience in Morazán: (1) the importance of literacy development that prioritizes meaning, expression through text, social interaction, and SEL over increasing reading speed; (2) the significance of teacher collaboration for mutual professional learning and support over centralized teacher training; and (3) the possibility of leveraging local knowledge and action with its unique history and cultural factors.

The way in which teachers incorporated SEL into learning experiences is not the way in which it has been conceptualized in frameworks from high-income countries, which tends to be competency-based or centred on the development of skills. As critics have pointed out, this competency-based approach of SEL stems from a Eurocentric cultural view of emotions as internal and individual states rather than a collective or shared experience. It tends to overemphasize the self (for example, awareness and control of one's emotions) rather than the relational dimension of emotions (Hoffman, 2009). While both approaches to SEL may be child-centred, emphasizing the relational dimension is recognizing children as social beings that learn through social interaction. In the words of Noddings (2006, p 240): 'It is not simply a matter of teaching students topics and skills associated with social-emotional learning. It is essentially a matter of showing, by our own acts and attitudes, that we care about what students are going through and that we are partners in the search for meaning.'

The sociocultural approach to literacy development employed by the teachers was also grounded in the students' lived experience. Rather than developing literacy skills through reading and writing texts unrelated to their reality, texts were grounded in the reality of the children, families, and teachers. As Sánchez (2013, p 10) explains: 'Learning to read is considered a tool with great potential, which prepares the learner to actively participate in society, understand and explain the events that occur in the environment and achieve a better coexistence in the community.'

Teachers could have employed a results-based approach to teaching and learning using only materials provided by MINEDUCYT, yet they provided students with meaningful learning experiences grounded in their social reality and their need for socioemotional expression. This local response contrasts with how education proceeded nationwide with government support and in line with the global trend for virtual learning during the pandemic: uncontextualized learner guides printed for distribution to students and centralized training for teachers to equip them for distance instruction. It also contrasts with the centralized way in which teacher training and support is provided by the government.

Teachers and students developed agency over their situation by putting it into words and sharing it within their education community, which also helped them to stay united at a time of isolation. ConTextos used a combination of methodologies to train and support teachers such as prioritization of dialogue, recognition of their ability to make decisions about teaching, and valuing experimentation and learning with new teaching practices. These teachers were driven to find solutions to ensure their students' wellbeing and continued learning. Not only did they create learner guides and materials for their students, but they also remained close and connected to them, and took on new roles to adapt to their needs. This caring and commitment may have stemmed in part from the history of northern Morazán during the war, yet it is also the vocation felt by many teachers around the world and should be commended. In the words of Mr Escoto: 'It makes me reaffirm my vocation as a teacher and commitment to the children and the educational community, that there is always something more to transform in the school to have better citizens.'

The teacher collaboration and dialogue that emerged in this experience raises questions about how to promote such an experience continually and in regular circumstances. The interactions between teachers in these spaces represent a disruption to what was done nationally at that time, which was training focused on technological empowerment of the teaching community yet neglecting their socioemotional health. In contrast, the teachers from Morazán kept questioning, searching, and learning new ways to support each other and their students. As Freire states (2004, p 39): 'As a teacher I must know that without curiosity, I neither learn nor teach. It is essential that students and teachers are epistemologically curious. Know that your posture is dialogical, open, curious, inquisitive, and not passive, while speaking or listening.'

Freire (2004) also points out the importance of considering the human dimension in teaching, which these teachers did with their students and amongst themselves. He emphasizes that there is a false separation between 'serious' teaching and the expression and recognition of emotions and feelings. It is necessary to cross these two elements for a more meaningful teaching with deep human connections: 'affectivity is not necessarily an enemy of knowledge or of the process of knowing' (Freire, 2004, p 125).

In contrast to education programmes supported by many large donors, PCF, through ConTextos, embraces alternative approaches to literacy and learning that emphasize meaning making and SEL, and are rooted in the local reality and history of teachers and students. When the pandemic hit, this support contrasted greatly with the national and international response and was leveraged through local knowledge and mobilization.

Conclusion

The tendency in Central America has been to organize teacher training in a centralized way so that teachers are passive actors in the educational system who follow the direction of educational authorities in terms of how and what they plan, what resources they use, and what student outcomes they should aim for (Zaccagnini, 2004). This chapter demonstrates how a group of teachers was able to respond successfully to adverse and unexpected situations through their own commitment, unity, organization, and creativity. It also demonstrates the value of donors tapping into local knowledge, history, and organized efforts to support education through alternative educational approaches.

It is important to consider what the necessary conditions are to build spaces between teachers to develop caring relationships, a sense of community, continual questioning, learning, and collaboration that allow teachers to effectively develop and assert themselves as professionals capable of building their own knowledge and reflecting on their own practice (Imbernon, 1998, 2005; Medina Moya, 2006). Ostovar-Nameghi and Sheikhahmadi (2016) propose ways to ensure such conditions: (1) school administrators can structure schedules and resources in a way that promotes dialogue between teachers; (2) ongoing meetings between teachers that focus less on administrative issues and more on sharing problems and solutions from practice; and (3) professional development through learning communities, study groups, and peer observation. This experience offers lessons that can be applied during a pandemic, but, above all, raises many questions about how to build the conditions proposed by these authors within a centralized educational context such as that of El Salvador, where teacher support tends to be limited to an administrative – and, in some cases, supervisory – function (Rosales and Trejo, 2007).

One way in which donors and local organizations can foster such conditions is through building on the strengths and social capital of the community. While large-scale bilateral donor efforts are valuable for helping improve learning conditions, donors and local organizations such as Pestalozzi and ConTextos are uniquely positioned to work both inside and outside the system through smaller-scale, localized efforts. The experience of the teachers of northern Morazán demonstrates that it is possible to foster meaningful learning experiences even within a resource-constrained context during an extreme situation, such as the one created by the COVID-19 pandemic. It offers guidelines for fostering and supporting such learning experiences for students across Central America and beyond, which is especially important after a pandemic that has left so many children and youth with greater socioemotional and academic needs. The pandemic spurred responses in education worldwide, many of which are learning opportunities. This experience shows the value of leveraging local dynamics to support quality learning, during a pandemic or in normal times, which remains a challenge for the donor community.

Notes

[1] This is using the quality-adjusted schooling (LAYS) metric, which combines quantity and quality instead of measuring only quantity.

[2] Child-centred pedagogy is defined in this chapter as the teacher understanding and adapting to the particular needs and interests of each student, and making learning a meaningful and social experience for each child (McCombs and Whistler, 1997).

[3] Since 2011, ConTextos has supported a network of 1,200 teachers from more than 100 schools in different parts of the country, but it was not until 2018 that it began to support the teachers in Northern Morazán.

[4] A physical notebook that was exchanged between students.

References

Ball, S.J. (2003). The teacher's soul and the terrors of performativity. *Journal of Education Policy*, 18(2), 215–228.

Candray, J. (2021). Sobre el decreto transitorio de plazas docentes: dudas interpretaciones y muchas preguntas. *Revista* Disruptiva, 28 June. https://www.disruptiva.media/sobre-el-decreto-transitorio-de-plazas-docentes-dudas-interpretaciones-y-muchas-preguntas/

Cassany, D. (2005). Investigaciones y propuestas sobre literacidad actual: multiliteracidad, internet y criticidad. *Cátedra UNESCO para la Lectura y la Escritura*, 1–10.

Dewees, A., Evans, E., and King, C. (1994). La educación básica y parvularia. *ECA: Estudios Centroamericanos*, 49(547–548), 411–435.

Dowd, A. J., and Bartlett, L. (2019). The need for speed: interrogating the dominance of oral reading fluency in international reading efforts. *Comparative Education Review*, 63(2), 189–212.

DIGESTYC (2020). *Encuesta de Hogares de Propósitos Múltiples 2019*. Ministerio de Economía.

Durlak, J. A., Weissberg, R. P., Dymnicki, A. B., Taylor, R. D., and Schellinger, K. B. (2011). The impact of enhancing students' social and emotional learning: a meta-analysis of school-based universal interventions. *Child Development*, 82(1), 405–432.

Freire, P. (2004). *Pedagogy of Freedom: Ethics, Democracy, and Civic Courage*. Rowman & Littlefield.

Freire, P. (2014). *Pedagogía de la Autonomía: Saberes Necesarios para la Práctica Educative*. México: Siglo XXI Editores.

Gaikwad, S., and Brantley, P. (1992). Teacher isolation: loneliness in the classroom. *Journal of Adventist Education*, 54, 14–17.

Hoffman, D. M. (2009). Reflecting on social emotional learning: a critical perspective on trends in the United States. *Review of Educational Research*, 79(2), 533–556.

Imbernon M. F. (1998). *La formación y el desarrollo profesional del profesorado. Hacia una nueva cultura profesional.* Editorial Graó.

Imbernon M. F. (2005). La profesión docente ante los desafíos del presente y del futuro. In C. Marcelo (ed.), *La Función Docente* (pp 27–45). Síntesis.

Luengo, J., and Saura, G. (2013). La performatividad en la educación: La construcción del nuevo docente y el nuevo gestor performativo. *REICE. Revista Iberoamericana Sobre Calidad, Eficacia y Cambio en Educación*, 11(3), 139–153.

Mar, R., Oatley, K., Hirsh, J., dela Paz, J., and Peterson, J. (2006). Bookworms versus nerds: exposure to fiction versus non-fiction, divergent associations with social ability, and the simulation of fictional social worlds. *Journal of Research in Personality*, 40, 694–712.

McCombs, B. L., and Whisler, J. (1997). *The Learner-centered Classroom and School: Strategies for Increasing Student Motivation and Achievement.* San Francisco, CA: Jossey-Bass.

Medina Moya, J. L. (2006). *La profesión docente y la construcción del conocimiento profesional.* Grupo Editorial Lumen.

Noddings, N. (2006). Educating whole people: a response to Jonathan Cohen. *Harvard Educational Review*, 76(2), 238–242.

Ostovar-Nameghi, S. and Sheikhahmadi, M. (2016). From teacher isolation to teacher collaboration: theoretical perspectives and empirical findings. *English Language Teaching*, 9(5), 197–205.

Parra Villalobos, S. (2018). *Modelo de formación para el desarrollo profesional docente y directivo.* Ministerio de Educación del Gobierno de Chile.

Red Interagencial para la Educación en Situaciones de Emergencia (INEE) (2020). *Nota técnica de la INEE sobre educación durante la pandemia del COVID-19: Versión 1, Abril de 2020.* INEE.

Rosales, L. and Trejo, M. (2007). Estrategias de desarrollo profesional docente en la reforma educativa. Tesis de maestría, Universidad Centroamericana 'José Simeón Cañas', no publicada [Master's thesis, Central American University 'José Simeón Cañas', not published].

Sánchez Chévez, L. E. (2013). La comprensión lectora: hacia una aproximación sociocultural. *Editorial Universidad Don Bosco*, 7(12), 7–16.

Technical Secretariat of the Presidency (STPP) and MINEDUC-DIGESTYC (2015). *Multidimensional Measurement of Poverty.* Technical and Planning Secretariat of the Presidency and Ministry of Economy, through the General Directorate of Statistics and Censuses.

Terigi, F. (2010). *Desarrollo profesional continuo y carrera docente en América Latina.* PREAL.

Trianes, M., and García, A. (2002). Educación socio-afectiva y prevención de conflictos interpersonales en los centros escolares. *Revista Interuniversitaria de Formación del Profesorado*, 44, 175–189.

Organización de las Naciones Unidas para la Educación, la Ciencia y la Cultura. (2020, 24 de marzo). 1.370 millones de estudiantes ya están en casa con el cierre de las escuelas de COVID-19, los ministros amplían los enfoques multimedia para asegurar la continuidad del aprendizaje. https://es.unesco.org/news/1370-millones-estudiantes-ya-estan-casa-cierre-escuelas-covid-19-ministros-amplian-enfoques

Vaillant, D. (2005). *Formación de docentes en América Latina: Re-inventando el modelo tradicional.* Ediciones Octaedro.

World Bank (2021). *Acting Now to Protect the Human Capital of Our Children: The Costs of and Response to COVID-19 Pandemic's Impact on the Education Sector in Latin America and the Caribbean.* World Bank.

Zaccagini, M. (2004). Reformas educativas: espejismos de innovación. *Revista Iberoamericana de Educación.* www.campus-oei.org/revista/deloslectores/338Zaccagnini

6

Learning *Convivencia* at School: Lessons on Peaceful Coexistence Policy Enactment from El Salvador

Pauline Martin

Introduction

In the last few decades, education policy in Latin America has moved from focusing primarily on increasing school enrolment and improving education quality to education as a force for transforming broader culture. Many policies and programmes related to school *convivencia*, defined as peaceful coexistence or positive school environment,[1] have been promoted in the last two decades (Morales and López, 2019). An important characteristic of education reforms in Latin America is that they are generally encouraged by regional and global institutions, with homogeneous agendas offered to multiple countries, in the hopes of adapting them to local and national contexts (Gillies, 2010). An ongoing field of research is how national policies – that is, macro-policies – are enacted and the kinds of results that are achieved in generating change at the school or micro-policy level (Ball, 1987; Blase, 2002).

The emphasis on the school as a place to learn *convivencia* can be traced back to the United Nations Educational, Scientific and Cultural Organization (UNESCO) report by Jacques Delors on the four pillars of education for the 21st century, which states that learning to live together is just as important as learning to learn (Delors, 1996). Learning to live together, or getting along, is considered an aim of education to combat violence, promote participation, cooperation, acceptance of diversity, etc. More recently, UNESCO has proposed fostering child-friendly schools and an improved learning environment, both in terms of physical school infrastructure and social interactions, while also highlighting that school-related, gender-based violence seriously undermines attempts to achieve gender equality in education (UNESCO, 2015). By late 2015, the United Nation's Sustainable Development Goals underscored the need for learners to obtain knowledge and skills considered nondisciplinary: human rights, gender equality, peace culture, nonviolence, global citizenship, cultural appreciation, and sustainable development (United Nations, 2015, Goal 4.7).

Another force behind the promotion of school *convivencia* policies is the situation of violence and inequality in the Latin American region. More than a third of intentional homicides occur in the Americas (UNOCD, 2013). The inequality levels in the region are only surpassed by Sub-Saharan Africa and are attributed to historical causes related to the distribution of wealth, income, and opportunities (de Farranti et al, 2004). In Latin America, schooling is viewed as an important resource for improving social cohesion (Gvirtz and Beech, 2014) and for building democracy through civics' education, although the responsibility (and ability) of the school to prevent violence in other spheres of society is questionable (Reimers and Villegas-Reimers, 2006). Nonetheless, as Morales and López (2019) state, there is no common concept of what school *convivencia* is, nor are there uniform approaches to how to translate this concept into policies and programmes.

This chapter will examine three school-based *convivencia* policy[2] efforts in El Salvador. These efforts are related to student participation in school governance, bullying, and sexual violence. The chapter examines their enactment and explains the challenges they have faced in practice. Each case of *convivencia* in schools will be examined using Bentancur's (2015) framework – focused on ideas, actors, and institutions – for explaining intentions and decisions around education policies. In brief, to understand the emergence and implementation of specific policies, the ideas that underlie the definition of the problem and the logic of the solution are key, while actors (beneficiaries, stakeholders, members of the education community, politicians, etc.) concretely make decisions and enact policies based not only on their roles, but also on their interests, preferences, and convictions. Finally, institutions and the way in which they are organized, their governance capacity and regulations are key in both defining policies and guaranteeing their subsequent enactment. The present chapter contributes to the aims of this volume in that it focuses, first, on the multilevel structures and relationships that shape educational reforms and, second, on the interests and discourse of key actors, while also being attentive, third, to the cultural dimension of seeking changes in social relations.

In terms of structure, this chapter will first present the context of *convivencia* education policies in El Salvador, both in terms of the need for this type of policy and the historical and structural constraints that enter into play. Then, the methods section explains the source of the data and the characteristics of each study included in the analysis. The results are presented using Bentancur's (2015) framework as a guide, followed by discussion and final considerations from the intersection of the three cases and dimensions of the analysis. Findings point out the complexity of addressing education policies that seek to impact interpersonal relationships; they also emphasize the need to see local actors, such as teachers, families, and communities, as holders of the real power of policy enactment.

The context for *convivencia* policies in El Salvador

The long-term history of colonization, social inequality, and political exclusion in El Salvador provides the backdrop for more recent efforts to contribute to peace and democracy building through education. This section will highlight some of the most relevant advances in education linked to the attempts to build a more just society in this small, densely populated country in Central America.

From a tumultuous history of education for economic, social, and political domination by an elite, oligarchy-based government (Gómez, 2012) to a force for modernization in a greatly inequitable society (Lindo-Fuentes and Ching, 2012), the 1983 Constitution establishes education as a responsibility of the state, a human right for all and a requirement for becoming 'useful citizens' (Article 56 of the Asamblea Legislativa de El Salvador, 1983). The bitter civil war from 1980 to 1992 that ended with the negotiated Peace Accords between the government and the guerrilla forces opened the way for multiple efforts for reconstruction and democracy-building, including an education reform. In 1995, the Ten Year Plan initiated major structural changes in education management and the curriculum, and for teachers, but also carried a clear mandate for consolidating peace and democracy while guaranteeing human rights (Ministerio de Educación, 1995).

In current times, the education system is organized centrally, with the Ministerio de Educación (Ministry of Education, or MOE) housing multiple administrative and technical support offices on specific programmes or areas, generally on the curriculum and special topics, such as *convivencia* and citizenship. This macro-policy level passes guidelines and resources to 5,143 public schools via 14 departmental offices that act as a subnational governance bridge. Even though the schools are administered by a school management committee (Consejo Directivo Escolar or CDE) that channels their requests back to the MOE through the departmental offices, they have little formal decision-making power or local resources to address their needs (Edwards et al, 2017). Moreover, education priorities tend to change every five years, along with the change in the executive branch, whether the same political party is in power or not. Adding to this instability is the fact that schools, on a micro-policy level, have very little autonomy to address their specific, contextual problems. Finally, the education system is characterized by a technical dependence on international organizations, which tends to limit contextualized, innovative, and problem-solving approaches.

Yet current economic challenges, migration, and insecurity demand that schools respond by offering quality services and fostering reciprocal relationships with families and communities. However, it is difficult to find specific strategies for promoting peaceful schools and *convivencia* in the official education plans prior to 2016. From 2004 to 2009, the strategy of the MOE – known at the time as the 2021 Education Plan – focused on human capital development and introduced strategies for effective school management and participation, but did not mention school violence as a challenge to address (Ministerio de Educación, 2005). The Social Education Plan, initiated by the government that came to power in 2009 alluded to a new integration of schools, families, and communities, but did not outline specific actions for getting along or confronting violence in education communities (Ministerio de Educación, 2009). In 2016 gender relationships were specifically addressed in the Gender Equity and Equality Policy (MINED, 2016b), but it was not until 2018 that the National Policy for Convivencia and Peace Culture was drawn up for more general getting along in the school setting (Ministerio de Educación, 2018b). Through a collaborative process and with the support of several international nongovernmental organizations (NGOs), the stated objective of this policy is to construct an inclusive school environment characterized by education quality, violence prevention, equity, participation, and harmonious relationships – all to improve both the internal environment and the external security of the school. As will be further discussed, the three cases analysed here span the period from 2008 to 2020, in this context of a weak policy framework.

Education in El Salvador continues to be considered an important means for economic opportunities and social cohesion, a space that fosters child and youth development, and a venue for transmitting values and social practices. Despite numerous challenges and ambiguous results, 97 per cent of respondents of a recent survey affirmed that education is a factor for success in life, while 70 per cent affirmed that public schools contribute to violence prevention in their community (IUDOP, 2019). These statistics confirm the collective belief that schools should and will contribute to a more peaceful and equitable society. These statistics also speak to the relevance of *convivencia* policies, despite unsuccessful enactment in recent years, as this chapter will show. The sources of the data and the methods used to demonstrate why the implementation of *convivencia* policy is limited are described further in what follows, after the presentation of the analytic framework in the next section.

Analytical framework

As noted previously, the comparative analysis for this chapter is based on Bentancur's (2015) framework, which focuses on the factors that affect the making and implementation of education policy in terms of ideas, actors, and institutions, as will be briefly described in what follows.

The role of ideas is most evident in the definition of the problem and the solution, that is, the way in which a problem is defined, and the logic of change proposed by the education policy. Specifically, with *convivencia* policies, the foundation of the problem and the solution is found in the underlying ideas, cultural norms, and beliefs about human interaction and the role of schools in modelling relationships for participation in broader society. The study of ideas can also extend to examining how the original policy is understood by actors at each level.

Education policy does not happen without the participation of different actors with varied roles (stakeholders, public officials, beneficiaries, principals, teachers, politicians, etc.) that play a part in planning and implementing a solution to a problem. Each actor brings a personal history, interests, beliefs, and preferences to the task. In addition to these factors, analysis must also take into account the more evident roles and responsibilities, or specific functions assigned to those individuals who make decisions and implement policy, but also how and why they enact policy. The subjectivity of each actor enters into play, especially with regard to a reform topic such as *convivencia*, which directly connects with beliefs about how to treat each other and how to achieve social change.

Finally, both ideas and actors operate within the reach and limits of institutions (that is, official organizations with a stated purpose), a regulatory framework, and a governance structure that proposes, implements, and evaluates policy. Institutions are situated in and act within a historical and cultural context, but also represent power structures that define decision making and enactment. In the three cases in the present chapter, the analysed institutions are the schools, the MOE and NGOs, all of which offer much-needed structure and operability to education, but which also constrain flexibility, local needs, and, often, results.

Methods

The data for this chapter are taken from three master's-level research projects produced in the context of the Education Policy and Evaluation Program at the Universidad Centroamericana José Simeón Cañas in El Salvador. Carried out in the period 2019–2020, they examine *convivencia* initiatives in local case studies of schools on three topics: participation through student governments; prevention of peer bullying; and the normalization of sexual violence. In all three cases, the findings show that policy enactment was largely unsuccessful. A summary of each research project is presented in Table 6.1.

The first study (Chicas, 2020) examines student participation through student government structures, characterizing the types of participation found in two public schools in the central part of El Salvador. The author links student participation to the aim of developing more solid democratic processes at the school level as an exercise of human rights that should translate into better citizenship skills on a macro-level. Student governments are grounded in support from the Inter-American Institute for Human Rights (IIDH), technical support from a global NGO (Plan International), and the framework provided by the 2021 National Education Plan (Ministerio de Educación, 2005).

The second study seeks to understand teachers' roles and social representations in preventing bullying among students (Galdámez and Lemus, 2020). Social representations are understood from the perspective of Jodelet (1986) as socially constructed, practical ways of thinking, communicating, understanding, and mastering the social, material, and ideational environment. The sample is made up of four schools in the western part of the country. The study compares schools' dynamics with the expectations embedded in the National Policy for School *Convivencia* and Peace Culture (Ministerio de Educación, 2018b). Since the MOE has no specific policy on defining, treating, and preventing school bullying, it coordinates interinstitutionally with the National Council for Boys, Girls and Adolescents (CONNA), the government child protection agency.

The third study explores the construction of hegemonic masculinity and its relationship with the legitimization of sexual violence in male teachers in two networks of public schools, in contrast with the aims of the MOE's Gender Equity and Equality Policy (2016), using both interviews and workshops with male teachers for data collection. The policy seeks the transformation of gender relationships in schools (through awareness-raising campaigns, training, policy and protocol design, curricular resources, etc.) that can transfer to broader society; the underlying idea is that teachers are the main social actors in promoting or hindering gender equality and environments free of sexual violence.

In addition to these three studies, the author of the present chapter systematically reviewed and analysed other documental sources to complete the analysis of why micro-policy enactment falls short of the macro-policy aims of promoting *convivencia* in schools. Both individual and cross-case analysis reveal dynamics among ideas, actors, and institutions in education policy that limit the capacity for a more peaceful school and society. Education policy is never a rational, objective process either in design or

Table 6.1: Methodological summary of each research project

Author and title	Type of study	Techniques	Sample	Main categories of analysis
Chicas (2020). *Approximation of the Participation of Student Governments in Rural Public Schools: Case Studies from Jicalapa, La Libertad, El Salvador (2008–2019)*	Explicative case studies	In-depth interviews Focus groups Content analysis of documents	12 teachers, former students, students, principals, technical advisors 2 focus groups 2 documents	Student participation Macro-policy Micro-policy
Galdámez and Lemus (2020). *Social Representations of Salvadoran Teachers on Bullying in Middle School Students in Salvadoran Schools*	Qualitative	In-depth interviews Participatory observation Document review	8 teachers 2 schools School internal documents	Understanding of bullying, response approach, training, regulations
Tejeda and Hernández (2020). *Hegemonic Masculinity and Legitimization of Sexual Violence by Male Teachers in the Salvadoran Public Schools*	Qualitative	In-depth interviews Workshops	2 school networks 11 key informants 37 male participants	Cultural imaginary, androcentrism, adult centrism, hegemonic masculinity, sexual violence, legitimation

Sources: Based on Chicas (2020), Galdámez and Lemus (2020), and Tejeda and Hernández (2020)

in enactment – and it is strongly influenced by historical, political, and economic contexts, as well as local dynamics and actors.

Case studies on school *convivencia* policies

For the three cases of interest, the findings are clear that *convivencia* efforts are very limited in their success; therefore, the analysis seeks to understand why this is so and how local interactions constrain the promotion of *convivencia* in public schools. In this section, each study is presented in relation to the ideas that orient the policy response, the actors who promote it, and the institutional support that sustains it.

Democracy through student governments

Student governments are considered a model for democratic society, as a means for practising dialogue, horizontal relationships, and representative participation for a more just and equitable society. School is an ideal setting to promote democratic forms of government; in schools, complex relationships and diverse situations and actors help strengthen citizenship skills (Chicas, 2020). Student governments are an educational initiative introduced several decades ago in El Salvador, even though there is no specific written policy to back them up. Introduced by the Ten Year Plan as a part of postwar education reform to foster civic values (Ministerio de Educación, 1995), it was not until the 2021 National Education Plan of 2005 that increasing student participation was clearly stated as a strategic goal (Ministerio de Educación, 2005).

The reasons for student participation can be framed in numerous ways. It can be framed as a human right, or it can be justified on grounds that are instrumental (to further the aims of schools) or political (to advocate for interests of specific groups). However, both in the macro-policy and supporting documents, the reason behind the promotion of student participation is not clear: only a single reference links student participation with 'enriching the internal democracy of the school (Ministerio de Educación/Plan El Salvador, n.d., p 6), while international reports point out gaps in the promotion of student governments in education planning (IIDH, 2011).

Even though the intention of student participation in El Salvador dates from the mid-1990s, in 2018 only 39.48 per cent of schools reported implementing strategies for student participation and 36.62 per cent had student governments that participated in decision making. Meanwhile, 66.51 per cent of public schools affirmed having formed student committees as a democratic exercise, but only 52.64 per cent indicated that they functioned even periodically (Ministerio de Educación, 2018a). At present, there are specific guidelines for putting student governments into practice; however, the aforementioned statistics show that they are not consistently enacted in the Salvadoran public schools.

The study by Chicas (2020) examines student governments in two rural public schools for the period 2008–2019, with a special focus on the participation of girls through the lens of human rights and state legitimization of student participation. When it comes to ideas, Chicas (2020) finds no consistent understanding of the concept of student participation, which creates confusion and a lack of consensus about how it should play out at the school level. For some, student governments are understood as political organizations, linked to a specific party rather than a depoliticized right to participate and be represented in school decision making. Without a clear conceptual basis, each school will do as it considers best and pleases, such as engaging in the practice of hand-picking the best-behaved, best-performing students as leaders. School staff also assign varied functions and activities to student leaders, such as helping with tasks like parents' assemblies, cleaning and decorating the school, and organizing celebrations, but student governments do not take part in decision-making spaces that determine schools' core activities. Unfortunately, one finding is that the students are the least informed about the concept, purposes, and scope of authority of the student governments in local school culture.

The impetus for implementation was provided by an international actor, the NGO Plan International. This organization provided technical assistance to produce student participation manuals from 2005 to 2009, during the period the 2021 National Education Plan was in force (Ministerio de Educación/Plan El Salvador, n.d), in addition to producing documents that present a broad conceptual framework as well as diverse strategies for forming student governments. The NGO also provided technical support for material development, teacher training, and some initial follow-up. However, the key school-level actor is the principal, who leads the process and provides guidelines on how to organize the student governments. Rather than empowering students in democratic skills, the findings point out that the process is adult-centred – that is, activities are planned by adults, including events relating to fundraising for school infrastructure needs.

Institutionally, student participation efforts need to be housed within existing structures to provide guidance and follow-up. Under the Social Education Plan launched in 2009 (Ministerio de Educación, 2009), the efforts for strengthening democracy and citizens' skills were coordinated centrally and overseen by subnational technical staff – located in the 14 administrative regions of the country – who were assigned to promote art, culture, recreation, sports, and citizenship – an interesting amalgam of topics oriented for violence prevention and socioemotional skills development. Monitoring and evaluation in El Salvador are generally assigned to subnational technical staff who oversee multiple processes. Certain instruments for guiding the enactment of student governments exist, but they are not consistently used by the schools. No signs of documenting actions and knowledge sharing are found in the case schools; the researcher found a lack of a paper trail to document the functioning of the student governments. With few monitoring, follow-up, and evaluation efforts, which demonstrate weak institutional commitment, there is little evidence that student governments either impact power relationships in school or model democratic practices.

The final reflection of Chicas (2020) is that even though the school is a key space to learn about democracy – given the convergence of actors and situations – achieving democratic practice requires a transformation of relationships in schools and the broader education system. With a lack of consensus of ideas, student governments are not enacted as an option for transforming power relationships or guaranteeing respect for human rights in schools. Adults, rather than students, are the key actors; findings reveal adult-centred decision-making, a prevalence of traditional power relationships (for example, students relegated to adults), stereotyped gender roles (for example, boys take leadership, girls take support roles), as well as a fear of politicized student governments. Moreover, institutionally, schools have scant autonomy to make their own decisions in a broader context of rigid hierarchies in education, with little voice in the broader system even for teachers and principals, which means that the MOE itself is not modelling the kind of democratic practices student governments are meant to promote.

Peer bullying

Schools are places where peers meet and interact, which helps or hinders a positive environment for learning. Bullying, in a broad sense, is understood as a type of relationship of violence, based on unequal power dynamics and ongoing aggressions that produce psychological and moral effects, and which causes a deterioration in the school social environment that is necessary for learning (CONNA, 2018). On a collective level, bullying is counterproductive to one of the social functions of the school, which is to educate in democratic values and respect for human rights. Interestingly enough, El Salvador does not have a specific education policy on bullying, as in other Latin American countries where the most-cited school-related violence problem is bullying (Morales and López, 2019). The National Council for Children and Adolescents of El Salvador provides guidelines for addressing bullying from a child protection approach rather than as an educational concern (CONNA, 2018), while the National Policy for a Harmonious School Environment (*Convivencia*) and Peace Culture does not address bullying or strategies to counteract it.

How broad of a bullying problem exists in El Salvador? In 2018, 28.5 per cent of schools reported that they have identified the types of bullying that are present in their schools, while only 8.09 per cent acknowledged that it was a problem among students, and only 0.48 per cent reported it as taking place among teachers (Ministerio de Educación, 2018a). Nonetheless, with data from 2015, Cuéllar and Góchez (2017) construct a violence map and affirm that psychological violence is one of the foremost types of violence present in Salvadoran schools. This map identifies 43 municipalities where 55 per cent of its schools are characterized by psychological violence among students, as well as 78 municipalities where between 35.8 and 55 per cent of schools report this kind of violence. Thus, in just under half of the 262 municipalities of the country, a third or more of schools are characterized by psychological violence among students, which contrasts sharply with the relatively low number of schools reported earlier that have a bullying problem. Psychological violence is not as visible in mass media as other expressions of violence, such as gangs and sexual abuse, as it is considered less violent or impactful, and even as normal student behaviour. In some cases, peer bullying is instigated by those associated with gangs – even in the case of younger students – who threaten or harass their peers and are backed up by their connections to the exceptional power and authority of gangs.[3]

The second study by Galdámez and Lemus (2020) examines bullying among students and how teachers' social representations of their role influence their response. Social representations provide a possible explanation of the differentiated reporting on levels of bullying in schools. This research analyses four aspects of the teachers' social representations – understanding, approach, training, and guidelines – showing how these influence prevention and intervention efforts. Galdámez and Lemus (2020) argue that the bullying found in schools reflects the different expressions of harassment found in broader society, and this contributes to accepting bullying in schools as a natural activity.

Galdámez and Lemus' findings point out that there is no uniform idea or conceptual comprehension of bullying and school harassment because each teacher uses personal parameters based on training, values, beliefs, mental structures, and even common sense. Teacher behaviour reflects a cultural belief in the survival of the fittest and the law of the strongest in hostile contexts, both of which are reinforced by prior experiences of being bullied or observing bullying. The tendency is to blame bullying on the family, mass media influence and the detrimental effects of technology (for example, as when individuals imitate inappropriate behaviour spread and encouraged through social media), or else to consider it normal behaviour. Bullying is a manifestation of conflicting values found in schools, families, and media, making a teacher's job overly complex (Tedesco and Tenti Fanfani, 2002). In addition to confusion about the concept of harassment and violence, the authors' findings revealed a lack of awareness about cyberbullying, as well as a conservative morality that discriminates when students are bullied for reasons of sexual diversity.

Key actors are teachers, whose social representations limit the prevention of bullying if they are influenced by personal and religious beliefs for intuitive and subjective responses, rather than what policy and professional training dictates. Even though the National Policy of Peaceful Coexistence and Peace Culture emphasizes positive attitudes, interpersonal relationships and accepting diversity for constructing peaceful *convivencia* (Ministerio de Educación, 2018b, p 20), in practice, it seems that teachers understand *convivencia* as the absence of conflicts. With social networks and the technology of the internet, school bullying transcends the physical space of schools where teachers can supervise and influence. While many interactions and connections occur in the schools, other relationships play out via virtual means and in the family and community space. Teachers, however, are important players in orienting relationships in school that can carry over into other spaces.

Institutionally, when teachers see certain practices as normal, there is little incentive to change their paradigm or basic concepts about human relationships. Consider, for example, that a broader culture of bullying is observed as teachers may also bully each other. Additionally, the vertical power dynamics of the MOE do not model democratic relationships.

In the same way, training for teachers is lacking, both pre-service and in-service, such that teachers do not have methodologies to address school violence (Ministerio de Educación, 2018a). Although only one in three schools report having received training on school violence prevention or peace culture, a greater percentage affirm the existence of tools to promote positive *convivencia*: 66 per cent of schools have *convivencia* plans (activities that foster better relationships) and 93 per cent use student handbooks to define rules and discipline measures, but only 19 per cent have access to psychological support services (Ministerio de Educación, 2018a). MOE and CONNA norms and guidelines for responding to bullying are confusing, unknown, and should be socialized and promoted to local actors as well. However, with little systematic follow-up from the MOE or the CONNA, mechanisms for appropriation, feedback, and evaluation are needed to support the schools.

An important conclusion of Galdámez and Lemus (2020) is that bullying is a problem of the school environment, not a student problem. Schools act on a collective belief system where individual beliefs and experiences converge; institutional responsibility needs to be strengthened. While policies and norms exist, schools should commit resources, define and implement actions to counteract aggressive and antisocial behaviour, and provide a school climate conducive to learning. As an education and social problem with multiple actors and agencies involved – that is, as both a child protection and an education issue – school becomes (or can become) a venue for convening children and significant adults, namely teachers, who can be part of the solution.

Addressing sexual violence

Gender equity has been broadly promoted in Latin America, where the school is considered a setting for learning *convivencia* practices, with the aim of equal treatment and opportunities in the face of deeply rooted cultural practices around men and women. In El Salvador, policies and programmes on gender emerged out of the 1995 International Women's Conference in Beijing, which gave the Salvadoran government a platform for action and led to the founding of the Salvadoran Institute for the Development of Women (ISDEMU), as well as strengthening the relationship between civil society women's groups and the government (Moreno, 1997). Gender equity has been linked to education indirectly through the ISDEMU, which defines key actions in the National Policy for Women focused on the development and rights of women (ISDEMU, 1998; ISDEMU, 2005, 2011). Gender policies are thus the result of negotiation among and influence from multiple organizations, though it should be noted that, at the macro-level, international agencies have historically played a key role in orienting national agendas (Edwards et al, 2015).

As a competency external to the MOE, for many years gender equity in education had little sound institutional support (Edwards et al, 2015). In more recent years, the specific policy framework in education includes a clause added in 2008 to the Teacher Career Law (Asamblea Legislativa de El Salvador, 1996) requiring training on violence prevention and discrimination.[4] Then, a 2011 addition to the General Education Law (Asamblea Legislativa de El Salvador, 2011) prohibited inequality between boys and girls based on prejudice, discriminatory practices, and stereotypes of gender roles, while stating that nonsexist language must be used in schools. Several guiding documents and curricular resources promote both gender equality and the eradication of sexual violence, such as the Action Protocol for Addressing Sexual Violence in Educational Communities in El Salvador[5] (Ministerio de Educación, 2013) and a cross-cutting sexual curriculum in 2014 (Ministerio de Educación, 2014).

The crowning jewel of the gender policy framework is the National Gender Equality and Equity Policy of 2016, which integrates a variety of topics such as equality, equity, prevention and treatment of sexual violence, gender violence, early pregnancy, sexually transmitted diseases, and human trafficking (Ministerio de Educación, 2016b). After a needs assessment and consultative process, the policy and implementation plan were drawn up as a condition for continued financing of the Millennium Fund II in El Salvador.[6] The National Gender Equality and Equity Policy addresses asymmetric gender relationships in education and focuses on 'eradicating the inequalities between men and women that exist in the national educational system' (Ministerio de Educación, 2016b, p 10). Despite a solid legal and policy framework condemning sexual violence, the statistics are not very encouraging. For example, in 2021, 75 per cent of the reported cases of sexual violence were schoolgirls under the age of 18. Gender equality is only ambiguously mentioned in other education policies – beyond those mentioned earlier – which do not specify what must be done and how.

The study by Tejeda and Hernández (2020) analyses the relationship between the construction of hegemonic masculinity and the legitimization of sexual violence by male teachers in the Salvadoran public schools, using interviews and workshops in two integrated school networks. They show that sexual violence has a tight relationship with cultural imaginaries related to gender. Their study affirms that if one differentially and asymmetrically values men/masculinity and women/femininity, this leads to abuse of power and sexual violence. Given that Tejeda and Hernández (2020) reveal heteronormative masculinity as a driver of gender violence by male teachers, their findings are important in terms of showing the difficulty of implementing gender equality in schools and the role of teachers when it comes to promoting gender equity in schools.

Findings highlight the complex, male-centred cultural imaginary that differentiates and asymmetrically values masculine and feminine traits, which then excuses and justifies violence against female students and women. Deep cultural beliefs – often military and religion-based – prevail and link masculine traits with power, force, and domination. As a result, shared ideas around what constitutes (or does not constitute) sexual harassment and abuse generate complicity among men and help to avoid punishment while also transferring guilt to women for their subordination and passivity in the face of harassment and abuse, in addition to directing judgement at the mothers who raised these men. Furthermore, the researchers identify serious conceptual gaps in teachers when it comes to understanding equity and equality.

Thus, as education actors, male teachers and supporting family members are influenced by the construction of masculinity and the strong cultural mandates that dictate how they should behave – all of which legitimizes sexual violence. Findings point out, first, that masculinity is understood in terms of the hunt, use of force, not expressing feelings, and absolute power, and, second, that adults – male or otherwise – are more important than children and youth. Male teachers participate in a cultural imaginary that reproduces the ideas, beliefs, images, practices, and archetypes that are transmitted from generation to generation, incorporated into individual and collective subjectivities. Teachers are important, frontline subjects in working with and transforming cultural imaginaries, but given that certain actors draw up policies while others enact it, it is difficult to secure commitment and behaviour change. Further to this end, and as noted in the case of the Millenium Fund II, international actors pressured and conditioned agendas, as described earlier in the financing of the National Gender Equality and Equity Policy, which led to a lack of ownership and practice at the school level.

On an institutional level, findings reveal that policy enactment is affected by an interest in protecting the school's image. Given that parents can choose any public school for their children, denouncing sexual violence, as called for in the 2013 Action Protocol mentioned earlier, is discouraged. Silencing and not questioning are signs of the installation of a hegemonic masculine culture in the school surroundings and the institution. Gender inequalities are observed to manifest in spatial and in discursive devices such as the use of recreational areas, types of music, activities that exalt beauty over ability, and in the written text, signs, etc. For institutional training efforts, gender is seen as a women's issue, so primarily female teachers are consulted and attend trainings. Once again, the lack of follow-up, technical support, and evaluation make for an incomplete policy cycle. Even though school is seen as part of a multisectorial effort for more equality, given that other government sectors and nongovernmental institutions also work on changing cultural practices and beliefs around gender, schools as a transformative cultural institution seem to be limited in impacting cultural imaginaries and social representations about power, violence, and relationships.

Tejeda and Hernández (2020) conclude that, despite a strong policy environment around gender equity and gender-based violence prevention, schools do not transform gender relationships, but rather reproduce imaginaries that sustain misogynistic and unequal relationships between men and women. Schools, families, and communities are links in a chain that reproduce and reinforce hegemonic masculinity and that legitimize sexual violence. In this chain, teachers are key in terms of reproducing or transforming relationships for gender equity, even in adverse institutional environments. These findings expose a tension between the dominant cultural imaginaries and schools as cultural institutions that should contribute to transforming culture.

Discussion

This chapter has examined three efforts to promote improved *convivencia* in schools in El Salvador immersed in a complex setting of social violence and cultural norms, where schools are expected to be key in promoting democracy, equitable relationships, and violence prevention. The use of Bentancur's (2015) dimensions of ideas, actors and institutions in education policy generates a series of reflections about why policies that aim to impact relationships in schools – in order to effect broader societal change – are largely unsuccessful. A cross-case and cross-dimensional analysis provides provocative insights on the complexity of addressing reforms in interpersonal relationships in schools which are embedded in an inconducive broader culture, even as schools are considered institutions for transforming culture.

The three cases demonstrate that it is difficult to separate the dimensions, in the sense that ideas are both personal and collective and knowledge is both formal and personal. Actors can be individuals but also institutions which have formal ideas based on their history and structure, yet individual actors within institutions may veer from the official posture based on their ideas and personal beliefs. Key local actors for enactment, such as parents and community members, are often ignored at the institutional agenda-setting table, and teachers are expected to implement something they have not been a part of creating, for which they have not received training, and about which they do not have shared understandings. In the absence of an effective meso-policy level, the distance between macro-level institutional decision-making and micro-level policy enactment interferes with how the actual ideas relating to the policy are communicated and understood at all levels.

This highlights how, in all three cases, there is no consensus among actors and institutions on the idea behind the policy or in terms of how it should be enacted. Different levels of actors had confusing and conflicting ideas about what democracy looks like in the first case, what constituted aggressive behaviour in the second case, and the roles of men and women in the third case. Formal institutional directives, such as policies and procedures, were found to be in dissonance with individual actor's beliefs and actions, and the lack of meso-level institutional support and guidance highlights the lack of functional program-level scaffolding to help schools address the macro-mandates and produce systems change. This confusion of ideas results in differing levels of buy-in and commitment, primarily at the school level, influenced by principals' personal knowledge and teachers' ideas on democracy, conflict, and gender.[7]

Just as broader education aims often lack clarity, the role of schools and educational processes in impacting general society are not clear. In the case of student governments, one apparent goal is to replicate the democratic processes that function in society, yet the actions taken are adult-oriented. In the second case, harmonious relationships among children and adolescents are formally a goal of the child protection agency, while the school is merely seen as a source of reporting and data about how children interact, not as a potentially transformative space wherein policy is enacted and *convivencia* is taught. Gender equity is a multi-agency task, where school is viewed as a place for learning new relationships; yet, without commitment from key players, such as teachers and family, schools remain a space for replicating a culture of violence.

Perhaps the most provocative aspect in the three cases presented is how these *convivencia* policies seek to transform very complex human relationships in the face of deep, historical cultural practices, such as authoritarianism, machismo, hierarchical school culture, and adult-centred power structures. These types of 'soft'[8] educational policies are also difficult to measure as their nature, aims, and content differ substantially from other traditional areas of reform, such as updating the curriculum, training teachers, new management structures, providing equipment such as computers, etc. Meadows (1999) argues that system change based on attitudes and cultural paradigms is much more complex than other kinds of change, but more effective and long-lasting, given that ways of thinking and paradigms that condition behaviour are transformed. As such, *convivencia* changes in schools and the goal of transforming broader society are the most difficult kinds of reform because they require transforming power structures and basic beliefs about human relationships.

Conclusions

The Salvadoran *convivencia* policies examined in this chapter show the dissonance of ideas, multiplicity of actors, and institutional complexities that challenge successful enactment.

Transforming relationships towards more equity, respect, and human rights through educational processes is a very complex task when broader culture is based on historical inequalities and unequal power dynamics. It is also important to recognize that other social organizations are providing an education as well – sometimes more powerfully than the school – such as family, religion, mass media, and local communities.

The preceding analysis underscores that the perspectives of those in the system at each level who are committed to making a difference should be considered, particularly the teachers who will enact policies in schools and families who educate at home. To reduce the distance between policy decision and policy enactment – preferably through strengthening the weak meso-policy level – other actors must be included and institutional initiatives must be synergized. If there is no consensus on aims for *convivencia*, rules about human relationships cannot be dictated from the macro-level to the micro-level in a top-down manner. Schools are in specific local contexts with their own social norms and practices that may enter into conflict with new *convivencia* patterns, so venues for creating consensus and commitment must be found.

For this reason, teachers are key, as they are found in the last link of the policy enactment chain and have the last word about what happens in the classroom. But teachers are also embedded in a management system and teacher culture that tends to assign additional functions and tasks to teachers without sufficient support systems, resources, or even time for more than classroom teaching (Martin and Bodewig, 2020). Teacher conditions limit their effectiveness, as Giroux (1990) points out, in that they are treated as technicians that carry out objectives and guidelines decided by experts who are unfamiliar with the classroom.

Successful reforms are not found only in material resources, but rather in the agents of change, that is, the teachers, in their mentalities, identities, and practices (Tedesco and Tenti Fanfani, 2002), where ideas and actors need to converge for effective change. Teachers are the most influential and powerful actors because in the end they decide what is taught and enacted (or not). But families are also influential in primary relationships with their children and may influence what is taught in the local school through direct complaints and formal denouncements made to the MOE, which may contrast with the aims established by international and national institutional actors. There is an opportunity for incorporating knowledge of micro-dynamics in the multidirectional nature of the policy process (Giudici, 2021).

These cases of *convivencia* policies, which seek the transformation of personal relationships, demonstrate the need to focus more on teachers, families, and local communities, and to increase their agency for participating in education policy decisions in order to contribute to successful enactment. Moving forward, more research must be carried out to understand the dynamics of school communities in policy enactment generally, not only in terms of *convivencia* issues, but also other reforms for improving education.

Notes

[1] As Morales and López (2019) state, the term *convivencia* is broadly used in education policy in Iberamerica, but is difficult to translate into English. The author prefers to use the word in Spanish, understanding *convivencia* as peaceful coexistence, 'getting along', a positive school environment and healthy social relationships.

[2] Education policy is understood as a response to a problem in education, generally proposed by the government, that justifies and responds to the demands of social actors or government agencies and contains an implicit educational theory (Espinoza, 2015).

[3] For more on the gang dynamics in schools, see Savenije, this volume.

[4] The legal document cited here still shows the year 1996, even though some clauses are newer.

[5] This protocol, which was designed by national and international public and private agencies, covers how to detect cases of sexual violence, process them in the legal system, handle specific cases, and prevent sexual violence, specifically in the school setting.

[6] Fomilenio II, or the Millennium Challenge Corporation Fund, was executed in El Salvador from 2015 to 2020, with a donation of $277 million from the US government, designated for infrastructure, investment environment, and human capital improvements in the southern part of the country.

[7] Even though some students were consulted in the studies, the primary focus was the effects of the policies from the perspective of teachers.

[8] The author suggests that these are soft policies, in that they are similar to the concept of soft skills – that is, reforms that seek to foster those character traits and interpersonal skills needed for positive human relationships.

References

Asamblea Legislativa de El Salvadaor (1983). Constitución de la República. Decreto 38. San Salvador.

Asamblea Legislativa de El Salvador (1996, 2008, 2011). Ley de la Carrera Docente. Decreto 665. San Salvador.

Asamblea Legislativa de El Salvador. (1996). Ley General de Educación. San Salvador.

Ball, S. (1987). *The Micro-politics of the School: Towards a Theory of School Organization*. Routledge.

Bentancur, N. (2015). Una contribución desde la ciencia política al estudio de las políticas educativas: el rol de las instituciones, las ideas y los actores. In C. Tello (ed.), *Los objetos de estudio de la política educativa* (pp 79–101). Autores de Argentina.

Blase, J. (2002). Las micropolíticas del cambio educativo. *Profesorado. Revista de Currículum y Formación del Profesorado*, 1–15. https://www.redalyc.org/articulo.oa?id=56751267003

Chicas, J. E. (2020). *Aproximación a la participación de gobiernos estudiantiles en centros escolares públicos rurales: Estudio de casos en el municipio de Jicalapa, La Libertad, El Salvador (2008 – mayo 2019)*. Universidad Centroamericana José Simeón Cañas. https://www.uca.edu.sv/mpe/tesis/67-chicas-j-2020-aproximacion-a-la-participacion-gobiernos-estudiantiles/

CONNA (Consejo Nacional de la Niñez y Adolescencia) (2018). *Lineamientos para prevenir el acoso (bullying) y ciber acoso (ciberbullying) a niñez y adolescencia en centros educativos públicos y privados en El Salvador*. Consejo Nacional de la Niñez y Adolescencia.

Cuéllar-Marchelli, H., and Góchez, G. (2017). *La pertinencia de las estrategias para prevenir la violencia escolar en El Salvador. Serie de investigación 1–2017*. FUSADES.

De Farranti, D., Perry, G. E., Ferreria, F. H., and Walton, M. (2004). *Inequality in Latin America: Breaking with History? World Bank Latin American and Caribbean Studies*. World Bank. http://hdl.handle.net/10986/15009

Delors, J. (1996). Los cuatro pilares de la educación. In UNESCO, *La Educación encierra un tesoro. Informe a la UNESCO de la Comisión internacional sobre la educación para el siglo XXI* (pp 91–103). Santillana/UNESCO.

DIGESTYC (2019). *Encuesta de Hograes de Propósitos Múltiples*. Ministerio de Economía.

Edwards Jr, D. B., Martin, P., and Flores, I. (2017). Education in El Salvador: past, present, prospects. In C. M. M. Posner (ed.), *Education in México, Central America and the Latin Caribbean* (pp 141–168). Bloomsbury Academic.

Edwards Jr, D. B., Martin, P., and Victoria, J. (2015). Differential support, divergent success: three case studies of international influence on education policy in El Salvador. In C. Brown (ed.), *Globalisation, International Education Policy and Local Policy Formation: Voices from the Developing World* (pp 39–58). Springer.

Edwards Jr., D. B., Victoria, J. A., and Martin, P. (2015). The geometry of policy implementation: L=lessons from the political economy of three education reforms in El Salvador during 1990–2005. *International Journal of Educational Development*, 44, 28–41.

Espinoza, O. (2015). 'Política', políticas públicas y política educativa: reflexiones y enfoques alternativos. In C. Tello (ed.), *Los objetos de estudio de la política educativa. Hacia una caracterización del campo teórico* (pp 143–159). Autores de Argentina.

Galdámez, R. M., and Lemus, C. L. (2020). *Representaciones sociales del docente salvadoreño sobre el acoso escolar entre estudiantes de tercer ciclo en la escuela salvadoreña.* Universidad Centroamericana José Simeón Cañas. https://www.uca.edu.sv/mpe/tesis/65-galdamez-r-y-lemus-c-2020-representaciones-sociales-docente-sobre-acoso-escolar/

Gillies, J. (2010). *The Power of Persistence. Education System Reform and Aid Effectiveness: Case Studies in Long-Term Education Reform.* USAID/Equip2.

Giroux, H. A. (1990). *Los profesores como intelectuales. Hacia una pedagogía crítica del aprendizaje.* Paidós.

Giudici, A. (2021). Teacher politics bottom-up: theorising the impact of micro-politics on policy generation. *Journal of Education Policy*, 36(6), 801–821. https://doi.org/10.1080/02680939.2020.1730976

Gómez, A. P. (2012). Educación para la Paz en el sistema educativo salvadoreño. *Ra-Ximhai*, 8(2), 93–126.

Gvirtz, S., and Beech, J. (2014). Educación y cohesión social en América Latina: una mirada desde la micropolítica escolar. *Archivos Analíticos de Políticas Educativas*, 2, 44. https://epaa.asu.edu/ojs/index.php/epaa/article/view/1754

IIDH (Instituto Interamericano de Derechos Humanos) (2011). *Informe Interamericano de la educación en derechos humanos. Un estudio de 19 países.* IIDH.

ISDEMU (Instituto Salvadoreño para el Desarrollo de la Mujer) (1998). *Política Nacional de la Mujer.* Instituto Salvadoreño para el Desarrollo de la Mujer.

ISDEMU (2005). *Política Nacional de la Mujer.* SaInstituto Salvadoreño para el Desarrollo de la Mujer.

ISDEMU (2011). *Política nacional de las mujeres: actualizada: medidas al 2014.* ISDEMU.

IUDOP (Instituto Universitario de Opinión Pública) (2019). *Entender el hoy para pensar en el mañana. Expectativas ciudadanas sobre la economía, la salud, la educación, la seguridad y la justicia.* Instituto Universitario de Opinión Pública UCA/Seattle International Foundation.

Jodelet, D. (1986). La representación social: fenómenos, concepto y teoría. In S. Moscovici (ed.), *Psicología Social II. Pensamiento y vide social* (pp 469–494). Paidós.

Lindo-Fuentes, H., and Ching, E. (2012). *Modernizing Minds in El Salvador: Education Reform and the Cold War, 1960–1980.* University of New Mexico Press.

Martin, P., and Bodewig, M. C. (2020). *La ecología de la profesión docente. Repensando el paradigma de la profesionalización docente en El Salvador.* Maestría en Política y Evaluación Educativa. https://www.uca.edu.sv/mpe/wp-cont ent/uploads/2020/06/Agenda-abril-2020-FINAL.pdf

Meadows, D. (1999). *Leverage Points: Places to Intervene in a System.* Sustainability Institute.

Ministerio de Educación (1995). *Reforma Educativa en Marcha. Documento III. Lineamientos generales del Plan Decenal 1995–2005.* Ministerio de Educación.

Ministerio de Educación (2005). *Plan Nacional de Educación 2021. Metas y políticas para construir el país que queremos.* Ministerio de Educación.

Ministerio de Educación (2009). *Plan Social Educativo. Vamos a la escuela.* Ministerio de Educación.

Ministerio de Educación (2010). *Política de Educación Inclusiva.* Ministerio de Educación.

Ministerio de Educación (2013). *Protocolo de actuación para el abordaje de la violencia sexual en las comunidades educativas de El Salvador.* Red interinstitucional para la prevención del acoso, abuso sexual y otras formas de violencia de género en las comunidades educativas.

Ministerio de Educación (2014). *Educación Integral de la Sexualidad.* Ministerio de Educación. https://www.mined.gob.sv/programas/educacion-integ ral-de-la-sexualidad/

Ministerio de Educación (2016a). ACUERDO No. 15–1257. San Salvador.

Ministerio de Educación (2016b). *Política de Equidad e Igualdad de Género. Plan de Implementación del Ministerio de Educación El Salvador.* Ministerio de Educación. https://www.transparencia.gob.sv/institutions/mined/docume nts/265940/download

Ministerio de Educación (2018a). *Observatorio MINED 2018 sobre los centros educativos públicos y privados subvencionados de El Salvador.* Ministerio de Educación.

Ministerio de Educación (2018b). *Política Nacional para la Convivencia Escolar y Cultura de Paz.* Ministerio de Educación. http://www.miportal.edu.sv/wp-content/uploads/recursos/convivencia/Politica/Pol_Nac_Con_2ed.pdf

Ministerio de Educación/Plan El Salvador (n.d.). *Manual de Participación Estudiantil para el Fortalecimiento de la Convivencia Escolar*. Ministerio de Educación.

Morales, M., and López, V. (2019). Políticas de convivencia escolar en América Latina: Cuatro perspectivas de Comprensión y Acción. *Archivos Analíticos de Políticas Educativas*, 27, 5. https://doi.org/10.14507/epaa.27.3800

Moreno, M. (1997). *La política nacional de la mujer (Alternativas para el desarrollo, No. 50)*. FUNDE.

Reimers, F., and Villegas Reimers, E. (2005). *Educación para la Ciudadanía Democrática en Escuelas Secundarias en América Latina. Trabajo Preparado para la Reunion del Dialogo Regional en Educación*. Banco InterAmericano de Desarrollo. https://publications.iadb.org/es/publicacion/14857/educacion-para-la-ciudadania-democratica-en-escuelas-secundarias-en-america

Reimers, F., and Villegas-Reimers, E. (2006). Sobre la calidad de la educación y su sentido democrático. *Educación para todos*, 90–107.

Rodino, A. M. (2013). Safety and peaceful coexistence policies in Latin American Schools: human rights perspective. *Sociologia, Problemas e Práticas*. http://journals.openedition.org/spp/970

Tedesco, J. C., and Tenti Fanfani, E. (2002). *Nuevos tiempos y Nuevos Docentes*. UNESCO.

Tejeda, W. V., and Hernández, A. V. (2020). *Masculinidad hegemónica y legitimización de la violencia sexual de docentes hombres en la escuela pública salvadoreña*. Universidad Centroamericana José Simeón Cañas. https://www.uca.edu.sv/mpe/tesis/66-tejeda-w-y-hernandez-a-v-2020-masculinidad-hegemonica-legitimacion-violencia-sexual/

UNESCO (2015). *La Educación para Todos, 2000–2015: logros y desafíos, informe de seguimiento de la EPT en el mundo, 2015, resumen*. New York: UNESCO.

United Nations (2015). *Transforming Our World: The 2030 Agenda for Sustainable Development*. United Nations. https://bit.ly/3xDuygj

UNOCD. (2013). *Global Study on Homicide 2013: Trends, Context, Data*. United Nations Office on Drugs and Crime. https://www.unodc.org/documents/gsh/pdfs/2014_GLOBAL_HOMICIDE_BOOK_web.pdf

7

When Schools Become Gang Turf: Schools and Government-Sponsored Prevention Programmes in El Salvador

Wim Savenije

Introduction

Diminishing gangs' influence and violence in society have been a long-time public security concern in El Salvador that has spilt over into the education sector. The National Council for Education (Consejo Nacional de Educación [CONED]) has assigned schools the role of being 'the central pillar of violence prevention', but recognizes that violence related to gangs directly affects students and teachers and admits that local schools do not have the resources to confront these challenges (CONED, 2016, pp 31, 35). During the last two decades, various government agencies and nongovernmental organizations (NGOs), supported by international agencies, have implemented numerous school-based violence and gang prevention programmes to counteract close relationships between students and gangs. However, little is known about how the school-based prevention programmes based on international models interact with the challenges of educating students directly or indirectly related to gangs in the Salvadoran context.

This chapter asks how local efforts, national programmes, and international models intertwine to prevent violence and gang influence in public schools in El Salvador. It juxtaposes the government-sponsored efforts – inspired by international models – to prevent violence and gang influence in school[1] with the challenges local teachers face when trying to avoid disrupting behaviour and conflicts with gang-related students in the classroom. It examines the ideas of prevention behind these programmes and their pertinence to the local context in order to understand their relevance. It concludes that, by employing a public security perspective that emphasizes individual decisions and responsibilities, these programmes typically disregard the social dynamics of the school, the families, and the nearby community. Although they can create the sensation that things are more or less under control, they can do little to prevent students from getting closer to gangs or to diminish gang influence in schools.

This analysis is based on the results of the Education in Risk and Conflict Situations research programme (2018–2022) at the Universidad Centroamericana José Simeón Cañas (UCA) in El Salvador. The research was directed at public primary schools with gang presence in the adjacent areas through a multiple-case design. Twenty-five public schools in seven regional departments were studied. A total of 177 semi-structured interviews were conducted with teachers, principals, parents, local organizations and stakeholders of government-sponsored prevention programmes. The research also included an online survey directed at teachers and principals of 61 comparable schools, a review of official documents and analytical workshops with informants.

This chapter is structured into four sections. The following section briefly describes how gang presence in neighbourhoods affects public education in El Salvador. The subsequent section discusses three government-sponsored programmes to prevent violence and gang influence in public schools. The third section then presents the experiences of local teachers in trying to avoid conflicts while educating gang-related students, the calming effect of police presence, and the consequences of anxiety and fear in the classroom. The final section discusses the extent to which the international models offer answers to the challenges local public schools face. Through a critical discussion of their assumptions, this chapter seeks to contribute to the development of more comprehensive prevention initiatives for primary schools in El Salvador and the wider Central American region where the gang phenomenon is extensive.

Gangs and education in El Salvador

Youth or street gangs are a phenomenon that is present in communities in different parts of the world (Klein et al, 2001), but is especially strong in the Northern Triangle of Central America (Bruneau et al, 2011). In some cases, gang dynamics spill over to the school grounds (Hutchison and Kyle, 1993, p 130; Trump, 2002; Savenije and van der Borgh, 2015). Although many gang members drop out of school early (Curry and Decker, 2003; Cruz et al, 2017), a school can also be claimed as 'turf' by the gang (Trump, 2002). In the case of El Salvador, even though active gang members are often not enrolled in school, the public school remains of particular interest to the gang. This is not just because it is a place where youth spend part of their time, where potential new gang members – that is, other youngsters with similar backgrounds and interests – can be found, or where drugs can be sold or consumed (Pérez Sáinz et al, 2018), but also because it is part of what the gang considers its territory and seeks to control (Savenije and van der Borgh, 2015).

In recent decades, the Mara Salvatrucha (MS-13) and 18th Street (18th St.) gangs have become powerful actors. These gangs originated in the US, extended internationally, and transformed the dynamics of many low-income neighbourhoods in Central America. During the 1980s, scores of youth – who were migrants of Central American descent growing up in poor areas in Los Angeles, California – started to join existing gangs such as the 18th St., a gang made up mostly of youths of Mexican origin. Later, they formed their own street-oriented groups, some of which joined ranks and became known as the MS-13 (Savenije, 2009; Ward, 2013; Dudley, 2020). In the 1990s, many gang-related youths were deported back to their native countries and founded gang chapters or 'cliques' of the MS-13 and 18th St. in the cities and towns they made their home (Coutin, 2007; Zilberg, 2011; Martínez and Martínez, 2018). In the years that followed, existing local gangs also converted into cliques of these two large gangs (Castro and Carranza, 2001; Savenije and van der Borgh, 2009).

Initially, the police force struggled with the new gang rivalries and rising violence; then, politicians also started to look to the north for new security policies (Matei, 2011). First, zero tolerance approaches were imported and translated into 'Mano Dura' (strong hand) policies, but later police-related prevention interventions were also adapted to the Central American context. The security policies followed a gang suppression model favouring a 'lock-'em-up' approach, to the detriment of social development programmes for the neighbourhoods that suffered the most from gang presence and violence (Durán, 2013). However, while filling up the penal system, these policies did little to stop the spread of these gangs. Nowadays, in El Salvador, they claim many neighbourhoods or even entire towns as their territory (Savenije and Beltrán, 2012).

Gang members are often the owners of the street: sometimes admired, often feared. Their presence profoundly limits the sociability of ordinary youth. The spaces that youth move through and where they meet with friends are often under the watchful eyes of gang members (Savenije and van der Borgh, 2015). Inhabitants will frequently meet visiting relatives at the community entrance and accompany them inside, while youth living in zones controlled by rival gangs are often prohibited from entering. So, seeing friends or participating in sports activities or community events – especially if it means going to other neighbourhoods – can imply serious security risks (Savenije and van der Borgh, 2015; INCIDE, 2016). Access to education has also become restricted (FUNDAUNGO et al, 2015; Pérez Sáinz et al, 2018) since gang members can ban young people from attending the local school because of their place of residence (PNUD, 2013; USAID-ECCN, 2016).

The gang phenomenon has local consequences in a public education system already characterized by poor outcomes, a weak policy environment (Fiszbein and Stanton, 2018), and a generalized concern about access and quality of education (Castaneda and Funes, 2017; FUSADES, 2017). Educational outcomes and teaching quality are closely linked to gangs and disorder (Howell and Griffiths, 2016). Approximately 43 per cent of public schools in El Salvador report the presence of gangs as a risk factor in the surrounding community, while 15,5 per cent report gangs as a security risk inside the school (MINED, 2018), producing stress and anxiety among students (Chacón et al, 2016) and staff (USAID-ECCN, 2016). However, the Ministry of Education has shown little interest in gang-related problems, while local and central level authorities lack comprehensive prevention-oriented policies. Official discourse often denies the existence of gang-related issues in schools; insecurity caused by gang presence is considered a problem in the surrounding communities (Flores and Menjívar, 2014).

However, schools are not insulated from the gang dynamics of the adjacent communities. Even though gangs are mainly a community phenomenon, inadequate education policies can influence local gang dynamics. Debarbieux and Blaya argue that a school effect 'contributes to the co-fabrication of a gang culture' (2008, p 219). Schools with 'higher levels of student victimization, sanctions, and poor student-teacher relations' (Howell and Griffiths, 2016, p 113) show a significantly higher number of students involved in gangs compared to other schools in similar socioeconomic contexts (Debarbieux and Blaya, 2008).

In El Salvador, a national public opinion survey reported that 71 per cent of the population surveyed agree that public schools help prevent violence in the community (IUDOP, 2019). However, even among low-income households, parents may send their children to nonstate – that is, private or religious – schools out of concern for their safety. Fifty-seven per cent of these nonstate schools have monthly fees below $30 per month, while around 11 per cent charge fees below $15 (Francis et al, 2018). In turn, nonstate schools try to prevent the enrolment of troublesome youth, a possibility that public schools do not have. As Francis et al report, 'some schools have entry requirements that exclude students who are low-performing, present behavioural problems, or do not have committed parents' (2018, p 5). Even if the number of affordable nonstate schools is low compared to public schools, this tendency underscores that in disadvantaged neighbourhoods, public schools receive the most socioeconomically disadvantaged youth.

Public schools are a space where students often bring gang loyalties with them (Howell and Griffiths, 2016; Monti, 1993). Even though they are not gang members, students may be close to a gang. It is therefore essential to make the distinction between *gang-involved* students (that is, active gang members), *gang-related* students (that is, wannabes, youth who identify with the gang or who have family members or friends in or close to the gang), and *ordinary students* (that is, those who have nothing to do with the gangs).

When gang dynamics take hold in the school setting, teachers and ordinary students face disruptive behaviour and potential conflicts influenced by gang loyalties (Martin and Savenije, 2021). When students feel threatened, they skip classes, avoid areas where gang members gather, leave school early, or even drop out (Hutchison and Kyle, 1993; PNUD, 2013). If they want to continue in school, they must observe the rules imposed by the gang, often involving dress codes and rules of conduct (Hutchison and Kyle, 1993; Savenije and van der Borgh, 2015).

Teachers face a complex situation when confronted by indiscipline or the disruptive behaviour of gang-related students. Teachers who comprehend the students' circumstances, understand street culture and how youth express themselves, and know how to treat them are usually respected, even by rebellious students. However, teachers who do not appreciate these characteristics, especially those who display aloofness and demand obedience, are often held in contempt and seen as weak (MacLeod, 1995). Sometimes unruly students threaten their teachers. Although these threats often do not lead to physical violence, they may generate feelings of anxiety and fear (Martin and Savenije, 2021).

The Salvadoran government implemented various violence and gang prevention initiatives to confront the insecurity surrounding public schools, the violence involving students, and the possibility of gangs disrupting educational processes (Oliva, 2015). Three vital government-sponsored programmes will be discussed in the next section.

Education and gang prevention

Implementing prevention programmes in schools makes a lot of sense in the context of insecurity and gang presence. Schools are not only a place to encounter children exposed to gangs in their communities but are also appropriate spaces to educate about gang affiliation and violence, offer alternatives for personal development, and foster life skills – all to keep violence at bay. Even though government policies and plans in El Salvador assign an important role to education in violence prevention (CONED, 2016),[2] an integrated strategy for reducing violence and gang-related influence in schools has never been drawn up. This section will explore three separate prevention programmes enacted in schools.

All three programmes discussed in this section share a public security perspective (Inter-American Development Bank, 2012; Cuéllar-Marchelli and Góchez, 2017) and are implemented by police officers.[3] The first, the Plan Escuela Segura (Safe School Plan [PES]), is a classic governmental response almost exclusively in security terms, but without recognizing the gang problem itself (Spergel, 1995). Although under different names, this strategy has been operating in El Salvador for nearly twenty years. The other two, the Liga Atlética Policial (Police Athletic League [LAP]) and the Gang Resistance Education and Training programme (GREAT),[4] are more recent innovations; both are sponsored by the United States Agency for International Development (USAID) and the US Bureau of International Narcotics and Law Enforcement Affairs (INL).

The Plan Escuela Segura

The PES dates back to 2004, when an agreement was signed between the Ministry of Education (MINED) and the National Civil Police (PNC) to reinforce security in and around public schools (Oliva, 2015). The plan primarily consists of preventive patrolling and police presence at the school entrance when students enter or leave the premises. When inaugurated, the PES was directed at 55 schools which experienced frequent violent encounters between different alliances of students (Savenije and Beltrán, 2007); in the following years, while more and more schools joined the plan, the PES focused more on the presence of gangs in and around the schools (Oliva, 2015). Its essence remained the same throughout the years: police presence deterring violence. The police search students' backpacks for arms or drugs and sometimes even check that their uniforms and haircuts respect the established norms. Occasionally police officers enter the classroom to check students' notebooks for gang-related signs or symbols and inspect bathrooms for graffiti. A police officer explains its workings:

'Two or three times a week, when the students arrive, there is police control at the school entrance. On other days, the police also show up unannounced in the classrooms for preventive inspections ... We always check the students' notebooks. In these, we have found several signs alluding to gangs. What we do is take note of this particular student. In other conversations, we will get more and more involved with him because of the sign found on him.'

In 2012, the Ministry of Defence joined the efforts to protect the security of public schools (Oliva, 2015). During this year, the army deployed its soldiers to help secure the surroundings of 778 schools in five of the 14 regional departments (Aguilar, 2019). In 2019, 1,123 public schools (about 22 per cent of the national total) were beneficiaries of this security plan, now called the School Protection Plan (Plan Protección Escolar) (Peñate, 2019). Despite some complaints about the mistreatment of students by security officials (Zetino Duarte et al, 2015; INCIDE, 2016; Pérez Sáinz et al, 2018), police presence is usually welcomed by the school staff members. They gain a sense of being protected against violent threats and supported in enforcing school rules and maintaining discipline.

Liga Atlética Policial

In El Salvador, the LAP is organised by the United Homeland Foundation (Fundación Patria Unida), the PNC, and the INL. It is modelled after the US Police Athletic/Activities League, whose mission is to promote the prevention of juvenile crime and violence by building relationships among youth, police, and community, and fostering positive engagement, providing mentorship, civic/service, athletic, recreational, enrichment, and educational opportunities and resources. It also aims to establish positive relations between youth and law enforcement officers (National Association of Police Athletic/ Activities League, 2022). In El Salvador, however, LAP was initiated in 2012 as a programme of 'prevention through sports' (Policía Nacional Civil, 2017). In 2017, the INL had donated more than US$1 million worth of sports gear to more than 3,500 children and adolescents (Salazar, 2017), and trained 220 police officers from the Division of Prevention as LAP instructors (Policía Nacional Civil, 2017).

In the LAP, police officers organize sports and artistic activities with students from communities with high levels of crime and gang presence, and emphasize the importance of team values and skills. Its aims include distancing them from participating in illicit activities and gangs (Patria Unida, n.d.). The main activities are soccer, modern dance, and choreography, but swimming and computer classes are sometimes offered (Sosa, 2019). At regional and national levels, the LAP organizes artistic and sports competitions among students from different schools or municipalities, but involves few classroom teachers, parents, or broader community members. The programme also strives to instil fundamental values such as discipline, perseverance, morality, and good behaviour (Patria Unida, n.d.). In 2019, the LAP reached 22,000 students (36 per cent girls and 64 per cent boys), while 2,000 students participated in modern dance and choreography (Sosa, 2019).

Gang Resistance Education and Training

Gang Resistance Education and Training (GREAT) is a prevention initiative intended as 'an immunization against delinquency, youth violence, and gang membership' (GREAT, n.d.). It focuses on teaching social skills to help students 'avoid using criminal behaviour and violence to solve problems' (Eguizábal, 2015, pp 86–87). It was initially developed in the US in 1991 by the Phoenix Police Department (Arizona). In 1992, the programme started to expand and train police officers as instructors across the US. In 2009, INL introduced GREAT to El Salvador. Since then, it has been implemented under various governments and changing security policies by the PNC in collaboration with the INL.

The objective of GREAT is to prevent the gang recruitment of children and youth through educational and recreational activities. The police officers are trained to follow a specially designed classroom curriculum providing a range of components, including a six-lesson upper elementary school programme (fourth and fifth grades) and a 13-lesson middle school (sixth to eighth grades) curriculum. GREAT gives students information about crime, violence, drug abuse, and gangs, and discusses the roles and responsibilities of the students in the family, school, and community. It focuses on the development of social skills and strategies – for instance, decision-making and communication skills, effective refusal skills, identifying whom to talk to for help, and anger management (GREAT, n.d.). Like LAP, GREAT also aims to foster positive relations between youth and law enforcement officers and students; as such, it involves few school teachers. GREAT also has summer and family components, although these have been implemented to a lesser extent in El Salvador.

In El Salvador, the extent of the programme is limited. It is offered to students in municipalities with high levels of insecurity and violence, but not in all schools or all grades; nor do participating schools have the guarantee that they will be involved the following year. However, since 2010, approximately 25,000 students have participated in GREAT (Eguizábal, 2015). A school principal explains: '[GREAT] is a very nice programme. It is a pity that there is so little coverage; only one grade participates. They start and remain in one grade until the programme finishes there.'

Although these three programmes are generally well received, it is not clear how far they can connect to the everyday experiences and necessities of the local schools and students. The following section looks at ways in which Salvadoran schools – with or without external interventions – cope with the reality of having gang-related or gang-involved students in the classroom and the challenges they pose.

Teaching gang-related youth

Establishing educational relations with disadvantaged students from insecure neighbourhoods can be difficult, even in the best situations. However, teachers often express that they have little need for special educational strategies or interventions as they often have long professional trajectories, sometimes having even taught the parents of the present-day students. For example, the online survey respondents were on average 50 years old and had been working for 17 years at the same school. Therefore, teachers intimately know the social and economic situations in which their students grow up and are usually well positioned to establish functional teaching and learning processes. But even so, gang presence in the neighbouring area adds another layer of strain.

This section shows that the presence of gang-related students can be more distressing for teachers than gang-involved students. Subsequently, it describes the principal strategies teachers use to avoid conflicts in the classroom and how police presence has a calming influence. Afterwards, it shows what happens when things get out of hand and reveals some consequences of the ensuing anxiety and fear in the classroom.

The challenges posed by gang-related students

Gang-related and gang-involved students are not so different from other students. They live in the same neighbourhood or town and come from roughly the same socioeconomic background. Public schools may have only a few active gang members attending; however, other students may have family members in the gang or be supporters. Gang-involved students often keep their association with the gang private and do not behave differently from other students. Teachers even admit that they are sometimes unaware that a student maintains these relationships. However, the behaviour of gang-related students can be more challenging. In the following quotes, school staff members tell about their experiences:

'Followers, yes, we have a lot. These are children who sympathize … who imitate what they do … But, thank God, I don't observe that they are totally involved in the gang. I think they are followers or family members of those who are.' (Director)

'We have two types [of gang-involved students]. One who knows that he has to study to be better. I have heard cases of: "This kid, I know that he is a gang member, but he is the one who works best, who studies most. When he enters the classroom, he comes to learn." But also, there is the other type who doesn't, who comes to mess things up … I have both kinds of students. There is no magical formula to say: "Because he is a gang member, he will behave this way." No.' (Teacher)

'Some students are gang members, and often these are the best-behaved students. They – maybe because their leader threatens them – respond or try to respond appropriately. Often those who are rebellious are probably just friends of gang members.' (Teacher)

Strategies to avoid conflicts

If a student mentions that family members or friends are involved in a gang, teachers often start to see them in a new light. They become more cautious because of the potential for gang members getting involved if a conflict arises. Street gangs are feared for the violence they inflict on those they see as enemies or who interfere with their affairs. Teachers certainly do not want to be seen in this way. One of the most critical strategies teachers use is avoiding conflicts and developing friendly and responsive relationships. Some teachers emphasize this:

> 'The best way is to place yourself in their context. That is my way of seeing it. It is to position myself without disrespecting or undervaluing my person or them. The aim is that they trust us, and we feel that we can trust them.' (Teacher)

> 'Be polite, have a word with them, and try to show that one is not their enemy but, rather, the contrary. Try to hold out one's hand a little bit, but also avoid being grabbed up to the elbow. Because that's how they are.' (Teacher)

> 'I have to find ways not to hurt or offend them, even though I will be humiliating myself. But I won't [talk like them] … "Hey, son!", I'll answer him, "Look how nice you are, don't speak that way". Though afterwards, he will say: "What does it matter to that old hag?" Because they don't conceal things when talking.' (Teacher)

Although friendly and responsive relationships should be the norm between all teachers and students, a significant motivation to form them here seems to be fear. Also, teachers often use the term 'respect' when asked how to treat gang-related students. One teacher affirms:

> 'Students, I don't treat him harshly; I don't mistreat them; on the contrary, with a lot of respect … Yes, at moments, I may feel frightened, but I have to overcome it. Because if they see that I, as a teacher, lower my guard and let everything happen … That cannot be.'

The experience of fear means that police presence and control at the school's entrance and through classroom visits, or even police involvement in prevention programmes can provide some reassurance to school staff. In these situations, disruptive students calm down, and their behaviour becomes less confrontational. Their presence helps the teachers ignore, to some extent, the relationship some students have with the gang and treat them as ordinary students. Staff members explain the calming influence of police being present:

> 'There are situations we as a school cannot handle: orderly behaviour, haircuts, and the clothes students wear. We cannot be very, very strict with them … But they [the police] can. They implemented various measures on the days they came, tidying up how the students were dressed.' (Teacher)

> 'Personally, I feel that police presence helps a little. It helps because knowing that the police are present, they [disruptive students] bother less.' (Director)

When things get out of hand

Nonetheless, in some situations, school staff members feel they need to adapt. When students manifestly impose themselves upon the classroom dynamics and disrupt learning processes to thwart the subject's objectives and the teacher's pedagogical strategies, new relations of power and authority appear. In students' provocative or disturbing behaviour, a struggle surfaces concerning who decides what happens in the classroom. Frequently this behaviour also influences other students to follow suit, even though they are not necessarily close to gangs. Some teachers explain how erratic or defiant conduct interrupts the processes of teaching and learning:

> 'He wanted to impose his rules. He didn't take notes, and he didn't bring his notebook, but he wanted to create his rules and bother the class because he knew that there was someone [a gang member] behind him who backed him.' (Teacher)

> 'It affects a lot because the other students want to follow in his footsteps [of a gang-related student]. They want to do the same as he does. If you don't stop this, the whole grade will become contaminated.' (Teacher)

Sometimes when teachers try to intervene and reassert control, they find themselves in a difficult position. Their efforts are resisted and framed as disrespectful or humiliating by the disorderly students; sometimes, they are even met with insinuations of violence or direct threats. A recurrent threat is to denounce the perceived ill-treatment to relatives close to the gang and mobilize them against the teacher. Merely an insinuation is often enough to convey the message; there is hardly any need to be explicit. A phrase such as: 'Look, don't mess with me. You don't know who my father is' (as described by a teacher) is sufficient to generate anxiety and fear. The notoriety of the gangs means that teachers do not want to get close to any kind of conflict. Some teachers confirm this:

'Recently, they [students] have threatened a colleague. The threat didn't come from one of the boys but from a girl whose brother is a gang member.' (Teacher)

'Some colleagues say: "No, I don't interfere with that guy because I know who his parents are." So, yes, there is fear. Teachers are afraid to order children around because behind them are the parents who are related to the gang.' (Teacher)

The teachers do not just fear the students themselves, but rather their brothers, fathers, or other relatives who are gang members or maintain close relationships with the local gang. These persons often support their kin, all the more so if they think that they were mistreated or disrespected. The ensuing anxiety and fear are directly related to what happens in the classroom because a student can feel wronged simply by a call to order or even a low score in an exam. Some teachers explain the limitations they face:

'You can't admonish nor try to correct this kind of problematic youth. Because you know that … this puts you in danger.' (Teacher)

'Last year, a student didn't pass, and immediately my colleague was threatened. We had to pass him to the next grade because they [gang members] threatened her. It was really dangerous.' (Teacher)

When anxiety and fear permeate educational relations, fostering bonds of trust with students becomes problematic. Because of the risk of being seen as disrespectful, teachers become more cautious in terms of how they interact with their students. Often, they do not want students to get to know them personally, so they will not share experiences or interests; instead, they maintain distance and evade sensitive topics. Some teachers assert:

'When these students come, we teach classes normally. We greet them; as I said before, one doesn't have to be their friend or enemy. You have to maintain distance and not confide in them.' (Teacher)

'We avoid confrontations with them. We treat them the best way possible, so they don't feel offended, although they are responsible for what they do.' (Teacher)

Ordinary students also suffer. They too receive threats when they do not give in to the demands of their gang-related peers. Out of fear, teachers do not dare support threatened students. They are unsure even about ordinary students since they may also have (direct or indirect) contact with gang members, which can cause difficulties. Also, teachers are sometimes anxious about students disclosing incidents of gang involvement in violent or criminal acts, since knowing too much will also put them at risk. Therefore, teachers opt to limit their contact with all students. A mother and school staff members recount the fear and uncertainty that is felt:

'Yes, some students may feel intimidated by peers involved in gangs and other stuff because they like to boss everyone around and threaten their fellow students. And, yes, these students feel unsafe and intimidated.' (Mother)

'You have to be careful with what you say to them [the students]. Because outside the school, you don't know them. You know them as students who attended our school for years. But as far as anything else, we talk about topics related to the lessons. Nothing else.' (Teacher)

'We are afraid. We are afraid when we leave school. But we try to speak respectfully to the students and the parents … Because only God knows who these youngsters really are, who they are when they take off their school uniform.' (Director)

Teaching under pressure

In these situations, the educational authority of the teacher is questioned or diminished. Fear provokes teachers as they do not dare to correct students' disruptive behaviour and will even cave in to their demands. Sometimes, teachers cannot teach the classes they have prepared or the topics they consider important. This situation validates the loss of authority the teachers have already suffered in the eyes of the gang-related students, provoking an additional loss of authority in ordinary students. A mother and school principal explain the consequences for the education the school can offer:

'So, teachers feel too intimidated to demand something from the students. They don't know if this person is involved in something. Consequently, the teachers feel somewhat fearful. This situation prevents them from offering better education.' (Mother)

'When a teacher plans his classes, he or she has a certain amount of time to teach specific units. So, if the class gets interrupted, the time is reduced, and it's not possible to meet curriculum goals.' (Principal)

The loss of control over the educational processes in the classroom by teachers who are afraid of gang-related or gang-involved students, combined with the already scarce resources available, sharply reduces pedagogical interactions and affects the quality of education public schools can offer. The following section analyses the extent to which the intervention programmes described in the previous section can provide answers to this problem.

International models, national programmes, and the limited weight of the local

The three prevention programmes mentioned previously constitute a nexus that connects international, national, and local ideas and practices of prevention, but where the local loses out. For the Salvadoran government, there are no fast and easy solutions available for the problems that gangs cause, so it is understandable that it looks for experiences and help outside the country. However, the international models followed view prevention mainly through a public security lens, and their solutions reveal relatively unsophisticated theories of change. This section will discuss concepts of prevention and the corresponding theories of change; shortcomings and constraints will also be highlighted.

As was discussed previously, the gang phenomenon and related insecurity have complex historical, social, economic, and political roots, so it is difficult to conceive that vigilance and search operations, complemented by educational, sports, and artistic activities, are crucial to preventing violence and gang affiliation. Of the three programmes, GREAT is undoubtedly the most sophisticated. Its general objectives are 'to prevent kids from joining gangs while providing them with life skills and decision-making tools. In addition, the program aims at improving the relationship between the police and the community' (US Embassy in El Salvador, 2021). Nonetheless, an evaluation of US Security Assistance to El Salvador in the 2009–2014 period argues that 'GREAT's usefulness is not because it helps youngsters in the community avoid being recruited by gangs ... The program's value lies in its confidence building among stakeholders aspect' (Eguizábal, 2015, p 87), especially between police officers, participating youth, and their families. This relational objective is shared with the LAP programme. Yet both involve only a few teachers, parents, or other community members. Another drawback is that having direct contact with police officers is risky in communities with an active gang presence. Anyone – be it students, teachers, or neighbours – seen interacting with the police can be considered an informant or disloyal.

The main criticism of all three programmes is not their overly ambiguous objectives, but their conceptions of prevention that reveal limited theories of change. PES understands prevention as deterrence through police and military patrolling the school's surroundings, maintaining a presence at the school entrance and searching students' belongings. LAP conceives prevention primarily as keeping youth engaged, especially in afterschool sports and artistic activities, so they do not have time to commit crimes or get involved in a gang. GREAT approaches prevention by raising awareness about the negative consequences of crime, drugs, and gang affiliation and also by teaching social skills as protection against gang propositions and peer pressure.

In all these programmes, police officers are in charge of patrolling and on-site visits, offering talks about gangs and gang membership, teaching social skills, organizing sports and dance events, and even tournaments involving students from other schools. Although some of these activities could form part of a more comprehensive and integrated school curriculum, the role of the school itself in preventing and maintaining a secure environment is overlooked, as well as the contribution of the family and the broader community. Even though LAP emphasizes team values and skills, and GREAT focuses on social skills – that is, both go beyond mere police presence and stress relationship values – the social dynamics among students, between students, their teachers and parents, and those taking place in the community are left out of the picture.

Even if these interventions achieve confidence among the stakeholders (Eguizábal, 2015), the method of police officers teaching social skills for relating with peers or family members is flawed. This is not only because little time is allotted for the intervention and only some grades participate, but also because these topics are not integrated with other subjects, teachers' pedagogies are not considered, and the opportunities for practising the skills in the local community are extremely limited. Theories of change that focus on the individual student lie at the heart of these shortcomings. On the one hand, police officers deter students from resorting to violence and associating with gangs through their presence and the inspection of personal belongings. On the other hand, police officers emphasize the individual choices that students face and try to raise awareness of their responsibilities and the negative consequences of violence, drugs, and gang membership. The underlying theories of change do not incorporate the school environment, the family, or the local community, nor do they recognize the importance of the adolescent identity processes or attend to the sociopsychological needs of belonging to a peer group and being appreciated by peers (Brown, 2004).

By emphasizing individual behaviour, these theories detach the students from their social environment and hold them personally responsible. They cannot explain how students can distance themselves from peer pressure, gang influence, and the temptations of associating with a gang. The students' basic social relations, their daily interactions, the social climate in their schools, families, and communities etc. all remain out of the picture.

To understand what these limitations mean for the aforementioned prevention programmes, it is necessary to go back to a fundamental question. What needs to be prevented in public schools with gang presence in their surroundings? Gang members often do not attend school, and those who do, do not always provoke significant problems inside the school's walls. Instead, issues frequently start with gang-related students who want to impose their will and, if challenged, threaten to mobilize relatives or friends involved in a gang. These conflicts produce anxiety and fear, question or diminish the educational authority of the teachers, often cause them to lose control over the educational processes in the classroom, and, at the same time, reduce effective teaching and learning relationships. Police presence and control at the school entrance and classroom visits by police officers usually reassure teachers by dissuading rebellious students. This presence helps them ignore some students' proximity to the gang and reinforces their authority. But this reassurance seems somehow elusive.

The main problem is that students grow up in a local environment with frequent violent episodes and gang presence and control. Some may even feel attracted to the gang in their community. Some have learned that using threats of violence or involving gang members in conflicts gives them power. The distress and fear provoked when this happens in the classroom put education processes and quality under strain. As a police presence can do little more than bring temporary relief to this problematic situation, teachers are acutely aware that they remain vulnerable outside the school or when the police are not present.

The international models cited in this chapter and the national prevention programmes based on them ignore the importance of local relationships in and between school, family, and community as fundamental components in violence and gang prevention efforts (Bursik and Grasmick, 1993; Spergel, 1995; Howell and Griffiths, 2016). By emphasizing the students' choices and responsibilities, they overlook teachers and schools as key players. Therefore, these prevention programmes have a limited impact and generate 'a dense fog that hinders seeing viable future solutions' (Oliva, 2015, p 36). While police officers are present, check the students' belongings, or offer sports, artistic, or other appealing activities, little violence happens, and gangs even may look unattractive. But in reality, nothing changes. The police officers leave. The teachers and students go back to their homes and communities. The gang looks on.

Some final reflections

Gangs are not a recent phenomenon in El Salvador, even though the arrival of deported gang members from the US in the 1990s changed the dynamics of gang conflict and control. Violence and economic insecurity during and after the civil war of the 1980s provoked a sizeable migration to the US of Salvadorans looking for a better future. The subsequent deportation of gang-involved youth, however, brought new and more violent conflicts to Salvadoran neighbourhoods between local groups that identified with the style, rules, and enmities of the MS-13 and the 18th St. gangs in the North. As a response, successive Salvadoran governments also looked beyond the border and adopted zero-tolerance approaches to inform their 'Mano Dura'-style security policies. Additionally, several violence and gang prevention programmes developed by the police in the US were adapted to the Central American context. Hence, the implementation of PES, LAP, and GREAT follows international models to deal with gang-related problems whose backgrounds likewise transcend local and national limits.

The interplay of local, national, and international forces constitutes the larger context of the gang-related problems faced by local schools and school-based prevention programmes in El Salvador. The national and international dynamics of gang development and anti-gang policies adversely affect the social fabric of neighbourhoods and educational communities. Gang presence and violence harm local social cohesiveness and collaterally damage educational processes by generating anxiety and fear, eroding trust, and diminishing the quality of education in public schools. At the same time, by favouring a public security perspective, government-sponsored prevention programmes can neither recognize nor address these damages.

The state of exception decreed by the Bukele government in March 2022 to deal with the gangs – which has resulted in the mass incarceration of suspected gang members and collaborators and the construction of a mega-prison to house 40,000 inmates – does little to mend the social fabric in the gang-affected neighbourhoods.[5]

Notes

[1] This chapter focusses solely on government-sponsored prevention-oriented programmes. The main reasons for this are as follows: 1. NGO-implemented programmes are very diverse in their form and implementation, often including objectives very different from prevention. To analyse these programmes, however important this may be, goes beyond the scope of the present chapter. 2. NGOs can only offer programmes of limited scope and duration, but governments can project prevention as a sustainable and long-term component of its education policies. Therefore, it is important to clarify the underlying logic of government-sponsored programmes and relate them to the everyday realities of the public schools.

[2] The National Education Council (CONED) defines the school as the main pillar of prevention (*eje principal de prevención*).

[3] Cuéllar-Marchelli and Góchez (2017) call it a *citizen security strategy*, which implies the meaningful and collaborative participation of local organizations or citizens in these initiatives (Inter-American Development Bank, 2012), so we prefer the concept of public security, which makes no such an assumption.

[4] Educación y Entrenamiento en Resistencia a las Pandillas, in Spanish.

[5] The state of exception, which started on 27 March 2022, was extended for the 17th time in August 2023 and has resulted in 72,000 persons being detained on suspicion of being gang members or collaborating with them, many of them innocent (Villarroel, 2022).

References

Aguilar, J. (2019). *Las políticas de seguridad pública en El Salvador, 2003–2018*. Heinrich Böll Stiftung.

Brown, B. B. (2004). Adolescents' relationships with peers. In R. M. Lerner and L. Steinberg (eds.), *Handbook of Adolescent Psychology*, 2nd edn (pp 363–394). John Wiley & Sons.

Bruneau, T., Dammart, L., and Skinner, E. (2011). *Maras: Gang Violence and Security in Central America*. University of Texas Press.

Bursik, R. J., and Grasmick, H. G. (1993). *Neighborhoods and Crime: The Dimensions of Effective Community Control*. Lexington Books.

Castaneda, J., and Funes, W. (2017). *Jóvenes fuera de la escuela*. FEDISAL. https://www.fedisal.org.sv/wp-content/uploads/2017/11/Jovenes_fuera.pdf

Castro, M., and Carranza, M. (2001). Las maras en Honduras. In ERIC-IDESO-IDIES-IUDOP (ed.), *Maras y pandillas en Centroamérica: Volumen 1* (pp 221–332). UCA Publicaciones.

Chacón, E. R., Olivar, M. A., MacQuaid, R. D., and Lobos Rivera, M. E. (2016). *Afectaciones psicológicas en estudiantes de instituciones educativas públicas ubicadas en zonas controladas por grupos pandilleriles*. Universidad Técnologica.

CONED (Consejo Nacional de Educación) (2016). *Plan El Salvador Educado. Por el derecho de una educación de calidad*. https://www.unicef.org/elsalvador/sites/unicef.org.elsalvador/files/2018-12/Plan_El_Salvador_Educado.compressed.pdf

Coutin, S. B. (2007). *Nations of Migrants. Shifting boundaries of Citizenship in El Salvador and the United States*. Cornell University Press.

Cruz, J. M., Rosen, J. D., Amaya, L. E., and Vorobyeva, Y. (2017). *The New Face of Street Gangs: The Gang Phenomenon in El Salvador*. Florida International University and FUNDE.

Cuéllar-Marchelli, H., and Góchez, G. (2017). *La pertinencia de las estrategias para prevenir la violencia escolar en El Salvador*. http://fusades.org/sites/default/files/SerieDES%20FINAL%20%281%29.pdf

Curry, G. D., and Decker, S. H. (2003). *Confronting Gangs. Crime and Community*, 2nd edn. Roxbury Publishing Company.

Debarbieux, E., and Blaya, C. (2008). An interactive construction of gangs and ethnicity: the role of school segregation in France. In F. van Gemert, D. Peterson, and L. Inger-Lise (eds.), *Street Gangs, Migration and Ethnicity.* Willan Publishing.

Dudley, S. (2020). *MS-13: The Making of America's Most Notorious Gang.* Hanover Square Press.

Durán, R. J. (2013). *Gang Life in Two Cities: An Insider's Journey.* Columbia University Press.

Eguizábal, C. (2015). The Central America regional security initiative: a key piece of US security assistance to El Salvador, but not the only one. In E. L. Olson (ed.), *Crime and Violence in Central America's Northern Triangle. How US Policy Responses Are Helping, Hurting, and Can be Improved* (pp 55–99). Woodrow Wilson Center.

Fiszbein, A., and Stanton, S. (2018). *The Future of Education in Latin America and the Caribbean: Possibilities for United States Investment and Engagement.* Inter-American Dialogue.

Flores, R., and Menjívar, V. (2014). 7 Estudiantes asesinados al inicio del año escolar. *La Prensa Gráfica,* 25 February, 2–3.

Francis, R., Martin, P., and Burnett, N. (2018). *Public Schools in Disadvantaged Neighbourhoods.* USAID/Results for Development and Education Development Center/Education in Crisis and Conflict Network.

FUNDAUNGO, STPP, and UNICEF (2015). *Percepciones de niñas, niños y adolescentes sobre su bienestar: ¿Apostando por el futuro de El Salvador?* Autores.

FUSADES (2017). *Informe de Coyuntura Social 2016–2017.* Fundación Salvadoreño para el Desarrollo Económico y Social.

GREAT (Gang Resistance Education and Training) (n.d.). *What Is G.R.E.A.T.?* Retrieved March 20th from https://www.great-online.org/GREAT-Home

Howell, J. C., and Griffiths, E. (2016). *Gangs in America's Communities,* 2nd edn. SAGE Publications.

Hutchison, R., and Kyle, C. (1993). Hispanic Street Gangs in Chicago's Public Schools. In S. Cummings and D. J. Monti (eds.), *Gangs. The Origins and Impact of Contemporary Youth Gangs in the United States* (pp 113–136). State University of New York Press.

INCIDE (Instituto Centroamericano de Investigaciones para el Desarrollo y el Cambio Social) (2016). *El Salvador: Nuevo patrón de violencia: afectación territorial y respuesta de las comunidades (2010–2015).* INCIDE.

Inter-American Development Bank (2012). *Citizen Security. Conceptual Framework and Empirical Evidence.* Inter-American Development Bank.

IUDOP (Instituto Universitario de Opinión Pública) (2019). *State of the General Situation of the Country.* https://uca.edu.sv/iudop/publicacion/encuesta-sobre-las-expectativas-hacia-el-nuevo-gobierno-2/

Klein, M. W., Kerner, H.-J., Maxson, C. L., and Weitekamp, E. G. M. (2001). *The Eurogang Paradox. Street Gangs and Youth Groups in the US and Europe*. Kluwer Academic Publishers.

MacLeod, J. (1995). *Ain't No Making It: Aspirations and Attainment in a Low-Income Neighborhood*. Westview Press.

Martin, P., and Savenije, W. (2021). El asalto a las relaciones pedagógicas. Educar en contextos de pandillas. *ECA Estudios Centroamericanos*, 76(766), 361–373.

Martínez, Ó., and Martínez, J. J. (2018). *El Niño de Hollywood*. Penguin/ Random House Grupo Editorial.

Matei, F. C. (2011). The impact of US anti-gang policies in Central America: quo vadis? In T. Brueau, L. Dammert, and E. Skinner (eds.), *Maras: Gang Violence and Security in Central America* (pp 197–210). Texas University Press.

MINED (2018). *Observatorio Mined 2018 sobre los centros educativos públicos y privados subvencionados de El Salvador*. MINED.

Monti, D. J. (1993). Gangs in more- and less-settled communities. In S. Cummings and D. J. Monti (eds.), *Gangs. The Origins and Impact of Contemporary Youth Gangs in the United States* (pp 219–253). State University of New York Press.

National Association of Police Athletic/Activities League (2022). *National PAL. The World's Foremost Leader in Engaging Kids, Cops & Community*. https://www.nationalpal.org/aboutus

Oliva, H. A. (2015). Matices cronológicos de la violencia escolar en El Salvador (Apuntes críticos para la comprensión del fenómeno). *Realidad y Reflexión*, 15(42), 11–38.

Patria Unida. (n.d.). *Liga Atlética Policial (LAP). Programa para la prevención de la delincuencia en El Salvador*. Patria Unida. http://patriaunida.org/liga-atletica-policial.html

Peñate, S. (2019). Educación cerró 2018 con 0.9% de deserción escolar. *La Prensa Gráfica*, 31 January, 24.

Pérez Sáinz, J. P., Alas Velado, W., and Montoya Hernández, M. (2018). Sobrevivir en la violencia. Jóvenes, vías laborales y estrategias de adaptación territorial en Soyapango, El Salvador. In J. P. Pérez Sáinz (ed.), *Vida sitiadas. Jóvenes, exclusión laboral y violencia urbana en Centroamérica* (pp 81–116). Facultad Latinoamericana de Ciencias Sociales.

PNUD. (2013). *Informe sobre Desarrollo Humano El Salvador 2013. Imaginar un nuevo país. Hacerlo posible. Diagnóstico y propuesta*. PNUD.

Policía Nacional Civil. (2017). *Más de 11,000 jóvenes participan en final de la Copa Liga Atlética Policial*. Policía Nacional Civil. http://www. pnc.gob.sv/portal/page/portal/informativo/novedades/noticias/ME1s %20de%2011000%20j%F3venes%20participan%20en%20final%20de%20 la%20Copa%20Liga%20Atl

Salazar, J. (2017). Fútbol para niños, niñas y adolescentes como mecanismo de prevención de la violencia. *Diario Co Latino*, 9 February. https://www.diariocolatino.com/futbol-ninos-ninas-adolescentes-mecanismo-prevencion-la-violencia/

Savenije, W. (2009). *Maras y barras. Pandillas y violencia en los barrios marginales de Centroamérica*. FLACSO El Salvador.

Savenije, W., and Beltrán, M. A. (2007). *Competiendo en Bravuras. Violencia Estudiantil en el Área Metropolitana de San Salvador*, 2nd edn. FLACSO El Salvador.

Savenije, W., and Beltrán, M. A. (2012). *Conceptualización del Modelo de Prevención Social de la Violencia con Participación Juvenil*. Instituto Nacional de la Juventud (INJUVE).

Savenije, W., and van der Borgh, C. (2009). Gang violence: comparing anti-gang approaches and policies. *The Broker*, 20–23.

Savenije, W., and van der Borgh, C. (2015). San Salvador: violence and resilience in gangland – coping with the code of the street. In *Violence and Resilience in Latin American Cities* (pp 90–107). Zed Press.

Sosa, R. (2019). La Liga Atlética Policial. *Diario El Mundo*. https://diario.elmundo.sv/la-liga-atletica-policial/

Spergel, I. A. (1995). *The Youth Gang. A Community Approach*. Oxford University Press.

Trump, K. S. (2002). Gangs, violence, and safe schools. In C. R. Huff (ed.), *Gangs in America III* (pp 121–130). SAGE Publications.

US Embassy in El Salvador. (2021). *INL in El Salvador*. US Embassy in El Salvador. https://sv.usembassy.gov/inl-in-el-salvador/

USAID-ECCN. (2016). *Rapid Education and Risk Analysis El Salvador. Final Report*. USAID/Education in Crisis and Conflict Network. https://irp-cdn.multiscreensite.com/5e8f9e5e/files/uploaded/RERA%20El%20Salvador%20Final%20Report%20.pdf

Villarroel, G. (2023). Legisladores aprueban la prórroga 17 a la excepción. *La Prensa Gráfica*, 10 August, 12.

Ward, T. W. (2013). *Gangsters without Borders: An Ethnography of a Salvadoran Street Gang*. Oxford University Press.

Zetino Duarte, M., Brioso, L., and Montoya, M. (2015). Dinámicas de violencia en los territorios salvadoreños. In J. P. Pérez Sáinz (ed.), *Exclusión social y violencias en territorios urbanos centroamericanos* (pp 99–144). FLACSO.

Zilberg, E. (2011). *Space of Detention: The Making of a Transnational Gang Crisis between Los Angeles and San Salvador*. Duke University Press.

8

Bridging the Curricular Divide: Open Educational Resources and the Digitization of Guatemala's National Basic Curriculum

Matthew Aruch, Felix Alvarado, Rachel Dyl, Shue-kei Joanna Mok, Katharine Summers, Kate Maloney Williams, and Michael Lisman

Introduction

In 2005, the Guatemalan Ministry of Education (MINEDUC) introduced the National Basic Curriculum (Currículo Nacional Base [CNB]). Responding to the previous decades of civil war, the CNB attempted to foster a more multicultural and inclusive education system by bringing culturally relevant and academically rigorous pedagogies to the forefront of the national strategy (Asturias de Barrios and Merida Arriano, 2007). While the CNB was a collaborative effort towards standards–based learning, financial and logistical challenges complicated its implementation in the classroom. In 2012, a Guatemalan living in the US,[1] recognizing the need for an accessible curriculum tool, developed cnbGuatemala.org (hereinafter 'cnbGuatemala'), a wiki[2] containing the full CNB, supplementary information, and hyperlinks to other open educational resources (OERs) that are aligned to elements of the CNB. The website, hosted by the Online Learning Initiative (OLI), is used by a broad network of public, private, and civil society actors, including schools, universities, governments, and nongovernmental organizations (NGOs). As cnbGuatemala has developed, the increase in site traffic demonstrates how individuals (for example, developers, supporters, and users) partners) and artifacts (for example, CNB and cnbGuatemala) drive the formation of global education networks and illuminate a set of global–local dynamics that include political and economic drivers and vested interests and actors in policy making and practice (see Chapter 2, this volume).

The chapter traces the history of cnbGuatemala from its ideation, design, and implementation across local, national, and transnational spaces (Bartlett and Vavrus, 2017). To understand the assemblages of actors involved, the chapter utilizes concepts from science and technology studies, and specifically Actor–Network Theory (ANT). In line with this perspective, we contend that, like public policy, technological artifacts are not neutral and only partially represent the intended form of their designers. Instead, technologies like cnbGuatemala become socially constructed as they are adopted, adapted, and utilized within the dynamics of actor networks (Bijker et al, 1987; Bijker, 2001; Latour, 2005). As Bartlett and Vavrus point out, 'ANT considers how, within networks, people and objects get invited, excluded and enrolled' and how they 'accept (at least temporarily) the interests and agenda as set by focal actors', in addition to how 'social acts curtail or facilitate future action' (2017, pp 45–46). In particular, the chapter utilizes the idea of four moments of translation (Callon et al, 2009; Rhodes, 2009) to demonstrate how the developer's and cnbGuatemala's networked relationships assemble, disassemble, and reassemble across translations of problematization, interessement, enrolment, and mobilization (see Figure 8.1). In problematization, an actor defines or frames a problem so that others recognize it as their own. Interessement represents the strategies used by actors to recruit and enrol allies in the 'problem'. Enrolment is the successful outcome of problematization and interessement, resulting in an expanded actor network. Finally, mobilization is the maintained commitment to the problematized cause of action (Rhodes, 2009). These four concepts of translations help readers to understand how networks are successfully assembled, expanded, or destabilized over time (Rhodes, 2009). These four concepts, together with the tenets of ANT mentioned earlier, have informed the analysis upon which this chapter is based, as well as the structure and presentation of findings in what follows, particularly in relation to the explanation of the factors that have influenced the emergence and influence of cnbGuatemala.

With this in mind, the chapter addresses the following research questions:

1) What social and technical factors led to the creation of cnbGuatemala?
2) Who uses cnbGuatemala and how are they using the platform for curriculum design, implementation, and interaction?
3) How does cnbGuatemala fit into a transnational network of education policy and practice at the local, national, and international levels?
4) Considering the COVID-19 pandemic, what are the potentials for OERs to transform regional and global educational landscapes more broadly?

Figure 8.1: cnbGuatemala's Actor Network

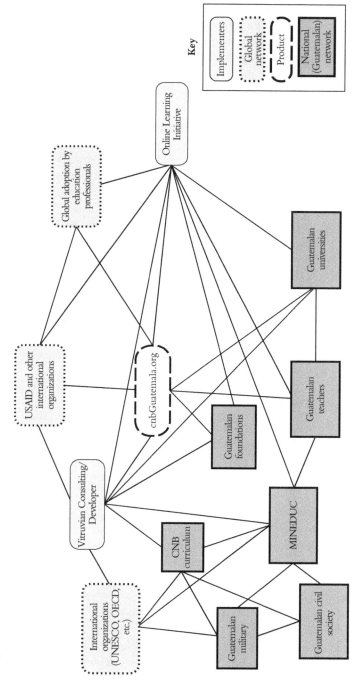

In answering these questions, the chapter seeks to provide a theoretically informed description of the evolution, usage, and influence of cnbGuatemala.

Our investigation relied on four data sources: historical documents, website traffic, user surveys, and focus groups. We reviewed 39 historical documents from the OLI archives between 2012 and 2014. The selected documents outline the origin and intent of the product design, as well as the later recruitment of various allies, including the MINEDUC, USAID, and Guatemalan universities and foundations (Callon et al, 2009). Additionally, we utilized Google Analytics to track and report website traffic, user locations, and specific page visits (Google, 2021), and analysed a 2020 OLI survey (n=320) of cnbGuatemala. Finally, we reviewed three focus groups conducted by OLI in January 2021.

This chapter first provides an overview of OERs. Next, the chapter briefly discusses the social, political, and historical context of K-12 education in Guatemala, focusing on the creation and dissemination of the curriculum. From there, it details the history of cnbGuatemala as initially designed, supported, and scaled up from 2012 to 2020 followed by an analysis on who uses cnbGuatemala today and how. This is followed by a discussion of cnbGuatemala's opportunities as a tool to facilitate dialogues and actions within Guatemala's educational spaces. The final sections then offer reflections on the ways that the socio-technical insights presented in previous sections (based on ANT) can be placed within the political economy of actor networks. In so doing, the findings of this chapter connect directly with the orienting framework of the present volume.[3]

Open educational resources

OERs constitute any medium of teaching, learning, or research materials (digital or otherwise) that 'reside in the public domain and have been released under an open license that permits no-cost access, use, adaptation, and distribution by others with no or limited restrictions' (UNESCO, 2020). Since the early 2000s, awareness and use of digital OERs have grown rapidly with approximately 1.4 billion licenses issued as of 2017 (Merkley, 2018).

This rise can partly be attributed to OERs' unique potential to improve access and usability in digital learning, particularly within education systems characterized by learning gaps and low resources. Many advocates argue that OERs have transformative features, such as enhanced interactivity and participation, adaptive assessment, and the ability to meet individualized learning needs (Choppin and Borys, 2017; Cronin, 2017).

While there are various types of OERs, wikis are hypertext systems designed for users to consult, link, and create web pages and restructure content (Leuf and Cunningham, 2001). This allows for multiple users to edit and contribute (synchronously and asynchronously), track content development, and manage different versions. In turn, wikis can support both capacity building and equitable knowledge distribution for teachers. Specifically, wikis challenge traditional conceptions of formal knowledge production by encouraging users to engage in the creation, interaction, and collaboration rather than establishing hierarchical or individual ownership and distribution (Duffy and Bruns, 2006; Parker and Chao, 2007). This promotes flexible online spaces and enhanced learner 'autonomy and reflective learning through … active participation and construction of meaning in the production of content … peer interaction and group work, [and] knowledge sharing and building' (Barajas and Frossard, 2018).

Background on Guatemalan education

Guatemala is an extremely ethnically, linguistically, culturally, and geographically diverse country. At times, this pluralism has created tension and conflict. From 1960–1996, civil war cost over 200,000 – mostly Indigenous – Guatemalans their lives (PBS, 2011). The war officially ended when the *Agreement on Firm and Lasting Peace* was signed by the government and the Guatemalan Revolutionary National Unity party in 1996 (United Nations, 1997). In the aftermath of the civil war, the MINEDUC – supported by national civil society actors (churches, NGOs), academic institutions, and military organizations – created the CNB. The social and technical processes of curriculum development was also supported by international organizations such as the Organisation for Economic Co-operation and Development (OECD), the United Nations Educational, Scientific and Cultural Organization (UNESCO), and the United States Agency for International Development (USAID) (United Nations, 1995; Asturias de Barrios and Merida Arriano, 2007; World Bank, 2007; Huerta, 2015; Edwards et al, 2020).

Supporters viewed the CNB and standards-based education reform as one vehicle for social transformation, recognizing the potential of education to support the peace accords (United Nations, 1995; Huerta, 2015). As stated in the CNB, 'the Education Reform emphasizes the ethnic, cultural, and linguistic context as an expression of national diversity that is recognized by the Constitution of the Republic (1985)' (CnbGuatemala, 2021). Beyond innovating through a competency-based design, planning, and assessment model, CNB stressed intercultural bilingual education, historical and sociological features on extant poverty and inequality, and encouraged local adaptation and implementation of curricular content.

Problematization and interessement

Once created, CNB dissemination presented several financial and logistical challenges. Initially, MINEDUC-sponsored teacher training provided teachers with hard copies of the curriculum; however, activities were interrupted due to financial constraints and shifting administrative priorities. One MINEDUC staff member recalled that in 2007, for '85,000 teachers, only 6,000 copies of the curriculum were printed' (OLI Focus Group 1, 2021). To compensate for the gap, MINEDUC shared (and continues to share) PDF versions of the curriculum on its website.[4] Another challenge is that the curriculum is divided into dozens of folders and zip files, complicating the navigation and downloading of materials. PDF formatting makes navigating documents difficult on smaller screens such as mobile phones. Moreover, PDFs are static and do not reflect real-time modifications to the curriculum. Finally, for those able to access the CNB, the curriculum provides little guidance on pedagogy, instruction, or curricular content to support teacher training, planning, or classroom implementation (Huerta, 2015).

In 2012, the developer (Felix Alvarado, coauthor of the present chapter) began taking important steps towards digitizing the CNB. Early website development included the following steps: securing a memorable web address (www.cnbGuatemala.org), financing web hosting, and transcribing texts, tables, and charts from the CNB, which was possible thanks to MINEDUC's open licensing policy regarding the CNB content (Vitruvian, 2013). Guatemalan educators quickly began using cnbGuatemala to access previously unavailable CNB resources. Within a year of its launch, website traffic had steadily increased. In June 2012, Google Analytics showed 369 visitors (43 returning). By August 2013, traffic increased to 7,896 unique visitors (1,621 returning) (see Figure 8.2).

With a growing user base, the developer sought to translate the problem to recruit and enrol political, financial, and technical allies from their networks at the MINEDUC, USAID, and Guatemalan universities and technical institutes.

MINEDUC as a natural ally for curriculum distribution

The developer regularly engaged MINEDUC during the development process. The developer used MINEDUC content to create cnbGuatemala and inquired about: (1) integrating cnbGuatemala into the MINEDUC website; and (2) leveraging ministry relationships with universities and technical institutes to support teacher training.

Specifically, between 2012 and 2013, the developer proposed transferring cnbGuatemala to MINEDUC to be further developed and maintained by university students in education. A ministry official graciously offered to help further search for institutional partners for cnbGuatemala.

Figure 8.2: cnbGuatemala visitors between April 2012 and December 2013

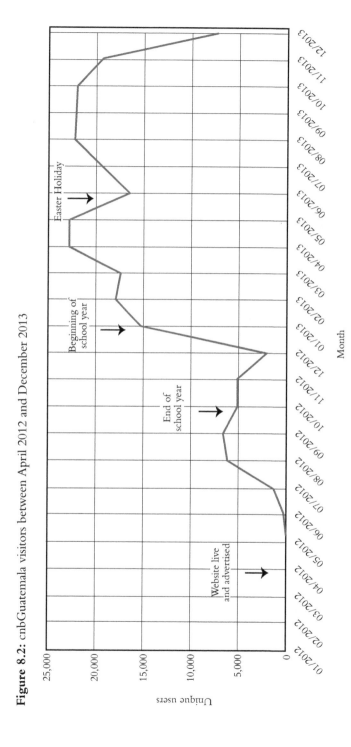

cnbGuatemala as a tool to disseminate USAID education priorities

The developer also contacted USAID about bolstering financial and technical support for cnbGuatemala. In 2013, an unsolicited proposal was sent to USAID with a rationale for financial and technical support. The proposal stated:

> Educators have demonstrated their interest in the online version ...
>
> To ensure sustainability, the resource needs to be consolidated ... More importantly, it needs to be integrated into the practices of a community of educators using it to provide quality education in classrooms and to be embedded in the Ministry of Education and other institutions in the education sector.
>
> The project proposed will contribute to USAID's commitment to education quality and access in Guatemala by tightening the relationship between materials and curriculum, providing a resource for effective teacher training and practice in classrooms, strengthening the link between the curriculum and bilingual education, alternative education, and assessment ... Given the large group of beneficiaries, I believe it presents a very reasonable investment for USAID. (Vitruvian, 2013)

USAID suggested a consultation with the Chief of Party for the USAID project 'Reforma Educativa en el Aula' ('Education Reform in the Classroom' [REAULA]) to develop a more comprehensive proposal, noting that:

> The emphasis of your proposal to increase the availability of the National Basic Curriculum in an open online platform is the starting point to provide useful tools for teachers to increase school performance. This is an area of acute need for the country and one that is being prioritized by USAID/Guatemala ... We certainly believe the tool you describe in your proposal can contribute to our objectives. (USAID Guatemala, 2013)

Based on this exchange, the USAID project implementer, Juarez and Associates, prepared a proposal supporting three areas:

a) to test the usability of the online CNB as a teacher- and school-level innovation;
b) to identify issues and options in creating a sustainable management for the online CNB; and
c) to identify options and means to incentivize teachers in the use of the online CNB (Vitruvian, 2013).

Between 2013 and 2014, USAID funded a set of consultants to analyse cnbGuatemala usage data, digitize content, develop technical solutions, test usability, and organize committee meetings to discuss, develop, and upload new content to cnbGuatemala. In addition, USAID funded uploading curriculum frameworks and content related to Intercultural Bilingual Education, early-grade reading comprehension, and other USAID-sponsored content.[5]

cnbGuatemala as a tool to support teacher education

Based on MINEDUC and USAID interest, in 2013, the developer solicited technical support from universities, viewing teacher training and technical institutes as an important part of the cnbGuatemala user community for the 'cultivation of an active user community' and 'a link with teacher training universities'. Specifically, the developer contacted Universidad Del Valle (UVG), Universidad InterNaciones, and Universidad del Istmo (UNIS) for support. A UVG administrator shared that they would 'involve the bachelor's degree students in Education'.[6]

In addition to Guatemalan universities, the developer contacted Fundación Sergio Paiz Andrade (FUNSEPA), a foundation committed to improving education through technology, outlining systemic teacher training and a team for technical support as important components for growth (FUNSEPA, 2021). Due to cnbGuatemala's assessment of the tightly coupled relationship between education and technology, FUNSEPA was viewed as 'an interesting and interested actor'.

FUNSEPA suggested other collaborators, including Campus TEC and the engineering faculty at UVG. UVG technology students participated in a programme that required 200 hours of internship work, and in 2014, a UVG student volunteer supported cnbGuatemala with a focus on '(1) the creation of one or more self-instruction tours for users, and (2) the creation of one or more forums for inexperienced users'.[7]

By January 2014, cnbGuatemala had obtained funding from USAID, acknowledgement and support from MINEDUC, Guatemalan universities, and foundations, and more than 400,000 unique website visitors per year. The initial actors within the CNB network had been translated, allied, recruited, enrolled, and mobilized (see Figure 8.1).

Network (de)stabilization and sustainability: creating the online learning initiative

From 2012 to 2015, cnbGuatemala's use continued to grow (see Table 8.1). However, the network of actors had begun to destabilize. In response, OLI[8] was set up in 2015 as a US-based nonprofit organization to support cnbGuatemala and other education technology initiatives for two reasons. First, USAID funding had ended, content on the site needed support,

Table 8.1: Number of visitors 2013–2020

Year (1 Jan–31 Dec)	Total unique visitors	Repeat visitors
2013	327,111	130,678
2014	405,008	233,365
2015	1,303,264	469,819
2016	1,654,663	616,263
2017	1,046,235	441,765
2018	1,320,420	586,070
2019	1,509,778	686,175
2020 *, **	2,920,348	1,230,451

Notes: * In March 2020, schools in many places around the world went virtual. ** As a comparison, as of 24 June 2021, the MINEDUC CNB website claims 1,650,821 total page views (not individual users and without a time range) to its curriculum page (MINEDUC, 2021).

Source: Google Analytics

and the 'friends of the curriculum' committee had been dissolved. Second, there were sustainability concerns. OLI's advisory board was convened partly because of the founders' concern about how to extricate themselves from the website's maintenance so it would not depend solely on them. In 2019 OLI replaced its board members and created several new initiatives to improve the product and better understand the profile of cnbGuatemala users and potential supporters (OLI, 2021b). In 2020, corresponding with the COVID-19 pandemic, there was a steady growth in web traffic, both inside and outside of Guatemala, as educators around the world sought resources for online distance learning and virtual support (OLI, 2021c).

In effect, the creation of OLI was an attempt to stabilize the network and reinitiate the processes of problematization and interessement to enrol additional allies to support the already-mobilized cadre of education professionals using the site across the world.

The mobilized network: who uses cnbGuatemala and how do they use it?

cnbGuatemala has a global user profile spanning more than 50 countries;[9] however, the website is mostly visited by users from Latin American countries. In addition to Guatemala (the top user location), Mexico, Colombia, Peru, and Ecuador round out the five countries with the most visitors (see Table 8.2). In 2020, the number of non-Guatemalan visitors increased from 25 per cent in 2019 to almost 40 per cent of total users.

cnbGuatemala saw a 182.22 per cent average increase between January–
October 2019 and January–October 2020 among top user countries (see
Table 8.2). Visitors from Mexico, Peru, Colombia, and Ecuador increased by
more than 150 per cent during that period. On the other hand, Guatemala
had a more modest increase of 55.33 per cent during the same period. Many
Guatemalans were already using the site prior to the pandemic, resulting
in a smaller rate of increase. At the same time, website data indicate the
growing importance of OERs, particularly curated Spanish-language OERs.
Such dramatic growth in non-Guatemalan users may indicate a growing
need for similar resources aligned to other countries' curricula and the use
of cnbGuatemala as a potential model for scale-up or replication in other
national contexts.

Analysed data from Google Analytics also highlighted how cnbGuatemala
was used as reference material or a quick stop for curriculum and content
across countries. Users did not browse often, but instead visited the site to
retrieve intended content. On average, 2.45 pages were visited per session.
The average duration for each user's visit to cnbGuatemala lasted 3.36
minutes and 4.39 minutes for Guatemalan users.

Content preferences also differed between Guatemalan and non-
Guatemalan users. To understand users' behaviours and identify popular

Table 8.2: Comparison of the 2019–2020 user base and the number of teachers
in the top five user countries

Country	All users 2020* (2019)	Percentage change (all users)	New users 2020 (2019)	Returning users 2020 (2019)	Number of teachers in the countries**
Guatemala	774,230 (498,449)	+55.3278	739,481 (299,443)	285,447 (128,513)	214,655
Mexico	248,415 (75,889)	+227.34	244,665 (52,516)	26,357 (5,915)	827,444
Colombia	104,017 (38,595)	+169.509	101,584 (24,912)	10,780 (2,562)	419,077
Peru	75,886 (27,676)	+173.941	76,297 (23,570)	7,311 (2,255)	309,338
Ecuador	39,757 (13,418)	+196.296	39,712 (10,344)	4,109 (852)	204,420
Total	1,242,305 (654,027)	+182.22			

Notes: * Between 1 January and 31 October 2020. ** From UNESCO Institute of Statistics
(2021). We do not account for people accessing on multiple devices (that is, computers and
mobile phones), which might explain the discrepancy in numbers vs. documented teachers.
Source: Google Analytics

content among Guatemalan and non-Guatemalan users, we investigated the top five landing pages for Guatemalan and other top-five country users (see Table 8.3).

Guatemalan users landed on pages aligned with CNB curriculum requirements. The most popular pages are curriculum frameworks, especially the *Basic Education*[10] *Curriculum Frameworks by Grade and Area*. This page is a catalogue which allows users to quickly find CNB curriculum content for low secondary levels, organized by subject area and grade. Users select the title of each area to see its detailed description and click the title of each grade to see the respective skills tables. The second most popular page in Guatemala is the cnbGuatemala homepage

Table 8.3: Top five landing pages for Guatemalan and non-Guatemalan visitors

Rank	Guatemala	Non-Guatemalan
1	Basic Education Curriculum Frameworks by Grade and Area (/wiki/Mallas_Curriculares_por_Área_y_Grado_-_Básico)	Reading comprehension strategies: identify or constructing the main idea (/wiki/Enseñanza_de_la_comprensión_lectora/Fichas_de_estrategias_de_comprensión_lectora/Identificar_o_construir_la_idea_principal)
2	Welcome to the CNB tour (/index.php?title=Bienvenidos_al_Currículum_Nacional_Baseandtour=inicio)	Graphic information organizers: Cognitive Map Mapa (sun shape) (/wiki/Inventario_de_organizadores_de_información/Mapa_cognitivo_tipo_sol)
3	CNB Basic Education Cycle (/wiki/CNB_Ciclo_Básic)	Reading comprehension strategies: differentiating between facts, opinions, and points of view (/wiki/Enseñanza_de_la_comprensión_lectora/Fichas_de_estrategias_de_comprensión_lectora/Diferenciar_hechos,_opiniones_y_puntos_de_vista_en_los_textos_leídos)
4	Primary Education Curriculum Frameworks by Area and Grade (Frameworks/wiki/Mallas_Curriculares_por_Área_y_Grado_-_Primaria)	Third grade: identifying similarities and differences (/wiki/Diferencias_y_similitudes_-_Tercer_grado/Identificar_diferencias_y_similitudes)
5	Landing page and Index (/index.php)*	Reading comprehension: finding the theme in the text (wiki/Enseñanza_de_la_comprensión_lectora/Fichas_de_estrategias_de_comprensión_lectora/Encontrar_el_tema_del_texto)

Note: * In the Guatemalan case, the index (homepage) came up as two separate instances, which ranked second and fifth respectively.

Source: Google Analytics

or 'index'. The index explains how to navigate the digital version of the curriculum. Apart from standardized content, such as the actual curricula and benchmarks, users can also click links to access more dynamic sections of the website, including 'Recent Publications' and 'The Latest', which provide a pool of teaching support materials. The homepage also features a search tool to facilitate website inquiry. The third most popular landing page was 'CNB Ciclo Básico', which allows users to quickly navigate through three aspects of the CNB curriculum: (1) curriculum reform and transformation; (2) a description of subject areas for lower secondary; and (3) methodological guidelines and evaluation elements. In short, Guatemalan users tended to use cnbGuatemala as a digital curriculum catalogue to supplement their needs within the framework of the official CNB curriculum.

In contrast, non-Guatemalan users tended to seek out tools for classroom implementation.[11] Users most often landed on reading comprehension or graphic organizers – the most popular page was entitled 'Identifying or Constructing the Main Idea'. Similarly, the second most popular landing page among non-Guatemalan users in 2020 was the 'cognitive map' page, which is shaped like the sun. The map serves as a guide for teachers to plan specific activities to enhance in-depth learning. The other three most frequent landing sites were also pages that supported reading comprehension, such as how to 'Differentiate Facts, Opinions and Points of View in Reading Texts', and 'Finding the Subject of the Text'. Overall, non-Guatemalan users gravitated towards their preferred curriculum content, some of which was created by USAID to support its early-grade reading initiatives.

The OLI user survey of Guatemalan education professionals

OLI conducted a survey of 320 cnbGuatemala users between 30 November and 3 December 2020 to capture more detailed demographic and user information for a subset of Guatemalan users. Of the respondents, 315 (98.4 per cent) were from Guatemala and represented a wide range of demographic categories, including in relation to education sector, grade level, areas of instruction, and years of teaching experience.

The survey results suggest that within Guatemala, the website was used across a broad spectrum of education professionals, grade levels, and curriculum areas. Notably, teachers of all levels of experience, from novice (less than five years) to extremely experienced (20+ years), used cnbGuatemala. However, there were areas of overrepresentation worthy of further analysis. For example, about 54 per cent (n =173) of participants noted some affiliation with the private sector. Similarly, while pre-primary and primary school teachers made up about 54 per cent of respondents (n= 174), both public schools and primary schools were underrepresented in the sample. One possibility was that private school and secondary school teachers in Guatemala, located in more resource-rich and urban areas, had easier access to cnbGuatemala and the survey itself.

The survey also provided useful data on the duration, frequency, and purpose of engagement with cnbGuatemala (see Table 8.4). Results indicated that the website user base has steadily increased. A total of 251 (78.4 per cent) respondents consulted the website at least once a month and 148 (46.3 per cent) respondents used it at least once a week for activities such as lesson planning or locating educational resources. Among frequent users (those who used cnbGuatemala at least once per week, n=148), 135 (91.2 per cent) identified 'class planning' as one of their primary reasons

Table 8.4: History, frequency, and purpose of using cnbGuatemala

Variable	Total (%)*
History of cnbGuatemala use	
Since 2012	93 (29.1)
Since 2013/2014	37 (11.6)
Since 2015/2016	60 (18.8)
Since 2017/2018	58 (18.1)
Since 2019/2020	72 (22.5)
Frequency of use	
Several times a week or once a day	52 (16.3)
At least once a week	96 (30)
At least once a month	103 (32.1)
Less than once a month	35 (10.9)
First time	34 (10.6)
Purpose of use	
Plan classes + find educational resources, and/or more	159 (49.7)
Plan classes	77 (24.1)
Find educational resources, and/or more	32 (10)
Train myself as a teacher, and/or more	12 (3.8)
Research	10 (3.1)
Design policies	2 (0.6)
Consult when you do not have the printed version at hand	1 (0.3)

Note: * n=320.

Source: OLI user survey (2021)

for using the site. Other main reasons identified were 'finding educational resources' and 'training as a teacher'. These results supported previously indicated and discussed trends from Google Analytics data, chiefly that Guatemalan teachers were using the wiki to consult and retrieve the curriculum for extra professional support. On the other hand, there was no survey evidence that users were creating or adding curricular content to cnbGuatemala.

Understanding users: 2021 OLI focus groups

Three OLI focus groups further illuminated the diversity of ways in which cnbGuatemala was utilized or underutilized by visitors. In January 2021, OLI conducted focus groups with: (1) a group of private school teachers and administrators (n=7); (2) MINEDUC officials (n=2); and (3) a set of teachers who participated in a cnbGuatemala workshop (n=8). Of the 17 participants, two were unfamiliar with and had not visited or used the website. Focus group discussions both confirmed and revealed gaps in the user base.

Many focus group participants shared a common, positive sentiment towards cnbGuatemala and its improved accessibility of the CNB. One participant expressed that navigating cnbGuatemala was much easier than the original CNB PDFs due to the separate sections on the site. Users also confirmed frequently revisiting the same pages to locate information and content of interest to use in the classroom. However, some participants noted discomfort in navigating the website beyond the known and familiar content areas (Focus Groups 1 and 3). Similarly, a MINEDUC participant (Focus Group 2) noted that many teachers were not equipped with the knowledge or training to navigate a tool like cnbGuatemala. Echoing MINEDUC, one teacher from Focus Group 3 noted that 'many teachers are fearful when looking for resources online. Because they are very "traditional" and do not know virtual tools'. The same teacher expressed privacy concerns among teachers regarding the sharing of online tools – for instance, '[once you] enter your data on a site, then they can extort money from you'. These responses revealed the need for support, guidance, and transparency to motivate users to explore and utilize all resources available within cnbGuatemala.

More practically, focus group participants shared two internet-related issues, illustrating the limitations of OERs. Participants from Focus Groups 1 and 3 noted that pages often loaded slowly or not at all because of disparities in internet access. On the other hand, participants discussed how cnbGuatemala made the curriculum more accessible for mobile users. For example, a participant from Focus Group 1 mentioned a WhatsApp[12] group of teachers that circulated cnbGuatemala resources.

Analysis: opportunities and limits of OERs

OERs,[13] such as cnbGuatemala, present noteworthy and low-cost opportunities for developing impactful global networks of education designers, practitioners, and policy makers. However, OERs are not a panacea – they are constrained by social (economic and political), technical, and environmental factors. The following text gives a description and discussion of four limitations and opportunities for OERs, both in general and for cnbGuatemala in particular.

Limit: OERs do not address systemic issues

OERs may reduce systemic inequalities within the education sector; however, they cannot fully eliminate them. In Guatemala, for example, indigenous students are particularly vulnerable to inequalities in access to resources and quality teachers in addition to historic marginalization (Hale, 2002, 2007). This has resulted in lower indigenous student performance. Only about 14 per cent of indigenous students reach national standards compared to 30 per cent of non-indigenous students (Amies, 2021). Similarly, on average, educational attainment for indigenous peoples is less than five years, with less than two years of education for indigenous women (Amies, 2021). The Guatemala Literacy Project (2023) found that 'for 10 children in Guatemala, only four will make it to middle school, and only two will complete high school'. cnbGuatemala can provide access to the curriculum and materials; however, it does not address disparities in resource allocation, teacher quality, and geographical location.

Opportunity: OERs reconfigure access, usability, and engagement

cnbGuatemala reorients access, usability, and engagement with CNB. If CNB in the original PDF or hard copy version is passive, the data presented in Table 8.5 revealed how cnbGuatemala facilitates active and dynamic exchanges of ideas and information around the curriculum.

Limit: OERs do not address inequities in infrastructure

OERs depend on necessary investments in connectivity and infrastructure to bridge the digital divide. cnbGuatemala users are concentrated in urban areas and the preliminary data indicate it is used more prevalently among better-resourced secondary and private school educators. It is estimated that 30 per cent of Guatemalans have access to the internet and that 21 per cent have a computer (Amies, 2021). These figures are likely to be much lower among marginalized (poor, rural, and indigenous) communities due to political, economic, geographical, and technical constraints. Despite its

Table 8.5: Comparison of CNB in hard copy or PDF and cnbGuatemala online

Access	• Users can download or print the curriculum and other documents from the ministry website (URL), but must first locate them in different pages and can search for content within each document.	• Users can navigate cnbGuatemala and visit page(s) with desired content, all in a single location.
Usability	• PDFs are text searchable. • PDFs are static documents (not updated with most recent changes). • PDFs do not include resources or materials.	• cnbGuatemala is text searchable and organized by different curriculum modules or resources. • cnbGuatemala can be periodically updated with both partial and full changes to the curriculum. • Useful OERs are hyperlinked to the curriculum content for aligned resources. • Access to content beyond the CNB curriculum.
Communication and content creation	• Content is deliberated and created amongst multiple selected, but limited local, national, and international stakeholders by MINEDUC. • Questions about curricular content are directed through a ministry email.	• With a user profile, any cnbGuatemala visitor can add or modify existing content to relevant resources or materials. • Communication is mediated through a cnbGuatemala administrator, but users can communicate directly with each other too. • Suggested content can be added by local (for example, teachers), national (for example, ministry), and international (for example, USAID) actors.

Source: Author

open-access nature, it is possible that cnbGuatemala may amplify existing educational and infrastructural inequities (Toyama, 2011).

Opportunity: OERs as a 'just in time' toolkit for 'the last mile' of instruction

cnbGuatemala is an important digital resource for teachers who do not have easy access to the CNB hard copy, PDF files, or education resources more broadly (both inside and outside of Guatemala). In practice, teachers need to plan out their daily activities aligned with curricular learning objectives. In this sense, cnbGuatemala is a useful and uniquely curated database of instructional resources for immediate planning and classroom usage. Assuming that the technology and resources are in place, OERs have the potential to reach even the most geographically challenging school facilities. Moreover, the digitized OERs are vetted for quality and relevance, thus helping to bridge the gap between research and practice – a particular imperative at the earlier grade levels and in contexts of poverty. The experience of cnbGuatemala illustrates the potential for relatively low-cost OERs to dramatically and immediately expand access to key tools in education reform and link the curriculum to improved classroom practices.

Limit: knowledge and technological barriers

OER effectiveness is limited by technical expertise. To fully utilize OERs such as cnbGuatemala, users must have: (1) awareness of the site or resource; (2) basic skills in web browsing and wiki site navigation; and (3) an understanding of the structure of curricular content such as CNB. OLI focus group data revealed that a significant subset of cnbGuatemala users were intimidated by the website, choosing to use Google rather than search and/or navigate through the website pages.[14] In addition, there are privacy concerns related to web browsing. Although cnbGuatemala can be used anonymously, focus group participants expressed fears related to the use of personal data and browsing histories.

Opportunity: OERs like Wikipedia are user-friendly and familiar

For many internet users, Wikipedia is a well-known web platform. In this respect, OERs like cnbGuatemala have a familiar design. Through a Google search, the navigation pane, or the search tools within cnbGuatemala, users can navigate to and retrieve information. Focus group participants revealed that despite the identified challenges, the cnbGuatemala site was a tremendous improvement from the cumbersome file folders of MINEDUC. In addition, software updates are simple and inexpensive when integrated with reliable third-party technology. Finally, OLI seeks additional financial or technical support, the familiarity of Wikipedia makes the website easily explainable to donors, contributors, or other parties interested in supporting or participating in the network.

Limit: Wiki users are not necessarily content creators

OERs like cnbGuatemala are designed to be democratic; however, the experience of Wikipedia, the most well-known wiki site, reveals that it is difficult to create a community of content creators. Even with its millions of visitors, a 2017 study found that 1 per cent of Wikipedia users are responsible for 80 per cent of the created content (Matei and Britt, 2017). Most users visit wiki, like cnbGuatemala, to access information rather than to add content. Initially, cnbGuatemala's developer sought a USAID-funded 'friends of the curriculum' committee composed of teachers and MINEDUC officials to dialogue and support content creation. However, this community never took shape and website content is still driven by the developer, OLI, and external actors such as USAID. Accordingly, cnbGuatemala's experience further illustrates the difficulties of developing an active community of content creators.

Opportunity: OERs can create transnational networks of collaboration

While users may not be active content creators, cnbGuatemala did create a common yet fluid understanding among transnational private voluntary initiatives, the public sector, and international aid organizations regarding how to improve education resources (Alvarado, 2015). cnbGuatemala facilitated a useful network of educators committed to building teacher capacity, resource exchange, and feedback loops for curriculum designers and planners. These networks exist within local WhatsApp groups, national policy discussions around curriculum frameworks, and international organizations that bring together diverse actor groups.

Discussion: cnbGuatemala and the political economy of actor networks

The history and usage of cnbGuatemala illustrates that the website is a socially constructed actor network. Its design and use continue to be influenced by a myriad of local, national, and international actors across three dimensions: (1) sociotechnical assemblages; (2) translated vested interests; and (3) network expansion through ongoing tensions and resolutions.

Sociotechnical assemblages of education intervention

The cnbGuatemala case illustrates the challenges of separating global, national, and local educational sociotechnical actor networks. CNB was created in response to decades of civil strife in Guatemala and with the support of international organizations. One member of the Guatemalan diaspora initially created a relatively simple website as a service to their country in response to financial, technical, and administrative constraints. Later, the developer and cnbGuatemala became the catalyst for an actor network where curricular content intersected with the social, political, and intellectual domains of teachers, ministries of education, and aid organizations.

The technical aspect of cnbGuatemala presents another layer of global–local interactions. Mediawiki (the software) was devised in the Global North as a tool for a generative encyclopaedia (Wikipedia). However, the software has now expanded to a variety of applications, including the Guatemalan curriculum. The software is free and open-source with the expressed intent of democratizing access to information. In this case, software from the Global North was adopted and adapted for use in the Global South by someone from the Global South living in the Global North.

Translating vested interests into policy making and enactment

In this chapter, we have detailed the complex navigation of the actor network as it was translated through the processes of problematization, interessement, enrolment, and mobilization. In particular, the developer was able to translate cnbGuatemala into a meaningful area of support and mobilization for diverse stakeholder groups.

As it pertains to the MINEDUC, cnbGuatemala was framed as a tool to disseminate the required curricular content more easily, as well as a platform to bridge government and academic stakeholders through content creation. MINEDUC engagement with cnbGuatemala was (and still is) highly dependent upon the interests and engagement of specific ministry personnel, which may vary for several reasons.[15] With regard to USAID, cnbGuatemala was carefully framed as a platform to meet USAID's strategic goals for early reading comprehension and Intercultural Bilingual Education. USAID helped to fund and create additional content and resources that contributed to its strategic objectives.

Website visitors, mostly teachers and administrators, needed a tool to access curriculum and resources aligned with their professional responsibilities. For Guatemalan users, cnbGuatemala was a platform to access the curriculum and other content, solicit answers regarding MINEDUC policies, or request content of interest. Visitors from outside Guatemala mostly used the site to retrieve specific content-area materials.

Expanding the network through the ongoing resolution of tensions

The preceding sections have traced the creation and stabilization of the cnbGuatemala actor network, primarily within the Guatemalan context, but also across the broader regional and global social arenas. From a sustainability perspective, the creation of OLI in 2015 shifted responsibility for the site from the developer to a board of experts responsible for guiding its growth and development with existing and future partners.

More practically, the network's strength comes from a mobilized and growing cohort of teachers using the site to resolve issues related to access and usability of the CNB, including access to content that might otherwise be difficult to obtain in any other format. In particular, the use of the curriculum is considered compulsory by MINEDUC for teachers in planning and assessment, and is also referenced in supervisory activities. However, in practice, the MINEDUC has difficulty ensuring that teachers are applying the CNB and/or know how to translate its content into effective teaching. The website is directly involved with these tensions of curriculum access, engagement, and availability. Thus, while cnbGuatemala may be neutral in its intent to present and distribute CNB and aligned OERs, the website is one artifact within a sociotechnical network responsible for education policy and practice in Guatemala (see Figure 8.1). cnbGuatemala operates within the same political and economic frameworks that define the implementers' decisions (and possibilities) about what OERs are included or adopted.

At the same time, this mobilized network of educators continues to expand beyond Guatemala. In March 2020, COVID-19 pushed cnbGuatemala into the global education arena. As schools around the world paused in-person learning, teachers scrambled to locate resources. In particular, the COVID-19 pandemic illuminates the potential for OERs like cnbGuatemala to expand beyond their original intent. COVID-19 created the conditions that drove regional educators to the webpage. The pandemic created a global, virtual ecosystem of educators – cnbGuatemala was uniquely positioned to capture and support these users. Our data indicate that many teachers in Latin America found their ways to cnbGuatemala in search of support for their virtual teaching. The shift to online learning suggests that OERs may become increasingly important as virtual learning and remote learning become mainstream.

Conclusion

Guatemala's CNB was a remarkable achievement in the aftermath of decades of civil conflict. The curriculum attempted to leverage education policy to promote reconciliation across a multi-ethnic and multicultural populace. Resource constraints hindered the process of delivering physical copies of the curriculum to all relevant social groups. cnbGuatemala, a wiki site containing both content and links to relevant OERs, democratized digital access and engagement with CNB. In its development, cnbGuatemala received support from Guatemalan teachers, universities, foundations, MINEDUC, and USAID, among others. This chapter has traced the history and trajectory of cnbGuatemala's transnational actor network. In addition, it has articulated an initial exploration of cnbGuatemala user data, suggesting that the website serves as a valuable 'grab-and-go' resource in Guatemala as well as Latin America more broadly.

Though the data may not include a representative sample, we offer ideas for a more comprehensive qualitative and quantitative analysis of OERs like cnbGuatemala and their regional usage in education policy and practice. Cross-national user behaviour is one area for further investigation which already demonstrates the potential for cnbGuatemala as a model in other national contexts. Furthermore, cnbGuatemala usage for teachers outside of Guatemala expanded considerably during the COVID-19 pandemic, illuminating the potential role of OERs in future emergencies and crises when schools may need to pause in-person instruction. Overall, the data indicate that cnbGuatemala has the potential for scale or replication in other national contexts.

The preceding discussion contributes to ongoing national (Guatemala), regional (Latin America), and global conversations about the potential of OERs to create effective research-policy-practice networks. With minimal social and technical infrastructure, even in resource-constrained environments, OERs are one means to improve the availability of educational resources. This chapter marks an important step in thinking about how global and local forces converge around OERs, and how sociotechnical systems can bridge the curriculum divide to facilitate dialogue, improve access, and provide relevant learning resources across the education landscape.

Notes

[1] Felix Alvarado developed the website. We use the term 'developer' throughout the chapter.

[2] The website runs on mediawiki, a free open-source software platform created so that users can 'collect and organize knowledge and make it available to people' (Mediawiki. org, 2021).

[3] It is acknowledged that there are tensions between the ontological foundations of ANT, on the one hand, and political economy perspectives, on the other hand (for example, relating to how space and causality are conceptualized). However, the stance taken here is that the relations highlighted by ANT (which assumes a flat ontology) can be placed within and analyzed in relation to the dominant political-economic structures that shape education reform.

[4] See https://www.mineduc.gob.gt/DIGECUR/?p=CNB.asp

[5] USAID content became some of the most downloaded, particularly for non-Guatemalan users.

[6] From email correspondence between developer and UVG administrator

[7] From 2014 documents from a UVG student, obtained from an OLI email archive

[8] OLI is committed to using OERs to 'bridge the link between curriculum, planning, and effective teaching and learning practice' (OLI, 2021a).

[9] For a dynamic view of cnbGuatemala's user profile, see https://online-learning-initiat ive.org/the-online-curriculum/

[10] Basic education corresponds to lower secondary education.

[11] While Table 8.3 indicates that Guatemalan and non-Guatemalan users utilize cnbGuatemala differently, it should be noted that Guatemala users consult pedagogical and content-related

pages to access classroom tools in large numbers, but visit the curriculum-related resources more frequently.

[12] WhatsApp is an internet messaging service typically utilized via mobile phones.

[13] Technically, OERs are inclusive of any freely accessible, open licensed instructional materials. However, they increasingly consist of digital resources that allow users to more readily edit, remix, and disseminate content. Our discussion of OERs specifically refers to the digital OERs that account for most of the current practice.

[14] Although this is not discussed here, analytics indicate that the search feature of the landing page is an underutilized feature, indicating that users prefer a generalized Google search or are unsure how to best navigate the page.

[15] While further investigation is required, there is some evidence of tension within the MINEDUC regarding the curriculum, and cnbGuatemala can get caught in the middle. As the developer shared, 'the tool/platform is confused with the content, when indeed it is relatively agnostic: anybody could put content on the website, but only some do'.

References

Alvarado, F. (2015). Enhancing access and use of the Guatemala national basic curriculum through online resources. Conference session, 2015 Comparative International Education Society Conference, Washington DC. https://convention2.allacademic.com/one/cies/cies15/index.php?progra m_focus=view_session&selected_session_id=988437&cmd=online_prog ram_direct_link&sub_action=online_program

Amies, C. (2021). The impact of the COVID-19 pandemic on indigenous children in Guatemala. *Human Rights Pulse*, 17 March. https://www.human rightspulse.com/mastercontentblog/the-impact-of-the-covid-19-pande mic-on-Indigenous-children-in-guatemala-chloe-amies

Asturias de Barrios, L., and Mérida Arellano, V. (2007). The process of developing a new curriculum for lower secondary education in Guatemala. *Prospects*, 37(2), 249–266. https://link.springer.com/content/pdf/10.1007/ s11125-007-9030-1.pdf

Barajas, M., and Frossard, F. (2018). Mapping creative pedagogies in open wiki learning environments. *Information and Educational Technologies*, 23, 1403–1419.

Bartlett, L., and Vavrus, F. (2017). *Rethinking Case Study Research: A Comparative Approach*. Routledge.

Bijker, W. E. (2001). Understanding technological culture through a constructivist view of science, technology, and society. In S. H. Cutcliffe and C. Mitcham (eds.), *Visions of STS: Counterpoints in Science, Technology, and Society*. MIT Press.

Bijker, W. E., Hughes, T. P., and Pinch, T. (1987). *The Social Construction of Technological Systems: New Directions in the Sociology and History of Technology*. MIT Press.

Callon, M., Lascoumes, P., and Barthe, Y. (2009). *Acting in an Uncertain World: An Essay on Technical Democracy*. MIT Press.

Choppin, J., and Borys, Z. (2017). Trends in the design, development, and use of digital curriculum materials. *ZDM Mathematics Education*, 49, 663–674.

cnbGuatemala. (2021). Hacía la Reforma Educativa. https://cnbguatemala.org/wiki/Hacia_la_Reforma_Educativa

Cronin, C. (2017). Openness and praxis: exploring the use of open educational practices in higher education. *International Review of Research in Open and Distributed Learning*, 18(5). http://dx.doi.org/10.19173/irrodl.v18i5.3096

Duffy, P., and Bruns, A. (2006). The use of blogs, wikis, and RSS in education: a conversation of possibilities. In *Learning on the Move: Proceedings of the Online Learning and Teaching Conference 2006* (pp 31–38). Queensland University of Technology.

Edwards Jr., D. B., Morrison, J., and Hall, S. (2020). The suspect statistics of best practices: a triple critique of knowledge production and mobilization in the global education policy field. *Globalsation, Societies and Education*, 18(2), 125–148.

FUNSEPA (2021). https://www.funsepa.org/

Google (2021). *Google Analytics.* https://analytics.withgoogle.com/

Guatemala Literacy Project (2023, September 15). *The Textbook Project.* https://www.guatemalaliteracy.org/the-project/textbooks/

Guatemalan Ministry of Education (MINEDUC). (2021). *Dirección General del currículo.* http://www.mineduc.gob.gt/DIGECUR/?p=CNB.aspandt=Curriculo_Nacional_Base_CNB

Hale, C. R. (2002). Does multiculturalism menace? Governance, cultural rights and the politics of identity in Guatemala. *Journal of Latin American Studies*, 34(3), 485–524. https://doi.org/10.1017/S0022216X02006521

Hale, C. R. (2007). *Más que un Indio: ambivalencia racial y multiculturalismo neoliberal en Guatemala.* Associación para el Avance de las Ciencias Sociales en Guatemala.

Huerta, L. C. (2015). *PISA for Development Capacity Building Plan: Guatemala.* OECD. https://www.oecd.org/pisa/aboutpisa/Guatemala%20CBP%20report_FINAL2.pdf

Latour, B. (2005). Reassembling the Social: An Introduction to Actor-Network-Theory. New York: Oxford University Press.

Leuf, B., and Cunningham, W. (2001). *The Wiki Way: Quick Collaboration on the Web.* Addison-Wesley.

Matei, S. A., and Britt, B. (2017). *Social Differentiation in Social Media: Adhocracy, Entropy, and the 1% Effect.* Springer Nature.

Mediawiki.org (2021). MediaWiki is a collaboration and documentation platform brought to you by a vibrant community. https://www.mediawiki.org/wiki/MediaWik

Merkley, R. (2018, May 8). A transformative year: state of the commons 2017. https://creativecommons.org/2018/05/08/state-of-the-comm ons-2017/

Online Learning Initiative (2021a). Online Learning Initiative. http://onl ine-learning-initiative.org/

Online Learning Initiative (2021b). Our work. https://online-learning-ini tiative.org/our-work/

Online Learning Initiative (2021c). The online curriculum by the numbers. https://online-learning-initiative.org/the-online-curriculum/

Parker, K., and Chao, J. (2007). Wiki as a teaching tool. *Interdisciplinary Journal of e-learning and Learning Objectsi*, 3(1), 57–72.

Public Broadcasting Service (PBS) (2011). Timeline: Guatemala's brutal civil war. *PBS News Hour*, 7 March. https://www.pbs.org/newshour/hea lth/latin_america-jan-june11-timeline_03-07

Rhodes, J. (2009). Using Actor Network Theory to trace an ICT (Telecenter) implementation trajectory in an African Women's micro-enterprise development organization. *Journal of Information Technologies and International Development*, 5(3), 1–20.

Toyama, K. (2011). Technology as amplifier in international development. Conference proceedings, 2011 iConference, Seattle.

UNESCO (2020). Open education resources. https://en.unesco.org/the mes/building-knowledge-societies/oer

UNESCO Institute of Statistics. (2021). Guatemala. http://uis.unesco.org/ en/country/gt

United Nations General Assembly Security Council (1997). *The Situation in Central America: Procedures for the Establishment of a Firm and Lasting Peace and Progress in Fashioning a Region of Peace, Freedom, Democracy and Development*. UN Peacemaker. https://peacemaker.un.org/guatemala-fir mlastingpeace96

United Nations Security Council (1995). *Agreement on Identity and Rights of Indigenous People*. UN Peacemaker. https://peacemaker.un.org/guatem ala-identityIndigenouspeoples95

USAID Guatemala (2013). *Response to Proposal*. OLI Archive.

Vitruvian Consulting (2013). *Expanding Access and Use of the Online Version of the Guatemala National Basic Curriculum*. Unsolicited proposal to USAID. OLI Archive.

World Bank (2007). *Guatemala: Education Quality and Secondary Education*. http://documents1.worldbank.org/curated/en/679221468039872822/ pdf/IPP1801GT0report1Annex0100August070006.pdf

9

Balancing Global Education Policy and Inclusive Education in Costa Rica: Capitalist Pressures, Social-Democratic Tendencies, and Technological Responses

Vanessa Pietras

Introduction

This chapter explores the impacts of global forces (such as international political–economic trends) on education and highlights the specific case of Costa Rica, where technology companies with capitalist motives were able to influence the country's education system. It also describes local efforts in Costa Rica to address or mitigate the effects of these global forces by establishing a new educational reform. Specifically, it presents how Costa Rica's political apparatus addressed the needs of the global economy while also attempting to increase educational equity. To this end, I highlight how the specific Tecno@prender programme, referred to in Costa Rica as the Programa Nacional de Tecnologias Móviles (National Programme of Mobile Technologies), was an example of inclusive education that was caught between global and local pressures.

By examining these issues, this chapter highlights various tensions during and since 2011 that Costa Rica has experienced due to global and local interactions in and through the making and implementation of its national education reform. The first tension, as will be discussed later on, resulted from the Public Education Ministry (Ministerio de Educación Publica [MEP]) actively ensuring that economic and political forces acted together to contribute to the country's education reform. The second tension resulted from the MEP attempting to address challenges in implementation to ensure reform efforts offered equitable opportunities. The tensions experienced by Costa Rica are not unique to this country and thus can help to shed light on the challenges faced by other countries in the region (and beyond) when it comes to developing and putting into practice policies that simultaneously respond to reform pressures with conflicting purposes (for example, economic growth vs. equity/inclusion).

To explain the role of multinational corporations and international standards in education reform and its impact in Costa Rica, this chapter is divided into five sections. In the first section, I present some initial background information by characterizing the immediate policy context. In the second section, I briefly comment on the theoretical approach around which this chapter is based. Then, in the third section, I provide an overview of Costa Rican public policy towards education to explain Costa Rica's relationship with both capitalist and social-democratic interests. In the fourth section, I describe the education reform effort in Costa Rica and introduce the concepts new to the country's national curriculum, such as digital technologies for the 21st century and planetary citizenship. In the fifth section, I mention the methodological basis for the insights subsequently shared about the Tecno@prender programme in the sixth section. Based on interviews with education specialists across the country, I explain how the Tecno@prender programme has sought to overcome obstacles presented by globalization. In the final two sections, I reflect on the case of Tecno@prender and offer concluding thoughts.

Immediate policy context

Costa Rica as well as other Central American countries suffer from social and economic inequalities due to the effects of globalization. Education, and more specifically access to education, is known to reduce social and economic inequalities and to increase human development. From this perspective, Costa Rica needed a global education programme to compete internationally, but it also sought an inclusive education programme to reduce structural (socioeconomic) inequalities within the country.

In 2015, global capitalist entities pressured the Costa Rican government to introduce a technology-focused curriculum (including access to state-of-the-art technology) in the education system. The country aimed to enhance the national curriculum and expand components related to technology to meet the needs of multinational corporations. The MEP was under extreme pressure to implement education reform that would satisfy these global economic forces operating inside Costa Rica. However, this new dynamic needed to be contextualized within local education programmes to avoid exacerbating inequalities in the education system – for instance, inequalities related to unequal access to technology that stem from the fact that some students could not afford to purchase a computer. Furthermore, the MEP needed to balance the needs of the population with those of the companies investing in the country.

In response, Costa Rica presented an innovate model of education, the new curriculum reform 'Educating for a New Citizenship'. However, conflicts and challenges were immediately experienced due to the difficulty of satisfying the local and global stakeholders. Costa Rica being a capitalist and social-democratic country (Lecouna and Momayezi, 2001), the MEP was responsible for constructing a capitalist curriculum that also incorporated social-democratic ideologies. As a result, the MEP created a humanistic curriculum with a focus on digital technologies for the 21st century and combined it with the guidelines for planetary citizenship from the United Nations Educational, Scientific and Cultural Organization (UNESCO). This curriculum was intended and legally mandated to provide equal opportunities for all students (including students with disabilities, those in vulnerable socioeconomic zones, adult education, and indigenous populations). The curriculum also satisfied global economic interests by teaching 21st-century skills, including the use of technology.

As this chapter will discuss later on, despite efforts to foresee potential difficulties and inconsistencies in implementation, local challenges still influenced the execution of the national curriculum, specifically the use of technology in the classroom. The MEP was legally bound to provide access to technology to all students and, to maintain its legitimacy, needed to develop the means for providing the country's most economically vulnerable students with technological resources. As a result, Tecno@prender arose as an internal policy to address outside global trends. This programme has promoted access to technology for vulnerable populations and contributed to the development of human capital across the country. But it has also attempted to meet the needs of multinational corporations. Costa Rica adjusted to global economic demands by identifying and strengthening local political resources to supplement central government funding and to try to ensure all of the country's students have access to quality education that would prepare them for employment in the 21st-century marketplace.

Globalization places governments under financial pressure to reduce spending (Verger et al, 2018). Interestingly, however, Costa Rica is an exceptional case with different outcomes from its experiences with globalization (Lehoucq, 2010). For example, in 2011, Costa Rica signed the Digital Social Agreement that produced a series of projects financed by the National Telecommunications Fund. One of the components of this Agreement focused on closing gaps in education (MEP, 2022). Costa Rica used this fund to prioritize vulnerable zones in the north and south (the Nicaragua and Panama border zones respectively) and indigenous populations (the Chorotega and Talamanca zones), with the purpose being to provide all students with access to education.

Because Costa Rica is a capitalist and social-democratic country, it has pursued less common educational reforms to satisfy the needs of global and local actors. That said, Costa Rica mirrored other countries across Central America and the Latin Caribbean in that its education reform was influenced by international forces. On this topic, Steiner-Khamsi explained how international standards have encouraged politicians to develop educational reforms: 'The terms "international standards", "21st century skills", and "best practices" greatly resonate with politicians and policy makers, and they resort to them at particular moments of agenda setting: Whenever there is need to generate reform pressure … [those terms] are politically powerful because they generate fear of falling behind in a global marketplace' (2014, pp 156–157).

Central American and Latin Caribbean countries are importing the 21st-century framework into their local education systems, and they are doing so to persuade companies to invest in them and ensure they do not fall behind economically. According to Akiba: 'Policymakers around the globe pay attention to the economic returns on investment in [education] quality' (2017, p 156). For our purposes, the point is that politicians, including those from Central American and Latin Caribbean countries, are using globalized and standardized approaches to education to attract investments, and Costa Rica is no exception.

Analytic approach

Just as with the framework that guides the present volume, the analytic framework employed in this case included three dimensions. The first dimension consisted of unpacking the political and economic forces at the national and international levels that structure and drive the process of educational reform (Dale, 1999; Edwards, 2014, 2018). The second dimension consisted of the negotiations between transnational companies (capitalism) and the MEP (social inclusivity) as the education reform was developed and implemented. Finally, the third dimension shifted away from the tensions between actors to focus on the challenges and conflicts created during the implementation of the reform (for example, related to educators' lack of knowledge regarding teaching technology in the classroom). As of 2022, Costa Rica is immersed in the third dimension and is working to resolve technological and educational obstacles at the local level.

Costa Rican public policy towards education

The Influence of national and international political and economic forces

The growing influence of multinational corporations has led to the MEP initiating efforts to modernize the country's education system. This actor experiences pressure from inside and outside of the country to implement and improve education reform efforts that enhance access to education and make that education more efficient, more effective, and more accountable (Dale 1997, 2000; Tarabini and Bonai, 2011).

On the one hand, Costa Rica seeks the benefits from the job creation and financial investment that globalization creates. Serving as a multinational technology hub can lead to the development of innovative technologies and can promote local and national wealth (Kellner, 2002). In addition, creating a workforce that is prepared to meet the needs of today's technology companies will not only strengthen the country's relationships with companies already operating in Costa Rica, but will also attract new companies to the country (Spring, 2008).

On the other hand, globalization can jeopardize the control and sovereignty traditionally wielded by developing nations (Verger et al, 2018). For instance, the MEP is considering the possible effects on access to education, specifically in the transition from traditional to more competitive and technology-focused curricula. This might provoke inequality and exclusion in the student population by producing a hierarchy in the education system (students who can and cannot afford the use of technology in the classroom).

As a result, in 2015, the MEP announced to the international community that Costa Rica was implementing a new curriculum with capitalist ideas, specifically 21st-century skills (MEP, 2018) to attract and retain technological companies. The new curriculum embraced digital technologies for the 21st century. It sought to introduce to students the types of knowledge and skills necessary to be successful in the technological and global marketplace of the 21st century, with the goal being to empower social groups, in part through the generation of technological networks in the community (Ministerio de Educación Pública, 2015).

However, Costa Rica is described as a 'hybrid socialist [(that is, social-democratic)], state-run capitalist system' when it comes to public policy (Lecouna and Momayezi, 2001, p 37). Thus, in order to align with the country's values, there had to be an emphasis on all students gaining experience and hands-on opportunities to access digital technology in the classroom. This emphasis provoked Costa Rica to create a humanistic education reform with both capitalist and social characteristics. However, in order to understand this reform, it is essential to review Costa Rican history to analyse the way in which capitalism and social democracy have interacted. A brief overview of public policy in Costa Rica from 1930 to 2015 is described subsequently.

On the one hand, the country has developed strong alliances with the US, with 75 per cent of foreign investment in Costa Rica historically coming from the US (Dewitt, 1980). According to Dewitt (1980), because of the vital role the US government plays in providing investments to Costa Rica, the US has had a significant impact on internal policy-making processes via international lending institutions. This influence often results in the adoption of programmes (for example, infrastructure initiatives) that require imports and that contribute to the country's trade deficit. In other words, the US and the Inter-American Development Bank support/approve projects that serve the US economic interests, but these projects also result in benefits for Costa Rica, such as 'industrial credit, agricultural credit (livestock development), roads, energy (largely the Arenal Hydroelectric Project), sanitation, pre investment, and education' (Dewitt, 1980, p 75). On the other hand, Lecouna and Momayezi explain that this country operates 'as efficiently as a private enterprise' (2001, p 36) and that the government oversees healthcare, education, telecommunications, electricity, and water. In other words, Costa Rica is a 'state-run monopoly of enterprises' (Lecouna and Momayezi, 2001, p 36).

According to Pietras (2016), Costa Rican capitalism started in 1930 with the national production of coffee and foreign investments for banana production from the US. Specifically, the United Fruit Company helped develop cosmopolitan cities, built highways, and constructed railroads to transport merchandise around the country. Additionally, English was the official language at the company. Salaries at the United Fruit Company were higher than salaries for most other jobs in the country, which drove migration to the Caribbean coast (Pietras, 2016). By 1940, Costa Rica had established a strategic alliance between President Calderon Guardia, the Catholic Church, and the Communist Party: 'The alliance only worked for a certain period of time and with the sole purpose of establishing social laws such as Social Guarantees, the Labor Code, among others' (Pietras, 2016, p 336). The idea was to establish social reforms to help the low and middle classes. As a result, Calderon created a free healthcare system, pensions, and government monopolies to maintain the welfare state and protect social reforms (Lehoucq, 2010). This was the beginning of social advancement and reform for the Costa Rican people.

Between 1940 and 1950, Costa Rica was governed by a welfare regime based on universal principles. The 'expansion of social policies took place across sectors, from education and training to social insurance and social assistance' (Franzoni and Anochea, 2013, p 153). Additionally, the accumulation of capital, along with public incentives (free education, free healthcare, pensions, and social guarantees) resulted in the development of a welfare regime with social-democratic policies focused on human development (Franzoni and Ancochea, 2013). Moreover, the Costa Rican military was abolished in 1948. Consequently, all expenditure previously allocated to the military shifted to state-owned enterprises, including infrastructure development, healthcare, and education (Lecouma and Momayezi, 2001).

Costa Rica was 'an exception, not only for the region, but also for the world in social development between 1950 and 1980' (Franzoni and Ancochea 2019, p 363). The country expanded universal social policies, such as high-paying jobs, free healthcare, high-quality pensions, and free education (Franzoni and Ancochea, 2019). Education was viewed as the cornerstone for job opportunities, and the economy took a new direction in 1965 with national attention on the opening of the National Institute of Learning (Instituto Nacional de Aprendizaje [INA]) (Franzoni and Ancochea, 2013). The Institute was the first in the country to create technical and technological degree programmes to meet the demand of international companies.

By 1970, the 'United Nations Development Program Human Development Index placed Costa Rica in the category of an upper middle-income country' (Lehoucq, 2010, p 53). After the US, Costa Rica is the longest=lasting democracy in the region (Lehoucq, 2010) Between 1971 and 1973, Costa Rica established the first national plan for public education, promoted by the Alliance for Progress. This effort was possible because of constitutional reform between 1946 and 1949 that made education mandatory. Educational planning helped to reduce patterns of inequality and strengthen work opportunities for people experiencing poverty and job insecurity. By 1982, the Costa Rican welfare regime was the most universal – and its society the least stratified – in all of Latin America (Franzoni and Ancochea, 2013). In the 1980s, Costa Rica continued refining its welfare regime; public spending on social policies was a top priority (Franzoni and Ancochea, 2013).

In the 1990s, Costa Rica began a process of privatization of state-owned companies and promoted foreign investment through an open banking system. This generated a shift in investment from agro-production to manufacturing and tourism, resulting in a large influx of capital investors interested in Costa Rica (Rivera, 2014). By 1998, the arrival of the technology company Intel in Costa Rica shifted the country from primary manufacturing to high-technology manufacturing, putting this small country on the map of technological production. According to Gonzalez et al (2016), Intel invested $300 million in Costa Rica. The main reasons Intel selected Costa Rica included the country's political and social stability, economic liberalization, previous experience in electronics production, a safe environment for foreign investment, and quality education (Gonzalez, et al, 2016).

By the 2000s, foreign capital came from the privatization of banks and the arrival of transnational banks and free trade zones, which drove the advancement of technology manufacturing, and call centres. Costa Rican success, according to Gonzalez et al (2016), was based on innovation and help from the US, specifically the United States Agency for International Development (USAID). For instance, this agency provided training for technicians, public workers, and university professors to promote investment. It also helped with the creation of a private agency to promote foreign investment, the Costa Rican Coalition of

Development Initiatives (Coalición Costarricense de Iniciativas de Desarrollo [CINDE]). USAID funds also provided support for the Foreign Trade Agency (Promotora del Comercio Exterior [PROCOMER]) and related free trade agreements between the two countries (Gonzalez et al, 2016). Siles González et al (2016) write that, in 2015, San Jose, Costa Rica was considered the most competitive city in the world in relation to the creation of communication technology. In addition to Intel, Hewlett-Packard, Schematic, and 95 other US companies were operating in Costa Rica, which accounted for $2.2 billion in investments and 24,000 employees (Gonzalez et al, 2016, p 420).

Human capital development, particularly in economies looking to move towards upper middle-income status, like Costa Rica, depends (at least in part) on access to quality education. The use of knowledge is key to producing innovation and technological advances in production and distribution. As such, education is considered a national resource – built with skills, knowledge, and creativity – that enables a country to compete in the global economy (Runde et al, 2017). In line with this view, in 2014, the Costa Rican government recognized the need to enhance the skills of its workforce. It developed strategies for the years 2015–2018 to promote innovation in the learning process through digital technology in order to further attract technology-related businesses and increase 21st-century job opportunities. Moreover, the MEP recognized that if Costa Rica was to remain competitive in the global marketplace, the country's educational efforts had to be more inclusive of the country's population.

Education reform: the new curriculum and Tecno@prender

As was noted earlier, Costa Rica developed a new curriculum reform, 'Educating for a New Citizenship', focused on technology in the classroom. As was also noted previously, in order to ensure technology was equally accessible to the entire population without discrimination, the MEP established Tecno@prender. This section is organized into three areas: the need to create an education reform that could satisfy global and national interests; the need to establish programmes like Tecno@prender to achieve inclusive education and validate the right of every citizen to a quality education; and the need for innovative technology policies to address local deficiencies that surfaced when the reform was initially implemented.

Education reform to satisfy global and national interests

According to the Directorate of Technological Resources in Education (Dirección de Recursos Tecnologicos en Educación), the education reform 'Educating for a New Citizenship' was intended to enhance the quality of life of all Costa Ricans by enabling citizens to participate in the global marketplace of the 21st century. This was to be achieved primarily through the focus of the new curriculum – known as 'Educating for a New Citizenship' – on digital technology. The curriculum was expected to enable Costa Rica to compete internationally for foreign investments and to be a leader among countries in the Latin American region (Programa Nacional de Tecnologias Móviles, 2021).

Referring to the 1949 Costa Rican Constitution, in 2016, the MEP declared that education is a human right and cannot only be economic but also serves a social-democratic perspective:

> In a globalized world, where everything seems to be done according to the laws of the market, we cannot forget that education should seek primarily the full development of people and the maintenance of peace. As established in the constitution, education is a human right of universal integral and indivisible enjoyment that constitutes a long-term aspiration in a developing country. (Ministerio de Educación Pública: Viceministro Académico, 2016, p 12)

Therefore, the aspirations of the Costa Rican government should not be solely capitalist in nature; they should also reflect the social-democratic sentiment that underlies education in Costa Rica (MEP, 2016).

While developing the country's education reform, agreement 07–44–2016 was presented to the government by the Superior Council of Education (Consejo Superior de Educación), an agency that approves curricular changes introduced by the MEP. This agreement called for a theoretical and philosophical foundation to be added to the digital technologies for the 21st-century curriculum to facilitate the implementation of the reform in different education contexts across the country. Furthermore, the MEP incorporated humanistic ideas from UNESCO in the curriculum to satisfy both capitalist and social-democratic interests.

The Superior Council of Education approved the new 'Educating for a New Citizenship' curriculum policy to promote curricular flexibility and the inclusion of all students in the education system. The resolution of the Superior Council of Education was intended to address an educational problem, specifically access to technology in the classroom, in order to satisfy both global and local actors. In response to this resolution, and using the concept of planetary citizenship from UNESCO, Costa Rica introduced an innovative and multidimensional model of education. According to UNESCO (2021), planetary citizenship appreciates cultural diversity and promotes cultural contributions to create and maintain sustainable development in countries. It is believed that planetary citizenship ensures the wellbeing of the global community and humanity.

For the MEP, the construct of planetary citizenship solved the tension surrounding inequitable education. Thus, the MEP introduced the term 'Global Citizenship Education' (GCE), which took inspiration from the concept of planetary citizenship and combined it with the framework of 21st-century skills. GCE formed the philosophical foundation for the new curriculum, 'Educating for a New Citizenship', as explained by the MEP:

> GCE is preparing learners for the challenges of the 21st century. It recognizes the relevance of education to understand and resolve global issues. It also considers their social, political, cultural, economic, and environmental dimensions. Beyond the development of knowledge and cognitive skills, GCE highlights the value of education as a generator of change. GCE focuses on strengthening the values, skills and attitudes in the education community that facilitate international cooperation and promote social transformation. This requires strengthening students' capacity to face the changing and interdependent world of the 21st century. (Ministerio de Educación Pública: Viceministro Académico, 2015, p 21)

Although not a direct translation of the concept of planetary citizenship, one can see parallels with this concept, in that the quote given earlier emphasizes the use of education to facilitate international cooperation and to promote social transformation. Moreover, while the MEP had specifically called for education reform to be guided by humanistic concepts, there was also a focus – rhetorically, but not in practice – on teaching technology to comply with economic interests from multinational corporations (MEP, 2016).

The MEP recognized the position Costa Rica was in and acknowledged that, in a globalized and interconnected world, boundaries between nation-states are permeated by digital information, communication technologies, and knowledge networks that are beyond the control of nation states (Di Castro, 2018). Thus, rather than attempting to control these technologies, the MEP stated a priority for using them as a way for the country to connect globally, a strategy which, at the same time, would also connect with the idea of planetary citizenship: 'The concept of planetary citizenship is based on connection and immediate interactions between people all over the world, anywhere and anytime, thanks to advances produced by digital technologies. This is how reality lives beyond local boundaries, through continuous technological digital forms' (MEP, 2015, p 19).

Interestingly, it stands out that both agendas are accommodated by the language of GCE. This is so in that it seeks to provide technological skills for capitalist development while also emphasizing technology access and technological use for planetary citizenship. By virtue of the fact that the language of GCE accommodates both agendas, it hides the tensions between them, for example, between capitalist growth and sustainable development.

The need for inclusive education

The MEP presented strategic directions for the period from 2015 to 2018 to create a digital citizenship curriculum with social equity at its core. This actor promoted the inclusion of digital technologies in education with the National Development Plan 2015–2018 during the Solís-Rivera Administration, which included the creation of the Tecno@prender programme as a way to blend the economic interests of global forces and the national interests of the country, as well as to ensure equal education for the nation (MEP, 2021). Between 2015 and 2018, the MEP and the Ministry of National Planning and Economic Policy (Ministerio de Planificación Nacional y Política Económica [MIDEPLAN]), the governmental agency that controls national expenditures, disclosed that Tecno@prender arose as an inclusive programme to help implement the country's new curriculum by specifically providing digital technology and promoting its inclusion in more vulnerable zones of the country.

Tecno@prender was implemented in 2018 and was built on existing governmental regulations and entities. These included the General Telecommunications Law of 2008, the 2011 Digital Social Agreement Law, and the National Telecommunications Fund (MEP, 2015). The Ministerio de Ciencia, Innovación, Tecnología, y Telecomunicaciones (Ministry of Science, Innovation, Technology, and Telecommunications [MICITT]) promotes public policies in the fields of science, innovation, technology, and telecommunications in the country. As a result, the MEP and the MICITT coordinated the funding for the reform generally and Tecno@prender specifically.

Prior to the introduction of Tecno@prender, the Costa Rican government established Executive Decree No. 340750 that assigned all control over the use of digital technologies in education to the Directorate of Technological Resources in Education (MEP, 2015). Therefore, in 2015, this actor assumed two important roles. First, it helped with the creation of Tecno@prender. Second, it transformed school libraries into resource centres for learning technology (MEP, 2015). According to the MEP, the Directorate of Technological Resources in Education promotes digital technologies for social inclusion locally and nationally (MEP, 2015). This curricular actor also helped implement public policy in the form of the new curriculum and promoted the country's vision of quality education by facilitating the implementation of the Tecno@prender programme so that even the country's most vulnerable students could receive comprehensive training in technology (MEP, 2015).

The need to address local deficiencies

The MEP experienced tension at the local level due to the impact of a global phenomenon – the COVID-19 pandemic, which affected education reform. The MEP was forced to establish online education in 2020 and a hybrid education (online and face to face) in 2021. The pandemic helped to highlight the need for access to technological resources and connectivity. The MEP solved tensions by providing technological resources to schools, improving infrastructure, and enabling internet connectivity, all of which are necessary not only for ensuring education in the context of a pandemic but also for the country to compete internationally and to satisfy national and international economic interests. At the same time, it should be recalled that the MEP also sought to implement digital technologies for all citizens to promote greater social equity and alleviate national tensions. Despite these ambitions, the implementation of the new curriculum and the Tecno@prender programme has experienced some challenges in practice. The chapter now turns in this direction, but first will briefly discuss the method.

Method

With insights from the previous sections in mind, the following sections present the preliminary findings from an exploratory case study of the Tecno@prender programme. Further research needs to be conducted because the education reform is still being rolled out across Costa Rica and the outcomes of its implementation have yet to be measured. The analysis is based on a series of interviews with professionals exposed to this educational reform's implementation. The main focus was to investigate Tecno@prender as an example of an inclusive education programme affected by the globalization process. The interviews took place in Costa Rica between July and August 2017 and in November 2021. These interviews illuminate how both internal forces as well as external forces, such as globalization, affect programme implementation. The investigation was based on semi-structured questions, such as: is Costa Rica an example of global education and Tecno@prender an inclusive education programme? How do globalization and international actors influence the reforms? What are some limitations that Tecno@prender experienced with the implementation of the new curriculum? Does Tecno@prender experience political internal pressure?

The case study described In this c"apte' has limitations. At the time of the data collection, Tecno@prender was relatively new, created between 2015 and 2018, with the implication that the programme has not been fully implemented for an extended period. Moreover, the perspectives shared here relate only to the experiences of governmental actors who have had direct contact with the Tecno@prender programme. However, the participants in this case study did have first-hand knowledge of Tecno@prender's development and trajectory in Costa Rica, a fact which allowed for an initial analysis of this inclusive educational programme.

Tecno@prender in Costa Rica

According to its director, Tecno@prender is a national, inclusive educational programme created by the MEP to incorporate technology into the new 'Educating for a New Citizenship' curriculum. Tecno@prender provides technology, such as access to computers and the internet, to vulnerable student populations across the country who could not afford technology in the classroom (R. Rodriguez, personal communication, 5 November 2021). This section addresses how the programme is supposed to work, how it is working, and what some of the current challenges are.

As stated by the programme's past director, 'Tecno@prender is free and open for all citizens and non-citizens of Costa Rica. This program provides access to technology in the classroom for all students no matter their gender, their citizenship, and socioeconomic status' (J. Castillo, personal communication, 8 August 2017). Mr Rodriguez, the director of Tecno@ prender, clarified how this programme seeks to remain inclusive and how relationships with government organizations have supported its legitimacy: 'The MEP works with the MIDEPLAN, which informs the MEP about which areas in the country experienced the highest levels of poverty based on census data. The MIDEPLAN control us with an action plan ... We have to deliver a quarterly report, inter-ministerial and inter-institutional, of how we are managing schools in vulnerable zones' (personal communication, 5 November 2021).

With this information from MIDEPLAN, the MEP then identifies economically disadvantaged students. Mr Rodriguez continued describing the relationship between the programme and education inclusiveness with the Mixed Institute of Social Assistance (Instituto Mixto de Ayuda Social), which is a national organization created to reduce poverty in Costa Rica. The Institute works to address poverty by executing a national plan – Law 4760 (Instituto Mixto de Ayuda Social, 2022). Mr Rodriguez mentions how equity programmes are coordinated between these entities:

'Tecno@prender delivers technology to an educational center ... We work with the Mixed Institute of Social Assistance. Only students in the Mixed Institute of Social Assistance database have access to the Tecno@prender computers. Other students bring their own technological devices to their classroom. These students are the most vulnerable in the country. These computers are not for all students, but those who are identified as very high risk. These students have no access to technology [otherwise], and they cannot be excluded from the educational reform.'

Important support comes from another governmental organization that tries to help maintain inclusiveness in education, namely, the Ministry of Science, Innovation, Technology, and Telecommunications (Ministerio de Ciencia, Innovación, Tecnología, y Telecomunicaciones [MICITT]). The MICITT's goal is to improve competitiveness of different sectors for the benefit of social welfare, equality, and the prosperity of Costa Rican society in the framework of digital transformation. In recent years, the MICITT has worked together with the MEP to manage a governmental fund with $200 million that is dedicated to the implementation of strategic policies in vulnerable zones (MEP, 2021). There is potential synergy between this fund and Tecno@prender in that this fund, according to Mr Quesada, advisor to the MICITT, should support both the building of infrastructure and the development of technology connectivity in remote areas, among other things. In addition, per Mr Quesada, 'the MICITT has invested nine million dollars in community centers, and the MEP began installing nine thousand computers in September 2017' (O. Quesada, personal communication, 14 August 2017). However, while both the aforementioned fund and the work of the MICITT generally align with the goals of Tecno@prender, more research is needed to understand the extent to which these initiatives are connecting with Tecno@prender in practice. For now, what is clear is that Tecno@prender is not the only programme dedicated to facilitating technology access in remote regions of the country.

More also needs to be done to address limitations that Tecno@prender has experienced with the implementation of the new curriculum. Mr Castillo, the past director of Tecno@prender, explained how internal tensions within the MEP contributed to the implementation of Costa Rica's education reform, 'Educating for a New Citizenship':

There are obstacles with the human resource ... the teacher's role has changed because of current demands. For example, getting access to technology for teachers located in remote areas who cannot come to workshops due to transportation reasons and travel expenses. Another limitation is the digital division of technology that separates educators by age: older, average, and young. Of all these groups, the older teacher is more likely to have difficulty learning technology or is not willing to learn. (J. Castillo, personal communication, 8 August 2017)

The Tecno@prender programme is thus having a hard time meeting its stated purpose/goal of inclusiveness, despite its focus on reaching marginalized communities.

Mr Castillo also commented on the vital role that technology in the classroom played in the new curriculum, but stated that this vision has not yet been realized because teacher training is lacking:

Tecno@prender has virtual training for teachers, and it goes from 40, 60, to 80 hours. The technological literacy trainings have a capacity from 700 to 1,500 teachers. This training consists of how to turn the computer on, turn it off, save a file, create a folder. How can the teacher bring the computer to the classroom? How does the teacher use technological devices in the classroom? How can the teacher use a phone or a laptop in the classroom? We still do not have an advanced level, only basic and intermediate level training courses. Training teachers is moving slowly. (J. Castillo, personal communication, 8 August 2017)

According to Ms Vargas, the advisor in educational research at the Superior Council of Education, teacher digital competence was still not sufficient for the full implementation of the curriculum in 2021:

Last year, under related research on teacher digital competence, it was determined that the majority of teachers are at initial and intermediate levels. They do not meet the expectation that is required to effectively implement technology in the classroom. Teachers are working well under pandemic circumstances where they have been trained more and have been forced to use the technologies. However, they are at an incipient level of digital competence development. (L. Vargas, personal communication, 5 November 2021)

Additional challenges, but also benefits, arose in the context of the COVID-19 pandemic, as noted by the director of Tecno@prender:

On one hand, the pandemic influences teachers to train in technological competencies. For example, management tools, such as Microsoft Teams, were available. However, educators did not use it. With the pandemic, Tecno@prender gave two workshops on Microsoft Teams where 60,000 teachers participated. In this sense, the pandemic has accelerated the digital skills of teachers. On the other hand, it has a negative aspect with a large budgetary reduction. In 2020, the Tecno@prender budget was reduced [by 40 per cent], and this year 2021 [51 per cent.] So, we do not have money to purchase equipment. At this moment, we have more than a thousand educational centers [participating in the program], so the money is not enough. Additionally, the educational centers don't have enough money to maintain existing equipment. This reality is not unfamiliar to Costa Rica. (R. Rodriguez, personal communication, 5 November 2021)

Costa Rica subsidizes the healthcare system in the country. It has created a contingency fund with 125 billion colones (US$195,479,375) allocated for the pandemic (Presidency of the Republic of Costa Rica, 2020). Nevertheless, other areas, such as education, have been negatively affected, as illustrated by Mr Rodriguez in the preceding quote. The pandemic is driving countries to cut education budgets around the world, but Costa Rica remains committed to pursuing its education reform despite funding challenges.

A closer look at Tecno@prender

According to Mr Rodriguez, the director of Tecno@prender, the MEP realized in 2020 that it needed to revise the reform to better account for specific characteristics of the Costa Rican education landscape. This was because students obtained access to technology with Tecno@prender, but teachers continued to struggle to incorporate this technology into the classroom (R. Rodriguez, personal communication, 5 November 2021). As a result, the MEP has been focusing on improving the quality of education by preparing educators to create lessons plans incorporating technology into the classroom. This coordination is to be provided by the Directorate of Technological Resources in Education, the entity that has provided technological and educational resources to Tecno@prender. Thus, at the beginning, Tecno@prender concentrated on providing access to technology to students, but now it is concentrating on strategies for teaching technology, since educators do not have the ability to implement it in advance technology levels in the classroom.

Over time, the MEP became aware of the country's technological limitations, particularly with regard to instructors using technology in the classroom. In response, in 2019 the MEP created a new policy proposal – the Policy for the Use of Digital Technologies in Education (Política para el Aprovechamiento de las Tecnologias Digitales en Educación [PATDE]) – which took inspiration from UNESCO's recommendations regarding the construction of digital policies in education (MEP, 2020). To work towards the goals of this policy, the MEP is formally evaluating, at the national level, all schools and assessing teacher digital competencies to generate an action plan specific to each school. The MEP is also implementing the National Development Plan and Public Investment (Plan Nacional de Desarrollo e Inversion Publica [PND]) 2019–2022, which consists of coordination among the Department of Documentation and Electronic Information, the Department of School Libraries, Learning Resource Centers, and, finally, the Department of Management and Production of Technological Resources to resolve technology deficiencies by preparing educators to teach technology in the classroom with the inclusion of digital technologies in education. In the words of Tecno@prender's director: 'this is the latest policy, approved two months ago (September 2021) by the Superior Council of Education. With a series of international and national consultations, research teams, and models from other countries, we are creating our own policy, not copied, according to our context' (R. Rodriguez, personal communication, 5 November 2021). Moreover, in order to improve student learning and to develop the digital skills required by teachers, the MEP is working to take into account the social and working conditions of teachers, as understood through teacher feedback, in order to help teachers incorporate the use of technology into their lessons plans (Dirección de Recursos Tecnológicos en Educación, 2021).

In summary, the dynamic process between actors (multinational corporations and government agencies) with conflicting interests (capitalism and social democracy) helped to produce an internal technological policy in the education reform in Costa Rica. However, in addition to challenges noted previously, and according to Ms Vargas, the advisor for educational research at the Superior Council of Education: 'There is no type of evaluation, experimental or quasi-experimental, that shows how Tecno@prender is positively or negatively impacting Costa Rican education ... we just do not have any type of studies' (L. Vargas, personal communication, 5 November 2021). Future research will thus need to look more closely at both the enactment and outcomes of the Tecno@prender programme.

Conclusions

The creation of the Tecno@prender programme was an example of how one country balanced tensions between global and local needs. The intent of this programme was to provide state-of-the-art technology and training on the use of that technology in the most vulnerable areas of the country. Without such a programme, indigenous populations, students from rural areas, special needs, adults, and those from low socioeconomic backgrounds are less likely to be able to access modern technologies and to acquire the knowledge required of 21st-century workers.

As noted earlier, the MEP was able to manage global and national tensions by pursuing an approach and by using language that could accommodate multiple agendas at the same time – namely, agendas related to worker preparation and skills development, on the one hand, and then planetary citizenship and equitable access to technology, on the other hand. Nevertheless, new tensions have arisen, in particular related to local challenges associated with the arrival of the global pandemic. Ultimately, Costa Rica continues to struggle with how to teach technology to students.

However, the MEP is aware of the challenges it faces and is creating new policies directed towards the construction of digital technology education in the classroom to address local technological tensions (MEP, 2020).

In conclusion, this chapter provides important details on how capitalist and social-democratic tendencies helped to create curriculum reform in Costa Rica. At the same time, it acknowledges that the impact of Tecno@ prender cannot be determined without additional data collection and analysis as the programme evolves. It will be interesting and important to continue examining Tecno@prender in order to analyse the acceptance and enactment of technology in the classroom, in the case of both students and teachers.

References

Akiba, M. (2017). Editor's introduction: understanding cross-national differences in globalized teacher reforms. *Educational Researcher*, 46(4), 153–168. https://www.jstor.org/stable/44971863

Dale, R. (1997). The state and the governance of education: an analysis of the restructuring of the state-education relationship. In A. H. Halsey, H. Lauder, P. Brown, and A. S. Wells (eds.), *Education: Culture, Economy, Society* (pp 273–282). Oxford University Press.

Dale, R. (1999). Specifying globalization effects on national policy: a focus on the mechanisms, *Journal of Education Policy*, 14(1), 1–17.

Dale, R. (2000). Globalization and Education: Demonstrating a 'Common World Educational Culture' or Locating a 'Globally Structured Educational Agenda'? *Educational Theory*, 50(4), 427–448. https://doi.org/10.1111/j.1741-5446.2000.00427.x

Dewitt. R. P. (1980). The Inter-American Development Bank and policy making in Costa Rica. *Journal of Developing Areas*, 15(1), 67–82. https://www.jstor.org/stable/4190845

Di Castro, E. (2018). Globalization, inequalities, and justice. In C. Roldán, D. Brauer, and J. Rohbeck (eds.), *Philosophy of Globalization* (pp 123–136). De Gruyter.

Dirección de Recursos Tecnológicos en Educación. Programa Nacional de Tecnologías Móviles Tecno@prender (2021). Perfil 2021. Personal email from Ronny Rodriguez to Vanessa Pietras, 9 November.

Eckstein, H. (1988). A culturalist theory of political change. *American Political Science Review*, 82(3), 789–804. https://doi.org/10.2307/1962491

Edwards Jr., D. B. (2014). How to analyze the influence of international actors and ideas in the formation of education policy? *Education Policy Analysis Archives*, 22(12), 1–34.

Edwards Jr., D. B. (2018). *The Trajectory of Global Education Policy: Community-based Management in El Salvador and the Global Reform Agenda*. International and Development Education series. London: Palgrave MacMillan.

Franzoni, J., and Ancochea, D. (2013). Can Latin production regimen complement universalistic welfare regimes? Implications from the Costa Rican case. *Latin American Research Review*, 48(2), 148–173. https://www.jstor.org/stable/43670080.

Franzoni, J., and Ancochea, D. (2019). ¿Cómo Costa Rica alcanzo la incorporación social y laboral? In M. Sagot and D. Arias (eds.), *Antología del pensamiento crítico costarricense contemporáneo* (pp 361–386). CLACSO.

Instituto Mixto de Ayuda Social (Mixed Institute of Social Assistance) (2022). Sobre la institución. www.imas.go.cr/es/general/sobre-la-institucion

Kellner, D. (2002). Theorizing globalization. *Sociological Theory*, 20(3), 285–305. https://doi.org/10.1111/0735-2751.00165

Lecuona, R., and Momayezi, N. (2001). Privatization in Costa Rica: political and economic impact. *International Journal on World Peace*, 18(2), 23–40. https://www.jstor.org/stable/20753301

Lehoucq, F. (2010). Political competition, constitutional arrangements, and the quality of public policies in Costa Rica. *Latin American Politics and Society*, 52(4), 53–77. https://www.jstor.org/stable/40925836

MEP (Ministerio de Educación Pública) (2016). *Educating for a New Citizenship*. https://'Educating for a New Citizenship' – mep.go.cr

MEP (2020). *Política en Tecnologías de la Información del Ministerio de Educación Pública: Transformación curricular, una apuesta por la calidad educativa*. Ministerio de Educación Pública.

MEP (2021). *Política para el Aprovechamiento de las Tecnologías Digitales en Educación (PATDE)*. Ministerio de Educación Pública Marzo.

Ministerio de Educación Pública, Dirección Recursos Tecnológicos Educación Programa Nacional de Tecnologías Móviles, Tecno@prender (2022). *Transformación Curricular, una apuesta por la calidad educativa*. Ministerio de Educación Pública.

Ministerio de Educación Pública: Viceministro Académico (2015). *Educar para una nueva ciudadanía. Transformación curricular: Fundamentación pedagógica*. https://www.scribd.com/document/341322184/Educar-Para-Una-Nueva-Ciudadania

Ministerio de Educación Pública, Gobierno de la República de Costa Rica (2018). *Memoria Institucional 2014–2018: Educar para una nueva ciudadanía una ponderosa transformación del sistema educativo*. www.mep.go.cr.memoria. memoria-2014-2018

Pietras, V. (2016). Mamita Yunai: La literatura del comunismo costarricense como parte de una vanguardia política. *Anuario de Estudios Centroamericanos*, 42, 327–355. http://www.jstor.org/stable/44735206

Presidency of the Republic of Costa Rica (2020). CCSS has executed more than 64 billion colones in the care of the COVID-19 pandemic. *En Comunicados de Prensa*. https://www.presidencia.go.cr/comunicados/2020/08/ccss-ha-ejecutado-mas-de-64-mil-millones-de-colones-en-la-atencion-de-la-pandemia-covid-19/

Rivera, F. (2014). Transformaciones y concentracion en grupos de poder económico en Costa Rica (1980–2012). *Revista Mexicana de Sociología*, 76(1), 37–58. https://www.jstor.org/stable/43495693.

Runde, F., et al (2017). Education and human capital development. In *Transforming Tomorrow's Developing Economies through Technology and Innovation*. Center for Strategy and International Studies. http://www.jstor.org/stable/resrep23182.6

Siles González, I., Espinoza Rojas, J., and Méndez Marenco, A. (2016). '¿El Silicón Valley latinoamericano'? La producción de tecnología de comunicación en Costa Rica (1950–2016). *Anuario de Estudios Centroamericanos*, 42, 411–441. https://www.jstor.org/stable/44735209.

Spring, J. (2008). Research on globalization and education. *Review of Educational Research*, 78(2), 330–363. http://www.jstor.org/stable/40071130

Steiner-Khamsi, G. (2014). Understanding policy borrowing and lending: Building comparative policy studies. In G. Steiner-Khamsi and F. Waldow (eds.), *Policy Borrowing and Lending in Education* (pp 3–17). Routledge.

Tarabini, A., and Bonal, X. (2011). Globalización y política educativa: Los mecanismos como método. *Revista de Educación*, 355, 235–255.

United Nations Educational, Scientific, and Cultural Organization (2021). *Global Citizenship Education*. https://en.unesco.org/themes/gced

Verger, A., Altinyelken, H., and Noveli, M. (2018). Global education policy and international development: A revised Introduction. In A. Verger, H. Altinyelken, and M. Noveli (eds.), *Global Education Policy and International Development: New Agendas, Issues, and Policies* (pp 1–34). Bloomsbury.

Edtech and Equity in Panama: Mobile Technology for Levelling the Learning Playing Field

Nanette Archer Svenson and Mariana Leon

Introduction

The Republic of Panama, like all of Central America, educates the majority of students in the public school system. In recent years, gaps in academic achievement between students attending public and private schools have become increasingly apparent and are reflected in national and international learning outcome evaluations. Panama's national standardized testing programme, the annual CRECER evaluation, shows clear evidence of this (MEDUCA, 2019), and similar tendencies appear in the Organisation for Economic Co-operation and Development (OECD) global Programme for International Student Assessment (PISA) results (MEDUCA/OECD, 2019). But the bigger problem is the general lack of accessibility to quality education and how this relates to inequality, social mobility and inclusion (Causa and Johansson, 2010; OECD, 2017).

Quality is a complex and subjective concept, especially for education. In this chapter, we use the United Nations Educational, Scientific and Cultural Organization (UNESCO) definition presented in the Sustainable Development Goals, which states that 'quality education specifically entails issues such as appropriate skills development, gender parity, provision of relevant school infrastructure, equipment, educational materials and resources, scholarships or teaching force' (UNESCO, 2022). Education quality issues and trends are not unique to Panama, and scholars are beginning to focus their attention on the numerous inequities associated with the quality of education typically offered in both public and private school systems worldwide. Their conclusions stress that students able to access quality education earlier on in their schooling tend to perform better in most types of evaluations (OECD, 2011, 2019). This, in turn, affects preparation for postsecondary learning opportunities, and, ultimately, options for employment and quality of life. The COVID-19 pandemic has exacerbated these disparities for many and threatens the present and future learning of an entire cohort of students.

With the forced school closures of the pandemic, remote learning became the new norm. Governments and schools around the world explored possibilities for incorporating different forms of information and communications technology (ICT), and education technology (edtech) became a familiar concept – as well as a determinant of families' abilities to access instruction. While ICT and edtech offer considerable promise (Yang et al, 2018), they also put those without adequate access to connectivity, ICT devices, and prior technological experience at a distinct disadvantage, potentially intensifying existing education inequality (Angrist et al, 2020; Azevedo et al, 2020; United Nations, 2020). Furthermore, ICT is merely a vehicle; alone, it does not affect educational quality. Rather, quality tends to be influenced by the professionals, processes, and materials involved. Thus, in order for ICT and edtech to offer broader promise for remote learning, this dyad of accessible connectivity and quality instruction is imperative (Amutha, 2020).

The COVID-19 pandemic has prompted thorny questions about the political economy[1] of edtech, digital inequality, and the future of learning (Williamson et al, 2020; Komljenovic, 2021; Wargo and Simmons, 2021). For a number of more privileged children worldwide who were able to access quality online instruction throughout the pandemic, their schools were able to proceed somewhat normally with curriculum completion, rate of learning, and evaluation. However, this scenario of continued virtual learning was generally not the case for most public school students in low- and middle-income countries, especially in remote areas (Seusan and Maradiegue, 2020; UNICEF/ITU, 2020; Williamson et al, 2020). For less privileged students in their early school years, this is troubling because of the obstacles posed for basic skills acquisition, which forms the foundation of subsequent learning (Cunningham and Stanovich, 1997; National Institute for Literacy and National Center for Family Literacy, 2008).

A means to leveraging edtech for more widespread, equitable remote learning is mobile technology. This offers a way to bypass more expensive, wired desktop connectivity and move directly to less expensive, portable wireless connections. Harnessed for learning purposes, mobile technology can become an accessible, low-tech mechanism for delivering to a greater number of people some of the benefits associated with high technology

(Ally and Samaka, 2013; Gómez Domingo and Badia Garganté, 2016; Yildiz et al, 2020).

This chapter discusses education equity and inclusion in Panama, presenting two mobile technology responses implemented at the primary level during the COVID-19 pandemic in which the authors participated as researchers. Within the context of the global pandemic, the programmes documented here were developed as creative collaborations of state and nonstate entities. Both interventions were products of joint ventures involving various institutions, including a nonprofit educational organization, an autonomous research centre, a higher education institution, and an edtech start-up. Both projects were also approved and openly promoted by Panama's Ministry of Education (MEDUCA), which allowed for national coverage and greater diversity of the participating population. Thus, these responses offer examples of interventions operating at the nexus of the global, the national, and the local. As such, they provide insights into how these types of innovative, nontraditional collaborations may contribute to and reshape the discussion surrounding edtech political economy. The chapter analyses these projects' characteristics, results, and potential for larger-scale implementation. It also explores how mobile edtech empowers end users – namely, teachers, families, and schoolchildren – and how this empowerment fits into broader political and economic discussions.

Following this introduction, the chapter provides background on Panama's primary education context and pandemic circumstances. It goes on to detail the two mobile technology interventions introduced, describing their methods, findings, limitations, and implications. It concludes with a discussion of the importance of these findings, both for Panama and for the world. It highlights possibilities for mobile technology policy and practice that could work to shift global edtech power dynamics. The conclusion emphasizes the nuanced global-local forces required to create the public-private-civic cooperation necessary to support this shift.

Context

Panama has just over 400,000 primary school students, around 85 per cent of them in public school. The COVID-19 pandemic forced a strict national quarantine and school closure in March 2020, and halfway into 2021 Panama held the dubious distinction of heading the global list of countries with the most consecutive days out of the classroom (de Hoyos and Saavedra, 2021; Svenson, 2021). From mid-March 2020, these children were stuck at home with little or no access to supplemental learning materials or programmes. The government announced an official return to class starting on 20 July 2020, with all activity managed through distance learning and schools to remain closed through December, the end of the Panamanian school year.

Given the prolonged school absence, these primary school students risk major academic setbacks. This is especially concerning for basic skills like reading, writing, and arithmetic, since these form the basis for further learning.

Panama's national CRECER evaluation, which since 2016 has annually measured reading, mathematics, and science learning outcomes in third and sixth graders, shows roughly half of public school third graders testing at low or very low levels for both literacy and mathematics (MEDUCA, 2019). This data also reveals achievement gaps. Private school and higher socioeconomic status (SES) third graders obtained significantly higher percentages in categories above basic than their public school and lower SES counterparts. Similar results are reflected in regional UNESCO-led evaluations (UNESCO, 2020).

In many countries, particularly within the OECD, the superiority of private schools with regard to improved educational outcomes disappears when controlling for SES and other background factors (Verger et al, 2020). In Panama, however, while the private school advantage diminishes when controlling for SES and other factors, it does not disappear. The UNESCO Third Regional Comparative and Explanatory Study (TERCE) and OECD Programme for International Student Assessment (PISA) results note that the impact of SES is more pronounced than the impact of the type of school (public or private), but that school type is still a relevant factor for outcomes even when controlling for SES and other factors (Villalba et al, 2018; MEDUCA/OECD, 2019).

These pre-pandemic studies highlight the inequities and low performance evident in Panamanian public schools. With prolonged absence from the classroom, there is a risk of students' attainment levels further diminishing across multiple academic outcomes (Carroll, 2010; Gottfried, 2014). The combination of pervasive underperformance and school closure heightens concern for primary school basics, such as literacy and mathematics, since learning in other subjects at all levels is linked to early comprehension in these areas. Setbacks at this stage are likely to negatively affect future learning (National Institute for Literacy, 2008).

Digital technology offers considerable possibilities for continued education even out of school (Yang et al, 2018). However, in order for this to be viable, connectivity must be available and accessible to students and families. In Panama, much of the population does not have access to fixed internet connection, computers, or even electricity. Only an estimated 40 per cent of public school students have internet at home and less than 30 per cent have computers (INEC, 2017). But cellular connection is far greater. In January 2020, market data reported a total of 4.86 million mobile connections nationwide, equivalent to 114 per cent of the total population (Kemp, 2020). This suggests that nearly every family, on average, has access to at least one mobile phone. However, accessibility varies by region, and data

Table 10.1: Estimated access of Panamanian public school students to mobile technology at home, by region, 2017

Region	% students with access	% students without access
Bocas del Toro	84	16
Cocle	89	11
Colon	96	4
Chiriqui	95	5
Darien	83	17
Herrera	94	6
Los Santos	96	4
Panama	97	3
Veraguas	84	16
Embera Comarca	74	26
Kuna Yala Comarca	59	41
Ngabe Bugle Comarca	53	47

Source: De Leon (2020, from INEC 2017 data)

from Panama's national statistics institute shows how indigenous *comarcas* and other nonurban areas are at a considerable disadvantage (INEC, 2017; de Leon, 2020), as Table 10.1 illustrates.

Even with the regional differences, these figures suggest enormous potential for mobile technology to serve as an existing, accessible education delivery vehicle – especially if coupled with innovative pedagogical and instructional tools. The COVID-19 pandemic has propelled new experimentation in this regard.

Pandemic mobile edtech interventions

The following section presents two pandemic projects developed and implemented in Panama with this objective: to leverage mobile technology to deliver quality educational material and instruction to public primary school children affected by school closures. We describe each intervention, the results, and the associated challenges, lessons, and implications. We hope these experiences and the resulting research will be useful in similar contexts where mobile technology offers a promising educational tool.

WhatsApp remote reading recovery

Most Panamanians with mobile phones also have access to WhatsApp, a free instant message application that operates across multiple platforms for text and multimedia transfer (Dichter & Neira Research Network, 2015). The accessibility of this inexpensive, user-friendly platform has made WhatsApp convenient for learning as well as messaging, and research is beginning to signal its potential as an educational tool (Bouhnik and Deshen, 2014; Gon and Rawekar, 2017). The first initiative presented here took advantage of mobile phone and WhatsApp ubiquity and developed a low-tech mobile solution to bolster primary school literacy.

In April 2020, three local nonstate actors united to design and implement the WhatsApp Remote Reading Recovery project: Panama's Centro de Investigación Educativa (Center for Education Research [CIEDU]), a recently founded public-private research centre; the ProEd Foundation, a UNESCO prize-winning nonprofit dedicated to K-12 teacher training; and Quality Leadership University (QLU), a locally and internationally accredited private university with considerable expertise in online delivery. This collaborative effort was supported by the Ministry of Education through a corps of 60 volunteer public school teachers and was the focus of an official teacher training programme.

Utilizing references from other programmes incorporating mobile technology and WhatsApp as didactic tools, this project sent grade-appropriate digital stories to 500 primary students (second to sixth graders) through their classroom teachers and caretakers for 12 weeks to stimulate daily reading practice during the COVID-19 quarantine. The goal was to preserve literacy so that the children would maintain (or expand) their reading skills and be better prepared for schools reopening.

The process began with the recruitment of teachers for project implementation. This involved the design and direction of a certificate course in action research within MEDUCA's teacher training portfolio, and included an applied component requiring teachers to be field implementers of the WhatsApp Remote Reading Recovery project. The teacher training portion consisted of approximately 80 hours of synchronous instruction and discussions, small-group coaching, and follow-up troubleshooting sessions. As an incentive to follow through with the requirements of and time dedication associated with this project, upon completion, teachers received a certificate of participation as well as professional points (Panama uses a points-based promotion system for public school teachers). Teachers were tasked with collection of pre-, mid-, and post-test data, in the form of WhatsApp video recordings where children read aloud benchmark passages provided by the researchers. Teachers were then responsible for sending PDF files with the daily readings to the parent or caretaker of each participating student, and keeping a daily record detailing receipt and completion of the readings.

Teachers video-recorded students reading sample passages three different times: prior to the start of the intervention, midway through the intervention (at the seven-week mark just prior to the official online reopening of classes), and at the end of the intervention (at the 12-week mark). These videos were stored in a cloud server and the project researchers trained five external evaluators (who were also teachers) to analyse each video and measure: (1) speed (judged by the number of words read per minute); (2) fluency (the number of errors noted); and (3) comprehension (the number of correct answers to subsequent story content questions). The researchers checked for inter-rater agreement to ensure the evaluator data was reliable and secured over 80 per cent agreement for both words-per-minute and fluency evaluations. Once the data were tabulated, cleaned, and checked, researchers conducted the statistical analyses.

Results from the quantitative pre- and post-test data, as well as the qualitative data collected from participating teachers, indicated high take-up and retention rates, reading rate and fluency improvements of up to 40 per cent over the intervention period, and strengthened teacher–family–student relationships that evidenced demonstrable learning gains. The study did not control for background characteristics in its analysis. Overall, with the five grades combined, the result was a statistically significant gain among all participating students, the highest gains being reported in the first seven weeks of the intervention. The mean number of words per minute was 81.5, with a reported increase at the end of the 12 weeks to 89.9, representing a 10.3 per cent increase in words read per minute. However, the number of words read per minute in week 7 was 95.2, which represented a 16.8 per cent increase at the midpoint of the intervention. These findings suggest that although some of the initial gains may deteriorate as the intervention advances, it is important to maintain consistency and fidelity for achieving significant progress.

Students in the second, third, and fifth grades showed statistically significant gains. Fourth graders achieved gains, but they were not statistically significant. Students in the sixth grade did not achieve gains. These results imply that reading interventions had a greater impact among students in early primary (second and third graders) and that gains – while still present – were less dramatic in upper primary grades (fourth to sixth graders). Other studies support the observation that gains in basic skills acquisition are likely to happen more quickly in lower grades (LoGerfo et al, 2006).

It is also important to note that the last five weeks of the WhatsApp Remote Reading Recovery intervention coincided with Panama's official reopening of the school year through distance learning. This reopening required teachers, families, and students to become familiar with new platforms, systems, processes, and materials for learning remotely – something never before attempted in Panama and for which MEDUCA and most of the country was ill-prepared. As a result, the end of July and August 2020 was a period of relatively high stress, disorganization, and harried relearning. It is possible that these circumstances distracted participating teachers, families, and students alike, and negatively affected students' progress.

Another measure tabulated was take-up (or rate of adoption), where researchers used data from a sample of 187 second- and fourth-grade students and found that, on average, students completed 84 per cent of the daily readings, or 51 of a total 60 readings. This measure is particularly important to international organizations that are interested not only in the gains obtained through reading interventions, but also the probability that participants will follow through with the intervention, in order to determine feasibility for wider future application (McKenzie, 2011, 2019).

Several factors observed and documented in the WhatsApp Remote Reading Recovery project make it notable in terms of its potential for future application on a broader scale. Retention and take-up rates were impressive: nearly 90 per cent of the teachers, families, and students who started followed the project through to its end, with an average completion rate of over 80 per cent on assigned tasks. The simplicity of the mobile edtech employed appeared to be instrumental in achieving these high rates, which bodes well for the incorporation of familiar devices and platforms at the low-tech end of distance learning. The thoroughness of the teacher training and coaching/mentoring follow-up that took place throughout also appears to have contributed to both retention and take-up rates, as evidenced by the commentary of participating teachers. Teachers noted that they had seldom participated in MEDUCA training that taught them concrete skills for measuring and monitoring literacy or that accompanied them through the process of applying these in practice. Finally, the excellence and attractiveness of the materials utilized for the literacy instruction caught the attention of teachers, families, and students, making it easier for everyone involved to take an interest in and commit to the implementation.

For these reasons, WhatsApp Remote Reading holds considerable potential for extended application in Panama, other low- and middle-income countries, and virtually anywhere. Its premise is simple and user-friendly, its appeal is easily understood and embraced, and its empirical results are promising.

Escribo Play Panama

Escribo Play is an evidence-based, gamified, early literacy and mathematics program that works with inexpensive personal mobile devices. The program was developed by Escribo Inovação para o Aprendizado, an edtech start-up based in Recife, Brazil. The start-up has been recognized by the Inter-American Development Bank (IADB) as one of the 12 best creative economy start-ups of Latin America and the Caribbean in 2016. The company took its international vision and successfully completed plans to translate the app to English and Spanish, seeking to cater to audiences outside of Brazil. Escribo partnered with the Quality Leadership University (QLU, one of the partners in the WhatsApp Remote Reading project detailed earlier) to offer free access to Escribo Play in Panama for kindergarteners and first graders. Parents registered their children for the program online and received individualized access to the app for a period of four months. Data from the games were digitally captured, enabling access to evaluation and impact through progressive improvement in the games, along with performance in a diagnostic game that the students played at the beginning and end of the trial period.

Half of the registered students were randomly assigned to the maths games first, and the other half were assigned to the reading and writing games first. These groups later obtained access to the reading and writing games, and maths games respectively, allowing for an experimental design of the study. The app did not require a consistent internet connection to play the games, but did require periodic internet connection in order to download new games and record results. Students played a total of 40 games, 20 focusing on maths and 20 focusing on reading and writing. Although almost 4,000 parents signed up, approximately 600 students completed all 40 games. In Brazil, Escribo Play demonstrated results of 68 per cent gains in reading and 48 per cent gains in writing (Amorim et al, 2020); similarly positive results were reproduced in Panama.

Before the application was launched in Panama, Escribo Play and QLU held various meetings with the MEDUCA to secure endorsement for the project, as well as support in countrywide dissemination through its official website. MEDUCA support for this project was key because its reach incentivized participation among the desired population and enabled the recruitment of a larger number of participants.

The project began with enlisting parents to register their children for the Reto Escribo (Escribo Challenge), which aimed to promote early reading, writing, and maths skills in boys and girls aged four to six, through free digital games. Parents were informed that participation was voluntary and could prove valuable for the learning of their children. All parents of participating children digitally signed an informed consent form. The project advertised the following benefits and incentives:

- The opportunity for the student to play fun digital games that build early literacy and maths skills.
- A report at the end of the study showing the student's progress in these skills.
- A digital certificate for the student upon completing the challenge.
- Free access for a specified period of time (about four months).

Upon granting consent, parents received a unique username and password to install the application so that their children could play the games. Parents were also responsible for ensuring that the device had intermittent internet access to download the games. The application ran on most iOS and Android devices (download data from the app demonstrated that the vast majority of the downloads were from Android devices).

Half of the students randomly received the literacy games first, while the other half received the maths games first. All students had the opportunity to play all 40 games (20 for literacy and 20 for maths) over the course of the project. Students were instructed to play one game per day and could repeat the games from the previous days. Before and after playing, students completed an initial test game and a final test game. These tests helped researchers understand how well the games worked, and provided the data necessary to explore if students achieved gains in literacy and maths through use of the games. Each game lasted approximately 10 minutes, and students played an estimated 20–30 minutes a day (leading to the assumption that they chose to play the same game multiple times).

The games were interactive, colourful, and age-appropriate. For example, students could play a game called *Baloncesto de los Fonemas* (*Phoneme Basketball*), where they joined two different phonemes to discover a new word (see Figure 10.1).

Another game, called *Gol de la Aliteración* or *Alliteration Goal*, asked students to choose the same beginning letter sound for a specific word, using illustrations for children who could not yet read. Children would then select *perro* as the word with the same beginning letter sound as *perico* (see Figure 10.2).

Almost 7,000 children participated in the Escribo Challenge, with equal participation among boys and girls. Children played the games a total of 131,759 times for an average of about 19 plays per child. Users reported the following descriptive data:

- *Age* – 67 per cent were five and six years old.
- *Special needs* – 5 per cent reported having special educational needs.
- *Geographical location* – approximately 50 per cent lived in the metropolitan areas of Panama (Panama Centre, North, East, West, and San Miguelito); 14 per cent were from Chiriquí, the second most-populated province in the country; and 13 per cent were from Coclé; the remaining 23 per cent were divided among other provinces and less than 4 per cent came from provinces predominantly inhabited by indigenous peoples (that is, the three *comarca* regions in Table 10.1 presented earlier).
- *Public versus private schooling* – 85 per cent belonged to the public school system.

Though this last figure reflects the general composition of the public-private student population, it may also be indicative of the greater need

Figure 10.1: Escribo Play Phoneme Basketball

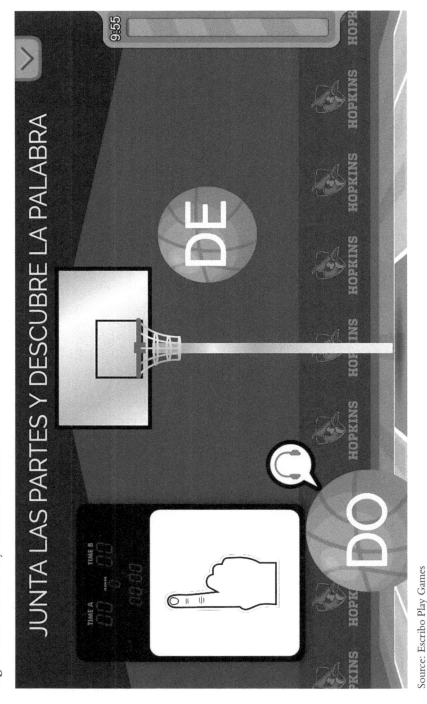

Source: Escribo Play Games

Figure 10.2: Escribo Play Alliteration Goal

Source: Escribo Play Games

perceived by public school parents during the pandemic to help their children learn the basic literacy and maths skills they were not obtaining through participation in the virtual, radio, or television classes provided by the public school system (UNICEF, 2021). The geographical distribution highlights the stark inequalities throughout Panama regarding access to technology and the internet: those outside of the urban areas are typically at a notable disadvantage, and those in the indigenous areas are often severely isolated from all ICT connections. While the games were free to play, users still needed to have a device where they could download and play the games, as well as periodic access to the internet. These requirements proved to be too restrictive in certain areas of the country, limiting participation among children who could have benefited most from this intervention.

Discussion and implications

Lessons learned

In both edtech interventions discussed here, valuable lessons emerged. First, with their accompanying quantitative research components, both provide empirical evidence to support the view that mobile technology, utilized under the proper circumstances, demonstrates considerable potential for levelling the distance learning playing field – and relatively quickly. Exploration of mobile technology within edtech literature has tended to focus on secondary- and tertiary-level learning, but the data presented here underscore their usefulness for the primary level as well, and with regard to certain critical basic skills. This evidence on primary-level application is important for demonstrating the foundational support mobile edtech can have, as well as its power to provide for subsequent learning.

Second, regarding the 'proper circumstances' mentioned earlier under which mobile edtech initiatives may be most effectively employed, several key factors in the two experiences documented appeared to be essential. Interestingly, though not surprisingly, these key factors for mobile edtech success are similar to those for educational success inside the classroom. And they all transcend country, language, culture, and grade-level differences, which further adds to their credibility as foundational programme characteristics:

- Complete and continued *capacity development*, provided virtually in these COVID-19 cases in the form of training, coaching, and follow-up for key implementers (teachers, families, ministry officials, evaluators, and researchers), helped ensure that participants had adequate base skills and information for implementation, as well as resources on hand for troubleshooting difficulties along the way.

- *Technological simplicity* with regard to platform, device, application, and software is critical; if familiar systems, apparatuses, and apps can be incorporated, even better. The user-friendliness of the edtech solution impacts take-up and retention rates. A major contributor to the success of the WhatsApp Remote Reading Recovery project was the fact that all participants already had access to WhatsApp and were highly proficient users; a new and/or more complex programme would likely not have had the same take-up. This simplicity also facilitates development of teacher–family–student connections.

- *High-quality instruction materials* are another key ingredient in the edtech equation. In both of the projects described, colourful, interactive, age-appropriate, and quality content seemed to make participation interesting and attractive for students and families. According to teacher reports, students felt both WhatsApp and Escribo Play tasks were more like recreation than homework. As mobile technology becomes a more viable vehicle for getting these kinds of materials to more public school students, we see how low-tech ICT can provide a means to bridging edtech gaps for quality instructional materials.

- *Focus on literacy* is important, especially since most subsequent learning depends on it. In crisis situations in particular, this critical skill must become a primary priority in order to maximize current gains as well as to minimize future complications. Also, the daily habit, even if it is of limited duration, is an essential and powerful tool for reading development and reinforcement, speed, and comprehension.

- *Incentives* for promoting healthy and communicative teacher–family–student interaction paved the way for fluid school–home interaction and mutual support for student learning. This is always helpful, but becomes vital in crisis or remote learning situations. In the cases explored here, these incentives took the form of applications, games, and digital books that households gained access to (during and after the projects), official certificates of participation, and noticeable improvements in student learning.

Last, but certainly not least, is the fact that access to ICT (through devices, connectivity, and data) is not as universal as we would hope in Panama, or in most low- and middle-income countries, and this affects which children get to participate in learning, especially during crisis situations such as the recent COVID-19 pandemic. This has direct implications for equity and inclusion at all levels. The lack of participation in both projects of children from Panama's outer-lying indigenous areas offers a visible case in point. Rectifying ICT access situation will require sizable political will and resources, as well as collaborative efforts on multiple public and private fronts. Establishing connectivity for remote, less populated, poor populations is not a profitable venture for any of those responsible for the decision making. However, it is an essential condition for expanding mobile edtech and any kind of internet-assisted instruction.

Taking these lessons and turning these mobile edtech innovations, which have had a proven but momentary impact on advancing public school primary school learning, into lasting solutions necessitates a deeper understanding of the edtech power dynamics at the global and local levels. It also entails curating the necessary conditions for productive collaboration among the multiple actors needed to contribute to and scale up such solutions.

Edtech power

Edtech is big business with US, European and Asian hubs leading the sector and much of the associated venture capital spending (Regan and Khwaja, 2019; Holon IQ, 2021). Valued in 2020 at nearly US$200 billion with an expected growth rate of 15 per cent and a projected market value of around US$400 billion by 2025, edtech is driven largely by proprietary digital products and services developed and sold by for-profit companies (Komljenovic, 2021). As a result, many new educational technologies are promoted and adopted not so much because there is solid documentation on their teaching and learning value proposition, but rather because they present an attractive market for vendors within a context that pressures educators to incorporate technology as a means to modernizing and improving outcomes (Regan and Khwaja, 2019). Mammoth companies like Google, Facebook, and Microsoft are moving into this space, along with large private foundations such as the Gates Foundation and the Chan Zuckerberg Initiative, educational publishers, niche corporations, private equity investors, venture capitalists, and international organizations like the United Nations and the World Bank (Regan and Khwaja, 2019; Komljenovic, 2021). With the effects of the COVID-19 pandemic on education systems worldwide, edtech businesses have ramped up marketing considerably to support online learning. These efforts have provided educators and parents with valuable tools and resources for continuing instruction during the crisis; they have also allowed the edtech industry to prove its worth, extend its reach, and grow its market share (Williamson et al, 2020). As is the case with most sectors, many early pioneers are now well positioned to shape the future of the industry, through the supply and distribution of products, the creation of barriers to entry for competitors and switching costs for customers, access to key resources, and influence over customer preferences, among other avenues of control.

Most edtech activity originated and has been concentrated in OECD countries, though low- and middle-income countries have also begun to explore and invest in edtech as a promising option for improving lagging outcomes. The key challenges facing non–OECD education systems are typically very different from those of OECD countries, so successful edtech interventions in one context may produce very different results in the other. Additionally, the majority of low- and middle-income country families and schoolchildren do not have access to computers or the internet, which are necessities for utilizing the level of programming and platforming usually associated with commercial edtech products (Rodriguez-Segura, 2020). Nevertheless, the spread of edtech and online learning in the non–OECD world (both before and after the pandemic) is being propelled by an array of coalitions and networks established to support the scaling up of distance learning delivery (Williamson et al, 2020). The Global Education Coalition recently launched by UNESCO is a prime example, as are complementary efforts of the World Bank and the OECD (OECD, 2020a; UNESCO, 2020; Muñoz-Najar et al, 2021). Google, Facebook, and Microsoft are associated with all of these, as are many other large global for-profit and nonprofit organizations.

Few, if any, major edtech actors have focused on mobile technology, even among the global development proponents. This seems paradoxical given the degree of mobile phone penetration in developing countries. The World Bank (2021) registers 107.5 mobile cellular subscriptions per 100 inhabitants worldwide. Neither internet usage (at less than 60 per cent of the global population) nor access to electricity (at 90 per cent of the global population) matches this. These indicators vary by region and country, but the point remains clear: more people have access to mobile phones than to either the internet or electricity. Following this trend, mobile technology for education delivery has become a topic of increasing interest among scholars and multilateral organizations (West and Chew, 2014; Alkhalifah et al, 2017; Rodriguez-Segura, 2020; Orozco, 2021), but comparatively little has been pursued in terms of research or implementation. This may be due to the repeatedly referenced obstacle of insufficient connectivity and mobile coverage, which involves a separate group of power players. As people everywhere increasingly connect to the internet through mobile broadband, local telecommunications providers of high-speed wireless access via mobile networks assume growing power in the world at large and especially in the context of edtech.

Collaboration to advance mobile edtech

Mobile edtech learning demonstrates the potential technology has to bridge certain gaps in global-local learning and knowledge attainment – gaps that technology itself and edtech political economy have helped to exacerbate (Jones, 2019; Williamson et al, 2020). By enabling dissemination of high-quality digital learning materials and instruction to least-common-denominator electronic screens, mobile technology offers a means of transferring knowledge previously reserved for those with access to computers and internet connections to a much broader audience. However, realizing this mobile edtech potential requires careful collaboration among a nuanced mix of actors, which may conflict in ways with the established dynamics of global and local edtech power. State support for pursuing this type of innovative objective, plus cooperation between government, private sector telecommunications providers and other international and civil society actors, as well as corresponding monitoring and evaluation activity are all critical for achieving more widespread mobile edtech solutions.

Often innovations are more likely to originate outside the government entities responsible for education delivery, since private sector and nongovernmental entities may be less constrained and better resourced for pursuing research and development activity (IDB, 2014). Often, too, there are bureaucratic impediments hindering collaboration between state and nonstate actors. Ironically, crisis situations can provide circumstances that better propel such cooperation. More examples of crisis–propelled cooperation have been studied from the perspective of how disaster can be capitalized upon by (predominantly) business enterprises to push self-serving agendas that would be more difficult to promote in less turbulent times (Klein, 2005). This is increasingly true for education, among other sectors, and illustrates how certain actors may utilize disruption to manifest and consolidate power within the process of crisis–induced policy change (Saltman, 2007). While this was likely true with the COVID-19 pandemic in Panama – and elsewhere – it is also possible to point to ways in which the crisis dynamic was utilized to promote greater public good in the Panamanian education sector, at least momentarily.

Nongovernmental and private sector involvement with MEDUCA that ordinarily would have required insurmountable bureaucracy was relatively streamlined for the sake of emergency response and resulted in various innovative public-private initiatives. The umbrella effort under which this took place was referred to as the Gran Alianza Educativa (Great Education Alliance), an initiative led at the start of the pandemic by MEDUCA and a group of Panama's more established education nongovernmental organizations. The mission of this cooperative effort was to work towards a country that provides 'quality and inclusive education for all' (LAGAE, 2021), and it was essential for developing and implementing much of the technological retraining of public school teachers nationwide to prepare them for remote teaching. This alliance created a more flexible, less bureaucratic space within which state and nonstate actors could work together to launch and scale innovative national projects more quickly than would normally be the case in noncrisis conditions. Among the projects enabled by this alliance are the two mobile edtech responses described previously.

Similarly, the Panamanian government and local telecommunications groups got together during the pandemic to establish 'Internet para Todos' (Internet for All). This response deployed 85 internet hubs to impoverished communities throughout Panama, ostensibly providing free wireless internet access and helping students attend classes remotely as they dealt with the effects of COVID-19 pandemic. Unfortunately, in spite of the well-intentioned agreements signed and promises made, relatively little on the ground has changed for the affected communities who have continued to face low connectivity and high levels of student attrition (Samaniego, 2020).

These types of collaborative creativity involving both state and nonstate entities, if properly supported, sustained, and evolved, have the potential to help education leapfrog technologically and substantively, but Panama's record with sustaining and expanding this type of collaboration is shaky. Various state-led collaborations over the years in different emergency situations have sought to widen the reach of internet connectivity in the country, most recently with the havoc wreaked by Hurricanes Eta and Iota in late 2020 that seriously impacted indigenous regions near the Costa Rican and Colombian borders. The impact of these initiatives has been limited and the benefit to citizens at the community level is consistently disappointing. This is primarily because of national-level political economy constraints that thwart expanded internet connectivity and device accessibility, as well as the incentives in place to perpetuate these constraints. The technology to solve these problems is available; the political will and sustained support are not.

When we contemplate using mobile technology to level the playing field, we must include our more vulnerable outlier populations: those who live in difficult to access areas, low density areas, or areas prone to suffering the effects from natural disasters. Increased effort must be dedicated to assessing actual interaction with distance learning in its various formats and to identifying which groups of students are not interacting and therefore are in danger of being left out. Although this effort is, presumably, a primary responsibility of the government and many international organizations, numerous power dynamics intervene to hinder progress in the direction of inclusiveness. These need to be overcome.

In his discussion of edtech political economy, Jones (2019) posits that overcoming or redirecting the global and local power dynamics involved in education reform will not be possible through technological change, civic action, and voluntary initiatives alone; strategic state action is critical. The successful mobilization of widespread digital education requires productive, collaborative engagement among political parties, educators, unions, international organizations, and social movements – the adoption of simultaneous, complementary top-down and bottom-up action to propel movement and change. This approach, Jones (2019) notes, is oddly similar to the one utilized by many states to introduce markets and quasi-markets into the education sector in the first place.

Conclusion

The two interventions explored in this chapter emphasize the potential for certain state and nonstate educational actors, in Panama and elsewhere, to develop, implement, and scale mobile edtech interventions at the national level, responding to and inspired by global objectives headed in the same direction. The interventions examined also emphasize the importance of their collaborative nature for helping shift some of the power dynamics typically associated with edtech. The results discussed serve to inform Panama, as well as other developing countries, on mobile ed tech distance learning options for propelling primary-level basic skills gains – and the types of collaboration necessary for bringing these about.

The knowledge generated is applicable to crisis–situation school closures, such as during the COVID-19 pandemic, as well as to supplemental coursework design during a regular school year. Part of the educational strategy for the medium and long term, beyond COVID-19 in Panama and the rest of the region, must include digital transformation of education delivery through ICT (Arias Ortiz et al, 2020). Mobile phone use and internet access will also likely continue to increase in most countries of the world, thereby facilitating the implementation of this type of intervention on a larger scale and subsequently offering a greater possibility for the reduction of existing educational inequity (West and Chew, 2014).

Taking mobile learning to the next level so that it truly begins to level the playing field will require enormous effort on many fronts. Political will and continued support for creative state–nonstate collaboration is crucial for achieving universal connectivity and more massified edtech implementation. Programming quality into the formula is a challenge that most developing countries continue to face with regard to public school education in general. Assuring quality with regard to mobile learning is no different and involves similar principles. Among the key components to consider for any mobile learning programme, regardless of size or scale, are adequate capacity development for all participants, relatively simple technology, the utilization of high-quality instruction materials, a focus on critical skills, and, finally, the incorporation of meaningful incentives. All of this is easier to discuss than put into practice, but the fact that certain programmes have produced evidence of success, quickly and in adverse conditions, offers proof that it can be done.

Note
[1] 'Political economy' is a term with many possible definitions. In this chapter, it will refer broadly to the ways in which political and economic processes interact in a society and the resulting distribution of power among different actors. This definition is in line with the political economy framework presented at the beginning of the book.

References

Alkhalifah, T., de Vries, D., and Rampersad, G. (2017). Mobile learning adoption in developing countries. ICETC 2017: Proceedings of the 2017 9th International Conference on Education Technology and Computers, December 2017, pp 89–93. https://dl.acm.org/doi/10.1145/3175 536.3175583.

Ally, M., and Samaka, M. (2013). Open education resources and mobile technology to narrow the learning divide. *International Review of Research in Open and Distributed Learning*, 14(2), 14–27. https://doi.org/10.19173/ irrodl.v14i2.1530

Amorim, A., Jeon, L., Abel, Y., Felisberto, E., Barbosa, L., and Martins Dias, N. (2020). Using Escribo Play video games to improve phonological awareness, early reading, and writing in preschool. *Educational Researcher*, 49(3),188–197. https://doi.org/10.3102/0013189X2090982

Amutha, D. (2020). The role and impact of ICT in improving the quality of education. Social Science Research Network (SSRN). https://pap ers.ssrn.com/sol3/papers.cfm?abstract_id=3585228#:~:text=ICTs%20 are%20making%20major%20differences,advantage20over20the20traditio nal20method.

Angrist, N., Bergman, P., Brewster, C., and Matsheng, M. (2020). Stemming learning loss during the pandemic: a rapid randomized trial of a low-tech intervention in Botswana. Columbia University. http://www.columbia. edu/~psb2101/Low-tech%20learning%20solutions%20-%20%20July%202 020.pdf

Arias Ortiz, E., Brechner, M., Perez Alfaro, M., and Vasquez, M. (2020). De la educación a distancia a la híbrida: 4 elementos clave para hacerla realidad. In *Hablemos de política educativa: América Latina y el Caribe*. Inter-American Development Bank. https://publications.iadb.org/publicati ons/spanish/document/Hablemos-de-politica-educativa-en-America-Lat ina-y-el-Caribe-2-De-la-educacion-a-distancia-a-la-hibrida-4-elemen tos-clave-para-hacerla-realidad.pdf

Astudillo, J., Fernández, M., and Garcimartín, C. (2019). La desigualdad en Panamá: su carácter territorial y el papel de las inversiones públicas. *Inter American Development Bank*. https://publications.iadb.org/es/la-desi gualdad-de-panama-su-caracter-territorial-y-el-papel-de-las-inversiones-publicas

Azevedo, J. P., Hasan, A., Goldemberg, D., Iqbal, S. A., and Geven, K. (2020). *Simulating the Potential Impacts of COVID-19 School Closures on Schooling and Learning Outcomes: A Set of Global Estimates*. World Bank Education Group. https://www.worldbank.org/en/topic/education/publication/ simulating-potential-impacts-of-covid-19-school-closures-learning-outco mes-a-set-of-global-estimates

Bouhnik, D. and Deshen, M. (2014). WhatsApp goes to school: Mobile instant messaging between teachers and students. *Journal of Information Technology Education Research*, 13, 217–231. https://doi.org/10.28945/2051

Carroll, H. C. M. (2010). The effect of pupil absenteeism on literacy and numeracy in the primary school. *School Psychology International*, 31(2), 115–130. https://doi.org/10.1177/0143034310361674

Causa, O., and Johansson, A. (2010). Intergenerational social mobility in OECD countries. *OECD Journal: Economic Studies*. https://www.oecd.org/economy/growth/49849281.pdf

Cunningham, A. E., and Stanovich, K. E. (1997). Early reading acquisition and its relation to reading experience and ability 10 years later. *Developmental Psychology*, 33(6), 934–945. https://doi.org/10.1037/0012-1649.33.6.934

De Hoyos, R., and Saavedra, J. (2021). It is time to return to learning. *World Bank Blogs*, 24 March. https://blogs.worldbank.org/education/it-time-return-learning

De Leon, N. (2021). Educación en Tiempos de COVID-19: Análisis para Políticas Educativas en la República de Panamá. Centro de Investigación Educativa (CIEDU). https://ciedupanama.org/wp-content/uploads/2020/09/Informe_Educaci%C3%B3n-en-Tiempos-COVID-_-CIEDU-1.pdf

Dichter & Neira Research Network (2015). Los adultos y el uso de WhatsApp en Panamá. https://www.dichter-neira.com/wp-content/uploads/2015/11/25.-Insider_PA_Uso-de- whatsapp.pdf

Gómez Domingo, M., and Badia Garganté, A. (2016). Exploring the use of educational technology in primary education: teachers' perception of mobile technology learning impacts and applications' use in the classroom. *Computers in Human Behavior*, 56, 21–28. https://doi.org/10.1016/j.chb.2015.11.023

Gon, S., and Rawekar, A. (2017). Effectivity of e-learning through WhatsApp as a teaching learning tool. *MVP Journal of Medical Sciences*, 4(1), 19–25. https://doi.org/10.18311/mvpjms/0/v0/i0/8454

Gottfried, M. (2014). Chronic absenteeism and its effects on students' academic and socioemotional outcomes. *Journal of Education for Students Placed at Risk (JESPAR)*, 19(2), 53–75. https://doi.org/10.1080/10824669.2014.962696

Holon IQ (2021). 10 charts to explain the global education technology market. https://www.holoniq.com/edtech/10-charts-that-explain-the-global-education-technology-market

INEC (Instituto Nacional de Estadística y Censo). (2017). INEC – Publicaciones. www.inec.gob.pa/publicaciones

Inter-American Development Bank (2014). Escalando la nueva educación: innovaciones inspiradoras masivas en América Latina. https://publications.iadb.org/publications/spanish/document/Escalando-la-nueva-educaci%C3%B3n-Innovaciones-inspiradoras-masivas-en-Am%C3%A9rica-Latina.pdf

Jones, C. (2019). Capital, neoliberalism and educational technology. *Postdigital Science and Education*, 1, 288–292. https://doi.org/10.1007/s42 438-019-00042-1

Kemp, S. (2020). DataReportal. Digital 2020: Panama. https://datarepor tal.com/reports/digital-2020-panama

Klein, N. (2005). *The Shock Doctrine: The Rise of Disaster Capitalism*. Picador.

Komljenovic, J. (2021). The rise of education rentiers: digital platforms, digital data and rents. *Learning, Media and Technology*, 46(3), 320–332. https://doi.org/10.1080/17439884.2021.1891422

LAGAE (La Gran Alianza Educativa). (2021). GreatFon. https://greatfon. com/v/lagranalianzaeducativa.

LoGerfo, L., Nichols, A., and Reardon, S. F. (2006). The Urban Institute. Achievement gains in elementary and high school. https://www.urban. org/sites/default/files/publication/50771/411290-Achievement-Gains-in-Elementary-and-High-School.PDF

McKenzie, D. (2011). Power calculations 101: dealing with incomplete take-up. *World Bank Blogs*, 23 May. https://blogs.worldbank.org/impact evaluations/power-calculations-101-dealing-with-incomplete-take-up

McKenzie, D. (2019). Take-up and the inverse-square rule for power calculations revisited: when does power not fall quite so drastically with take-up, and when does lower take-up increase power? *World Bank Blogs*, 23 September. https://blogs.worldbank.org/impact evaluations/take-and-inverse-square-rule-power-calculations-revisi ted-when-does-power-not

MEDUCA (Ministerio de Educación de la República de Panamá). (2019) *Resultados de pruebas CRECER 2018*. MEDUCA.

MEDUCA)/OECD (Organisation for Economic Co-operation and Development) (2019). *PISA Panamá: Programa para la Evaluación Internacional de Estudiantes*. https://www.oecd.org/pisa/pisa-for-development/Panama _PISA_D_National_Report.pdf

Muñoz-Najar, A., Gilberto, A., Hasan, A., Cobo, C., Azevedo, J. P., and Akmal, M. (2021). *Remote Learning during COVID-19: Lessons from Today, Principles for Tomorrow*. World Bank.

National Institute for Literacy and National Center for Family Literacy (2008). *Developing Early Literacy: Report of the National Early Literacy Panel*. https://lincs.ed.gov/publications/pdf/NELPReport09.pdf

OECD (Organisation for Economic Co-operation and Development) (2011). PISA in Focus. Private schools: Who benefits? https://www.oecd. org/pisa/pisaproducts/pisainfocus/48482894.pdf

OECD (2017). *Multi-dimensional Review of Panama – Volume 1: Initial Assessment*. Chapter 3 – Social inclusion in Panama. https://www.oecd-ilibrary.org/development/multi-dimensional-review-of-panama_978926 4278547-en

OECD (2019). 100 things we've learned from PISA. *OECD Education and Skills Today*, 17 September. https://oecdedutoday.com/pisa-100-findings-education-learning/

OECD (2020a). Education responses to Covid-19: embracing digital learning and online collaboration. https://www.oecd-ilibrary.org/education/education-responses-to-covid-19-embracing-digital-learning-and-online-collaboration_d75eb0e8-en

OECD (2020b). Publications. Programme for International Student Assessment. https://www.oecd.org/pisa/publications/pisa-2018-results.htm

Orozco, V. (2021). Mobile-based solutions can strengthen human capital gains disrupted by COVID-19 in developing countries. *World Bank Blogs*, 29 September. https://blogs.worldbank.org/digital-development/mobile-based-solutions-can-strengthen-human-capital-gains-disrupted-covid-19

Regan, P. M., and Khwaja, E. T. (2019). Mapping the political economy of education technology: a networks perspective. *Policy Futures in Education*, 17(8), 1000–1023.

Rodriguez-Segura, D. (2020). Educational technology in developing countries: a systematic review. University of Virginia, Curry School and Batten School EdPolicy Works Working Paper. http://curry.virginia.edu/sites/default/files/files/EdPolicyWorks_files/72_Edtech_in_Developing_Countries.pdf

Saltman, K. (2007). *Capitalizing on Disaster: Taking and Breaking Public Schools*. Paradigm.

Samaniego, A. (2020). Deserción escolar, mayor riesgo frente a la pandemia. La Prensa. https://www.prensa.com/impresa/panorama/retencion-escolar-otro-reto-educativo-frente-a-la-pandemia/.

Samaniego, A. (2021). 'Reparar la brecha educativa llevará años': Nanette Svenson. *La Prensa*, 31 May. https://www.prensa.com/impresa/panorama/reparar-la-brecha-educativa-llevara-anos-nanette-svenson/

Seusan, L. A., and Maradiegue, M. (2020). Education on hold: a generation of children in Latin America and the Caribbean are missing out on schooling because of COVID-19. United Nations Children's Fund (UNICEF), New York, 2020. https://www.unicef.org/lac/media/18746/file/Education-on-hold-web-0711-1.pdf

Svenson, N. (2021). Panamá, el país con más tiempo sin aulas del mundo. *Agenda Pública*, 12 May. https://agendapublica.es/panama-el-pais-con-mas-tiempo-sin-aulas-del-mundo/

United Nations (2020). Policy brief: education during COVID-19 and beyond. https://www.un.org/development/desa/dspd/wp-content/uploads/sites/22/2020/08/sg_policy_brief_covid-19_and_education_august_2020.pdf

UNESCO (United Nations Educational, Scientific and Cultural Organization) (2020). Global Education Coalition. https://globaleducationcoalition.unesco.org/

UNESCO (2022). SDG resources for educators – quality education. https://en.unesco.org/themes/education/sdgs/material/04

UNICEF (United Nations International Children's Emergency Fund) (2019). Derecho a la educación. In *Situación de los derechos de la niñez y la adolescencia en Panamá*. https://www.unicef.org/panama/media/1621/file

UNICEF (2021). Situación de las Familias con Niños, Niñas y Adolescentes durante la pandemia por COVID-19 en Panamá – Tercera Encuesta de Hogares, Junio 2021. https://www.unicef.org/panama/informes/tercera-encuesta-de-hogares

UNICEF/International Telecommunication Union (ITU). (2020). How many children and young people have internet access at home? Estimating digital connectivity during the COVID-19 pandemic. https://data.unicef.org/resources/children-and-young-people-internet-access-at-home-during-covid19/

Verger, A., Moschetti, M. C., and Fontdevila, C. (2020). How and why policy design matters: understanding the diverging effects of public-private partnerships in education. *Comparative Education*, 56(2), 278–303.

Villalba, D., Luzardo, M., Fajardo, E., Villarue, J., and Tuñon, C. (2018). Impact of the factors associated with the third comparative and explanatory regional study in Panama. *Revista Espacios*. http://www.revistaespacios.com/a18v39n40/18394006.html

Wargo, E. S., and Simmons, J. (2021). technology storylines: a narrative analysis of the rural education research. *Rural Educator*, 42(2), 35–50.

West, M., and Chew, H. E. (2014). Reading in the mobile era: a study of mobile reading in developing countries. https://reliefweb.int/report/world/reading-mobile-era

Williamson, B., Eynon, R., and Potter, J. (2020) Pandemic politics, pedagogies and practices: digital technologies and distance education during the coronavirus emergency. *Learning, Media and Technology*, 45(2), 107–114.

World Bank (2021). World Development Indicators. https://data.worldbank.org/indicator/IT.CEL.SETS.P2

Yang, X., Kuo, L., Ji, X., and McTigue, E. (2018). A critical examination of the relationship among research, theory, and practice: technology and reading instruction. *Computers & Education*, 125, 62–73.

Yıldız, G., Yıldırım, A., Akça, B., Kök, A., Özer, A., and Karataş, S. (2020). Research trends in mobile learning. *International Review of Research in Open and Distributed Learning*, 21(3), 175–196. https://doi.org/10.19173/irrodl.v21i3.4804

11

Education as an Antidote to Underdevelopment, and the Epistemicide That It Has Entailed

Tobias Roberts

Introduction

Many children's first year of schooling is a mixture of excitement, wonder, and a bit of apprehension at the novelty of being away from the comforts, reassurances, and familiarities of life at home. In most cases, however, the child quickly assimilates to their new surroundings, integrating seamlessly into the educational atmosphere. Despite the novelty of unfamiliar settings and new faces, the school environment is customarily similar to the homes and communities from where they have come.

Yet, for an indigenous Mayan child from rural Guatemala, that first school experience presumably leads to foreseeable distress at the substantial variances between the community/family life they have known and the school environment they perceive. The difference in language is, of course, the first palpably felt shock. Though there may be a bilingual teacher that helps the child ease into the new language, the majority of classes from the beginning are taught in Spanish. Thus, the first years of schooling serve as a compulsory introduction into a language that is not their own, a language that is a requisite for entry into the world of education. The child quickly learns to segregate and compartmentalize the two languages: their Mayan language for home use and Spanish as mandatory for their schooling.

The physical structure of the school environment is also different. In rural communities, where adobe and wood homes abound, the tidily painted cinder block walls of the school are yet another striking disparity that the child perceives. Tile floors that smell of bleach and disinfectant certainly do not resemble the earthen floors and walls permeated with the smell of smoke from the constant wood fire of their home kitchen.

As the school's central authority figure, the teacher is also unmistakably different from the parents, grandparents, and other elders within their community. Though the teacher is most likely of shared ethnic identity, she may not wear traditional dress and may only intermittently throw in a few words of the children's mother tongue while doing her best to look and speak like a Ladino.[1]

After these initial, corporeal impressions begin to fade into a new and enforced normalcy, the educational content of the subsequent years of schooling also creates a sense of discord from the place and culture of the child's upbringing. There is no 'career day' where parents come to talk about their jobs or professions throughout the school year because the vast majority of those parents are subsistence farmers who are subtly derided by the official educational system. The educational curriculum strategically omits lessons about the significance of land/territory or the value of the *milpa* (traditional cornfield) to Mayan identity and livelihoods. As the child progresses through schooling, most subjects are taught with a subliminal undertone that encourages rising above those rural, agrarian, and primarily indigenous places. The child hastily perceives that schooling is a heralded opportunity for getting ahead ('salir adelante') and serves as a prospect to transcend and leave behind those cornfields, adobe homes, and other supposedly archaic aspects of land-based livelihoods.

After several years of this daily education, is it any wonder that this indigenous child struggles to communicate with her elderly grandmother, who once taught her the stories and values of her people? Should society find it strange that she is ashamed of her mother's inability to write or her father's insistence on going into the cornfield every morning to come back late at night with *guisquil*[2] leaves and *hierba mora*[3] to feed the family? After finishing her primary education, it should come as no surprise that the child begs her family to let her go into the nearest urban area to live with a distant aunt or perhaps rent a room while she pursues her high school diploma, likely never to return permanently to the village she leaves behind.

But why is this applauded? Why does society consider this normal? Why will so many people see this child's story as yet another testament to human willpower and the desire to overcome the limitations of his or her upbringing? Why, instead, is this 'educational journey' not seen as a continuation of years of dispossession, destruction, and genocidal violence against Mayan peoples and cultures? Though there may be a public outcry regarding the violence of residential schools and other genocidal educational programmes of past decades and centuries, rarely are the ways in which modern-day schools continue to participate in the extermination of the alternative epistemologies and lifestyles of indigenous peoples across the world taken into consideration.

This chapter argues that the Western development paradigm, which so profoundly shapes the epistemological framework of the modern-day capitalist and globalized civilization, proscribes Western-raised and educated people from understanding, valuing, and respecting the alternative epistemologies of indigenous people and communities. In the first part of this chapter, I explore how the governing rationality of the Western paradigm has contributed to the denigration and disparagement of rural, peasant, and indigenous communities in Guatemala. More specifically, I aim to identify how educational norms contribute to this disparagement. Throughout this section, I will be following the work of different postdevelopment thinkers, including Gustavo Esteva, Arturo Escobar, Boaventura de Sousa Santos, and the critical theory of Wendy Brown. The second section of this chapter will briefly look at what is being lost due to the homogenizing effects of the Western development paradigm and the role of education in furthering this governing rationality. Specifically, I look at how indigenous thought and praxis diverge from that of the predominant Western rationality. The last section will analyse two concrete examples of educational resistance to the homogenizing impositions of official education in Guatemala. Both the Ixil University and the Utz Kaslimaal Collective challenge the hegemony of Western educational norms and seek to create educational alternatives that respect, value, and esteem the specific, territorial epistemologies of place-based cultures.

The information and analysis for this chapter has stemmed from the experience of having lived and worked between El Salvador and Guatemala for the past 16 years. While living in the Maya Ixil region of Guatemala (the northern Quiché department), I spent five years working as a consultant with the Ixil University during its early years of formation, and accompanying Ixil students in their final year of study. I also currently co-head the Utz K'aslimaal Collective based in Santiago Atitlan, Guatemala, a grassroots educational organization in Guatemala that engages in diverse efforts to promote and make visible Mayan expressions and articulations of The Good Life (Buen Vivir).

The education/development connection

In this first section, I will look at the origins of the development discourse. From its roots in the post-Second World War restructured political landscape, the idea that progress and development were the birthright of every human being, and that value and worth were connected to those goals quickly became widely adopted. I then turn my attention to the role of education in furthering the development discourse and how in more recent years neoliberalism has even further buttressed the hegemony of Western rationality.

The origins of the development discourse

Gustavo Esteva from the Universidad de la Tierra in Oaxaca, Mexico, says that: 'For two-thirds of the people on Earth, to think of development – any kind of development – requires first the perception of themselves as underdeveloped, in a subordinate position, after comparing their own situation with an established standard' (Esteva, 2018, p 3).

Forms of Western colonialism and hegemony have unremittingly manifested the supposed superiority of the Western standard and paradigm since 1492. In more recent decades, as part of an effort to reduce the most tangible and violent expressions of this colonialism, the concept of underdevelopment has been used as a tool to disparage alternative expressions of livelihoods. From the vantage point of progress and development, Western powers have assumed the monopoly over detailing and defining what a 'good life' entails.

However, it is essential to recognize that this dominating narrative is relatively contemporary. The concept of developed and underdeveloped nations did not gain traction until the post-Second World War years. A 1951 document prepared by the United Nations Department of Social and Economic Affairs reads:

> There is a sense in which rapid economic progress is impossible without painful adjustments. Ancient philosophies have to be scrapped, old social institutions have to disintegrate; bonds of caste, creed, and race have to burst; and large numbers of persons who cannot keep up with progress have to have their expectations of a comfortable life frustrated. Very few communities are willing to pay the full price of economic progress. (United Nations Department of Social and Economic Affairs, 1951, p 19)

From its very beginnings, the development industry, which sought to foster economic progress at all costs, unapologetically demanded the disintegration of 'social institutions' and 'ancient philosophies' of rural and indigenous cultures worldwide. In the ensuing decades, 'the full price of economic progress', which the document alludes to, has been paid through the destruction of territorial lifestyles and the elimination of alternative epistemologies in order to make way for the homogenization of the globalized, free-market world that has encroached upon every corner of the planet.

The assumed benignity of progress and development

This development discourse has become a fundamental pillar of Western rationality in the subsequent seven decades. Rarely do people call into question the assumed benefits of progress, economic growth, rising affluence, and the expectations of a comfortable life. Poverty is an evil that must be defeated; better incomes and more purchasing power led to more satisfaction; higher standards of living must be irrevocably pursued to improve the human condition; and all of these beliefs are foregone conclusions in the Western governing rationality that is homogenizing the world.

Arturo Escobar, speaking of how this development discourse has comprehensively penetrated the Western worldview and understanding of reality, writes: 'One could criticize a given approach and propose modifications or improvements accordingly, but the fact of development itself, and the need for it, could not be doubted. Development had achieved the status of a certainty in the social imaginary' (Escobar, 2011, p 5).

Though this Western governing rationality is undoubtedly multifaceted, its main attributes include an acclamation of the individual over the community and a firm attachment to a competitive economic system focused on unrelenting growth, industrialism, and market primacy. In a world where everything is a commodity, economic growth is a requisite for progress, affluence, and wellbeing, which is the primary economic indicator of the health of society. Today, Western levels of consumption, comfort, and lifestyle patterns are almost universally coveted. Political parties of all colours and ideologies worldwide construct policies that blindly pursue economic growth to achieve the prosperity summarized in the emblematic American Dream.[4] Of course, structural adjustment policies, debt management, and other instruments of coercion and intimidation by the neocolonialist financial powers of the day also help to further advance the political agenda of the development discourse. Any economic constraint or obstacle to increased individual consumption and growth is seen as a throwback to the primitive and stagnant lives that modernity has allowed modern-day civilization to conquer and overcome.

Escobar continues by saying that: 'A type of development was promoted which conformed to the ideas and expectations of the affluent West, to what the Western countries judged to be a normal course of evolutions and progress ... By conceptualizing progress in such terms, this development strategy became a powerful instrument for normalizing the world' (Escobar, 2011, p 26).

Western nations assumed the hegemonic authority to define the parameters of poverty and prescribe formulas to 'defeat' that poverty. This has contributed to a deepening sense of subordination and inequality, especially amongst the rural, agrarian, and predominantly indigenous communities of Central America. This Western crusade against 'underdevelopment' has been advanced by several institutional authorities, including structural adjustment policies of international financial institutions, public development programmes of national governments, and by the thousands of nonprofit development organizations working around the world.

This 'development offensive' has led millions of people across Guatemala and the rest of the 'underdeveloped' world to have normalized the prevailing assumptions and tenets of this governing Western rationality. The combination of mass media, an encroaching capitalist economy, increased access to technology, and the standards and aspirations imbued through public schooling have all taught them to equate happiness and value with increased consumer capacity. However, there are still large sectors of the population, predominantly peasant and indigenous communities in rural territories, who sustain traditional livelihoods that contradict the postulations of the dominant development discourse.

In Guatemala, these alternative livelihoods arise from land-based cultures where a sense of territorial belonging has impeded 'upward' socioeconomic mobility, which requires rootlessness and an unfettered ability to move to wherever the next economic opportunity lies. These livelihoods also arise from an epistemological framework that is fundamentally different from the predominant Western development paradigm. Because of these foundational differences, the agrarian or indigenous epistemologies of Guatemala's Mayan and peasant communities are often energetically attacked by the hegemonic Western rationality.

Mining, energy, and other large transnational corporate interests often deride and ridicule Mayan communities who oppose these types of mega-projects in their territories, accusing them of rejecting the opportunity for a better life (or a higher salary) for the youth in their community. As a more camouflaged critique, schools often urge students to use their education to escape the supposed drudgery of the rural, agrarian lifestyles of their parents and preceding generations. It is not uncommon at parent–teacher conferences in Guatemala for educators to attempt to convince parents that schooling offers a better future for their children. This automatically assumes that the place-based, territorial lifestyles that have sustained these cultures for thousands of years are inherently inferior to the promises of increased 'progress' that education brings.

The author Boaventura de Sousa Santos defines 'epistemicide' as the murder of knowledge. According to him: 'Unequal exchanges among cultures have always implied the death of the knowledge of the subordinated culture, hence the death of the social groups that possessed it' (de Sousa

Santos, 2014, p 149). The continual encounter of Western development rationality with indigenous, land-based cultures is certainly imbalanced, with a disproportionate amount of power and influence given to the former.

De Sousa Santos continues: 'Whatever knowledge does not fit the image [of Western scientific knowledge] is discarded as a form of ignorance … The epistemological privilege that modern science grants to itself is thus the result of the destruction of all alternative knowledges that could eventually question such privilege' (2014, p 243).

The role of education in advancing the hegemony of the development discourse

So what exactly does education have to do with all of this? In Guatemala, as in other parts of the 'underdeveloped world', official forms of education have played a fundamental role in advancing and establishing the hegemony of the Western development rationality. Schools have been one of the primary vehicles for the imposition of the development discourse that has led to the epistemicide of alternative worldviews and livelihoods. Official schooling has contributed to the disparagement and degradation of formerly resilient rural communities, and the territorial rootedness that arises from that reality. How exactly does this happen? In most rural communities of Guatemala and other parts of Central America, the educational curriculum integrally promotes the core tenets of the Western development paradigm, including individualism, competition, the requisite for sustained economic growth, material progress, and market primacy. Young people from rural, agrarian, and indigenous communities often gather, through their schooling, that the lifestyles, values, and livelihoods of their communities are inherently at odds with the 'good life' that is to be pursued through education.

During the past four decades, the percentage of Guatemalan children enrolled in public schooling has increased from 58 per cent attendance in 1980 (n.d.; Inter-American Commission on Human Rights, 2022) to almost 81 per cent of children finishing primary school in 2020 (n.d.; The Global Economy, 2022). This has led to an even further exodus of young people from their rural areas of origin as young people move to urban areas where professions can be practised. This exodus also occurs psychologically, through a change of epistemological framework that depreciates traditional forms of land-based knowledge. In their book *Escaping Education*, Madhu Suri Prakesh and Gustavo Esteva look at how education encourages and stimulates a sense of progressing beyond roots and origins, denoting a clear hierarchical standard of worth and value:

> Mobility overcomes marginalization – goes the familiar global chant of education. Mobile individuals, like their cultures, escape the

marginalization of people going nowhere; of cultures stuck in their past; dwelling rather than pursuing progress by 'moving and shaking'. Through their education, however, children learn to leave home, not to stay home. The psychological and cultural price of this impact cannot be measured. The new social norm implies that the child's destiny is not to succeed the parents, but to outmode them; succession is substituted for supersession. Neither school nor University looks toward passing on an unimpaired cultural inheritance. Instead, they push and promote the professional career. This orientation is 'necessarily theoretical, speculative, and mercenary'. The emphasis is on earning money in a provisional future that has nothing to do with place, commons, or community. Parents and children are separated from each other; made useless to one another. (Prakash and Esteva, 2008, p 6)

Education, then, is perhaps the primary pathway for fostering the authority and hegemony of the Western 'development paradigm'.

Returning to the hypothetical description of the impressions of schooling on a young Mayan child, many of the ways in which education furthers the Western development agenda and the standards that it enforces are symbolic in nature. Education, especially past primary/elementary grades, takes place almost exclusively in Spanish-speaking urban areas. This forces young, indigenous children and youth out of their rural communities and into the urban, increasingly commercial centres that have largely adopted the tenets of the Western development paradigm. The forced geographical migration that continued education compels leads to the expulsion of young people from their rural communities of origin and is undoubtedly a contributing factor to the rapid urbanization of Guatemala. Furthermore, this integration into Western-centric urban areas where schools are located separates young people from the traditional governance, economics, and even spirituality of their rural upbringing. Once in the city, the mayor and other government-elected political figures are the final authority, superseding the traditional authorities and elders from their communities. The land-based wealth of corn, land, and animals is superseded by salaries and access to money in a monetized economy. And the Catholic or Evangelical churches tend to succeed the Mayan spiritual guides who continue to practise traditional elements of Mayan cosmovision in the sacred sites that dot the mountains of rural villages.

Furthermore, the educational content in schools further disconnects young people from the land-based, indigenous worldviews that they inhabited from birth. Education is intimately tied to the job market, as it seeks to prepare young people for jobs that are effectively non-existent in rural areas. Increasing one's economic status is equivalent to salvation in the hegemonic Western rationality. The assimilation of the development paradigm and neoliberal rationality has led many indigenous parents in Guatemala to favour Western education to prepare their children for wage employment.

Prakesh and Esteva further the argument: 'The global mission of the educational system is secular salvation. The noblest variety of secular salvation saves the mind of the individual from remaining stunted or from rotting; while the most "practical" or "pragmatic" is defined by the market for employment: the holy "job market"' (2008, p 16).

Mayan children and youth, then, are physically removed from their rural communities to attend a school that prepares them for a professional career that, in effect, expels them from that community. Along the educational journey, they more intensely internalize the supposed superiority of Western rationality that promises them a pathway towards professionalization, material comfort, and greater affluence. Parents, grandparents, and elders, foundational sources of wisdom in indigenous, land-based cultures, are derided for their ignorance and outmoded lifestyles. This often leads to generational discord, essentially interrupting one of the primary avenues for transmitting knowledge: from elder to youth.

The effect of neoliberalism

In more recent years, the spread of neoliberalism has only further cemented the implication of education as a promoter of hegemonic Western rationality. Most people equate neoliberalism with an economic theory prescribing the privatization of public services, deregulation, globalization, free trade, austerity, and reductions in government spending. However, the political theorist Wendy Brown (2017) believes that neoliberalism has gone beyond a simple economic paradigm or formula to constitute foundational rationality that governs the thoughts, actions, and forms of organizing Western livelihoods. In her book *Undoing the Demos*, she says that neoliberalism as a governing rationality:

> transmogrifies every human domain and endeavor, along with humans themselves, according to a specific image of the economic. All conduct is economic conduct; all spheres of existence are framed and measured by economic terms and metrics, even when those spheres are not directly monetized. In neoliberal reason and in domains governed by it, we are only and everywhere homo economicus ... an intensely constructed and governed bit of human capital tasked with improving and leveraging its competitive positioning and with enhancing its (monetary and nonmonetary) portfolio value across all of its endeavors and venues. (Brown, 2017, p 9)

Neoliberal rationality thus amplifies and extends the essential traits of the Western development discourse discussed earlier. Capital accumulation and increased individual affluence are now to be achieved by the commodification of everything, including ourselves. Young people born into this neoliberal paradigm intrinsically learn that in order to prosper in life, one must sell oneself as part of a personal branding strategy. Young people are taught to see themselves as an economic asset. The ideal of the entrepreneurial individual is fetishized, and education is geared towards the ends of this rationality. Education, then, is just another part of a personalized branding strategy.

Brown argues that education in this context is primarily focused on capital development for individuals, businesses, or corporations: 'Knowledge is not sought for purposes apart from capital enhancement, whether that capital is human, corporate, or financial. It is not sought for developing the capacities of citizens, sustaining culture, knowing the world, or envisioning and crafting different ways of life in common. Rather, it is sought for "positive ROI" – return on investment' (Brown, 2017, p 177).

This type of education has little regard for place-based epistemologies and livelihoods that do not seek to maximize the efficiency of capital gain for individual benefit. Traditional epistemologies, which focus on respecting proper limits and boundaries that a territorial and community-based life obliges, are ridiculed in the eyes of an educational system that encourages adherence to the neoliberal rationality and whose primary focus is the preparation of young people to sell themselves in increasingly competitive job markets.

What is being lost?

De Sousa Santos argues that 'dominant epistemologies have resulted in a massive waste of social experience and, particularly, in the massive destruction of ways of knowing that did not fit the dominant epistemological canon' (2014, p 371). The modern-day neoliberal rationality that dominates the globalized economic systems, that guides Western epistemological understanding of the world and humanity's place in it, and that conditions how educational systems are shaped has unfortunately ravaged the wealth of alternative forms of knowing that arise from the particularities of place-based cultures. Some sectors of academia and science might indeed show token respect for the traditional ecological knowledge (TEK) of indigenous peoples. However, the depth and complexity of alternative, indigenous epistemological frameworks are most commonly annihilated by the 'dominant epistemological canon'. The Western mind, attuned to the all-encompassing framework of the development discourse, fails to grasp the far-reaching implications of alternative epistemologies and livelihoods.

In the 1870s, Nathan Meeker, an Indian agent working for the Federal US government, was tasked with 'civilizing' the Ute people of present-day Colorado and Utah. Meeker's mission, with which he engaged with religious zealotry, was to corral the nomadic, buffalo-following Ute people into cooperative agrarian colonies, thus freeing up land for Mormon settlers in the West. However, after several years of failure in this mission, Meeker wrote to the Commissioner of Indian Affairs: 'Their needs are so few that they do not wish to adopt civilized habits. What we call conveniences and comforts are not sufficiently valued by them to cause them to undertake to obtain them by their own efforts ... the great majority look upon the white man's ways with indifference and contempt' (quoted in Brown and Sides, 2007, p 374).

What followed, of course, was the barbaric genocidal policies of massacring buffalo herds and stealing Indian ponies so that roaming and hunting their ancestral territory became impossible to sustain their traditional livelihood. Though malicious intent and insatiable greed for land indeed drove policies against indigenous communities throughout the Americas, Meeker's statement given previously also suggests a genuine incapacity to comprehend alternative livelihoods and the governing rationalities that made them possible. As de Sousa Santos (2014) reiterates, this inability (and/or unwillingness) to comprehend what is foreign and different is most often characterized by an imposed hierarchical order wherein the Western values as denoted by the development discourse come out as the superior expression of human striving. Native Americans were seen as lazy, indolent, and too injudicious to maximize their benefit, as defined by the White man.

The homogenizing and exhaustive influence of the predominant Western rationality essentially disabled the capacity to solicitously consider other epistemologies and vantage points of relationality to the surrounding world. Quite simply, the domineering effects of this mindset make it close to impossible to understand that which contradicts the fundamental postulations upon which the development discourse rests.

The early governments of El Salvador expressed similar sentiments. In the late 19th century, ambitious government policies were enacted to exhaust every possibility for coffee production in order to introduce the country into the global commodity economy. In 1881 and 1882, the government of El Salvador, under the presidency of Rafael Zaldívar, enacted a series of laws decreeing the extinction of the communal lands (*ejidos*) collectively held and owned by the indigenous population. This decreed expropriation of the lands of indigenous communities opened up vast areas of the country for coffee production by wealthy landowners with connections to the oligarchic class.

The textual 'justification' within the Law of Extinction of Communities enacted on 23 February 1881 is telling: 'The division of lands owned by (indigenous) communities prevents the development of Agriculture, hinders the circulation of wealth and weakens the ties of the family and the independence of the individual' (Ley de Extinción de Comunidades – Wikisource, 2021, author's translation).

Again, the voracious greed for indigenous lands was the driving force behind the law. However, there also seems to be an authentic confusion as to why the indigenous communities did not willingly participate in the full exploitation of their lands to maximize production and profit. The response to this confusion was again to disparage the communal nature of indigenous epistemologies for not allowing the 'independence of the individual', a foundational aspect of Western rationality. In essence, the refusal to maximize individual standing, profit, and benefit was considered subhuman.

It is important to assert that the centuries of violence that Western powers have inflicted on indigenous communities is a necessary and expected derivative of religion preached with a sword, wealth and resource extraction by brutal force, and a globalized economic system that requires expendable populations and unlimited access to natural resources. This positivist, racist ontology upon which the Western worldview is constructed unsurprisingly leads to continued violence against indigenous peoples around the world today.

Lamentably, the same arguments and reasoning continue to be espoused by transnational corporations pursuing mining, hydroelectric, and other mega-project interests on the ancestral territories of indigenous communities throughout Guatemala, Latin America, and around the world. However, this brief historical account attempts to show that this violence is also partly due to the failure to comprehend or esteem the alternative epistemologies that resulted from place-based cultures. Part of the violence of the Western mindset is its deafness towards other cultures and epistemologies.

Beyond the obvious negative consequences for indigenous communities, the homogenizing, established standards of the Western development discourse have also prevented people in the West from learning from the civilizational paradigm of indigenous conceptions of The Good Life (Buen Vivir). The concept of 'Buen Vivir' is most often associated with the Quechua and Aymara indigenous communities of the Andes Mountains of South America. However, most indigenous peoples around the world share similar conceptualizations of what a good life entails. While offering a definition would be limiting, most indigenous formulations of a 'good life' refute the traditional concepts of the development discourse and focus on situating communities in correct relationship to the natural world and the surrounding community. Contrasting the guiding principles of each rationality is often the best way to begin to appreciate the foundational differences.

Consider the realm of economics. In today's neoliberal governing rationality, the commodification of everything is just the latest iteration of the economic growth paradigm that grew out of the development discourse. Economic growth is a requisite for progress, affluence, and wellbeing, the primary economic indicator of society´s health. The indigenous conceptualization of 'Buen Vivir', on the other hand, is founded on a requisite understanding of the biophysical limitations of the places, territories, or ecosystems where individuals and communities live. Community structures and norms are devised and implemented to enforce the collective observance of those necessary limitations. The concept of limitations or economic restraint is almost entirely negative in Western rationality. However, for the Mayan communities of Guatemala, limitations are necessary and the foundation for a cosmovision that requires a right relationship to the place that sustains.

Many of the most pressing ecological crises that are faced today arise from blind adherence to the economic growth paradigm and the increasing pressure placed on the ecosystems and natural resources that this system requires for its perpetuation. With an increasing focus on job preparedness, most education and schooling are unsuspecting of the growth paradigm and uncritically encourage young people to participate in this system.

The resulting suppression and veiling of the cultural traditions and the civilizational paradigms of healthy, rooted, territory-based lifestyles affect all people. Rooted, indigenous communities like the Maya Ixil offer a time-tested, sustainable lifestyle based on the acceptance of necessary limits. Most of Western history is a continuous repetition of the frontier mentality: abuse a place until it has nothing left to give, and then move on to conquer and abuse another place. In today's iteration, the ambition of upward mobility requires rootlessness and the ability to move to wherever the next economic opportunity lies. However, for the Maya Ixil, the territory is the foundational factor governing identity and requires an ethic of placed-ness.

The gravity and imminence of the impending ecological crises have essentially forced Western society to confront the fact that it has run out of new frontiers to exploit. The models of modernity are exhausted and cannot offer solutions to modern problems. The possible solutions to the global conflicts and crises of today necessarily have to include sources of knowledge different from the Western paradigm. Instead of trusting in science or some other type of technosolutionism to solve the increasingly grave problems arising, the rooted traditions that arise from indigenous onto-epistemologies offer a practical opportunity to learn and subsequently re-evaluate some of the guiding assumptions of the development discourse. The Ixil University is one such example.

The Ixil University: an attempt to rescue ancestral epistemologies and livelihoods

For the Maya Ixil people, the concept of 'a good life' is encapsulated in the word 'Tiichajil', which is most often translated simply as 'life'. For elders in the Ixil region, explaining the concept of Tiichajil to outsiders is often challenging, as a good life is experienced instead of theorized. Tiichajil requires growing one's own corn, beans, and herbs, and having access to fresh water and sufficient firewood. All of this, of course, also entails the common work of caring for their traditional territories that provide these sources of sustenance. An ethic of caring and respecting the land allows soils to be replenished to continue offering future harvests, springs to continue to run clear, and forests to thrive. A good life is also lived in a community, with proper respect shown to elders and traditional authorities. Thus, traditional systems of justice and governance are also a fundamental aspect of Tiichajil, allowing the community to resolve its problems and conflicts without outside interference.

The Ixil University was founded in 2011 after a group of elders, traditional authorities, and young people began to question why the values and ethics of 'Tiichajil' were entirely excluded from the official education system. As was explained earlier, schools created friction between the generations and expelled young people from the rural areas and livelihoods that defined the Ixil people for thousands of years.

However, the critical fracture in the educational/development rationality was that it simply was not working for the vast majority of young people. In this tiny corner of northern Guatemala, the local or regional job market was simply not able to provide any sort of stable, economically relevant employment for the hordes of young people who were buying into the prevailing logic and promise of the development discourse. Young people were leaving their communities and agrarian identities to pursue higher education, but were unable to find any sort of decent employment.

Every year, hundreds of young people from the Ixil region graduate as teachers to compete for the five or ten teaching jobs that the Ministry of Education makes available. The failure of schooling to live up to its promise to provide wage employment has led to a multitude of unemployed young people disconnected from their agrarian heritage, ashamed to go back to the land and the lifestyle that their education motivated them to surmount, and a generational rupture between elders and youth.

Given this bleak situation, the founders of the Ixil University rightly began to question the basic tenets and promises of the official education system. Whereas many young people ask, 'Where are the promised rewards and the pathway to prosperity and progress that we were assured?', the Ixil University questioned why the values, ethics, and practical livelihoods associated with Tiichajil were abandoned in the first place. Despite years of colonial violence, genocidal civil war from the 1960s to the 1990s, and continued dispossession of their lands, the founders of the Ixil University believed that the values and ethics of Tiichajil and the resulting agrarian lifestyle offered a better future to young people in the region.

Unfortunately, the generational rupture between elders and young people meant that many young people no longer had an intimate, experiential knowledge regarding the basic tenets of Tiichajil. The sacred transmission of knowledge between generations had been severed. The Ixil University sought to reconnect elders and young people, thus helping Ixil youth to 'valorar lo nuestro' (value what is ours).

In the process of creating an autonomous, alternative university, the Ixil people unabashedly sought to reclaim ancestral knowledge and reject the imposition of Western educational norms and epistemologies. This decision led to some educational techniques that outsiders might find unorthodox. The University has no physical campus with classrooms, blackboards, and overhead projectors for PowerPoint presentations. Instead, classes are held amongst the cornfields, in a sacred cave, next to a river, or in a community lodge. Though there are facilitators, those who impart knowledge and teaching are the midwives, spiritual guides, ancestral authorities, leading farmers, and the 'Alcaldía Indígena' (a group that administers and oversees traditional justice). The most important books are the brains and the memories of the elders in the community. Instead of merely studying Western authors and supposed experts of a given subject, the Ixil University prioritizes the unwritten knowledge that the community protects.

Introductory classes focus exclusively on reintroducing young people to the territories where they live. Young people spend hours hiking through forests and mountains to discover their communities' 'mojones' (boundaries). Subsequent classes focus on diverse subjects such as resource management, traditional spirituality, gender issues, traditional justice patterns, and others. Elders point out the different types of trees that grow in the forest and where the headwaters of springs are found. Midwives patiently explain the natural medicines that grow amongst the fields and forests. Ancestral authorities explain the collective governance of commons such as forests and pasturelands. Spiritual guides reintroduce young people to the importance of the Mayan calendars and take students to sacred sites for traditional ceremonies.

Because Tiichajil is necessarily experiential, students also are required to participate in the life of the community. They sit in on the sessions of the 'Alcaldía Indígena' to see how conflicts are resolved traditionally without relying on the police or Guatemalan court system. They participate in the 'faenas', or communal labours related to cleaning freshwater springs, protecting communal forests, and other tasks that ensure their communities continue to enjoy the necessities to thrive. Moreover, they are also encouraged to re-engage with 'xula', traditional labour-sharing practices between farmers where neighbours work together in the cornfields.

By the end of the first two years of the programme, students of the Ixil University can once again value and esteem the traditional lifestyles of their people. Furthermore, young people are rediscovering the 'functionality' of territorial governance systems, including ancestral forms of agriculture with a focus on local commercialization, the good governance that comes with ancestral authorities and traditional justice practices, and the sustainable resource management practices of their people. During the third and final year of the programme, students are encouraged to appraise their home community and identify a specific problem that their community faces. The last year of the programme is dedicated to a dissertation wherein the student interviews elders and other relevant community members to delineate the problem and offer a proposed solution based on the core tenets of Tiichajil. The dissertation is primarily oral, though students are also encouraged to put their dissertation into writing. The dissertation is defended in front of a diverse group, including ancestral elders from their community, traditional authorities of the Ixil people, and outside academics.

The Ixil University is actively discredited by the official education sector, with the Ministry of Education refusing to grant its status as a recognized, official university. Despite this form of epistemic violence, the University's success is tangibly felt within the communities and the wider Ixil region. Countless graduates of the Ixil University have returned to their communities of origin and are participating actively with their ancestral authorities and elders. Several graduates have also accepted 'cargos', or traditional responsibilities within their communities, thus ensuring the perpetuation of ancestral forms of governance. Others have conquered the shame associated with farming and have returned to their family cornfields. These young farmers have also been instrumental in mounting a thriving farmers' market in Nebaj to create local commercialization opportunities to improve the economic lot of the farmers. Other young people have become active in social movements related to territorial defence, accompanying elders and other community leaders in political struggles against mining and hydroelectric mega-projects in their territory. Lastly, and perhaps somewhat ironically, many Ixil University graduates have also been able to find decent wage employment upon graduating. Both governmental agencies and nonprofit organizations have come to recognize and appreciate the unique depth of knowledge that these graduates possess, and their connections to the local community and grassroots actors.

The Utz Kaslimaal Collective

The Ixil University is a prime example of an indigenous community that has identified the deceptions of the Western development paradigm, examined the role that official education plays in disturbing a mostly functional way of life, and developed a unique educational alternative that seeks to 'value our own' (*valorar lo nuestro*) in the process of reclaiming an autonomous epistemological framework. But what about people born into the modern-day Western world who are also interested in engaging with alternative epistemological visions of what a Good Life entails?

The Utz Kaslimaal Collective, founded in 2016, seeks to create educational spaces where Mayan communities can share their wisdom with students from Western academia. The Collective partners with different indigenous communities around Guatemala to design unique educational journeys where Western student participants step back, recognize their worldview in light of an encounter with an indigenous, non-Western cosmovision, and are hopefully provided an entirely new set of questions with which to challenge their commonly held assumptions about reality.

Most study-abroad and international service-learning programmes in Guatemala provide students with a provocative encounter with issues such as the poverty and injustice resulting from years of historical, state-led, and international structural violence against the Mayan people. Though the Utz Kaslimaal Collective certainly recognizes and acknowledges this genocidal history, the emphasis of the educational programmes deliberately avoids the temptation to victimize the indigenous population of Guatemala. Instead, the Collective unreservedly affirms that the Mayan communities that students visit and learn from are holders and inheritors of unique forms of ancestral knowledge.

Instead of coming to 'study' the Mayan people, Utz Kaslimaal encourages students to humbly absorb the reservoirs of knowledge and wisdom that Mayan communities embody. Instead of instinctively seeing only need, hardship, and poverty, the Utz Kaslimaal programme of study encourages students to challenge their conceptual framework to encounter the alternative cosmovision of the indigenous highland communities of Guatemala. Through engagement with an indigenous, non-Western cosmovision, participants are afforded the space to begin to identify and explore assumptions related to their commonly held presuppositions about reality.

One powerful example of this relates to the issue of the contamination of Lake Atitlan, a stunningly beautiful volcanic lake located in the Western highlands of Guatemala and the ancestral homeland of the Mayan Tz'utujil and Kakchiquel people. In recent years, massive algae blooms have been linked to increasing contamination of the lake ecosystem due to agricultural runoff and a lack of effective sewage treatment systems.

Due to Lake Atitlan's prominent economic role in the tourism industry, the contamination issue has attracted the attention of several powerful actors within the country. A consortium of private universities, government interests, and nonprofit organizations have subsequently created a plan to build a 'mega-collector', essentially a massive sewage treatment system that would collect solid waste from all the towns around the lake and pump this waste to a treatment plant in the coastal area. The proposal has been met with massive resistance by indigenous communities around the lake, who distrust the intentions of any mega-project and denounce the lack of proper consultation. Significant hostility and political tensions have arisen due to this issue.

Students who participate in a study-abroad educational program with the Utz Kaslimaal Collective meet with proponents on both sides of this debate. First, the technical solutions to the issue of lake contamination are presented by environmental engineers, biologists, academics, and other advocates for the massive infrastructure proposal of the mega-collector. Students generally tend to immediately sympathize with this vantage point as it resonates with some of the predominant characterizations of Western rationality. Specialized scientific knowledge coupled with the power of industry and technology is seen as the paramount authority to respond to the socioeconomic-ecological issues affecting humanity. This 'technosolutionist' response to the specific issue of lake contamination has parallels with other global ecological crises such as climate change and biodiversity loss to which students can relate. Big problems require big solutions and a technoscientific elite to deal with those solutions.

After meeting with proponents of the mega-collector proposal, students then spend a few days meeting with different members of the Tz'utujil community of Santiago Atitlan. They meet with groups of fishermen who care for the rapidly disappearing reed beds that used to shelter the coast of the lake before tourists, wealthy elites, and other massive hotel resorts began to privatize the beautiful coastal lands of Lake Atitlan. Though much less scientific in their explanations, the students hear how these reed beds used to act as a natural filter for the sedimentation that drained into the lake. They also provided local employment as local artisans would weave the reeds into mattresses (*petate*) used by families. The students also meet with the Tz'utujil ancestral authorities who mount political resistance to the mega-collector project and who situate their resistance to the mega-collector within the long history of dispossession and lack of respect for the rights of indigenous peoples. The particular issue of the contamination of Lake Atitlan offers a unique opportunity for young, Western students to grapple with two very different solutions to a common problem – solutions that arise from differing rationalities and reveal some of the fundamental differences between the prevailing development discourse and the rooted, territorial wisdom of the Mayan conception of the Good Life.

Though students quickly identify with the large-scale, technological, and scientific solutions presented by the Western academics with whom they meet, the inherent territorial wisdom of the Tz'utujil people begins to come into view by the end of the course. The local solution of restoring community control of the lakefront and re-establishing the reed beds might not appear as scientifically sophisticated as a massive sewage mega-project;

however, the practicality of a territorial-based solution that is holistic, integral to the local economy, long term in scale, and appropriate to place invites both an individual and communal responsibility that is part of a cohesive, territorial sense of belonging. The solution to the problem is not 'outsourced' to the techno-industrial elites but is instead intimately bound to the particular local livelihoods and responsibilities of the Tz'utujil people. After witnessing the community-driven response that arises from the 'Good Life' of the Tz'utujil people, the students, often for the first time in their lives, can question and engage with some of the elementary aspects of the Western rationality they have inherited.

Conclusion

Throughout this chapter, I have attempted to show how the established standard of neoliberal rationality and the development discourse is enormously influential on educational norms and practices in Guatemala. The Ixil University provides an inspiring example of an indigenous community that questions this standard and seeks to protect and rescue epistemological norms and praxis that have governed a functional, sustainable, and healthy way of life. The Utz Kaslimaal Collective seeks to create opportunities to share and disseminate the wisdom that springs from Guatemala's Mayan communities' alternative epistemologies and lifestyles.

As indigenous communities throughout Guatemala, the rest of Central America, and around the world, continue to organize and defend their territories and livelihoods from epistemic and structural violence, the establishment of autonomous educational institutions will most likely continue to expand. The increasing visibility of indigenous epistemological alternatives will not only stand to benefit the indigenous communities themselves, but also offers a unique opportunity for people brought up in the dominant Western rationality to encounter and learn from their profound wisdom.

Notes

[1] A Hispanicized person of Latin American origin.

[2] A commonly eaten vine in Central America (*Sechium edule*).

[3] Nightshade (*Solanum nigra*).

[4] The American Dream, defined by James Truslow Adams in 1931, mentions that 'life should be better and richer and fuller for everyone, with opportunity for each according to ability or achievement' (Clark, 2007). The American Dream equates values such as freedom with the prospect of unconstrained prosperity, economic success, and constant upward social mobility. Today, the American Dream (Sueño Americano) is considered by many marginalized people in Latin America as an opportunity to more fully participate in the capitalist-consumer globalized economy.

References

Brown, D., and Sides, H. (2007). *Bury My Heart at Wounded Knee: An Indian History of the American West*. Picador.

Brown, W. (2017). *Undoing the Demos: Neoliberalism's Stealth Revolution*. Zone Books.

Clark, J. (2007). In search of the American Dream, *The Atlantic*, June. https://www.theatlantic.com/magazine/archive/2007/06/in-search-of-the-american-dream/305921/

De Sousa Santos, B. (2014). *Epistemologies of the South: Justice against Epistemicide*. Routledge.

Esteva, G. (2018). Special feature: colonialism, development, and educational rights: a 'Dialogue under the Storm'. *International Journal of Human Rights Education*, 2(1). https://core.ac.uk/download/pdf/216990367.pdf

Escobar, A. (2011). *Encountering Development: The Making and Unmaking of the Third World*. Princeton University Press.

Global Economy, The (2022). Guatemala: primary school completion rate. https://www.theglobaleconomy.com/Guatemala/Primary_school_completion_rate/#:~:text=The%20latest%20value%20from%202020,62%20countries%20is%2091.11%20percent

Prakash, M. S., and Esteva, G. (2008). *Escaping Education: Living as Learning within Grassroots Cultures*, 2nd edn. Peter Lang.

United Nations Department of Social and Economic Affairs (1951). *Measures for the Economic Development of Under-developed Countries*. United Nations Digital Library System. https://digitallibrary.un.org/record/708544

PART III

The Latin Caribbean

12

The Impact of the Opening of the Market Economy on Education and Teachers in Cuba: An Analysis of the Special Period

Changha Lee

Introduction

Education in Cuba is one of the hallmarks of its revolution in 1959. The literacy rate on the island is 98 per cent and Cuban students easily outperform their counterparts in neighbouring countries (Carnoy et al, 2007). According to the international student assessment in which Cuba participated in 2006,[1] third- and sixth-grade students scored roughly one standard deviation higher than the regional average in reading and maths (LLECE, 2008). Moreover, unlike other countries in the region where there is a significant rural and urban divide in terms of students' achievement, in Cuba, rural students scored slightly less than urban students and the difference was minimal compared to the other countries (for example, third-grade reading: 7 points [Cuba] vs. 26 points [Honduras] vs. 28 points [Colombia]; LLECE, 1998).

The reason for Cuba's academic success largely derives from the government's exceptional interest and investment in education. Numerically speaking, when government expenditure on education as a percentage of gross domestic product (GDP) is compared, in 2010 Cuba invested more than double the global average (12.84 per cent in Cuba vs. 4.54 per cent for the global average) and more than that of high-income countries (5.31 per cent).[2] In addition, the government is heavily involved and centrally manages what goes on in the classroom; the national government mandates that teachers practise a child-centred approach, which is strongly associated with quality education as measured by student achievement exams (Carnoy et al, 2007). In such a context, where the government imposes tight quality control over education, socioeconomic background has a weak influence on students' academic achievement; in Cuba, regardless of the years of education their parents received, almost all students finish their schooling on time (LLECE, 1998).

Furthermore, the highly competent teachers in Cuba, who are also the beneficiaries of the government's heavy interest in education, influence students' academic success. They are regarded as professionals and enjoy a relatively high social status. Not only are they paid generally on a par with other well-compensated professionals, but they also go through many years[3] of a systematic, demanding, and competitive training process that is just as rigorous as that for persons in other occupations such as lawyers and doctors, who are often referred to as monetarily well rewarded and well respected (Gasperini, 2000).

However, as this chapter will argue, the preceding point may only apply to teachers who taught prior to the demise of Soviet Union in 1991, when the loss of the strongest ally pushed the country into a steep economic downturn, also referred to as the *Special Period*, which is considered the darkest, most challenging years in the history of Cuba. This chapter aims to analyse how the global economic pressures experienced during and after the Special Period have influenced Cuban politics and policies, including those related to education and teachers, and, ultimately, trickled down to the occupational decision making of individual teachers in Cuba, resulting in a chronic teacher shortage during the past three decades (González, 2013). To immediately enhance the coverage, the government lowered the entry bar to the profession, diversified the supply chain by accepting teachers with few or no qualifications, and shifted responsibility towards the remaining teachers by imposing extra work to make up for the insufficient number of teachers. Many of these measures have also been pursued in countries in Central America and the Caribbean, which suggest dim prospects for Cuba – that is, a continued teacher shortage in the education system.

As a guiding methodology,[4] I primarily relied on document analysis, reviewing relevant academic journals, official newspapers, and magazines published by the Cuban Communist Party (*Granma, Juventud Rebelde*, etc.), numerical data from the National Office of Statistics in Cuba (La Oficina Nacional de Estadísticas de Cuba [ONE]) as well as official announcements and reports from the Ministry of Education (MINED). A limitation of these data sources is that they are collected, monitored, circulated, and authorized by the Cuban government.

This chapter is organized according to the monumental events in Cuban history: the demise of the Soviet Union and the Special Period, the Battle of Ideas by Fidel Castro, and Cuba under Raul Castro. Each section outlines the dynamic between global economic forces and those from the political sphere, and introduces the relevant education policies generated as the result of their relationship. The chapter closes with a discussion of the emerging patterns.

Education policies and teachers in transitional Cuba

The demise of the Soviet Union and the Special Period

According to García Ramis (2004), in his report on 'The Situation of Pre-service and In-service Teacher Training in Cuba', the enrolment numbers in tertiary-level pedagogical institutes (ISP) grew to 48,000 students in 1994 and dropped to 38,000 in 1996, and again to 35,000 in 1998 (ONE, as cited in García Ramis, 2004). The graduation rate for the students who enrolled in 1994 and 1995 was only 12 per cent and 14 per cent, respectively, meaning that only one out of seven or eight students graduated from ISP on time. What happened in the ISPs in the 1990s? Was the program too demanding for students to graduate on time? What accounts for the falling number in enrolment?

García Ramis (2004) argues that the decline in both enrolment and graduation rates can be attributed to the economic crisis that Cuba encountered due to the collapse of socialist countries in the late 1980s and, most significantly, that of the Soviet Union in 1991. Scholars on Cuban education (Gasperini, 2000; Erikson et al, 2004; García Ramis, 2004; Lutjens, 2007; Goldstein, 2012) unanimously point to the economic crisis in the early 1990s as the tipping point when teachers fled to tourism-related employment for better-paying jobs, and teaching began to lose its attraction for the younger generation, which manifested itself in the decline in both the numbers of enrolment and graduation.

To elaborate further on the economic crisis in the 1990s, the loss of its strongest ally alone locked Cuba into a severe economic depression, since 85 per cent of Cuba's trade was with the Soviet Union, not to mention the dependence on its fuel, which accounted for up to 60 per cent of overall consumption on the island (Lutjens, 2000). As a result, 'Cuba's transportation networks and the heavily petroleum dependent agriculture ground to halt' (Sobe and Timberlake, 2010, p 356). Coupled with this economic downturn was the ever-strengthening US embargo (or blockade), namely the Cuban Democracy Act in 1992 and the Helms–Burton Act in 1996, which prevented and penalized foreign companies trading with Cuba.

As a response, Fidel Castro developed various economic reforms that were designed to address Cuba's excruciating economic constraints, and many of these reforms reflected those practices typically carried out in a transition economy (Moreno et al, 1997). Transition economies are those where countries are transforming their centrally planned economies into market economies, with common ingredients being privatization (transferring the ownership of state firms to private hands), liberalization (allowing prices to be determined in a free market), and other institutional reforms (redefining the role of state and introducing appropriate competition policies) (IMF, 2000; Estrin et al, 2009; Trivić and Petković, 2015). With the official name of the 'Special Period in Peace Time' (Período Especial en Tiempo de Paz), the newly introduced policies included opening up certain sectors of national industry to foreign investments, expanding the tourism industry, legalizing private employment in 150 occupations, liberating the circulation of US dollars, creating farmers' markets, and developing agriculture cooperatives (Moreno et al, 1997).

Changes in the economy signify changes in the labour market. The aforementioned reforms brought about a different landscape in the labour market, and the teaching force, traditionally made up of the most competent workers/citizens in Cuba, was affected. Teachers' monthly salary, which was 350 Cuban pesos or about US$13.50, despite being almost equivalent to other respected, public/state sector professionals such as doctors and lawyers, was simply not enough to prevent teachers or potential teachers from flocking to other sectors (Lutjens, 2000). They began to shift their interest to tourism where they could enjoy direct access to foreign currency. Compared to their local Cuban peso, US$1 (or 1 Cuban Convertible Peso [CUC]) was worth 24–25 times more.[5]

As education was the top priority in Cuba, even under the severe economic constraints, the Cuban government never ceased to invest in public education. For instance, in 1999, teachers' salaries were increased by 30 per cent, to the equivalent of approximately US$20 a month, with the hope of preventing an ever-expanding exodus amongst teachers (Sobe and Timberlake, 2010); however, the influx of dollars in tourism-related activities continued to draw teachers away from the classrooms. Throughout the 1990s, the annual teacher attrition rate was 4–8 per cent (Gasperini, 2000). Cuba has never recovered from the teacher losses during this time (González, 2013).

The 'Battle of Ideas' by Fidel Castro

During the latter half of the 1990s, the Cuban economy slowly recovered from the economic decline generated by the demise of Soviet Union. The GDP of Cuba, which dropped to US$22 billion, again reached its 1990 level (US$29 billion) by 1995 (World DataBank). Moreover, its strong ties with Venezuela and active investment by China alleviated the government's main concern of securing oil imports and gave Cuba confidence in the possibility of continuous economic recovery (Anderson, 2006; Font, 2008; Mesa-Lago and Pérez-López, 2013). Witnessing the improving economic situation, Cuban authorities quickly began to undo the liberalizing measures applied during the Special Period and criticized them for creating social problems relating to inequality.

Functioning upon Fidel Castro's campaign of 'Battle of Ideas' (1999–2006), countermeasures on economic fronts focused on limiting the access to hard currency which was considered the cause of growing inequality on the island. Ludlam explains that:

> With most ordinary national peso (CUP) salaries insufficient to live on decently, a fragmented labor market contains an aristocracy of labor characterized not by high levels of skill but by access to hard currency, convertible Cuban pesos (CUC) acquired through pay bonuses in key sectors, or tips in the tourism sector. And in well-stocked hard currency shops, Cuba's nuevos ricos (new rich) can be encountered who no longer work at all, having access to unearned CUC income from remittances or corruption. (Ludlam, 2012, p 45)

As a response, the government restricted circulating dollars by imposing a 10 per cent penalty on the amount and by shutting down small-scale entrepreneurs, including 2,000 private street stalls and other businesses, by 2005 (Font, 2008). As a result, the number of licensed entrepreneurs and foreign businesses halved.

On the social and educational fronts, the government reinforced revolutionary values and socialist norms, as many of these had been lost during the Special Period (Kapcia, 2005; Breidlid, 2007; Font, 2008; Ludlam, 2012; Ginsburg and Garcia Batista, 2019). Over a decade of individualist resolution of daily problems, as well as the fracture in the link between normal work and decent income, severely damaged and discouraged the commitment to the revolution (Breidlid, 2007; Ludlam, 2012). Fidel Castro noted the emphasis of the Battle of Ideas being the reorientation towards socialist ideology: 'We must continue to pulverize the lies that are told against us ... This is the ideological battle, *everything* is the Battle of Ideas' (quoted in Anderson, 2006, p 44).

The main aspect of the Battle of Ideas included mobilizing youth to take the lead, as the lack of revolutionary spirit, as well as the high level of youth unemployment, was considered a growing concern. Fidel Castro and other leaders realized that by capitalizing on youth as an ideological weapon, the country could not only win them back to the ideas of the revolution, but also tackle the social problems caused by their disengagement (Kapcia, 2005; Breidlid, 2007). The political objectives of programmes created as part of the Battle of Ideas were largely twofold: 'to give a potentially lost generation a stake in the system and guaranteed well-paid employment in socially useful tasks' (Kapcia, 2005, p 401).

In December 1999, the Battle of Ideas was officially launched, and shortly afterwards it was followed by a new educational revolution (Ginsburg and Garcia Batista, 2019). As part of the Third Educational Revolution (2001–2009), the government spending on education as a percentage of GDP doubled from 7 per cent at the beginning of Battle of Ideas in 1999 to 14 per cent in 2008 in the last year of Fidel Castro's presidency (World DataBank). During this time, the network of emergency training schools (Escuelas Emergentes),[6] upper secondary-level institutions, were established to respond to the immediate needs of the society, covering five specific areas: social work, primary teaching, nursing, cultural education, and instruction of information technology. In terms of primary teaching, *emergente* primary school teachers were prepared 'to reduce the class size to a promised [20] to a class and to address staff shortages caused by the exodus from the public sector to the dollar economy' (Kapcia, 2005, p 401).

Moreover, access to higher education was widely expanded through offering university courses through TV channels (University for All [Universidad para Todos]) and extending higher education centres to all municipalities (*municipios*), where courses could be provided by the university staff during flexible times (Kapcia, 2005; Breidlid, 2007; Font, 2008). As a result, the gross tertiary enrolment rate in Cuba exploded from 22 per cent in 2000 to more than 100 per cent in 2007 (World DataBank). The dramatic expansion of tertiary education played an ideological role similar to that in the 1960s of primary education and of secondary education in the 1970s (Quintero López, 2012). It embodied the ethos of Education for All, which was central to socialist development in transitional Cuba (Kapcia, 2005).

Another essential element in the Third Educational Revolution[7] was the introduction of a comprehensive junior secondary teacher position, Profesor General Integral (PGI),[8] the holder of which was expected to teach all subjects, in contrast to the earlier system where teachers only taught their specialized subject (Breidlid, 2007; Martín Sabina et al, 2012; Ginsburg and Garcia Batista, 2019). The student teachers in the PGI course were admitted after finishing the twelfth-grade in upper secondary school and then spent their first year in the programme at the main campus of their university. From the second to the fifth year, they combined work and study by teaching full time in a junior secondary school (seventh to ninth grade) and taking university courses in the municipalities once a week. The focus was to provide general knowledge and interdisciplinary teaching through technology such as TV, video, and computers. Moreover, attention was paid 'to the social aspect of learning, where the idea of inclusion plays an important role in the rhetoric around the new reform' (Breidlid, 2007, p 624), and this was facilitated by keeping a small student-teacher ratio – a maximum of 15 students per teacher.

Cuba under Raul Castro

Strategies employed as part of the Battle of Ideas began to wind down as Fidel Castro fell seriously ill in 2006 and ceded power to his brother Raul Castro as acting president. Even before he was elected as the next president in 2008, Raul Castro was known to be in favour of reforms (Font, 2008). He agreed to the ideas presented by the reformers who were largely economists and other social scientists, and saw market reforms as an opportunity to check the state monopoly in certain areas, promote competition, increase efficiency, generate productive employment opportunities, and spur economic growth (Mesa-Lago and Pérez-López, 2013).

During his speech given on 26 July 2007, Raul Castro acknowledged that salaries are insufficient to meet basic needs and announced that reforms were carefully underway (Font, 2008). There he emphasized efficiency as a new approach for the country to solve complex problems:

> what has been achieved in recent years ... [was possible] with a clear conscience about our problems, our inefficiencies, our errors and our bureaucratic and/or slack attitudes ... *Efficiency* largely depends on perseverance and good organization, especially of systematic controls and discipline, and in particular on where we have succeeded in incorporating the masses to the struggle for efficiency. (Emphasis added)[9]

Translating the concept of efficiency, the Guidelines of the Socioeconomic Policy of the Party and the Revolution (Lineamientos de la política económica y social del Partido y la Revolución; hereinafter 'Guidelines') were approved at the Sixth Party Congress of the Communist Party of Cuba in April 2011 and shaped the following education reform. The overall message was that Cuba would preserve the accomplishments of the Revolution, focusing on education and health, but with a differentiated approach driven by efficiency (Backer, 2011). Section 143 of the Guidelines, for example, noted an essential need for the social sphere, including education, to eliminate excessive costs and find means to generate revenues for their continuous improvement (PCC, 2011). On education in particular, section 145 outlined how to make the most out of the existing labour force, and section 148 called for reducing spending on students' transportation, food, and basic living costs (PCC, 2011). These signalled the reduction or removal of some symbolic programmes which were launched and emphasized in the preceding decades.

First, the University for All programme introduced during the Battle of Ideas was scaled back, and measures to raise the bar and improve the quality of admitted students were emphasized, such as strengthening entry exams and academic rigour in secondary schools and universities (Martín Sabina et al, 2012; Ginsburg and Garcia Batista, 2019). The resources saved from reduced enrolment were instead devoted to expanding technical vocational programmes (agronomy, computer science, education, medicine, etc.) (Martín Sabina et al, 2012; Ginsburg and Garcia Batista, 2019) and moving students into more practical careers to reduce costs and fill gaps in the workforce (Frank, 2012). As a result, the gross tertiary enrolment in Cuba almost halved[10] from 120 per cent in 2008 to 63 per cent in 2012 and continued to plummet to 34 per cent in 2016 (World DataBank).

Another major change that occurred during the presidency of Raul Castro was the closure of the iconic programme, Schools in the Countryside (Martín Sabina et al, 2012; Ginsburg and Garcia Batista, 2019). The programme appeared at the height of revolutionary Cuba in 1971 and was designed to finance itself based on the revenues generated through crops harvested by the students. However, due to reduced student interest in engaging in agriculture, coupled with deterioration in the overall agricultural sector in Cuba, schools were criticized for their excessive cost and inability to finance themselves – a goal that has never been met since the inception of the programme (Carnoy, 1990).[11] Consequently, rural boarding schools were phased out in 2011, relocated to the urban areas, and their land was leased to farmers (Martín Sabina et al, 2012).

In teacher training, the government removed fast-track *emergentes* and PGI programmes (Espinosa Chepe, 2011) and reopened upper-secondary pedagogical schools (Preuniversitarios vocacionales de ciencias pedagógicas) all across Cuba which had been closed in the 1990s, 'when teacher preparation became a tertiary education activity exclusively' (Ginsburg and Garcia Batista, 2019, p 11). In 2010, 22 pedagogical schools were reopened with the purpose of more quickly channelling teaching personnel to pre-primary, primary, and special education schools. Later, they expanded to preparing primary-level English teachers in 2013 as well as lower secondary teachers of subjects with shortages of teacher (namely, history and mathematics) in 2017 (Ginsburg and Garcia Batista, 2019).

The four-year curriculum at these institutions includes academic subjects such as Spanish, history, mathematics (absent in the English teaching track) and pedagogical subjects such as psychology, pedagogical theory, and practice; from the second year, students engage in student teaching in local primary schools (Ríos, 2013). As for the graduation requirement, students need to score above the average of 80–85 per cent in the final test, and generally more than half of graduating students get to teach in schools that they selected as their first choice (Ministerio de Educación, 2010). Students who graduate from a teacher formation school are also granted access to higher education at the Pedagogical Science University (in the case of Havana) or in a school of education in provincial universities (Ginsburg and Garcia Batista, 2019). The following section outlines the shortage of teachers that persisted throughout the years under President Raul Castro.

Teacher shortage issue in contemporary Cuba

The problem of retaining teachers, also referred to as a teacher exodus, continued as access to the CUC economy widened and private tutoring became legal in Cuba. According to Rodríguez Guerrero (2013) in *Granma*,[12] the official gazette of the Cuban Communist Party (*Gaceta Oficial de la República de Cuba*), first announced private tutoring to be legal in 2010. This legalizing measure allowed for underground private tutors[13] to surface and resulted in a continuous departure of teachers. This is because, except for languages, teachers of other subjects are not allowed to give private lessons unless they leave the public system. The same article reported that by 2013, the government had authorized 1,023 people to hold licences to work as private tutors.

Coupled with the issue of teacher retention, recruiting and preparing future teachers became more problematic as youth were less attracted to teaching (Ludlam, 2012). Indeed, the Battle of Ideas, which was designed to instil revolutionary values and social consciousness in the young, was not successful, as their daily struggles continued, and inequality grew based on the access to the CUC economy (Font, 2008). Cuban youth became less interested in sacrificing themselves for national goals and entering teaching; they simply wanted to live their lives on their own terms (Font, 2008; Ludlam, 2012). As a result, recruiting future teachers in Cuba became more difficult over time, and this was evident in enrolments in the official teacher training institutes, such as pedagogical schools and pedagogical universities or colleges of education in provincial universities, where teachers are trained.

In higher education, the number of students enrolling and graduating with a degree in education decreased over time. According to ONE (2009; 2018a), the number of university students majoring in education reduced significantly from 113,000 in 2008 to 44,000 in 2017. What should be noted along this enrolment trend is the government's policy to limit the available seats and make college entrance more competitive (Martín Sabina et al, 2012; Ginsburg and Garcia Batista, 2019). Nevertheless, students' reduced interest in entering teaching was captured when calculating and comparing the graduation rate of those who entered university during the Battle of Ideas (2000–2003) against those who entered during the first years of Raul Castro (2008–2011). When calculating their graduation on time in five years and juxtaposing the two rates, that of the former group was much higher than the latter: it ranged from 21 to 33 per cent (2004–2007), while the latter was between 6 and 13 per cent (2012–2015) (ONE, 2009; 2018a).

In addition, the graduation rate differed significantly depending on where the training institutes were located; that is, the provinces that had low graduation rates in pedagogical schools, for example, aligned with those that suffered from severe teacher shortages. According to Barrios (2017) in *Rebel Youth* (*Juventud Rebelde*, an official newspaper published by the Union of Young Communists founded by Fidel Castro in 1965), the provinces that experienced teacher shortages during the 2016–2017 academic year were Havana, Matanzas, Camaguey, Artemisa, and Mayabeque, and they imported teachers from other provinces that produced enough teachers. For example, during the same academic year, Guantanamo produced 309 teachers in addition to its internal needs and managed to export teachers to the provinces in need: out of 309 teachers, a vast majority (85 per cent) were relocated to Havana, and the rest were split between Matanzas and Mayabeque (Merencio Cautín, 2016).

Despite the reopening of pedagogical schools and the relocation of teachers across provinces, the shortage of teachers remained, and it called for a diversification of the supply chain of teachers in Cuba. Ena Elsa Velazquez, the Minister of Education in Cuba, reiterated at the beginning of each school year that the coverage was met through alternative measures, yet the quality of teaching was compromised and therefore these alternative measures were not a long-term solution (Barrios, 2017; Juventud Rebelde, 2019). For instance, according to the report from the MINED, a total of 7,400 teachers left the profession in 2013, and for the following academic year (2013–2014), 15,200 teachers were needed (Lotti and de las Nieves Galá, 2014). Out of the numbers required to meet the coverage, only a third was made up of the graduates of teacher training institutes and two-thirds included a group of retired teachers who returned to contribute to the coverage among others who were not directly related to teaching (Lotti and de las Nieves Galá, 2014).

The ongoing battle of teacher coverage in Cuba

The shortage worsened with the increased departure of teachers. The teacher coverage rate for the academic year of 2018–2019, without the alternative measures mentioned previously, was 91.9 per cent, which was significantly lower than the two previous years: 95.5 per cent in 2017–2018 and 94.2 per cent in 2016–2017 (Barrios, 2017; MINED, 2019). The provinces that have traditionally been short of teachers – namely, Havana, Matanzas, Artemisa, and Mayabeque – continued to face their problems and relied on teachers travelling from afar. The number of teachers who left teaching during 2018–2019 was 12,000, which represented an increase from 11,700 in the previous academic year (MINED, 2019) and significantly more than the figure of 7,000 in 2013–2014 (Lotti and de las Nieves Galá, 2014). To make up for the loss of teachers, 13,900 were newly incorporated into the teaching force, 38 per cent of whom were graduates of teacher training institutes, while the rest were a group of people from other fields recruited to make up for the shortage.

In sum, the trend has been that coverage was met through compromising and undermining the quality of teaching in the classroom: lowering the entry bar for the teaching profession, diversifying the supply chains and accepting teachers with little or no education profession qualification, and shifting responsibility towards remaining teachers by imposing extra work to make up for the insufficient number of teachers.

The teacher shortage is to some extent unsurprising given that the official teacher salary was significantly lower than the national average. Unlike what is widely known about teachers' salaries – that is, that teaching is one of the best paid professions in the socialist regime (Gasperini, 2000; Bruns and Luque, 2014) – 2014 was the first year when the average monthly salary of state professions was higher than that of teachers: 584 CUP (US$24) vs. 527 CUP (US$22) (ONE, 2017). In 2017, the salary gap between the national average (US$32) and teachers (US$22) widened to US$10, and as a reference, jobs in sugar refining (1,236 CUP, US$52) and mining (1,219 CUP, US$51) industry were the highest-paid (ONE, 2018b).

Another reason that may explain the issue of teacher recruitment and retention in relation to salary would be that the monthly salary for teachers had plateaued over the past two decades since Fidel Castro increased it to US$20 in 1999 (Sobe and Timberlake, 2010; ONE, 2017; 2018b). During a similar time period (2005–2017), the average salary of people working in the public sector in Cuba doubled, and for those working in Havana, it almost tripled (2018b).

Responding to this salary gap between teachers and the other occupations in the public sector as well as the ongoing teacher coverage battle, the Cuban government announced an increase in teachers' salaries at the end of the 2018–2019 academic year. It was increased to 783 CUP (US$33), a 34 per cent boost compared to the previous year (583 CUP, US$24) – higher than the average state worker's salary in 2018 and still lower than the same in 2019 (ONE, 2020). According to Barrios (2019), after the announcement, more than 9,000 teachers either returned or withdrew their resignation request. Thousands of teachers who had dropped out previously and expressed their interest to rejoin had to go through a selection process in order to verify whether they were suitable to return.

Thanks to the significant rise of the teacher salary, which became slightly more competitive within the pay scale of the state system,[14] the teacher coverage rate in Cuba increased to 95 per cent from 92 per cent from the previous academic year (Barrios, 2019). To fill the remaining 14,500 teaching positions, the alternative measures from the previous academic year continued, including hourly contracts, support from university students, and additional paychecks for teachers with a higher teaching load in the classroom.

The 2019–2020 academic year ended abruptly on 24 March, due to the rapid spread of COVID-19 on the island of Cuba (UNICEF, 2020). Only 70 per cent of the annual curriculum was covered at the time, and the rest was offered in the distance learning mode. All academic subjects were delivered through public TV channels with national coverage (that is, Canal Educativo and Tele Rebelde), and Q&A sessions were offered live on TV shows addressing students and parents with questions or concerns. This modality continued until the beginning of the next academic year (1 September 2020) and for the provinces like Havana, until 1 November, where the cases of COVID-19 remained relatively high.

It is still too early to draw conclusions on the implications of school closure and the adaptation to the distance learning mode on teacher retention and recruitment during and after the pandemic. However, based on the available information, what has been found is that the provinces that have traditionally experienced severe teacher shortage have continued with the shortage (for example, Havana and Matanzas), while those that struggled relatively less (for example, Cienfuegos and Villa Clara) either continued with or encountered an improved situation. According to Yonia Falcóns, the Provincial Director of Education in Havana, for the new academic year, the city recruited 2,800 teachers from the other provinces, and there were still roughly 2,000 teaching positions that remained unfilled.[15] The province of Villa Clara, which prior to COVID-19 experienced a relatively mild teacher shortage, began its school year with a similar experience, whereas Cienfuegos managed to secure all teaching positions necessary in the classroom (Chaveco, 2020).

Discussion and implications

The overall economic picture has been consistent since the Special Period in the 1990s. The trend has been that Cuba slowly but gradually introduced measures that mimicked the open market economy. The first three years after the collapse of the Soviet Union wrecked the Cuban economy with consecutive negative GDP growths ranging from −10 per cent to −15 per cent (World Databank). Prevost has commented on the severity of the situation: 'Outside the context of war, no modern economy had been so devastated in the 20th century' (2019, p 9). Another global force that has long shaped economic constraints in Cuba is the US embargo, which has existed since 1958, since the triumph of the Cuban Revolution. The practice of sanctioning corporations for trading with Cuba continues to the present day. Under the Trump Administration, more than 240 measures were newly imposed (even in the context of the pandemic that resulted in Cuba suffering an 11 per cent decline in GDP), and it is back on the US list of state sponsors of terrorism (Frank, 2021; Yaffe, 2021).

Prior to the COVID-19 pandemic, Cuba steadily grew and managed to expand its economy fourfold between 1996 and 2018 (World Databank). Liberalizing measures harnessed this economic growth, including opening to foreign investments, expanding the tourism industry, legalizing private employment in some occupations, and liberating the circulation of US dollars (Moreno et al, 1997), many of which were temporarily removed by Fidel Castro during the Battle of Ideas for causing inequalities and later revamped under the leadership of Raul Castro. Compared to Fidel, Raul was more in favour of market reforms and promoted competition, efficiency, and productivity, the three principles that continue to guide the Cuba government under the new president, Miguel Díaz-Canel, since April 2018.

Efficiency became the ethos of Cuba following the Sixth Party Congress of the Communist Party in 2011, and permeated all aspects of society, including education. Education is one of the key accomplishments of the Revolution and continues to play a central role in the country. However, programmes that were considered costly for the government, such as Schools in the Countryside and University of All, both of which are iconic projects of Fidel Castro that emphasized the combination of work and study and guaranteed learning opportunities for all respectively, were either scaled down or removed due to their inefficiency. Consequently, tertiary enrolment in Cuba plummeted from 95 per cent in 2010 to 36 per cent in 2015 (World Databank), and entrance to the university level became extremely competitive.

With regard to teacher recruitment and retention policies, again Fidel and Raul Castro assumed a different approach. in the late 1990s, Fidel Castro increased the teacher salary to mitigate teacher exodus and intended to make teacher preparation a tertiary education activity exclusively; although for primary school teachers, he opened emergency training schools which were upper secondary level in order to make up for the teacher shortage caused by teacher exodus and reduced class size. Raul Castro, on the other hand, responded to the phenomenon by lowering the education level of teachers and reopening the upper secondary pedagogical schools that were closed in the 1990s when teacher preparation became tertiary. Following the reopening in 2010, they trained primary school teachers and have now expanded to the upper level, training secondary school teachers on subjects that lack teachers (for example, history and mathematics).

In addition, under Raul Castro, the government paid active teachers to take on more students and hours, retired teachers to continue teaching and receive double paychecks (full paycheck plus pension), and individuals with little or no education background to teach students, all of which had to do with compromising and undermining the quality of teaching in class. All these efforts notably failed to reverse the outbound wave of the teaching force until 2019, when the new President Miguel Díaz-Canel increased the monthly salary for teachers to match the average of workers in the state system. This salary increase indeed temporarily reduced the magnitude of the shortage (that is, the coverage rate increased from 92 per cent to 95 per cent); however, it did not act as a silver bullet in terms of resolving the issue. The 34 per cent salary increase was rather symbolic, comparing how the education sector ranks against the other sectors in the state system: it is currently ranked at 14th, which was previously 15th out of 18 categories prior to increase, which indicates that teaching continues to be poorly paid in relation to the rest of the public sector.

It is likely that the problem of teacher recruitment and retention will continue when considering the plight of teachers in relation to the economic and political forces elaborated earlier. Prevailing political and economic conditions will negatively influence teachers' occupational decision making and will likely serve as reasons for departure. Teachers will leave as long as market economy measures are in place: the existence of the convertible peso (CUC) to which private tutors have access – and which has a value that is 24 times higher than the local one (CUP), which is used to pay the schoolteachers – will continue to attract teachers to the private sector. Moreover, teachers will leave due to education policies that burden teachers with additional hours (including after retirement), continuously underpay them relative to other professions, and reduce their social status by lowering the entry bar and accepting instructors without qualifications, which ultimately undermines the overall professionalism of the teaching force.

The aforementioned practices mimic many of the predicaments that countries in Central America and the Caribbean face with regard to teacher shortages in their education systems. Virtually all countries in the region underpay teachers compared to the national average (for example, Honduras −5 per cent, El Salvador −15 per cent, Costa Rica −25 per cent, Panama −25 per cent, and Nicaragua −55 per cent) and report difficulties in finding sufficient teachers for specialty subjects such as secondary school maths and science, and almost half of students from teacher training schools do not pursue teaching after their graduation in countries like Costa Rica and Panama (Bruns and Luque, 2014).

For example, since 2000, Jamaica has experienced a teacher shortage rate of 1–4 per cent as thousands of teachers in subject areas of mathematics, science, and foreign languages have fled predominantly to the US and the UK and to other developed countries in need of English teachers. The government response has been ineffective, as its strategy resembled that of Cuba – simply relying on the replacement rather than the retention of qualified teachers. Teachers in Jamaica, too, struggle with 'poor remuneration, heavy workloads, poor working conditions, feeling of disempowerment, low status and disrespect' (Gentles, 2020, p 197).

If Cuba does not revert to the approach taken to teacher retention from before the Special Period – that is, if it does not actively invest in teachers by paying them on a par with other highly qualified professions, increasing their social status, and making teacher preparation rigorous and competitive – it will not reverse the exodus, as has been witnessed in the neighbouring countries.

Conclusion

The date of 1 July 2021 marked the first day that the convertible peso (CUC) is no longer accepted in Cuba. In December 2020, President Díaz-Canel announced that after 26 years of operating with a dual currency, the CUP and the CUC would be unified, a decision made in October 2013 but that finally took effect from 1 January 2021 (Gámez Torres, 2020). Cubans were given six months to spend or exchange their CUCs to CUPs (24:1) and the next six months to only exchange in banks in order to retrieve the remaining 20 per cent circulating in the market (*Granma*, 2021).

Eliminating the dual currency was long advocated as a top priority, due to growing inequalities and other ramifications in the society, including the teacher exodus. How would this new economic and political force play out for teachers in Cuba? What does the elimination of the CUC economy mean to public teachers as well as private tutors? Will it deter them from leaving if other economic, political, and cultural forces remain constant, such as the poor work environment, low pay in relative terms, and lowered social status? Or will it end the vicious cycle and improve the aforementioned forces to play in favour of retaining and recruiting teachers?

Until the Special Period, Cuban teachers enjoyed a high social status, were generally paid on a par with other well-paid professionals, and went through a selective and rigorous training process, which together embodied high professionalism and ensured the recruitment and retention of quality teachers in the classroom. Cuba has the answer to its teacher shortage issue. It always did.

Notes

1. Latin American Laboratory of Evaluation of Quality of Education (Laboratorio Latinoamericano de Evaluación de la Calidad de la Educación [LLECE]).
2. Based on the World Bank's Country and Lending Groups, the countries with a gross national income (GNI) per capita of $12,536 or more are classified as high-income economies. See https://datahelpdesk.worldbank.org/knowledgebase/articles/906519-world-bank-country-and-lending-groups
3. After the reopening of pedagogical schools in 2010, many teachers at the pre-school, primary, and lower secondary level start their classroom roles after only an upper secondary level of pedagogical school training, though the vast majority continue to pursue university-level pedagogical degrees.

[4]   Based on a previous study conducted during 2018–2020 (Lee, 2020).

[5]   As an example, based on salary and, more importantly, tips, a housekeeper in a hotel might earn double or triple a teacher's salary (Carnoy et al, 2007, p 32).

[6]   https://www.ecured.cu/Maestros_Emergentes

[7]   The previous two educational revolutions began in 1961 and 1975, respectively (Ginsburg and Garcia Batista, 2019).

[8]   The programme was discontinued under Raul Castro due to concerns related to the age and the professional knowledge and experience of PGIs who are only trained full time for a year after graduating from upper secondary school (Backer, 2011; Buchberger, 2013).

[9]   http://www.walterlippmann.com/rc-07-26-2007.html (author's translation).

[10]   This decline in the gross tertiary enrolment rate also in part resulted from the large expansion of university graduates in the population that took place prior to 2008, and thus the proportion of the population that 'needed' to enrol in higher education was reduced.

[11]   http://www.juventudrebelde.cu/cuba/2009-09-03/amplias-expectativas-genera-el-regr eso-de-los-institutos-preuniversitarios-urbanos; https://www.cibercuba.com/videos/ noticias/2018-09-18-u1-e186450-s27061-cuba-ha-sido-preuniversitarios-campo

[12]   The official newspaper of the Central Committee of the Cuban Communist Party.

[13]   Their official term is 'Reviewers' (Repasadores) as the Official Gazette in 2013 defines their role as follows: they help students study the materials of all levels of education defined in the national curriculum and help them enter higher education institutions (Rodríguez Guerrero, 2013).

[14]   Out of 18 different occupation categories, education ranked 15th in 2018 and the 14th after the salary increase in 2019.

[15]   See https://www.radiociudadhabana.icrt.cu/2020/10/22/a-habana-abraza-con-mucho- entusiasmo-nueva-etapa-docente/

References

Anderson, J. (2006). Castro's last battle. *New Yorker*, 31 July.

Backer, L. C. (2011). 'Order, discipline and exigency': Cuba's VIth Party Congress, the lineamientos (guidelines) and structural change in education, sport and culture? *Consortium for Peace and Ethics Working Paper* (2011–2012).

Barrios, M. (2017). ¿El maestro fuera del área de cobertura? *Juventud Rebelde*, 26 June. http://www.juventudrebelde.cu/cuba/2017-06-26/el-maestro-fuera-del-area-de-cobertura

Barrios, M. (2019). Ningún aula queda sin maestros. *Juventud Rebelde*, 21 December. http://www.juventudrebelde.cu/opinion/2019-12-21/nin gun-aula-queda-sin-maestros

Buchberger, H. (2013). Teacher Development in Cuba: An analysis of two strategies. Stockholm University. https://www.diva-portal.org/smash/get/ diva2:643823/FULLTEXT01.pdf

Breidlid, A. (2007). Education in Cuba – an alternative educational discourse: lessons to be learned? *Compare: A Journal of Comparative and International Education*, 37(5), 617– 634. https://doi.org/10.1080/030579 20701582491

Bruns, B., and Luque, J. (2014). *Great Teachers: How to Raise Student Learning in Latin America and the Caribbean*. World Bank Publications.

Carnoy, M. (1990). Educational reform and societal transformation in Cuba, 1959–89. In M. Carnoy and J. Samoff (eds.), *Education and Social Transition in the Third World* (pp 153–208). Princeton University Press.

Carnoy, M., Gove, A. K., and Marshall, J. H. (2007). *Cuba's Academic Advantage: Why Students in Cuba Do Better in School*. Stanford University Press.

Chaveco, O. (2020). Más cobertura docente en nuevo curso escolar en provincia de Cienfuegos. *ACN*, 28 October. http://www.acn.cu/cuba/ 71900-mas-cobertura-docente-en-nuevo-curso-escolar-en-provincia-de-cienfuegos

Erikson, D., Lord, A., and Wolf, P. (2004). *Cuba's Social Services: A Review of Education, Health, and Sanitation*. Background paper for the World Development Report.

Espinosa Chepe, O. (2011). Insufficient and Unclear Guidelines. From the Island, Vol. 1 (Havana) (Cuba Study Group) 14 June. http://www.cub astudygroup.org.

Estrin, S., Hanousek, J., Kocenda, E., and Svejnar, J. (2009). Effects of privatization and ownership in transition economies. Policy Research Working Paper. The World Bank.

Font, M. (2008). Cuba and Castro: beyond the battle of ideas. In M. Font (ed.), *Changing Cuba in a Changing World* (pp 43–72). CUNY Graduate Center.

Frank, M. (2012). Cuba cuts education spending, shifts priorities. *Reuters*, 3 October. https://www.reuters.com/article/us-cuba-education/cuba-cuts-education-spending-shifts-priorities-idUSBRE89217O20121003

Frank, M. (2021). Coronavirus slashes Cuba sugar harvest, piles on economic woes. *Reuters*, 11 May. https://www.reuters.com/article/cuba-economy-sugar/coronavirus-slashes-cuba-sugar-harvest-piles-on-economic-woes-idUSL1N2MX2PH

Gámez Torres, N. (2020). After 26 years, Cuba does away with artificial hard currency, raises workers' salaries. *Miami Herald*, 11 December. https:// www.miamiherald.com/news/nation-world/world/americas/cuba/artic le247776195.html

García Ramis, C. L. J. (2004), *Situación de la formación docente inicial y en servicio en la República de Cuba*. Instituto Central de Ciencias Pedagógicas.

Gasperini, L. (2000). The Cuban education system: lessons and dilemmas. *LCSHD Paper Series*, 48. World Bank, Latin America and Caribbean Regional Office.

Gentles, C. H. (2020). Stemming the tide: a critical examination of issues, challenges and solutions to Jamaican teacher migration. In *Exploring Teacher Recruitment and Retention: Contextual Challenges from International Perspectives* (pp 197–209). Routledge.

Ginsburg, M., and Garcia Batista, G. (2019), Reforming education and teacher education in Cuba: revolución and perfeccionamiento. In C. Ornelas (ed.), *Politics of Education in Latin America: Reforms, Resistance and Persistence* (pp 215–243). Sense Publishers.

Goldstein, A. S. (2012). Teaching in the shadow of an empire. In M. Ginsburg. *Preparation, Practice, and Politics of Teachers: Problems and Prospects in Comparative Perspective*, vol. 3 (pp 31–47). Springer.

González, I. (2013). Growing number of private operators in Cuban education. http://www.ipsnews.net/2013/12/growing-number-private-operators-cuban-education/

Granma (2021). Se ha recogido más del 80 % del CUC circulante. http://www.granma.cu/cuba/2021-05-04/se-ha-recogido-mas-del-80-del-cuc-circulante-04-05-2021-00-05-28

Guardia, L. (2016). La Habana importará 2.000 profesores de otras provincias. *Radio Televisión Martí*, 7 September. https://www.radiotelevisionmarti.com/a/habana-importara-profesores-secundaria-provincias/129450.html

Juventud Rebelde (2019). Presidente cubano asiste a reunión preparatoria del próximo curso escolar. http://www.juventudrebelde.cu/cuba/2019-04-25/presidente-cubano-asiste-a-reunion-preparatoria-del-proximo-curso-escolar-1

International Monetary Fund (IMF). (2000, 3 November). Transition economies: an IMF perspective on progress and prospects. https://www.imf.org/external/np/exr/ib/2000/110300.htm#II

Kapcia, A. (2005). Educational revolution and revolutionary morality in Cuba: the 'new man', youth and the new 'battle of ideas'. *Journal of Moral Education*, 34(4), 399–412.

Lee, C. (2020). The teacher shortage issue in Cuba: how the changes in its economic system impacted teachers decision to enter, remain, or leave the profession. Doctoral dissertation, University of Maryland.

LLECE (Laboratorio Latinoamericano de Evaluación de la Calidad de la Educación) (1998). *Primer Estudio Internacional Comparativo sobre Lenguaje, Matemática y Factores Asociados en Tercero y Cuarto Grado*. UNESCO.

LLECE (2008). *Segundo Estudio Internacional Comparativo sobre Lenguaje, Matemática y Factores Asociados en Tercero y Cuarto Grado*. UNESCO.

Lotti, A. M., and de las Nieves Galá, M. (2014). ¿Por qué te vas?: El éxodo de maestros (I). *Trabajadores*, 14 September. http://www.trabajadores.cu/20140914/por-que-te-vas-el-exodo-de-maestros/

Ludlam, S. (2012). Aspects of Cuba's strategy to revive socialist development. *Science & Society*, 76(1), 41–65.

Lutjens, S. (2000). Política educativa en Cuba socialista: lecciones de 40 años de reformas. In M. Monereo Riera and J. Valdéz Paz (eds.), *Cuba: Construyendo Futuro* (pp 1–23). Fundación de Investigaciones Marxistas/Viejo Topo.

Lutjens, S. (2007). Schooling and the Third Revolution. Recapturing the personal: essays on education and embodied knowledge in comparative perspective, 163. https://books.google.com/books?hl=en&lr=&id=__ knDwAAQBAJ&oi=fnd&pg=PA163&dq=Lutjens,+S.+(2007).+School ing+and+the+Third+Revolution.+Recapturing+the+personal:+essays+ on+education+and+embodied+knowledge+in+comparative+perspect ive,+163.&ots=xE_ILx_qKQ&sig=W

Martín Sabina, E., Corona González, J., and Hickling-Hudson, A. R. (2012). Cuba's education system: a foundation for 'the capacity to share'. In A. R. Hickling-Hudson, J. Corona Gonzalez, and E. Martin Sabina (eds.), *The Capacity to Share: A Study of Cuba's International Cooperation in Educational Development* (pp 53–72). Palgrave Macmillan.

Merencio Cautín, J. L. (2016). Más de 300 educadores guantanameros apoyan la docencia en otras provincias. *Granma*, 21 September. http://www.granma.cu/cuba/2016-09-21/mas-de-300-educadores-guantaname ros- apoyan-la-docencia-en-otras-provincias-21-09-2016-23-09-25

Mesa-Lago, C., and Pérez-López, J. F. (2013). *Cuba under Raul Castro: Assessing the Reforms*, vol. 6. Lynne Rienner.

MINED (Ministerio de Educación) (2010). Cuba: Abrirá sus puertas Escuela Formadora de Maestros Primarios en Pinar del Río. https://www.eumed. net/rev/caribe/2017/08/formacion-maestros-cuba.html

MINED (2019). Área de resultado clave I. Proceso de Dirección Educacional. https://www.mined.gob.cu/wp-content/uploads/2019/06/Evalu aci%C3%B3n-ARC.docx

Moreno, J., Pérez Rojas, N., Ginsburg, M. B., and McGlynn, F. (1997). *Political Economic Challenges and Responses within the State and Civil Society in Cuba. Cuba in the Special Period.* College of William and Mary.

ONE (Oficina Nacional de Estadísticas, República de Cuba) (2009). *Educación en la Revolución.* La Habana.

ONE (2017). *Anuario Estadístico de Cuba 2016. Empleo y Salarios.* La Habana.

ONE (2018a). *Anuario Estadístico de Cuba 2017. Educación.* La Habana.

ONE (2018b). *Anuario Estadístico de Cuba 2017. Empleo y Salarios.* La Habana.

ONE (2020). *Anuario Estadístico de Cuba 2019. Empleo y Salarios.* La Habana.

PCC (Partido Comunista de Cuba) (2011). VI Congreso del Partido Comunista de Cuba, Lineamientos de la política económica y social del partido y la Revolución. http://www.cuba.cu/gobierno/documentos/ 2011/esp/l160711i.pdf

Prevost, G. (2019). Cuba in an Age of Economic Reform. In *Oxford Research Encyclopedia of Politics*. https://oxfordre.com/politics/display/10.1093/acref ore/9780190228637.001.0001/acrefore-9780190228637-e-1518?rskey= 6MXCdo

Quintero López, M. (2012). Education in Cuba: foundations and challenges. *Estudos avançados*, 25, 55–71.

Ríos, C. (2013). Escuela Formadora de maestros ¿La esperanza pedagógica cubana? https://www.cubahora.cu/sociedad/escuela-formadora-de-maest ros-la-esperanza-pedagogica-cubana

Rodríguez, L. and Suárez Rivas, R. (2014). Elegir el camino del magisterio. *Granma*, 5 May. http://www.granma.cu/cuba/2014-05-05/elegir-el-cam ino-del-magisterio

Rodríguez Guerrero, L. (2013). La hora de los repasos. *Granma*, 11 October. http://www.granma.cu/granmad/2013/10/11/nacional/artic06.html

Sobe, N., and Timberlake, R. (2010). Staying the (post) socialist course: global/local transformations and Cuban education. *International Perspectives on Education and Society*, 14(14), 351–367.

Trivić, J., and Petković, S. (2015). Different features of transition economies: Institutions matter. In L. Dana and V. Ramadani (eds.), *Family Businesses in Transition Economies* (pp 71–96). Springer International Publishing.

UNICEF (United Nations International Children's Emergency Fund). (2020). *Educación en tiempos de COVID-19: La experiencia Cubana.* UNICEF.

World Databank. https://databank.worldbank.org/home

Yaffe. H. (2021). Day zero: how and why Cuba unified its dual currency system. *London School of Economics*, 10 February. https://blogs.lse.ac.uk/ latamcaribbean/2021/02/10/day-zero-how-and-why-cuba-unified-its- dual-currency-system/

13

Contrasting Trends of Low-Fee Private Schools in the Dominican Republic and Honduras: Dialectical Relationships and the Ethos of Privatization

Alejandro Caravaca, Mauro C. Moschetti,
D. Brent Edwards Jr., and Xavier Bonal

Introduction

Research on education privatization in low-income country contexts has tended to distinguish between privatization processes resulting from governments enacting pro-privatization policies, on the one hand, and privatization processes that have occurred without government intervention, on the other hand (Rose, 2005; Verger et al, 2016). The latter has been characterized as 'default', 'de facto', or 'grassroots' privatization, emphasizing the lack of proactive policy making involved in its development, especially when compared to 'traditional', neoliberal policy making actively creating educational markets and encouraging different forms of private provision (Caddell and Ashley, 2006; Tooley and Dixon, 2006; Tooley, 2013). This trend of default privatization has manifested itself through the proliferation of what are frequently known as 'low-fee (or low-cost, or affordable) private schools', among other somewhat more idiosyncratic names (for example, 'garage schools' or 'marginal schools'; see, for instance, Srivastava, 2007; Härmä, 2013; Languille, 2016). In essence, low-fee private schools (LFPSs) are privately owned and privately run schools targeting lower-income households or marginalized populations that often live in areas underserved by public schools. LFPSs are most frequently an urban phenomenon and ownership can vary across different contexts ranging from enterprising individuals to nongovernmental organizations (NGOs) and faith-based organizations. However, in recent years, many international aid agencies, development banks, corporations, and philanthropic organizations have started to promote this type of school as a cost-effective means of extending educational access. This support has resulted in the expansion of for-profit chains of LFPSs, at times through direct funding of the LFPS sector from governments and international actors (Riep, 2014; Junemann and Ball, 2015; Srivastava, 2016).

By now, LFPSs are a widely documented phenomenon. Much research has been produced examining the origins, quality, inclusivity, and affordability of LFPSs across different contexts, mostly in Sub-Saharan Africa and Southeast Asia, where LFPSs account for a significant part of the schooled population (for a review, see Day Ashley et al, 2014; Tooley and Longfield, 2015; Verger et al, 2016). Some researchers have also looked at the phenomenon in South America, where they have shed light on the interdependencies between LFPS expansion and government deregulation and subsidizing in Peru and Argentina (Moschetti, 2015; Balarin, 2016; Balarin et al, 2019; Moschetti and Lauría Masaro, 2020). However, when compared to these other regions, there is very little research on how this trend has shaped educational provision in Central America and the Caribbean. Arguably, the region is ripe for LFPS expansion, given that universal access to basic public education is still a major challenge for many countries and that government inaction provides an opportunity for private involvement in education.

Available exploratory research in El Salvador (Francis et al, 2018) and the Dominican Republic (Flores, 1997; Guzmán and Cruz, 2009) suggests the existence of a vast LFP sector which is either faith-based – most frequently Catholic and on occasion publicly subsidized – or nonreligious, owned by individual citizens. Research also shows that governments are either unwilling or unable to regulate the LFPS sector, if not largely unaware of its existence – especially in the case of the nonreligious private subsector, which operates on a self-funding basis, primarily through fees charged to families. As Francis et al (2018) show for the case of El Salvador, even though this may create a challenging scenario for unsubsidized LFPSs to proliferate, there is evidence that the inadequacy of government schools, together with a perception of LFPSs offering a safer environment, drives families in low-income and marginalized neighbourhoods to choose LFPSs, especially in areas affected by gang violence.

Yet, while these studies offer some initial clues about the characteristics of this trend, there is much that remains unknown when it comes to the extent of the phenomenon and the factors driving it in the region. This chapter responds to this gap by explaining and comparing LFPS trends and developments in Honduras and the Dominican Republic, and by situating these changing dynamics within the larger and deeper conditions and characteristics of these two contexts, which, as we will show, are witnessing new forms of privatization as opportunities emerge at the intersection of global and local constraints. To do so, we share and combine insights from two recent studies. The first of these studies focused on the case of Honduras and aimed to map out and explain the various kinds of privatization that are have affected the education system in the country (Edwards et al, 2019). While the study drew initially on a global governance approach, it later included a broader framework synthesizing elements from political economy perspectives, world systems theory, and postcolonial literature that made it possible to understand and explain the deeper foundations upon which privatization and globalization dynamics manifest themselves (Edwards et al, 2023). The second study focused on the case of education privatization in the Dominican Republic (Caravaca et al, 2021; Edwards et al, 2021). Although the initial focus of the study was broad in that we sought to map out – as in the case of Honduras – the different manifestations of education privatization in recent decades (with a focus on the time since the 1990s), it was ultimately narrowed to allow for a deeper analysis of what appears to be the most prominent form of privatization in the country, that is, the increasing involvement and influence of a range of nonstate actors in the formulation of education policy. Drawing on a political economy framework and on the notion of network governance, we identified and analysed the origins of this trend in the Dominican Republic, the growing tendency of hybrid public-private governance structures, and the emergence of new philanthropy engaging directly with the state – both formally and informally – and in state-controlled spaces as part of its efforts to influence policy formulation.

However, importantly for this chapter, in both studies LFPSs appeared as an unexpected yet relevant trend operating in somewhat different directions, with Honduras witnessing an expansion of the phenomenon and the recent emergence of LFPS chains, and the Dominican Republic experiencing a decline in what used to be a pervasive LFP sector. Notably, these trends cannot be isolated from deeper forces and political-economic structures at play in each country. With this in mind, in the next section of this chapter, we revisit our findings[1] and extract the most salient features of the default privatization/LFPSs phenomenon in Honduras and the Dominican Republic. The subsequent section offers a substantive discussion that reflects on – but also goes beyond – the core findings in the sense that it also considers: (a) how the nature of privatization is shifting and combining with other forms of privatization; (b) the origins of states in the region and the way in which their colonial-capitalist foundations have produced states that are permeated by what we call an 'ethos of privatization'; and (c) the implications of these two factors when considered dialectically with the findings of this chapter on how/why the privatization of education in Honduras and the Dominican Republic has evolved in recent decades. Our goal in, first, characterizing

LFPS trends and, second, analysing their implications in the ways just described is to produce insights that complement the focus of the present volume on the global-local dynamics that drive education reform in Central America and the Latin Caribbean.

State weakness and expansion of LFPSs: the Honduran case

As part of a broader default privatization process, Honduras is experiencing a rapid proliferation of LFPSs. In order to understand the process, some contextual data regarding economy and education must be taken into consideration. First, the literature defines Honduras as a 'weak state', that is, a state that struggles to provide public services, ensure public safety, and prevent political corruption (Rotberg, 2004). As will be further discussed later on, this, together with a historical dependence on external resources since the very foundation of the modern state, is essential for understanding the difficulties of the Honduran state to provide universal public education that is considered to be of high quality.

Specifically in the educational field, the weaknesses delineated earlier can be inferred in multiple ways, including a generalized sense of misgovernment and a deep underfunding of the education system (Edwards et al, 2019, 2023). Regarding the first of these – misgovernment – there are several dynamics that generate a lack of political stability and inconsistent leadership, including: (a) the high turnover of Ministers of Education and the lack of experience in the educational field of some of them; (b) the coexistence and overlapping of different decision-making structures in the education system, with unclear purposes and functions; and (c) the trend towards system decentralization, with the creation of new decentralized administrative structures that are, at the same time, inoperative and underfunded (Morales, 2013; Edwards et al, 2019, 2023). Regarding underfunding, despite Honduras ranking among the countries of the region with a highest share of public spending on education – about 6 per cent of gross domestic product (GDP) in recent years (GPE et al, 2017) – the absolute investment remains minimal due to the relatively low value of the country's GDP. Additionally, teachers' salaries consume most of the national budget for education – 93 per cent in 2017 (Díaz et al, 2018) – which leaves little room for other expenses, such as infrastructure and equipment (GPE et al, 2017).

These factors resulted in low public supply at all educational levels, but especially in pre-primary and middle education. Notably, however, there have been strategies to increase educational access in Honduras since 2003; in pre-primary education it rose from 36 per cent to 76 per cent between 2002 and 2015 (Econometría Consultores et al, 2016).[2] Nevertheless, the deficit in educational coverage is still immense: it is estimated that, at the 2005–2014 growth rate, Honduras still needs 289.7 years to achieve the Organisation for Economic Co-operation and Development (OECD) coverage level in pre-primary education, 114.2 years in the third cycle of primary education, and 63.1 years in lower secondary education (ERCA, 2016). This situation has created the perfect scenario for default privatization trends and, specifically, the proliferation of LFPSs. In words of one of the interviewees:

'We have default privatization because all the demand that the State does not cover finds a fertile field in private actors who, of course, see this as a business, because it is in fact a business ... The State leaves this room; it is a default privatization process that the State tolerates ... Since the State can't cover the demand, private actors enter.' (Scholar 10)

Thus, the proliferation of LFPSs is not surprising in the context of a clear lack of universal public coverage.

We also identified other factors related to underfunding which contribute to the perception of public schools as being of low quality. In line with previous research (for example, Phillipson, 2008; Balarín, 2015), these factors include the lack of teaching materials (for example, whiteboards, textbooks, and computers) and poor infrastructure in public schools (Edwards et al, 2019, 2023). Relatedly, in contexts of high insecurity such as some areas of Honduras (OUDENI, 2018a, 2018b), the incorporation of security staff into the school is essential to prevent them from being the focus of violence. In the words of two interviewees:

'One problem that is affecting us much is the lack of security ... In our school we do not have a person, staff, in charge of this service. What we only have right now is the parents' support: they give a voluntary collaboration [that is, monetary donation] to pay for a cleaner and a security guard. We only have one guard at night ... and we have been robbed. So yes, there's quite a deficiency in terms of that.' (Semi-rural school principal)

'The parental association is responsible for ... Look, they charge the parents 50 Lempiras [about €1.80] every month. These 50 Lempiras are used to pay for a cleaner and a guard, because the government hasn't given us a cleaner or a guard.' (Rural school principal)

Thus, for schools, the lack of public funding for cleaning and security staff is a common concern. In many cases, these staff are compensated with fees paid by families. Such fees represent a form of privatization, one that highlights the tension between the need of public schools to charge fees to families and the legal prohibition of doing just that – because Honduran education law establishes that public schools should be free of charge. In fact, the state is promoting some control and accountability mechanisms in this regard, such as a telephone line for families to report illegal fee collection (Edwards et al, 2019).

It is therefore inferred that in Honduras, the proliferation of LFPSs is mostly related to a deficiency of public educational coverage, as well as to the perception of low-quality education, lack of safety, and hidden costs in public schools.[3] All of these causes are directly or indirectly related to the lack of funding and public education provision, as set out in the following quotation:

> 'With education it has been similar [to other sectors]: almost no budget for infrastructure and security has been assigned. Well, the guards have to be paid by the parents … Lots of basic things of the school, sometimes even the whiteboards … So many parents are opting for private schools, which give them… a slightly safer environment … In general, the social perception is that [low-fee] private schools at least give children a safer environment, less risk, supposedly, less risk of bullying, of danger, less risk of drugs, less risk of abuse … [LFPSs] provide buses to take them home.' (Scholar 12)

Despite these possible benefits for families, some problems related to LFPSs in terms of quality and equity, partly linked to the lack of state control, have been identified. First, in practice no state actor regulates the conditions under which LFPS teaching takes place, nor does it ensure that teachers have the appropriate training. Second, teaching staff from LFPSs are not unionized, thus limiting their ability to demand improvements in working conditions; rather, they are only subject to market rules. Third, because LFPSs totally depend on fees, in the event of nonpayment, some LFPSs have established legal mechanisms that even allow the repossession of families' assets (Edwards et al, 2019).

It is also important to highlight the state's low capacity to regulate and control the Honduran education system. Although the Education Law ensures the right to create private schools in practice, the state is unable to effectively monitor these schools and to hold them accountable. One consequence is that many schools operate illegally and are not included in the official register. For this reason, although the expansion of LFPSs is well known, its actual scope remains unclear. Despite limited data, there is no doubt about the widespread – and growing – nature of LFPSs in Honduras.

Increasing public education spending, decreasing private schools

The case of the Dominican Republic

The current situation of LFPSs in the Dominican Republic is the opposite of the Honduran situation, although the trend was virtually identical some years ago. It is necessary to explore two distinct stages, with 2012 as a turning point, to understand this phenomenon in the Dominican context.

Historically, public spending on education in the country has been low compared to the rest of Central America and the Caribbean. In 1991, for example, after decades of civil authoritarian control (1966–1978) and constrained democratic politics (1978–1990), only 0.97 per cent of GDP was allocated to education, a consequence of large budget reductions since 1970, when the allocation reached 2.8 per cent (EDUCA, 2016). This resulted from a long period of Structural Adjustment Programs promoted by the World Bank and the International Monetary Fund (IMF). In order to reverse this downward trend, after strong demands by part of the education community in the country, a committee was created in the early 1990s to write a new Education Law. This law, which was finally passed in 1997, required the investment of 4 per cent of GDP or 16 per cent of the total public spending – the highest of the two – in pre-university education. However, for many years the government did not comply with this legal mandate, and until 2012 only about 2 per cent of GDP was allocated to education (EDUCA, 2016).

The education underfunding of this first stage generated a scenario with many similarities to the Honduran case: dynamics of default privatization emerged, which included in the proliferation of LFPSs in response to a lack of state investment in the sector. This can be illustrated in the following quote:

'[LFPSs grew] because of two situations: one, because [in] some areas the State did not supply [universal, public education]. This happened, above all, in marginalized neighborhoods: there were public schools, but they didn't provide sufficient access for the number of students. Therefore, we had more [low-fee] private schools in the Santo Domingo area, where the big cities are, in La Romana ... Because there wasn't enough provision [of public schools]. And second, other schools [appeared] for one reason: let's say, family safety and comfort. In which sense? "I have this private school that is closer, with classes every day, with no strikes, which perhaps is smaller, with less violence" ... Because there has also been an issue of violence in the schools – in all [the schools] but in the public sector it has been more noticeable. So they preferred to take [their children to LFPSs].' (Government Representative 1)

This quote describes a context that recalls the Honduran case: lack of public school access in some areas as well as safety problems, to which interviewees add the perception of the low quality of public schools. Interestingly, for many years, the Dominican state tried to seek an intermediate solution to the problem of lack of school infrastructure by creating a schedule of multiple shifts in each school. In other words, the same school infrastructure hosted different groups of students every day in blocks of four hours. This led to numerous conflicts related to competition over limited spaces and resources (Secretaría de Estado para la Educación, 2008), and it meant a considerable reduction in the school hours that each student received, which, consequently, generated more pressure – in terms of time and care – on families. These developments have further incentivized families to enrol their children in LFPSs, which have longer school days.

Nevertheless, this default privatization trend began to change in 2012, when there was a massive and coordinated social movement that brought together several civil society actors under a unitary claim: increasing educational investment to 4 per cent of GDP. In the face of the impending presidential elections, this movement pressured all candidates to sign a document committing to increase the percentage of GDP in education to the levels required in the 1997 Education Law (Lapaix Ávila, 2018; Edwards et al, 2020). Consequently, since 2013, 4 per cent of GDP has been allocated to pre-university education. This recent substantial increase in the funds for education has been primarily earmarked for three purposes: (a) the construction of new school infrastructure; (b) the progressive transition from shorter school shifts to the extension of school hours, along with the provision of free lunches in public schools; and (c) the recruitment of more teachers, who, after intense demands articulated through the union, have seen their salaries raised considerably in recent years (EDUCA, 2016).

This new situation has led to a significant expansion of educational coverage rates for pre-primary education (that is, from 40.34 per cent in 2012 to 50.11 per cent in 2018), secondary education (from 63.82 per cent to 70.61 per cent) and tertiary education (from 48.63 per cent to 59.92 per cent) (UIS, 2020). In this way, some of the structural deficiencies which generated default privatization dynamics in previous decades have been alleviated. Indeed, many families have shifted back to the public school sector, as the following quote indicates:

'With the extension of school hours, some of these "neighborhood schools" [as LFPSs are sometimes termed] have disappeared ... Why have they decreased? Because the extension of school hours has been too attractive ... for that kind of students with parents working. So, "here, at least, there's a school where [the children] spend eight hours, where I leave the children and I stay calm, and I don't have to look for someone to look after them".' (Government Sector Representative 1)

All the actors interviewed agreed that many of the students who were enrolled in LFPSs moved to public schools once this sector began to receive additional funding. Summarizing the points made previously, the reasons for this shift in enrolment pattern are related to the provision of free lunches at school, which is an economic relief for many families; the construction of new school infrastructure in some neighbourhoods; and the extension of school hours. There is a broad consensus on the fact that the increased investment in public education has led to the closure of some LFPSs. The following quote from a teacher in a marginalized school serves as an example:

'I owned a [LFPS]. And when public schools started having water and such things, parents started taking their children out of [LFPSs] to find a space in public schools – and with all their rights, because they don't have to pay here [in public schools] and they have a lot more advantages. I mean, a lot of [LFPSs] had to close ... My [LFPS] started with fifty students more or less, but then some went away; but we did reach about a hundred students. Then it started going down again, so there was a time when it became unsustainable and it had to be closed down.' (Marginal school teacher)

Unlike in Honduras, the Dominican state has a more comprehensive register of private schools that could be accessed. However, the register does not distinguish schools by the fees they charge, so it is impossible to determine how many of them are LFPSs. Nevertheless, according to the National Bureau of Statistics, the Dominican Republic recorded the peak of private schools – of all types, elite private schools included – in the 2012–2013 academic year, with a total of 4,484 schools. Interestingly, by the 2017–2018 academic year, the number had already fallen to 3,709, a 17.28 per cent decrease. Despite it not being possible to attribute all this decrease to the closure of LFPSs, it can be inferred that, after the expansion of the public education budget, there was a considerable reduction of private education provision – a fact on which all the interviewees agreed.

As a final point, it should be noted that in addition to the migration of demand from LFPSs to public schools, there has been a similar phenomenon regarding teaching staff: with the increased need for teachers in public schools, aggravated by the closure of some of the LFPSs where they worked, many teachers moved to the public education system. The teacher quoted previously falls into this category, as well as another teacher from a semi-marginal school, who comments: 'In my case, we didn't have health insurance [in the LFPS], we had nothing ... You're an employee and if they [LFPS managers] don't want you there because you don't serve them anymore, they fire you' (semi-marginal school teacher). Thus, both the student population and the teachers working in LFPSs are in very precarious positions, as are the schools themselves, which are subject to the whims of the market, including parents' ability and willingness to pay (Edwards et al, 2017).

The political economy of education reform

Dialectical relationships and the ethos of privatization

The preceding sections focused on the political-economic dimensions of the cases of LFPSs in Honduras and the Dominican Republic. In what follows, we revisit and extend the comments made along these lines. In We reflect on: (a) how the nature of privatization is shifting and combining with other forms of privatization; (b) the origins of states in the region and the ways in which their colonial-capitalist origins have produced states that are permeated by what we call an 'ethos of privatization'; and (c) the implications of these two factors for how/why the privatization of education in Honduras and the Dominican Republic has evolved in recent decades as it has.

Honduras

As mentioned earlier, in the case of Honduras, the emergence of LFPSs can be seen as an outcome of continued low investment in public education. Not only are there too few public schools, but those in operation typically lack basic supplies. This is not surprising since the majority of the budget for public education is consumed by teachers' salaries. This situation is particularly common in schools in marginalized and underserved areas. On the political side, it is also notable that there is no agency that has been charged with regulating and overseeing LFPSs – which are a relatively recent phenomenon that has developed in the past ten years or so, although traditional private schools have always been a core feature of the education system.

Even if LFPSs are a relatively new phenomenon, insufficient funding to public education and reliance on aid and economic investment from international actors is not. Indeed, Honduras' history, since at least the late 1800s, has been closely intertwined with and dependent on aid agencies and transnational corporations (Edwards et al, 2023). The marginalized position of Honduras was a reality even when the country was under Spanish rule.[4] And since the country's founding in 1838, there has not been interest from either politicians or transnational corporations (who have a disproportionate influence on politics in this country) to dedicate significant sums to the education sector. In a recent book on the relationships among globalization, privatization, and the Honduran state, we suggest that neither the aforementioned dynamics nor the contemporary trend of LFPS can be understood without first understanding the role of the 'ethos of privatization' (Edwards et al, 2023). In short, the central idea behind the ethos of privatization is that there is a self-serving logic that drives the behaviour of actors who are employed by or are connected (via their networks) to the state. This self-serving logic puts the interests of private individuals – who are in a position to derive benefit from the state – ahead of the interests of the 'public good'. Unsurprisingly, the ethos of privatization can be seen as the legacy of the origins of the Honduran state, which has grown out of a foundation of colonialism and capitalism (for more on this, see Edwards et al, 2023).

As we further explain in our aforementioned book by drawing on literature from political economy, world systems theory, and postcolonial studies, the state apparatus, including the education system, must function in order to reproduce the capitalist mode of production while also managing the tensions at the heart of the capitalist economy. In many countries, the tendency of capitalism to concentrate the benefits of the economy in the hands of a few is legitimated through the idea that individuals who dedicate themselves to getting an education and to working hard will succeed. To validate this message, public schools must be of a sufficient quality, otherwise the message rings hollow. Honduras, in contrast, and as we have noted, has never invested in much in the public education system. Here, as in other postcolonial countries, rather than legitimating the promise of capitalism by investing in public education, the state distributes benefits via clientelistic practices related to the ways in which teachers' positions are assigned, schools are built, and contracts for educational resources are awarded (for more on this, see Edwards et al, 2023). The fact that the public education system in Honduras is the largest employer in the country is one indication of the structural role that the education system plays. With part of the middle class invested in the status quo – that is, in maintaining and deriving benefit from the mediocre status of the Honduran education system through their employment by this system (as teachers, administrators, etc.) – and another part not necessarily employed by the state but opting for private education, there is little incentive on the part of the government to dedicate itself to improving public education; in other words, there is no great tension for the state to resolve. In this way, the ethos of privatization militates not only against the improvement of the public education system but also against the monitoring and regulation of the private school system. When the state knows that it is not providing sufficient educational access for its student population, what sense does it make to persecute those private actors who are filling in for its deficiencies? LFPSs in Honduras are doing the state a favour.

When it comes to the focus of the present chapter, a key implication of the ethos of privatization is that analyses of education reform must be sure not to assume that reforms are always globally imposed or coerced. Certainly, there is a long history of influence being leveraged by international organizations and by transnational corporations. And, certainly, there are examples of policy actions that have been required by international organizations such as the World Bank and the IMF (for example, related to Structural Adjustment Programs and budget cuts). But it is also true that the education system, at the level of practice – that is, at the level of daily operations – is intractable in that it operates according to a logic that does not respond (beyond, perhaps, lip service) to the priorities and preferences of international actors. It is for these reasons that we suggest that any fruitful analysis of education reform in Honduras or other postcolonial countries must first take into account the foundational layers and logics of the state, the way that the state is situated within the global economy, and the role that education – including different forms of privatization – plays in maintaining and resolving the tensions that necessarily arise as a result of capitalism and colonialism.

The Dominican Republic

The same kind of analysis can be applied to the case of the Dominican Republic. To start with, it should be recalled that, with regard to LFPSs, the Dominican Republic was previously in a similar situation to where Honduras is now. The difference is that the Dominican Republic drastically increased funding to public education starting in 2012 in order to comply with the legal commitments codified in law in 1997. While low investment had encouraged a large private school sector, including for low-income families, this trend was reversed in the 2010s.

An important implication of the Dominican Republic case is that civil society and social movements can constitute influential actors in the politics of education. These actors can insert themselves into the reform conversation and, in so doing, can disrupt the balance of power and the manner in which the invested interests in the system serve themselves. Although it took some time – 15 years from the passage of the law that required investment in education to be dramatically increased – the Coalition for a Dignified Education succeeded in channelling frustration around meagre public education investment into a movement that took advantage of the political window provided by the presidential elections of 2012, at which point the Coalition pressured all the presidential candidates to commit to complying with the letter of the law.

At the same time, and in keeping with the dialectical thinking highlighted by the framework of this volume, it must be noted that the state and the private sector did not 'lose'. Education politics are not a zero-sum game. Increasing the budget has allowed the government to enact many of its reform priorities, including extended school days, the construction of new schools, hiring more teachers, curricular reform, teacher training, and professional development. Notably, many of these reform strategies can serve to bolster support for the government and for the status quo in that they can serve a patronage function – that is, they can reinforce the ethos of privatization – in addition to being defensible on the grounds that they improve the quality of education. Increasing and using the education budget in these ways has thus been politically valuable in multiple ways.

Meanwhile, increased funding to education has also attracted the attention and the interest of other actors, who have dedicated themselves to shaping the government's reform agenda. Participatory strategies for developing education sector plans that were first piloted in the 1990s have evolved into institutional arrangements through which philanthropic organizations have been able to insert themselves into the decision-making processes of the Ministry of Education in the Dominican Republic. No longer does the government only meet with education sector working groups, whose members are international development organizations. Rather, in the context of increased education funding – a context that has implied a decline in the influence of such organizations – the government now works closely with both an education-related think tank – Educa – that advances the interests of private companies, and with a government-led network of nonstate actors who represent international cooperation agencies, the business sector, and civil society.[5] This network is known as the Dominican Initiative for Quality Education and serves as a space to propose specific policies or plans for the education sector, in addition to being a vehicle through which to monitor and evaluate the enactment of these policies and plans. Although such examples can be labelled as forms of privatization 'through' policy making in that they reflect the increased involvement of private sector and/or other nonstate actors (Ball, 2012), what stands out with regard to the focus of the present chapter is that each of these actors, by participating together in such processes, serves not only to legitimate the involvement of the others but also to legitimate the policies and plans that result – even if they do not address the underlying crisis of the legitimacy of the capitalist mode of production.

But what about the foundational layers and logics of the state to which we alluded in the previous subsection? A final example from the Dominican Republic case is of relevance here. We refer to Inicia Educación, the philanthropic arm of the Vicini Group, a business conglomerate controlled by the Vicini family, who immigrated to the Dominican Republic in the 1860s, invested in sugar cultivation, and are now the wealthiest family in the country. The Vicini Group has subsidiaries in the banking, financial services, and agro-industrial (coffee and sugar) sectors. What stands out about Inicia Educación is, first, that it has evolved from a traditional philanthropic approach, rooted in the donation of resources, into an approach that is more akin to an investment fund, in that it seeks to dedicate its resources – or the resources of the government, with whom it is in constant contact – to those factors that are most likely to influence the performance of the education system, as determined by metrics for return on investment that it has developed (Edwards et al, 2021). Second, it is notable that Inicia Educación has shifted to include a focus on profit generation through the creation of a consulting company, known as '512', that can bid on government projects and can provide services (for example, professional development) for a fee.[6]

While 512's modus operandi reflects the capitalist orientation of its parent company, the Vicini Group, simply highlighting this parallel is insufficient. What is needed is recognition of the fact that although education funding has been increased to a level where the trend of LFPSs has been curbed, structurally, education reform in the Dominican Republic, as in Honduras and elsewhere, is still subject to unequal power relations between the state and the private sector, power relations which are, in turn, rooted in historical tensions that connect to the way in which the Dominican state and its export-oriented economy have evolved together. This kind of analysis highlights the way in which the global economy and domestic politics have consistently rewarded those who control exports (for example, those from which the Vicini family has benefited, such as sugar and coffee), while at the same time incentivizing those who control the state to use their powers in self-serving and clientelistic ways, rather than building the power and independence of the state apparatus, including the education system and education reform processes, which are caught in the middle and serve to legitimate the capitalist economic system in the ways mentioned earlier. Moreover – and dialectically – it is, in part, because of the nature of the global economy and the fact that profit-driven companies like the Vicini Group have been able to benefit disproportionately from it that actors from the business world, including private philanthropies, are now able to exert such influence on the making of public education policy.

Conclusions – or insights and opportunities

This chapter began with a focus exclusively on the phenomenon of LFPS. Although the empirical focus here has been on the cases of Honduras and the Dominican Republic, the discussion earlier in the chapter also emphasized that one might expect this trend to spread to other areas of Latin America – if, indeed, it has not already done so (although we may not know this because of a lack of research on this topic). However, this chapter has also shown that this trend is not inevitable. While LFPSs are a growing trend in Honduras, they are receding in the Dominican Republic, with the difference being that the latter country has significantly increased funding to public education since 2012. The mobilization of civil society and emergence of a social movement at an opportune moment – just before the presidential elections – in the Dominican Republic was a key factor in reversing the LFPS trend.

Although the first half of the chapter took into account some of the political-economic drivers to which the advance (or regress) of LFPSs, the second half of the chapter took a step back to place this trend in broader perspective. Discussions of the privatization of education often focus on: (a) how public education is being outsourced to private companies (exogenous privatization); (b) how the public sector is incorporating principles and practices from the business world (endogenous privatization); or (c) how education reform plans are developed or influenced by nonstate actors and their agendas (Ball and Youdell, 2008). However, what we have sought to show is that there is a deeper form of privatization, one that goes beyond surface-level manifestations. This form of privatization – which we have labelled the 'ethos of privatization' – speaks to the way in which individuals who work in, or are connected to, the state use their positions to generate private benefit rather than seeing their post as serving the public good. This insight, paired together with the observation that the state must maintain the legitimacy of the capitalist mode of production, leads to the (perhaps surprising) realization that, from the perspective of the state, LFPSs can be seen as a welcome development, in that these schools tend to cater to areas and populations that are underserved by the state itself, a state which, as was noted earlier, not only has little motivation to invest in the provision of public education, but which has even less motivation to dedicate itself to regulating private actors who are working on the fringes of the system and who, if anything, help to uphold the belief that getting a 'good-quality' private education can lead to success in a capitalist system that inherently tends towards inequality and the concentration of power.

As the case of the Dominican Republic shows, even where the state has been pressured into reversing underinvestment, both the ethos of privatization and the legitimating function of education reform can still be seen, even while claims of improved education quality are made. As has already been noted, the additional funding to the education system is being used in ways that: first, are defensible because they can be labelled as investments that improve the education system (for example, by expanding educational access, hiring more teachers, offering professional development, developing new text books, and purchasing additional resources); second, help to maintain the stability and legitimacy of both the education system and the capitalist mode of production (not only by expanding the number of people employed by the system but also by making it easier to claim that the education being offered is of higher quality than it was before and thus provides opportunities for advancement and success in the capitalist system); and, third, do not disrupt the underlying ethos of privatization (in that the strategies mentioned in the first point can be put into practice in ways that accord with clientelism, patronage, and self-serving tendencies). The same three points are relevant to the way in which private actors (think tanks, corporations, and philanthropies) have intensified their collaboration with the Ministry of Education in recent years: first, the utilization of business practices (for example, metrics related to return on investment) to guide educational investments can be defended on the grounds that they will lead to better outcomes; second, the collaboration of government with a range of nonstate actors legitimizes the processes for reform formulation as well as the reform content itself; and, third, by both strengthening relationships with government and inserting themselves into the decision-making processes, private actors such as think tanks (Educa), philanthropies (Inicia Educación), and consulting companies (512) can serve their own interests (for example, by winning contracts and then awarding them to their own subsidiaries or to others in their networks, as 512 and Inicia Foundation have done; for more on this, see Edwards et al, 2021).

In concluding, we suggest that, going forward, more research is needed that attends to the dynamics discussed earlier. Much is missed if one analyses education reform without attention to the larger political–economic constraints, dialectical relationships, and the ethos of privatization. This kind of research will help to shed light on (and to problematize) the often simplistic assumptions and concepts that are employed to make sense of global–local dynamics in education policy, both in the so-called Global South and Global North. For, indeed, as Wallerstein (1974), Poggi (1978), and others have pointed out, the evolution of states in the Global North has likewise been intertwined with the ethos of privatization and the development of the global economy.

Notes

[1] Both studies are based on extensive on-site fieldwork which included more than 90 interviews with various state and nonstate actors, a thorough document and literature review, and data-gathering visits to schools in urban and semi-urban areas. For more information, see Caravaca et al (2021) and Edwards et al (2021, 2023).

[2] This is due to the introduction of two alternative modalities of pre-primary education: the Community Pre-Basic Education Centres – with a large presence especially in rural areas – and Educación en Casa/Education at Home (or EDUCAS, a homeschooling programme; see Econometría Consultores et al, 2016).

[3] Other secondary aspects linked to social differentiation, such as the willingness of some families to enrol their children in bilingual English-Spanish schools, were also identified.

[4] The territory now known as Honduras gained independence from Spain in 1821.

[5] The private sector in Honduras has taken on a similarly protagonist role in the 2010s (Edwards et al, 2023).

[6] In a striking development, 512 has also begun to work in other countries, such as Colombia and Peru, where it seeks to use its knowledge and skills to similarly influence education reform (for more on this, see Edwards et al, 2021).

References

Balarín, M. (2015). *The Default Privatization of Peruvian Education and the Rise of Low-Fee Private Schools: Better or Worse Opportunities for the Poor?* Open Society Foundations.

Balarín, M. (2016). La privatización por defecto y el surgimiento de las escuelas privadas de bajo costo en el Perú. ¿Cuáles son sus consecuencias? *Revista de Sociología de la Educación*, 9(2), 181–196.

Balarin, M., Fontdevila, C., Marius, P., and Rodríguez, M. F. (2019). Educating on a budget: the subsistence model of low-fee private schooling in Peru. *Education Policy Analysis Archives*, 27(132), 1–43. https://doi.org/10.14507/epaa.27.4328

Ball, S. J. (2012). *Global Education Inc: New Policy Networks and the Neo-liberal Imaginary*. Routledge.

Ball, S. J., and Youdell, D. (2008). *Privatización encubierta en la educación pública*. Education International.

Caddell, M., and Day Ashley, L. (2006). Blurring boundaries: towards a reconceptualisation of the private sector in education. *Compare*, 36(4), 411–419. https://doi.org/10.1080/03057920601024750

Caravaca, A., Moschetti, M. C., and Edwards Jr., D. B. (2021). Privatización de la política educativa y gobernanza en red en la República Dominicana. *Education Policy Analysis Archives*, 29, 1–19. https://doi.org/10.14507/epaa.29.6421

Day Ashley, L. et al (2014). *The Role and Impact of Private Schools in Developing Countries*. Department for International Development.

Díaz, H. A., Buezo, R., Bueso, C., Valladares, N., Cruz, J. D., Chinchilla, B., … Alas, M. (2018). La deuda social en Honduras y los desafíos actuales y futuros que tiene el país con el financiamiento en educación. *Observatorio de La Educación Nacional y Regional*, 3, 1–8.

Econometría Consultores, Banco Mundial, and Gobierno de la República de Honduras (2016). *Consultoría Internacional para la Evaluación del Resultados del Plan Educación para Todos EFA Honduras 2003–2015*. Econometría Consultores, Banco Mundial, and Gobierno de la República de Honduras.

EDUCA (2016). *Calidad del Gasto Educativo en la República Dominicana: un análisis exploratorio desde la vigencia del 4%*. EDUCA.

Edwards Jr., D. B., Caravaca, A., and C. Moschetti, M. C. (2021). Network governance and new philanthropy in Latin America and the Caribbean: reconfiguration of the state. *British Journal of Sociology of Education*, 42(8), 1210–1226. https://doi.org/10.1080/01425692.2021.1990014

Edwards Jr., D. B., Klees, S., and Wildish, J. (2017). Dynamics of low-fee private schools in Kenya: governmental legitimation, schools-community dependence, and resource uncertainty. *Teachers College Record*, 119(7), 1–42. https://doi.org/10.1177/016146811711900702

Edwards Jr., D. B., Moschetti, M. C., and Caravaca, A. (2019). *La educación en Honduras: entre la privatización y la globalización*. Education International.

Edwards, D. B., Moschetti, M. C., and Caravaca, A. (2020). *Tendencias de privatización en la educación dominicana: heterarquías, gobernanza en red y nueva filantropía*. Education International.

Edwards Jr., D. B., Moschetti, M. C., and Caravaca, A. (2023). *Globalization, Privatization, and the State: Education Reform in Post-colonial Contexts*. Routledge.

ERCA (2016). *Quinto Informe Estado de la Región Centroamericana en Desarrollo Humano Sostenible*. Costa Rica.

Flores, R. (1997). *La escuela básica de la zona marginal de Santo Domingo. IADB Working Papers*. (No. R-304). IADB.

Francis, R., Martin, P., and Burnett, N. (2018). *Affordable non-state schools in El Salvador*. USAID Education in Crisis and Conflict Network by Results for Development and Education Development Center.

GPE, IIEP-UNESCO, and Gobierno de la República de Honduras (2017). *Análisis del Sistema Nacional de Educación y Formulación del Plan Estratégico del Sector Educación 2017–2030 de la República de Honduras*. GPE, IIEP-UNESCO, and Gobierno de la República de Honduras.

Guzmán, R., and Cruz, C. (2009). *Niños, niñas y adolescentes fuera del sistema educativo en la República Dominicana*. Foro Socioeducativo.

Härmä, J. (2013). Access or quality? Why do families living in slums choose low-cost private schools in Lagos, Nigeria? *Oxford Review of Education*, 39(4), 548–566. https://doi.org/10.1080/03054985.2013.825984

Junemann, C., and Ball, S. (2015). *The Mutating Giant: Pearson and PALF*. Leverhulme Trust.

Languille, S. (2016). 'Affordable' private schools in South Africa: affordable for whom? *Oxford Review of Education*, 42(5), 528–542. https://doi.org/10.1080/03054985.2016.1220086

Lapaix Ávila, D. (2018). *La forma del sistema educativo por venir: un ensayo*. Oficina de planificación educativa (RD).

Morales, R. (2013). *Los cambios en la gobernanza del sistema educativo en Honduras: la política de desconcentración de la educación pre-básica, básica y media (1990–2010)*. Universidad de Oporto.

Moschetti, M. C. (2015). Private education supply in disadvantaged areas of the city of Buenos Aires and 'low-fee private schooling': comparisons, contexts and implications. *Education Policy Analysis Archives*, 23(126), 1–26. https://doi.org/10.14507/epaa.v23.1981

Moschetti, M. C., and Lauría Masaro, M. (2020). A cultural political economy of supply-side subsidies for private schools in Argentina. *Education Policy Analysis Archives*, *28*, 1–34.

OUDENI (2018a). *Boletín Informativo nº 5*. Universidad Pedagógica Nacional Francisco Morazán.

OUDENI (2018b). *Boletín Informativo nº 6*. Universidad Pedagógica Nacional Francisco Morazán.

Phillipson, B. (2008). *Low-Cost Private Education: Impacts on Achieving Universal Primary Education*. Commonwealth Secretariat.

Poggi, G. (1978). *The Development of the Modern State: A Sociological Introduction*. Stanford University Press.

Riep, C. B. (2014). Omega Schools Franchise in Ghana: 'affordable' private education for the poor or for profiteering? In I. Macpherson, S. Robertson, and G. Walford (eds.), *Education, Privatisation and Social Justice: Case Studies from Africa, South Asia and South East Asia* (pp 259–278). Symposium Books.

Rose, P. (2005). Privatisation and decentralisation of schooling in Malawi: default or design? *Compare: A Journal of Comparative and International Education*, 35(2), 153–165. https://doi.org/10.1080/03057920500129890

Rotberg, R. I. (2004). Failed states, collapsed states, weak states: causes and indicators. In R. I. Rotberg (ed.), *State Failure and State Weakness in a Time of Terror* (pp 10–19). World Peace Foundation/Brookings Institution Press.

Secretaría de Estado de Educación (2008). *Plan Decenal de Educación 2008–2018 (6ª revisión)*. Secretaría de Estado de Educación.

Srivastava, P. (2007). For philanthropy or profit? The management and operation of low-fee private schools in India. In P. Srivastava and G. Walford (eds.), *Private Schooling in Less Economically Developed Countries: Asian and African Perspectives* (pp 153–186). Symposium Books.

Srivastava, P. (2016). Questioning the global scaling up of low-fee private schooling: the nexus between business, philanthropy, and PPPs. In *World Yearbook of Education 2016* (pp 268–283). Routledge.

Tooley, J. (2013). Challenging educational injustice: 'grassroots' privatisation in South Asia and Sub-Saharan Africa. *Oxford Review of Education*, 39(4), 446–463. https://doi.org/10.1080/03054985.2013.820466

Tooley, J., and Dixon, P. (2006). 'De facto' privatisation of education and the poor: implications of a study from Sub-Saharan Africa and India. *Compare*, 36(4), 443–462. https://doi.org/10.1080/03057920601024891

Tooley, J., and Longfield, D. (2015). *The Role and Impact of Private Schools in Developing Countries: A Response to the DFID-Commissioned 'Rigorous Literature Review'*. Pearson.

UIS (2020). Dominican Republic: education and literacy. http://uis.unesco.org/en/country/do

Verger, A., Fontdevila, C., and Zancajo, A. (2016). *The Privatisation of Education: A Political Economy of Global Education Reform*. Teachers College Press.

Wallerstein, I. (1974). *The Modern World-System: Capitalist Agriculture and the Origins of the European World-Economy in the Sixteenth Century*. Academic Press.

14

Educational Policies on Gender Perspective in Puerto Rico in the Face of the Transnational Anti-Gender Crusade

Loida M. Martínez Ramos

Introduction

Since the 1970s, women's and feminist movements worldwide have driven public policy development to recognize women's human rights. The United Nations' (UN) World Conferences on Women have been important milestones in this agenda. These policies are entwined with theoretical transformations within feminism and historical developments across different countries.[1] The addition of *gender perspective*,[2] also known as *gender mainstreaming*, is an example of these transformations and the efforts to interconnect discourses and practices related to the rejection of racism, xenophobia, transphobia, classism, and homophobia. These developments gave rise to intersectional feminism,[3] which advocates for gender agendas addressing local issues. As with other discursive struggles, conflicting stances seek to gain ground in the political, economic, and cultural arenas.

Progress has not gone unopposed. Although the opposition is not a recent development, since the 1990s, it has been grounded in a framework that aims to intervene against gender perspective policies (Bracke and Patternote, 2018). The anti-gender crusade has created the concept of *gender ideology* to delegitimize equity and gender perspective policies. Gender ideology has affected local-level politics, especially in Latin America, where it has been associated with the rejection of educational policies (Barrientos Delgado, 2020; Campana, 2020; Corrêa and Parker, 2020b).

Within this context, this chapter aims to analyse educational policies related to gender in Puerto Rico and their trajectory since the 1970s. In addition, it discusses how recent neoliberal reforms are characterized by anti-democratic tendencies that have local effects while, at the same time, being part of the global reform agenda. First, I examine the discursive debates gender policies have sparked and their ties to international organizations that promote equity from a gender perspective. Second, I address the anti-gender discourses in some countries and their repercussions in Puerto Rico. Finally, driven by the need to further equity and gender perspectives in education, the development of human rights, and democracy, I assess the current situation. I assume a critical approach towards anti-gender discourse and the patriarchal system within which it is produced. At the heart of the anti-gender crusade is the erosion of democracy (in the sense of making society less inclusive) and the depoliticization of public life (by attempting to take gender politics out of public policy). These effects on political culture are intertwined with the neoliberal policies that have threatened vulnerable groups worldwide, including women and sexual minorities.

The sources for the analysis are documents issued by the Puerto Rican government, press articles and webpages on the subject, UN documents, and academic studies published in the region. Public policy analysis from a feminist and historical perspective contributes to the study of policies on gender and education. Such an analysis by a Puerto Rican scholar adds a critical Caribbean perspective – a region that has not received much attention. The historical study of discourses on educational policy on gender reflects their progress, regressions, tensions, and interrelations to concrete and situated contexts. How the discussion of gender becomes woven with other discursive knots, leading to different lines of inquiries, questions, and challenges, is considered in this chapter.

Women's rights and educational rights

The international context as seen from the margins

The international community's participation in advancing equity policies is grounded in UN agreements between constituent countries. The 1975 World Conference on Women held in Mexico was a milestone in the history of women's rights; the issue of women's equality was the starting point of the conference, which addressed the subject of education. In 1979, the UN General Assembly approved the Convention on the Elimination of All Forms of Discrimination Against Women, which includes the need to 'take all appropriate measures to eliminate discrimination against women to ensure their equal rights with men in the field of education' (UN, 1979, Article 10).

Subsequent conferences addressed topics and issues championed by women's and feminist movements, including (1) judicial equality vs.

discrimination and equality across diverse social contexts; (2) the integration of *gender* as a relational concept that alludes to sociocultural constructs; (3) the link between discrimination and violence against women; and (4) women's heterogeneity. Progress was made in analysing other problems related to women's human rights (namely, sexual and reproductive rights, family diversity, gender-based violence, and education). The interconnections between these issues and other forms of discrimination (for example, ethnic and racial minorities, differently abled persons, sexual orientation, and cultural and gender identities) attracted attention. The Beijing Conference (1995) introduced a *gender perspective* in the approved Platform for Action. Its 79th clause states that 'governments and other actors should promote an active and visible policy of mainstreaming a gender perspective into all policies and programmes' (UN Women, 2014, p 46).

Education for All (EFA) was a significant statement by the international community regarding education agreed upon in Jomtien and adopted in Dakar in 2000 (UNESCO, 2008). It stressed the need to educate girls and boys – women and men – to increase opportunities for well-being and development in all dimensions of life. In 2015, the World Education Forum approved the Incheon Declaration (UNESCO, 2015). This Declaration expands upon Goal 4 of the 2030 Sustainable Development Goals and establishes the need to 'ensure inclusive and equitable quality education and promote lifelong learning opportunities for all' (UNESCO, 2015, p 20). This document promotes expanding educational levels and condemns the disparities between genders. It also points to the intersection of gender with the life experiences of differently abled, ethnically, and racially diverse marginalized populations.

To address the concerns of the LGBTTQIA+ movement and expand gender policies to be inclusive of sexual diversity, the Office of the High Commissioner for Human Rights (OHCHR) published *Born Free and Equal*, which establishes nations' obligations anchored in the Universal Declaration of Human Rights (UDHR). The fourth obligation states that countries should: 'Prohibit and address discrimination based on sexual orientation, gender identity, and sex characteristics by enacting relevant, comprehensive legislation and policies … [in addition to] combatting stigma and discrimination, including through training, education, and awareness-raising activities for public officials and the general public' (ONU, 2012, p 7). Among its areas of concern, it includes education in recognition of the multiple discriminatory and stigmatizing experiences of which LGBTTQIA+ persons are victims during their school years.

The changes the international community demands echo the social movements spreading across different countries. However, opposition quickly arrived, leading to widespread anti-gender policies. In Latin America and the Caribbean, educational policy on gender is fused with policy on sexual education. Nearly all countries have policies or programmes related to these topics. However, feminist and conservative groups' influence results in policies that oscillate back and forth in the extent they reflect gender perspectives, recognize sexual diversity, are transversal (meaning that they attempt to embed a gender perspective across different issues and policies), and focus on human rights. Argentina and Paraguay[4] are emblematic cases (Báez, 2015). According to the Observatorio de Igualdad de Género de América Latina y el Caribe (2017), Brazil, Ecuador, Honduras, Mexico, and Bolivia have had policies of this sort, albeit through various lenses. The following section will briefly describe the experiences with the anti-gender crusade in the region.

The anti-gender crusade

The threat to gender policies has a long history. Some studies point towards historical origins that pre-date their inception in the international discussion associated with the UN (Bracke and Patternote, 2018; Campana, 2020; Gil Hernández, 2020). However, the turning points in this barrage are the International Conference on Population and Development held in Cairo in 1994 and the World Conference on Women held in Beijing in 1995. In Cairo, the Vatican upheld a rigid perspective on the family, the discourse on the complementarity of men and women, marriage for procreation (Vatican, 1994), and the rejection of sexual and reproductive rights (Bracke and Patternote, 2018; Campana, 2020; Gil Hernández, 2020).

The Catholic Church took a stand against gender to maintain the naturalization of sex, the man-woman binary, and ascription to rigid gender characteristics and traditional gender roles. Moreover, their positions aimed to erase the analytic complexity contributed by the concept of gender. To this end, they resorted to *gender ideology* as a rhetorical tool that delegitimizes social movements using *gender* to analyse, condemn, and change centuries of inequality. As Bracke and Patternote assert: ' "Ideology" performs a particular rhetorical labor here, as it conjures a vision in which the spheres of beliefs and ideas are separated from the sphere of reality, and gender is allocated to the former, thereby undermining the knowledge production and truth claims of many decades of gender studies scholarship' (2018, p 144).

The erasure of knowledge developed with the concept of gender served as a mechanism for transnational political mobilization through which religious groups formed alliances to oppose gender policies.

In Latin America and the Caribbean, gender policies related to sexuality, sexual and reproductive rights, marriage equality, and gender identity triggered anti-gender reactions. The Catholic Church served as a breeding ground for many anti-gender campaigns. However, there is a crossing of denominational borders. Military tradition plays a role in some countries, as in Brazil (Corrêa and Kalil, 2020).

The anti-gender crusade is entangled with other national issues. For example, in Colombia, the negative outcome of a referendum to approve peace agreements with the Revolutionary Armed Forces of Colombia (RAFC) was closely connected to anti-gender discourses (Gil Hernández, 2020). In Costa Rica, political parties emerged to bolster overtly religious agendas opposed to the gender perspective approach (Arguedas Ramírez, 2020).

In public discourse, the anti-gender crusade has attempted to link gender policies to Marxism (Campana, 2020) and other leftist ideologies, echoing discursive strategies used by the Catholic Church during the Cold War (Bracke and Paternotte, 2018). It also employed discourses on anti-imperialist struggles and denunciations of colonialism, previously associated with the left and deeply rooted in Latin America and the Caribbean (Vitieri, 2020; Gil Hernández, 2020), and replicated strategies used by right-wing organizations in the US to co-opt the civil rights movement of the 1960s. Of particular concern is the obstruction of a gender perspective in educational policies by the anti-gender crusade in many countries (Báez, 2015; Corrêa and Kalil, 2020; Carreaga Pérez and Aran, 2020).

The strategies used by anti-gender crusades share several patterns: mobilizations in support of the traditional family, the use of social media to spread fake news, and the promotion of a template letter to be signed by parents opposing their children's participation in educational initiatives with a gender perspective (Campana, 2020; Corrêa and Kalil, 2020).

The most toxic effect of anti-gender crusades is the erosion of political culture across the region. One of its strategies is propagating conservative religious beliefs and agendas in the public sphere, as in the case of Mexico (Careaga Pérez and Aranda, 2020). These changes to the political culture are interwoven with precarity, deteriorating quality of life, fiscal crises, neoliberal policies in economic and budgetary matters, increased authoritarianism with a moralist agenda (Vitieri, 2020), and restriction of freedoms. However, multiple forces have served as a retaining wall against anti-gender crusades, including gender policies advanced by grassroots and allied feminisms, related international commitments, and the tradition of separation of church and state instituted in the Constitution of some of these countries. Nevertheless, anti-gender efforts have worn down an active political culture (Arguedas Ramírez, 2020; Corrêa and Kalil, 2020).

Policies in Puerto Rico

Background

In Puerto Rico, the rise of second-wave feminism in the 1970s coincided with the beginnings of the electoral alternation of the Popular Democratic

(PDP) and the New Progressive (NPP) parties.[5] This decade also witnessed the founding of multiple women's and feminist organizations, such as Woman Get Involved Now (Mujer Intégrate Ahora) in 1972, the Federation of Puerto Rican Women (Federación de Mujeres Puertorriqueñas) in 1975, and the Feminist Alliance for Human Liberation (Alianza Feminista de Liberación Humana) in 1977. Linked in various ways to the working-class discourse of the era, these organizations launched campaigns advocating for the reform of family laws, the opening of childcare centres, the transformation of domestic labour, and the elimination of the double shift. They also worked against the mass sterilization of women,[6] the objectification of women's image in the media, and sexist education (Crespo Kebler, 2001). Despite the vestiges of liberal feminism that advocate for the individual subject, the influence of Marxist and radical feminisms in the analysis of class and patriarchy also left a mark. In the 1980s, the issues of domestic violence and sexual and reproductive rights gained momentum. Since the 1990s, the analysis of these topics has become more sophisticated, increasing the connection with other marginalized identities (Rivera Lassén and Crespo Kebler, 2001).

Regarding education, research conducted in the 1970s at the Commission for the Improvement of Women's Rights, a governmental body created during a PDP administration, constituted the first denunciation of sexism in school textbooks. These studies set the ground for subsequent work on various aspects of formal education (Santiago-Centeno and Martínez Ramos, 1990). Implementing gender-focused public policies relating to education remains a work in progress. However, the spirit of educational reform that filled the air in the 1980s contributed to advancing women's agenda when the Organic Law of the Department of Education, Law No. 68 of 28 August 1990, was approved. It asserted: 'There shall be an education that liberates the students from all types of prejudices based on race, sex, religion, politics, or social condition. The issue of sexist stereotyping will be given particular attention by implementing this policy (Legislatura de Puerto Rico, 1990, Article 1.02).

However, the Organic Law of the Department of Education, Law No. 149 of 1999 (Legislatura de Puerto Rico, 1999) substituted the law approved in 1990 and excluded the previous statement. After years of advocating for the inclusion of gender equity in public policy and nearly ten years since its approval, the mandate was dropped.

The new millennium: gender policy gains momentum in education

In 2006, an amendment to Law No. 149–1999 was approved. The amendment held the Secretary of Education responsible for establishing, in coordination with the Women's Advocate Office, an education curriculum for gender equity and domestic violence prevention. Following this law, policies on equity and gender perspectives within the Puerto Rican Department of Education shift according to the governing political party. Ultimately, policies approved by the more liberal party (PDP) are subsequently abolished by the more conservative side (NPP).[7]

In 2008, the first equity and gender perspective policy of the Puerto Rican Department of Education (PRDE) was approved. It was signed by Rafael Aragunde, Secretary of Education, four months before the 2008 general elections (Circular Letter 03-2008-209). In the context of the electoral campaign, this policy was subject to intense attacks by religious fundamentalist groups that opposed the concept of gender perspective. However, the idea of gender ideology had not yet been so widespread. The statements of Marcelina Vélez, President of the Pontifical Catholic University of Puerto Rico, merit special attention. She agreed with the concept of equity but not gender perspective. She thought this concept did not capture the 'essential reality' that only two sexes and two genders exist, which is evidence of her heteronormative discourse (Mercado Sierra, 2011). Such discourse excludes decades of research that show that gender perspective is a tool to uncover, denounce, and deconstruct the historical experience of gender-based discrimination and subordination.

The administration of NPP governor Luis Fortuño (2009–2013) repealed Circular Letter 03-2008-2009 policy on gender perspectives. For those four years, the topic of gender in K-12 lay dormant in public policy. However, academics, students, feminist activists, and various organizations kept the discussion alive through research and demand for equity and gender perspective policies.

When a new administration assumed power in 2013 under the leadership of Alejandro García Padilla (PDP), the demands by feminist groups gained strength. As a result, in 2013, Senator Mari Tere González (PDP) presented Bill 484, which proposed that students be exposed to a curriculum grounded in equity and gender perspectives focusing on gender-based violence, particularly violence against women. The idea was that the new approach would uncover the hidden gender curriculum. It would highlight the need to integrate women's knowledge into educational content and practices and the importance of opportunities for women to access traditionally male-dominated careers. The proposed measure recognised the complexity of Otherness, the omnipresence of gender in daily life, and the construction of a canonized body of knowledge from an androcentric worldview.

During García Padilla's last two years as governor, the Secretary of Education approved a second policy (Circular Letter, 19-2014-2015) on gender perspective. Gender Equity Manuals (Manuales de Equidad de Género; DEPR, 2015) were assembled for each academic subject. This policy was supported by three teachers' organizations, the Department of Family Affairs, the Commission on Civil Rights, and the American Civil

Liberties Union, as well as other professional organizations and specific religious figures.

Analysing the context for this second policy allows us to examine contemporary debates that permeate subsequent policy texts. When Rafael Román, then Secretary of Education, signed this policy, religious fundamentalist groups launched a campaign of vehement resistance (Mujeres por Puerto Rico, 2016). They argued that the policy meant schools would use reprehensible materials to teach sex education. However, the PRDE's policy on sex education at the time was to use Crooks and Baur's (2009) book *Our Sexuality* to train teachers – not students – in sex education (Lilibeth Vega, personal communication, 16 February 2021). PRDE's position was opposed by some religious groups[8] who claimed the topic was a family matter. These groups disregarded criticisms about the lack of a gender perspective and focus on human rights to promote equity (Grupo Internacional de Currículo en Sexualidad y VIH, 2011). Conservative groups stressed the family as the 'natural socialising agent'.[9] This discourse toyed with the anxieties of multiple groups that believe that teaching sex education awakens youths' sexuality, which ignores the complexity of sex education.

Other PRDE policies during García Padilla's tenure used LGBTTQIA+ inclusive language. The first was related to school uniforms. It established that 'the use of particular clothing items shall not be imposed upon students who feel uncomfortable with them due to their sexual orientation or gender identity' (PRDE, 2015, p 4) – this type of discussion about gender opened to include the LGBTTQIA+ community in educational contexts. Prioritizing this diversity dimension became apparent just days before a new NPP administration assumed power in 2016. A new policy (Carta Circular 24, 2016-2017) was issued to 'guarantee that all students within the public education system would not be victims of discrimination nor bullying due to their perceived sexual orientation or gender identity' (PRDE, 2016, p 1). It also sets school communities' norms to ensure compliance. Although legislation cannot guarantee that vulnerable communities will receive a practical benefit in their daily lives, its impact on public discourse and political culture is undeniable.

LGBTTQIA+ inclusive policies aligned with the US government's initiatives against transgender discrimination in education. In May 2016, the US Secretary of Education and the Attorney General cited the prohibition of discrimination in Title IX of the Education Amendments Act of 1972 when they asserted that 'this prohibition [Title IX] encompasses discrimination based on a student's gender identity, including discrimination based on a student's transgender status' (US Department of Justice and US Department of Education, 2016, para. 1).

It is essential to point out that homophobia is at the core of religious fundamentalist factions' opposition to policies that strengthen the secular state's adoption of policies to guarantee human rights. Corrêa and Parker (2020a) and Bracke and Paternotte (2018) have noticed this trend in other parts of the world. For example, a 'gender equity' policy (Carta Circular, 36, 2016-2017) in education was approved by the PRDE in 2017, a month into the new NPP administration headed by Ricardo Rosello Nevárez.[10] With it, the new administration abolished the gender equity and gender perspective policy approved by the previous one, including the ability of LGBTTQIA+ students to choose clothing outside of traditional gender norms (for example, skirts for girls and trousers for boys). This shift delivered a blow to the claims of the LGBTTQIA+ community and those who advocated for pro-gender perspective initiatives.

Between 2016 and 2020, the legislature rekindled a discussion on the need for policies in support of gender equity. Senator Zoé Laboy Alvarado sponsored Law No. 62–2017 (Legislatura de Puerto Rico, 2017) to develop a project for coeducational schools aiming to promote gender equity. It instructed the PRDE and the Women's Advocate Office to institute a pilot project in ten elementary schools located in areas with high rates of gender-based violence. Unfortunately, its implementation was delayed due to the devastation caused by Hurricane Maria in September 2017. However, looking at its overt and underlying discourses is imperative to understand the initiative's logic and reach.

The concept of coeducation was developed during post-Franco Spain's transition to democracy. It referred to the classroom integration of boys and girls (mixed education) and was mandated through the Spanish General Education Act of 1970 (González Pérez, 2018). In recent decades, its meaning has transformed due to the advocacy for gender policies in the Iberian country. It now explicitly incorporates the themes of equity and gender perspective (Álvarez Uria et al, 2019). In Puerto Rico, Law No. 62–2017 asserted the education system's responsibility to guarantee boys' and girls' equal access to opportunities. This law aimed to eliminate 'discriminatory mechanisms and styles', promote 'nonviolence towards women', and emphasize the family's role in socialization. Conspicuously, the term 'gender perspective' was not present. Instead, the word 'coeducation' was used. This omission contrasts with the goals of groups advocating for gender policies in the country where coeducation was conceived.

The emphasis on the family as an abstract and quasi-universal concept is worth noting. Defined as the 'natural socializing agent', the law required the education authorities to notify families in the ten participating schools to allow them to withdraw their children from activities with which they disagreed. This notification reacted to worldwide anti-gender campaigns that strategically advocated for parents to sign letters demanding their children be excluded from equity and gender-perspective curricular sequences. Even so, the educational materials developed as part of this pilot project adhere to a liberal worldview of society that has a place that accommodates emancipatory struggles, feminists, and the LGBTTQIA+ communities.

Policies on equal access and opportunity have played an essential role in allowing many people and groups to access diverse spheres of social life. However, when there is job scarcity, as is characteristic of neoliberal economic reforms (such as those passed in Puerto Rico), education neither guarantees employment nor the liberal aspiration to social mobility associated with the education-work dyad (Aronowitz, 2004). Thus, the approach of the 2017 law is problematic as it does not consider the roots and historical trajectories of marginalization and diversity. Moreover, it risks getting mired in cosmetic issues tinged by individualist ideals central to neoliberal education policies (Kenway, 1996; Apple, 2000; Aronowitz, 2004).

Another important topic in Law No. 62–2017 is the institution of a group 'composed of diverse sectors from the school community' to develop strategies to address gender-based discrimination (Article 1). It includes the representation of interdenominational groups, a clear allusion to religious groups, as an attempt to cater to the factions represented by religious fundamentalists that oppose gender perspective policies. It dilutes the political strength of equity and gender-perspective discourses by fitting potentially antagonistic discourses within the same space. However, 2017 saw the unfurling of a new reality in Puerto Rico. Only weeks after the approval of Law No. 62–2017, the country suffered the blows of Hurricanes Irma and María, which interrupted the implementation of this law. The pilot project finally began in August 2018 in 11 schools. The experience with these projects has not been published and thus represents an avenue for future research.

The new decade and ongoing debates

On 26 October 2020, Wanda Vázquez Garced, governor and former head of the Women's Advocate Office, signed an Executive Order that declared combating violence against women an urgent priority in Puerto Rico. It alluded to Law No. 62–2017 and instructed that the 'specialized coeducational schools' curriculum be expanded to the entire school system by August 2021. However, due to the COVID-19 pandemic, implementing this order became a precarious effort.

In 2021, Puerto Rico's new governor, Pedro Pierluisi Urrutia (NPP), addressed feminist groups' demands and declared a state of emergency by Executive Order. This order committed to a curriculum with a gender perspective and established the Prevention, Support, Rescue, and Education on Gender-Based Violence Committee (PSRE) for educational programmes. This marked the first time an NPP administration made a statement using such language. As expected, it was attacked by anti-gender groups. The discussions, escalating through candidate debates during the 2020 general election, captivated the country. Anti-gender groups, strengthened by having two female supporters (Joanne Rodríguez Veve and Janet Burgos) in the Legislative Assembly, intensified their crusade. These senators, elected as members of the Project Dignity Party, initiated a lawsuit against the governor, claiming the Executive Order violated the constitutional separation of powers because the Legislative Assembly had not received a report on the results of the Law 62–2017 pilot project. Carlos Ramos González, a constitutional law professor at the Inter-American University of Puerto Rico, argued that this lawsuit was a 'paradigmatic example of a judicial action that does not meet the necessary conditions of constitutional litigation to be adjudicated' (*El Nuevo Día*, 13 March 2021). The court threw out the lawsuit, which is now being appealed.

In the second half of 2021, Bill Proposal 714 was submitted to the Legislative Assembly to amend the Educational Reform Law of Puerto Rico, Law No. 85–2018 (approved in the last four-year term and replacing Law No. 149–1999). This proposal, sponsored by three PDP members, aimed to clarify the language of Law No. 85–2018 (3 LPRA sec. 9802c, clause b-35). The proposal amended the obligation of the PRDE to coordinate, along with the Women's Advocate Office, an educational programme aimed at advancing equality, managing conflict or anger, and preventing domestic violence. The amendment proposed 'an educational program or *curriculum with a gender perspective* that holds as its objective the advancement of *gender equity* and *gender-based violence prevention*' (Puerto Rican House of Representatives, Bill Proposal 714, p 3). The debate that had taken place in the first decade of the 21st century gained relevance once again. In a move to please the religious fundamentalist factions that equated gender perspective with 'gender ideology', the Legislative Assembly retreated, and the project did not pass. The outlook is not optimistic. In 2021, the governor and the Interim Secretary of Education declared that the new curriculum would focus on 'values' to 'promote respect and equity' and insisted on not including the concept of gender perspective (*El Nuevo Día*, 7 November 2021; González, 2022). The introduction of 'values' in the discourse of gender is regarded as code for teachings based on conservative religious moral standards.

Discussion: towards a local agenda with transnational referentiality

The 1990s saw the surfacing of an anti-gender crusade rooted in Catholic dogma and joined by fundamentalist Evangelical Protestants and other conservative groups. This fundamentalism presupposes that notions of gender, women, and sexuality remain static. According to López (2021), these groups attempt to obstruct the link between discourse, thought, and action: 'fundamentalism halts relational movement by becoming a doctrine; believing itself the owner of an absolute and invariable truth that rejects any connection with otherness … fundamentalism tries to destroy any possibility of connection through hatred, exclusion, condemnation, or death' (Provocación 5).

For these groups, women's roles are tied to compulsory procreation and enacting the heterosexual family. The Other is opposed in an attempt to erase it. This position led them to orchestrate a worldwide anti-gender movement with interconnected webs that attacked through a media showcase of lies, the entanglement of arguments, and the co-opting of discourse, to name but a few.

In the first decades of the 21st century, the anti-gender crusade has relentlessly used various discursive and political strategies against gender policies in education. The focus of the anti-gender crusade varies across countries, evidencing the ways that international forces affect and are mediated by national/local levels. However, their discourses and impact on public policy coalesce in practice. The mobilization against sexual identity, reproductive rights (abortion in particular), and equity and gender perspective educational materials in school contexts have familiar leading figures, ideological origins, and strategies. The anti-gender discourses spreading worldwide share qualities with those in Puerto Rico. They include a gender binary anchored in a discourse on what is 'natural', the family as the institution for conversations about sexuality, men's and women's complementarity, the alignment of gender perspective with gender ideology, and the placement of fake news on educational content relating to the gender perspective.

At a time when we experience decreased quality of life and the weakening of social policies to protect vulnerable populations, anti-gender policies have both diluted and caused the regression of gender policies, as well as the discourse of political parties that had previously supported these policies. This situation coincides with increased political authoritarianism, and values imposition and a single religious worldview, eroding the democratic (inclusive) discourse that has been costly to humanity. As posited by Corrêa and Parker (2020b), citing Cooper (2017), there is an interconnection between neoliberalism and conservatism, and its effect is to de-democratize the public sphere regarding gender and sexuality policies. In education, this interconnection focuses on forming a power bloc composed of capital market factions, neoconservative intellectuals, fundamentalists, authoritarians, populist religious persons, and sectors of the professional middle class (Apple 2000). This bloc has promoted policies (standards, educational vouchers, school choice, and charter schools) that have further impoverished the most vulnerable groups. The bloc shares a wish to return to a past of traditional homes, families, and schools. In the modern, conservative worldview, man/woman complementarity and binary are the foundations for this discourse. According to Cooper (2017), this discourse aims to 'ensure that the duty of protection and care returns to families – or, more specifically, to women – when States, under the impact of neoliberalism, reduce social protection policies to a minimum' (cited in Corrêa and Parker, 2020b, p 7).

The promise of a democracy strengthened through greater inclusion – one that expands through education – appears to be losing ground to restrictions against the participation and representation of historically marginalized groups.

In Puerto Rico, these concrete and contextualized narratives encourage gender-based violence and are shaped by the country's colonial/territorial situation. In 2016, the US Congress imposed the Financial Oversight and Management Board as part of the Puerto Rico Oversight, Management, and Economic Stability Act (US Congress, 2016). Under the pretext of paying off an unpayable debt of $74 billion in bonds, extreme austerity measures subjected the population to uncertain healthcare, education, and housing conditions and dramatic increases in the cost of living. The Fiscal Supervisory Board has absolute power over Puerto Rico's budget. It controls all laws and regulations of the Puerto Rican government that affect the budget despite no democratic representation of Puerto Rico's constituents in the US Congress, disproportionately impacting poor, vulnerable populations. Women across all possible intersections, albeit in different forms, carry the weight of this imposition.

Education gender policies in Puerto Rico have been promoted in response to gender-based violence. Goudreau Aubert (2021) argues that it is necessary to establish the relationship between this violence, human rights violations, and the broader economic crisis, which diverse groups of women experience in an embodied and lived way. This situation is not limited to physical or psychological violence women endure in individual and private ways but also structural violence that encompasses all spheres of life. As Contreras Capó states:

> To talk about gender violence is not only to talk about the 'Ley 54' [Law for the Prevention and Intervention with Domestic Violence]. We also need to talk about cuts in TANF [Temporary Assistance for Needy Families] benefits because they mainly affect female-headed households; we need to talk about the closing of schools because more than 75% of teachers are women; we need to talk about layoffs in the public sector because most of them are women. (2021, p 168)

Conclusions

The struggle for gender policies acts as a retaining wall against anti-gender policies. A conversation among the Global South, including Central America and the Caribbean, would benefit the development of common agendas to oppose anti-gender efforts. The use of information, communication technologies, and social media has the potential to strengthen that retaining wall and advance democratizing agendas.

The next decade will likely bring further polarizing of discourses and material actions regarding these political forces. On the one hand, the anti-gender crusade; on the other hand, the parties that advocate for equity and gender perspective at the local, national, and international levels. Mobilizing young people is an essential strategy. However, this cannot be done through traditional approaches. Feminist organizations need to work together with other movements. Throughout Latin America, there are concrete efforts to this effect and an understanding of the links between gender issues and the global tendencies aimed at de-democratizing society. Information technologies have played an essential role in connecting people across issues and organizing efforts. This is an important avenue to explore going forward – both in practice and research.

Feminisms have shown the capacity to establish alliances and blocs, sustain dialogues, and coordinate strategies to address specific problems with a vision that expands and connects issues affecting various marginalized populations. As a result, feminisms have generated more subtle and intersectional theoretical understandings. These, in turn, contribute to developing and refining the movement's agenda, enabling it to include the marginalization of which we all, in different ways, are a part. Herein lies its deeply democratic character.

Notes

[1] Puerto Rico has a colonial/territorial relationship with the US. Puerto Rico is under the territorial clause of the US Constitution, which means that the ultimate power over the archipelago is the US Congress. The geographical archipelago of Puerto Rico is not a member of the UN. Regardless of the positions that the metropolis assumes with respect to the UN, the discourses that emerge from this organization resonate in the country. Through nongovernmental organizations, groups in Puerto Rico have participated in the UN and related agencies. Puerto Rico is also an associate member of the Economic Commission for Latin America and the Caribbean (ECLAC).

[2] The term 'gender perspective' was adopted at the Fourth International Conference on Women held in Beijing in 1995. It is an analytical methodology that calls for mainstreaming gender in the development and implementation of policies and practices. More than a focus on quantitative participation of gender, it places emphasis on the effects of policies and practices on gender, as well as the experiences of gender in people's lives.

3   According to Viveros Vigoya (2016), intersectional feminism accounts for the multiplicity of forms of oppression and resistance that intersect, interact, and are articulated in specific contexts at the individual and institutional levels. Its origins can be traced to 19th-century writings, although the current use of the concept can be attributed to the African-American lawyer Kimberlé Crenshaw. It criticizes oppression's hierarchical structures, the theoretical conception of adding oppression and resistance, and the epistemological dichotomy that characterizes Western thought. It proposes a heterogeneous feminism, promotes forming alliances, and considers 'openness to differences a condition, not a limitation, to intersectionality' (Purschert and Meyer, cited in Viveros Vigoya, 2016, p 15).

4   In Argentina, Law No. 26-150 of 22006 (the Comprehensive Sexual Education Law) is in force, which embraces gender perspective and human rights. In Paraguay, the Governing Pedagogical Framework for Comprehensive Sex Education of 2010 contained similar guidelines but was rejected by conservative factions who deemed it 'ideologization'. It was replaced by the National Plan for Sexual and Reproductive Health, the main axis of which is prevention (Báez, 2015).

5   The Popular Democratic Party leads the formulation of the current political status of the country, the Commonwealth (Estado Libre Asociado), while the New Progressive Party advocates that Puerto Rico should become a state of the US.

6   Since the 1960s, women in Puerto Rico have been subjected to massive sterilization campaigns, an issue that has been analysed from two angles: the use of women as guinea pigs as a result of colonial/imperial relations with the US, and the impacts on women's development opportunities as the number of children is reduced.

7   It is worth noting that liberal and conservative are used as somewhat lax categories. The crossings across different aspects are very remarkable. However, the trends do exist.

8   Religious groups in Puerto Rico are heterogeneous. On the one hand, there are the historic Evangelical Protestant churches that are grouped in the Council of Churches of Puerto Rico, to which eight Christian churches belong alongside two churches that 'live in unity through diversity.' In their preaching and practices, some of these churches have embraced discourses in favour of women, sexual, and gender diversity. In addition, there is the Fraternity of Pentecostal Councils, made up of Pentecostal, neo-Pentecostal and non-Pentecostal conciliar denominations, most of whom oppose education with a gender perspective. Finally, there is the Catholic Church, within which, despite the opposing stances adopted by some priests and nuns, there are priests who have rejected gender perspective and encouraged their parishioners to actively participate in activities against it.

9   It is necessary to comment on the qualification of 'natural' socializing agent to refer to the family. This assumes an inflexible vision of the family, as if it were the same across all places and eras. A historical-critical look at the family as a concept would account for its transformations and conflicts. It would consider underlying problems with the association of consanguinity that has existed throughout the history of the family and the major political issues that this view has produced. A similar analysis could account for the historical evolution of other 'socializing agents' whose adjective 'natural' could be equated to that of the family: peer groups, the media, schools, and other social institutions.

10 Roselló Nevárez resigned as governor 18 months prior to the end of his term due to a series of events relating to a group chat he shared with several close associates, which led to national mobilizations for his resignation. The content of this chat contained sexist and homophobic language.

Acknowledgement

The author would like to thank Camila Guillama-Capellas for the translation of this chapter.

References

Álvarez Uria, A. Vizcarra Morales, M. T., and Lasarte Leonet, G. (2019). El significado y la evolución del término 'coeducción' con el cambio de siglo: El caso de los centros escolares de Vitoria-Gasteiz. *Tendencias Pedagógicas, 34*, 62–75. Doi: 10.15366/tp2019.34.006

Apple, M. W. (2000). Reform through conservative modernisation: standards, markets, and inequality in education. In J. Boaler (ed.), *Multiple Perspectives on Mathematics Teaching and Learning* (Kindle). Ablex.

Apple, M. W. (2001). *Educating the 'Right' Way: Markets, Standards, God and Inequality*. Routledge Falmer.

Arguedas Ramírez, G. (2020) Ideología de género', lo 'post-secular', el fundamentalismo neopentecostal y el neointegrismo católico: La vocación anti-democrática. Observatorio de Sexualidad y Política. Género & Política en América Latina. http://www.sxpolitics.org

Aronowitz, S. (2004). Against schooling: education and social class. *Social Text, 22*(2), 13–35.

Báez, J. (2015). *Políticas educativas, jóvenes y sexualidades en América Latina y el Caribe: Las luchas feministas en la construcción de la agenda pública sobre educación sexual*. CLACSO.

Barrientos Delgado, J. (2020). *Políticas antigénero en América Latina: Chile ¿Estrategias en construcción?* Observatorio de Sexualidad y Política. Género & Política en América Latina. http://www.sxpolitics.org

Boletín administrativo Num. OE-2020–013 [La Fortaleza, Oficina del Gobernador]. Declarando un estado de emergencia ante el aumento de casos de violencia de género en Puerto Rico. 25 de enero de 2021.

Boletín administrativo Num. OE-2020–078 [La Fortaleza, Oficina de la Gobernadora]. Para declarar servicios prioritarios la lucha contra la violencia a las mujeres en Puerto Rico. 26 de octubre de 2020.

Bracke, S., and Paternotte, D. (2018). Desentrañando el pecado del género. In S. Bracke and D. Paternotte (eds.), *¡Habemus género! La iglesia católica y ideología de género: Textos seleccionados* (pp 8–25). Género y política en América Latina. http://www.sxpolitics.org

Campana, M. (2020). *Políticas antigénero en América Latina: Argentina.* Observatorio de Sexualidad y Política. Género y política en América Latina. http://www.sxpolitics.org

Caro González, L. (2022). Educación confirma que el currículo para la educación con perspectiva de género no se llamará así. *El Nuevo Día*, 18 January. https://www.elnuevodia.com/noticias/gobierno/notas/educac ion-confirma-que-el-curriculo-para-la-educacion-con-perspectiva-de-gen ero-ya-no-se-llamara-asi/

Careaga Pérez, G., and Aranda, L. E. (2020). Políticas anti-género en América Latina: México. Género y sexualidad en el centro del huracán. Observatorio de Sexualidad y Política. Género y política en América Latina. http://www.sxpolitics.org

Contreras Capó, V. (2021). Debt and structural gender violence. *Critical Times*, 4(1), 167–169. https://read.dukeupress.edu/critical-times/issue/4/1

Cooper, M. (2017). *Family Values: Between Neoliberalism and the New Socialconservatism*. Zone Books.

Corrêa, S., and Parker, R. (eds.) (2020a).*¡Habemus género! La iglesia católica y ideología de género: Textos seleccionados*. Observatorio de Sexualidad y Política. Género & Política en América Latina. http://www.sxpolitics.org

Corrêa, S., and Parker, R. (2020b). Prefacio. Serie Políticas anti-género en América Latina. *Observatorio de Sexualidad y Política*. Género & Política en América Latina. http://www.sxpolitics.org

Corrêa, S., and Kalil, I. (2020). Políticas anti-género en América Latina: Brasil. *Observatorio de Sexualidad y Política*. Género & Política en América Latina. http://www.sxpolitics.org

Crespo Kebler, E. (2001). La liberación de la mujer: Los feminismos, la justicia social, la nación y la autonomía en las organizaciones feministas de la década de 1970 en Puerto Rico. In A. I. Rivera Lassén and E. Crespo Kebler (eds.), *Documentos del feminismo en Puerto Rico: Facsímiles de la historia* (pp 39–95). Editorial Universidad de Puerto Rico.

Crooks, R., and Baur, K. (2009). *Nuestra Sexualidad*. Cengage Learning Editores.

Departamento de Educación de Puerto Rico (2015). *Manuales de Equidad de Género*.

El Nuevo Día (2021). Obispos católicos se expresan en contra de las terapias de conversión. 1 April. https://www.elnuevodia.com/noticias/legislatura/ notas/obispos-catolicos-se-expresan-en-contra-de-las-terapias-de-convers ion-y-tambien-rechazan-el-proyecto-que-las-prohibe/

El Nuevo Día (2021). Educación trabaja en un currículo que promueve el 'respeto y la equidad'. 7 November. https://www.elnuevodia.com/notic ias/gobierno/notas/educacion-trabaja-en-un-curriculo-que-promueve- el-respeto-y-la-equidad/

Gil Hernández, F. (2020). *Políticas antigénero en América Latina: Colombia – Agentes conservadores contra los derechos sexuales y reproductivos*. Observatorio de Sexualidad y Política. Género & Política en América Latina. http://www. sxpolitics.org

Goudreau Aubert, A. (2021). We women who don't owe anyone: Las Propias in times of public debt and austerity. *Critical Times*, 4(1), 130–147. https://read.dukeupress.edu/critical-times/issue/4/1

González Pérez, T. (2018). Políticas educativas igualitarias en España. La igualdad de género en los estudios de magisterio. *Archivos Analíticos de Políticas Educativas*, 26(2), 1–21. http://dx.doi.org/10.14507/epaa.26.2764

Grupo Internacional de Currículo en Sexualidad y VIH (2011). *Un solo currículo: Pautas y actividades para un enfoque integrado hacia la educación en sexualidad, género, VIH y derechos humanos*. Population Council.

Kenway, J. (1996). La educación y el discurso político de la nueva derecha: Enseñanza privada frente a enseñanza estatal. In S. J. Ball (ed.). *Foucault y la educación: Disciplinas del saber* (pp 171–207). Morate.

Legislatura de Puerto Rico (1990). Ley Orgánica del Departamento de Educación del Estado Libre Asociado de Puerto Rico (Ley Núm. 68–1990). https://www.lexjuris.com/LEYORG/lexeduca.htm

Legislatura de Puerto Rico (1999). Ley Orgánica del Departamento de Educación de Puerto Rico (Ley Núm. 149–1999). https://www.lexjuris.com/lexlex/Ley1999/lex99149.htm

Legislatura de Puerto Rico (2017). Ley para disponer el desarrollo de un proyecto piloto de escuelas coeducativas dirigido a promover la equidad de género. (Ley Núm. 62–2017). https://www.lexjuris.com/lexlex/Leyes2017/lexl2017062.htm

López, F. (2021). Provocación 5. Fundamentalismos de todo tipo. En Observatorio móvil del Instituto de Investigación Violencia y Complejidad. *Provocaciones para pensar la violencia*. https://observatoriomovil.com/2021/03/20/provocaciones-para-pensar-la-violencia/

Luvis Nuñez, A. (2021, 16 marzo, *El Nuevo Día*). Terapias de conversión: a reparar nuestra inhumanidad. https://www.elnuevodia.com/opinion/punto-de-vista/terapias-de-conversion-a-reparar-nuestra-inhumanidad/

Mercado Sierra, M. (2011). La perspectiva de género en la educación: un análisis con método mixto de las políticas educativas de equidad de género en Puerto Rico. Doctoral dissertation, University of Puerto Rico.

Mujeres por Puerto Rico (2016). Ideología de género en la enseñanza: Manuales en 'equidad de género' Departamento de Educación de Puerto Rico. PowerPoint, 12 May. https://www.encuentrodefamilia.com/uploads/2/7/4/3/27436853/edg_en_el_depr_manuales.pdf

Observatorio de Equidad de Género Puerto Rico (2021). Feminicidios, desaparecidos y violencia de género 2021. https://img1.wsimg.com/blobby/go/d3c2458f-94d2-43aa-a679-5965a68f49c5/OEG%20-%20Lista%20de%20Feminicidios%20por%20categoria-0005.pdf

Observatorio de Igualdad de Género de América Latina y el Caribe (2017). *Planes de igualdad de género en América Latina y el Caribe: Mapas de ruta para el desarrollo*. CEPAL. https://www.cepal.org/sites/default/files/events/files/planes_de_igualdad_de_genero_en_america_latina_y_el_caribe._mapas_de_ruta_para_el_desarrollo.pdf

Organización de Naciones Unidas, Derechos Humanos, Oficina de la Alta Comisionada (2012). *Nacidos libres e iguales: Orientación sexual e identidad de género en las normas internacionales de derechos humanos.* https://www.ohchr.org/Documents/Publications/BornFreeAndEqualLowRes_SP.pdf

Puerto Rican Department of Education (2015). Directrices sobre el uso del uniforme escolar en el sistema público de enseñanza en Puerto Rico. DEPR, Carta Circular Núm. 16 de 2015–2016.

Puerto Rican Department of Education (2016). Politica pública sobre el trato igualitario para estudiantes transgénero y contra el discrimen por razón de orientación sexual o identidad de género en el sistema público de enseñanza en Puerto Rico. DEPR, Carta Circular Núm. 24 de 2016–2017.

Puerto Rican House of Representatives (2017). Bill Proposal 714. https://aldia.microjuris.com/wp-content/uploads/2021/06/PC714-Radicado.pdf

Ramos González, C. (2021). La constitución, la dignidad humana y la perspectiva de género. *El Nuevo Día*, 13 March. https://www.elnuevodia.com/opinion/punto-de-vista/la-constitucion-la-dignidad-humana-y-la-perspectiva-de-genero/

Rivera Lassén, A. I., and Crespo Kebler, E. (2001). *Documentos del feminismo en Puerto Rico: Facsímiles de la historia.* Editorial Universidad de Puerto Rico.

Santiago Centeno, Z., and Martínez Ramos, L. (1990). *Mesa redonda: Estrategias para la equidad por sexo en la educación.* Comisión para los Asuntos de la Mujer del Gobierno de Puerto Rico.

Senado de Puerto Rico. (2022). P del S. 727. Ley de integración de valores y ética. https://ntc-prod-public-pdfs.s3.us-east-2.amazonaws.com/F1xwGLGQnPdbEbLlPW0FDbkJzZI.pdf

UNESCO (United Nations Educational, Scientific and Cultural Organization) (2008). *Un enfoque de la educación para todos basado en los derechos humanos.* https://unesdoc.unesco.org/ark:/48223/pf0000158893

UNESCO (2015). Declaración de Incheon: Educación 2030: Hacia una educación inclusiva y equitativa de calidad y un aprendizaje a lo largo de la vida para todos. (2015). https://unesdoc.unesco.org/ark:/48223/pf0000245656_spa

United Nations, General Assembly (2015). Resolution 70/1. Transforming our world: the 2030 Agenda for Sustainable Development. https://unctad.org/system/files/official-document/ares70d1_es.pdf

United Nations, Human Rights, Office of the High Commissioner (1979). Convention on the Elimination of All Forms of Discrimination against Women New York, 18 December 1979. https://www.ohchr.org/sp/profe ssionalinterest/pages/cedaw.aspx

UN Women (2014). *Beijing Declaration and Platform for Action, Beijing +5 Political Declaration and Outcome.* https://www.unwomen.org/-/media/ headquarters/attachments/sections/csw/bpa_s_final_web.pdf?la=esan dvs=755

US Congress. Puerto Rico Oversight, Management, and Economic Stability Act (PROMESA), Pub. L. No. 114–187, 130 Stat. 549 (2016).

US Department of Justice and US Department of Education (Civil Rights Divisions. (2016). Dear Colleague Letter on Transgender Students. 13 May. http://www.ed.gov/ocr/letters/colleague-201605-title-ix-transgender.pdf

Vatican (1994). Reservas de la Santa Sede al documento final de la Conferencia de el Cairo sobre Población y Desarrollo. https://www.vati can.va/roman_curia/secretariat_state/archivio/documents/rc_seg-st_1994 0913_conferenza-cairo-riserve_sp.html

Vitieri, M. A. (2020). Políticas anti-género en América Latina: Ecuador. La instrumentalización de la 'ideología de género'. Observatorio de Sexualidad y Política. Género & Política en América Latina. http://www.sxpolitics.org

Viveros Vigoya, M. (2016). La interseccionalidad: una aproximación situada a la dominación. *Debate Feminista*, 52, 1–17. https://doi.org/10.1016/ j.df.2016.09.005

PART IV

Conclusions and Future Directions

15

The Dialectics of Education and Development in Central America and the Latin Caribbean

D. Brent Edwards Jr.

Introduction

One characteristic of the relationship between education and development in Central America and the Latin Caribbean (CALC) is its dialectical nature. Although research on the region rarely speaks to this characteristic (see Chapter 1), it is clearly evident when looking across the cases presented in this volume. By dialectical nature, I am referring, first, to the reality that education helps to resolve or reduce tensions between the state and capitalism (as was first discussed in Chapter 2) and, second, to the fact that the ways in which this tension is resolved repeatedly creates new opportunities for a range of international actors to insert themselves into education reform dynamics in the region. Involvement by these actors, together with counterparts from state agencies, then proceeds – typically while ignoring or without input from teachers, students, and families – until a new crisis emerges, at which point the cycle repeats itself.

The purpose of the present chapter is, first, to make the aforementioned dialectical dynamics clear, which are summarized in Figure 15.1. Second, and relatedly, the purpose is to highlight the challenges that accompany this dynamic when translating policies and programmes into practice. These purposes will be addressed by engaging in an analysis of the chapters in this volume. The guiding framework for the discussion is the one presented in Chapter 2. The key points of this framework are summarized and further elaborated upon in the next section.

In that the chapters of this volume take the international political economy framework detailed in Chapter 2 as their point of departure, it is argued that

Figure 15.1: The dialectic of reform

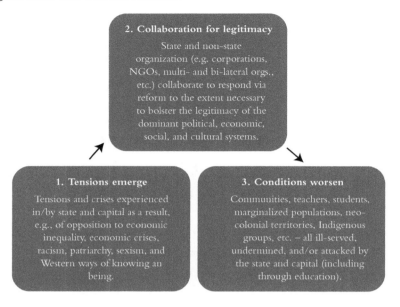

2. Collaboration for legitimacy
State and non-state organization (e.g. corporations, NGOs, multi- and bi-lateral orgs., etc.) collaborate to respond via reform to the extent necessary to bolster the legitimacy of the dominant political, economic, social, and cultural systems.

1. Tensions emerge
Tensions and crises experienced in/by state and capital as a result, e.g., of opposition to economic inequality, economic crises, racism, patriarchy, sexism, and Western ways of knowing an being.

3. Conditions worsen
Communities, teachers, students, marginalized populations, neo-colonial territories, Indigenous groups, etc. – all ill-served, undermined, and/or attacked by the state and capital (including through education).

a contribution to the literature on education and development in CALC has already been made. This chapter seeks to make a further contribution by harnessing and bringing together the insights from each study. The goal is to make explicit that which is typically unacknowledged or insufficiently addressed in research on education in CALC – that is, the extent to which education, in its reform and implementation (or lack thereof), is inextricably linked to and constrained by tensions and incentives produced as a result of the relationship between the state and the global capitalist economy. In that the discussion in this chapter is based not on the analysis of one or a few cases, but rather on the analysis of 12 studies spanning nine countries (that is, all the Spanish-speaking countries of CALC), it is hoped that the reader perceives the relevance and necessity of grasping these dynamics if one wishes to achieve a meaningful and profound understanding of the limits and potential contributions of education in the region.

Before discussing the themes embedded in each chapter, the next section revisits and extends the explanation of the guiding analytic framework for this volume as presented in Chapter 2. The key features and insights of each chapter are then discussed. Rather than analysing each chapter in the order in which it is included in the volume, the discussion proceeds based on the commonalities and thematic connections across chapters. Those chapters which directly address the role of education in managing tensions between the state and capital are discussed first. This discussion is then followed by the excavation of insights from the other chapters, focused, for example, on technology, gender, and gangs. While all chapters have relevance for the state-capital dialectic, the implications were, in some cases, implicit or secondary. The present chapter thus rounds up and extends the relevant insights from all chapters in order to generate a region-wide perspective on how this dialectic influences education reform. The next and final chapter then reflects on where education and development can and should go from here.

Education between the state and global capitalism

Before proceeding with the insights that emerge from across the studies included in this volume, it may be helpful to remind the reader of the analytic orientation presented in Chapter 2. There, it was explained that there are three dimensions of analysis that take priority: first, the processes of policy making and how these are affected by such considerations as geopolitical constraints, capitalist pressures, and international organizations; second, the ways in which different reform visions are communicated, interpreted, and experienced; and, third, the manner in which tensions across political-economic forces and interest groups are resolved (and in ways that are frequently problematic in the long run). More specifically, this last dimension refers to the way that education helps to mediate and resolve tensions that arise between the state and capital in the context of capitalist development.

Since the implications of the third dimension may not be obvious, a bit of additional commentary, drawing on Chapter 3, is in order. In Chapter 3, it was noted that while education cannot – due to structural constraints inherent to capitalism – offer the majority of students the promise of meaningful employment or economic advancement, it is still the case that the rhetoric and reform of education play key roles in the dialectic between the state and capital. Rhetoric and reform here refer to the policies and programmes promoted by the government and international organizations. These entities are aware of the structural constraints within which education operates. But, in order to manage expectations and to preserve social stability, these policies and programmes extend the promise of a better future by focusing on such things as the acquisition of 21st-century skills, technological competencies, job preparation, and entrepreneurship, among other themes highlighted in earlier chapters of this volume (and critically discussed later on). Policies and programmes thus circulate a certain discourse about how education is central both to better opportunities at the individual level and to the success of national economic growth. To the extent that education is successful in advancing these and other beliefs that contribute to preserving (or insignificantly modifying) the status quo, it helps to maintain the stability (and if not also the perceived legitimacy) of a system that tends towards inequality and concentration of power at multiple scales, from the local to the global.

The guiding concern in the analysis that follows is to demonstrate how, in each and every case contained in the present volume, education is affected by this dialectic, that is, the dialectic whereby the state has to facilitate the workings of the global capitalist system (in other words, the accumulation of capital) while also sufficiently taming (or averting attention away from) the worst tendencies of that system. Of course, states do not typically acknowledge this tension, which is not surprising given that doing so would inherently draw attention to it. Rather, as the studies in this volume have shown, liberal capitalist states and other actors involved in education reform emphasize the potentially salutary effects of their policies and initiatives – which are always and necessarily focused on other issues (gender-based discrimination, peer bullying, sexual violence, student governments, mobile technologies, gang prevention, teacher training, etc.). The present chapter not only locates these reforms within the dialectic between the state and capitalism but also, in so doing, uses the tensions inherent in this dialectic to explain why some reforms have advanced and have affected practice more than others. Where reforms do not connect with the logics and incentives that animate national and international actors, they are much less likely to move towards enactment.

The absence of any mention in the previous paragraph of local-level actors should not be taken to mean that actors at this level are left out of the analysis. On the contrary, and as was emphasized in Chapter 2, it is essential that the perspectives and experiences of actors at this level also be taken into account. Indeed, as has been repeatedly shown in this volume, the perspectives and expectations of students, families, school directors, and teachers help to explain why policies do or do not move towards enactment. Moreover, and to connect back to the dialectic noted previously, the actions of actors such as unions, social movements, indigenous peoples, and rebel groups can serve as sources of pressure that motivate states to act. States, acting in their own self-interest and in the interests of capital, may take the offensive against such groups (see, for example, Chapter 3), but such groups can also be successful in pushing states to act in ways that they are not initially inclined, as when a social movement pressured the government of the Dominican Republic to significantly increase its investment in education (although even this investment has dialectical implications, as will be discussed later on and as was addressed further in Chapter 13). Additionally, although no less importantly, it is imperative to consider not only how the actions of local as well as national and international actors are caught in the dialectic between the state and capital, but also how these actions are entangled with other systems of discrimination with which capitalism is entwined, and from which it benefits, such as patriarchy, sexism, and racism. Where possible, the present chapter makes such connections.

As a final point here, the meaning of the state should be clarified. Although the discussion in this and previous chapters has referred, for example, to political actors, the government, policy makers, etc., to be clear, the understanding of the state employed in the discussion that follows derives from a neo-Marxist approach. Here, the state is seen as both a pact of domination and a product of class conflict, rooted in historical dynamics, while at the same time it mediates class conflict and does so through semi-autonomous state apparatuses that have an administrative nature, take organizational forms, and are defined as 'specifiable publicly financed institutions' (Dale, 1989, p 54). Moreover, as noted in the comments made earlier, it is assumed that the state is embedded within the global capitalist system and that states are differentially able to take advantage of their position in that system depending on their historical context. Finally, it should be noted that states – that is, the institutions, policy makers, networks, and other actors who populate their agencies – continue to reflect, or at least to function in the service of, the colonial (extractive and exclusionary), modernizing (rational-functionalist), and capitalist (profit- and growth-oriented) logics upon which they have been constructed. These foundations and their connection to education are discussed at length in Chapter 11 of the present volume. They are also addressed extensively together with a discussion of state theory in a recent companion volume (Edwards et al, 2023). The chapters in the present volume help to draw out the importance and interconnections of each of these aspects of the state, as will be shown in the following discussion.

Economic transformation and a new paradigm for education

Any discussion of the dialectics of education in CALC needs to recall the shift in the development paradigm that took place in the 1980s and 1990s. This issue was taken up in Chapters 2 and 3. As noted there, a fundamental tension present throughout the region relates to the fact that the current paradigm of development undermines the ability of governments to provide a well-resourced education. This is so in that, during these decades, at the same time that countries in the region were making efforts to shift from conflict and authoritarianism to peace and democracy, a simultaneous economic transition was occurring that, in effect, would undermine the ability of these states to address the root causes of conflict, including economic inequality. Incorporation into the global economy transformed the nature of the government's relationship to the economy. State agencies went from being the director or manager of the economy to serving as a facilitator for global capital. This shift eschewed the question of structural transformation of the economy in favour of those who had been historically dispossessed and disadvantaged by capitalist accumulation.

Concurrently, these reforms combined with and reinforced colonial tendencies, where the economic and political elite saw the state as a vehicle for their own advancement. Not only were the economic and the education systems of the region to be put in the service of the global economy, but these same systems would also be used to enrich members of the upper classes, just as they always had been. Perhaps nowhere is this more clear than in Honduras (see Chapters 4 and 13). With political parties themselves having been founded by banana companies in the late 1800s, the state has historically operated as a vehicle for the benefit of those in power together with their networks. The case of Honduras is discussed further later on.

For now, this first point about economic transformation needs to be drawn out and connected to its implications for education. Generally, international development banks and the US (for example, through its bilateral aid agency) were pushing the countries of CALC to open their economies to international imports and foreign investment, to privatize state agencies, to minimize and modernize their bureaucracies, and to cut social spending (see Chapter 2). In the realm of education, the dominant strand of thought pushed by those in the development industry was, first, that education should, above all, contribute to the development of human capital in order to contribute to individual and national economic success. Second, and following from the general reform priorities just enumerated, the education system itself should made to operate more efficiently, effectively, and accountably (see Chapter 3). Ideally, this was to be done by putting into practice the principles of New Public Management.

Approaches based on New Public Management would, among other things, seek to move decision making away from the central bureaucracy and to lower levels of administration in order to make the provision of education more responsive to the needs and preferences of schools and communities. Such approaches, it was thought, would also lead to cost savings: there would be less waste of financial resources since those in charge of incurring expenditures would only purchase what was needed and what they could afford, as opposed to central office officials purchasing the same materials for all schools. A further focus of New Public Management is the need to collect data that can be used both for decision-making purposes (as when parents choose a school for their children) and for holding individuals accountable (as when evaluating teachers).

In the present volume, multiple chapters examine reforms that embody the logic of New Public Management. Chapter 3 shares findings on (failed) standardized testing reforms in Honduras as well as school- and community-based management reforms in El Salvador, Guatemala, and Nicaragua. Through these latter reforms, committees composed of parents (in El Salvador and Guatemala) or teachers and principals (in Nicaragua) were given the responsibility for making decisions at the school level that were previously handled by higher levels of the system (teacher hiring/firing, purchasing school supplies, etc.). Chapter 4 likewise focuses on how administrative decentralization in Honduras, through which certain responsibilities were to be transferred to intermediate levels of the education system, should have made the system more efficient and responsive to the needs of teachers and schools.

While the authors of these chapters underscore the difficulty of putting these reforms into practice (a point that will be revisited later on), their relevance at the moment is that they represent manifestations of the approach of New Public Management. As opposed to focusing on inputs such as funding, an equitable distribution of resources, teacher professional development, free school meal programmes, conditional cash transfers, wraparound services for students and families, new infrastructure, curriculum reforms, or cultural differences between the home and school environment, among many other possible foci, these New Public Management reforms took as their focus efficiency (spending), effectiveness (test scores), and accountability (of teachers, but in the absence of sufficient materials, training, and support). The larger point, which should not be overlooked, is that a focus on these outcomes is the natural consequence of the changing relationship between the state and the (now global) economy. An additional point, also noted at the outset of this chapter, is that the process of resolving state-capital tensions (related to reducing government bureaucracy and attempting to make it more efficient, etc.) opens up space for the further involvement of international development organizations, such as the World Bank, which were central to developing and financing school- and community-based management reforms in El Salvador, Guatemala, Honduras, and Nicaragua.

Moreover, in all cases, what we can see is that the enactment of New Public Management reforms did not lead to the elimination of the state, but rather to a transformation of its role, where it is expected to govern according to principles (efficiency, effectiveness, and accountability) that are characteristic of a particular economic approach to education.[1] However, and to reiterate, although these reforms have garnered significant attention, often sapping energy and resources away from other efforts, it is also the case that the approach of New Public Management has not been entirely (or even mostly) successful in transforming the way in which education systems operate in the region. Yet this reality has not prevented governmental actors and international organizations from formulating policies and circulating discourse that connects with this approach.

Policy-making and knowledge production processes
Providing legitimacy, diverting attention, and undermining the opposition

Formal policy-making processes and the official strategy documents that result from them can help to bolster the legitimacy of the state, while at the same time diverting attention away from the fact that the real reform action and emphasis are placed elsewhere. The preferred reform initiatives of development organizations and the government may enter through the proverbial backdoor with the assistance of pilot programs, think-tank advocacy, and research conducted or contracted by international organizations. This was the case in the school- and community-based management reforms in Guatemala, El Salvador, and Nicaragua. All began as pilot programmes which were developed and financed in the early 1990s with support from the United Nations Development Program, the World Bank, and the United States Agency for International Development (see Chapter 3). Moreover, during these same years, there were other, public-facing policy-making processes that paid lip service to how education could help to overcome the damage done by the civil wars in the preceding decades. In El Salvador, for example, the Ten Year Plan that was finalized in 1995 after a lengthy, high-profile, and participatory process included four general areas of emphasis: educational access ('coverage'); institutional modernization; quality improvement; and education for human, ethical, and civic values. Who could argue with these priorities, particularly in the aftermath of a civil war and given its negative effects on enrolment, for example? But that is precisely the issue – that such declarations, and the processes through which they were produced, served to divert attention away from the real action – that is, the evolution and scaling-up of pet programmes favoured by governmental representatives and international organizations.

Once pilot programmes were underway, international organizations were able to maintain focus on them and to highlight the supposed virtues of the underlying programmes thanks to their capacity and resources. This was done in El Salvador and Nicaragua through the production of numerous advanced quantitative programme evaluations that touted the efficiency, effectiveness, and accountability of the school- and community-based management models. Meanwhile, in the case of Honduras, the World Bank, together with the German Development Bank, financed the creation of an evaluation unit affiliated with the Secretary of Education that would promote the need for the evaluation of educational outcomes (for example, through standardized testing). Thus, as was noted in Chapter 3, when not sending out messages themselves in an attempt to influence reform priorities, international organizations can create the research infrastructure necessary at the country level so that surrogate entities will advance their perspectives.

Moreover, the advanced quantitative studies produced by international organizations often carry more weight than locally produced research, which is scant to begin with and which typically does not meet the standards held by the technocratic development experts who control resources and who make decisions based on the data that they deem to be more credible and objective.[2] Whereas in the Global North it is not uncommon for studies to be carried out by researchers and professors affiliated with universities and independent research centres, in the Global South, there are multiple challenges to this model. Universities tend not to have the financial resources available to sponsor research, and the professors or researchers available tend not to have the training, expertise, or disposition necessary to carry out the kind of quantitative studies required by funders. Another common scenario is that professors are overburdened with the demands of teaching: the model of a research university where a significant portion of a professor's time is dedicated to research is not widespread in the Global South. The implication of this situation is frequently that not only the funding but also the human resources necessary to conduct development research come from outside the country and are beholden to the preferences and knowledge production processes of the international development organizations that provide the funds (and the paycheck).

In these ways, policy-making and knowledge production processes enhance the legitimacy of both the state and the reform priorities of international organizations, all while the principle of equity, as discussed in Chapter 3, is sacrificed in the name of efficiency, effectiveness, and accountability. However, this is not to say that there is no potential for overlap, at least conceptually: the same reform language can speak to multiple principles and priorities simultaneously, and this has served the state well. School- and community-based management reforms, for example, allowed governments to quickly expand access to education in the postwar period and with an emphasis on areas that had been affected by the conflict. Agility in the government's response was a result of the fact that these reforms were isolated programmes that had international organization support and operated outside of the normal education bureaucracy, making them more nimble. Another factor that facilitated a quick scaling-up of access is that these programmes encouraged community participation when it came to such tasks as building and maintaining school spaces. School- and community-based management programmes thus (a) addressed the political priority of access and (b) did so in areas that were more marginalized, all while (c) still connecting with the guiding reform principles of New Public Management, as discussed earlier.

Additionally, it should be noted that education reforms can be held up for their benefits while at the same time being used to undermine opposition groups – opposition groups that challenge the legitimacy and the reform priorities of the state. This dual function of reform was made evident in all three cases of school- and community-based management discussed in Chapter 3. In Nicaragua, school-based management was seen as a way to change the nature of the relationship between the state and citizens, and, in so doing, to erase the vestiges of the approach to education of the (socialist) Sandinista revolution. In El Salvador, community-based management, in the postwar period, undermined the rebel groups that sought recognition for their schools and teachers. If the communities in rebel-controlled areas of the country wanted government support for their schools, they had to agree to join this new programme. While parental committees managing schools had the authority to hire teachers, they were prohibited from hiring their own teachers because they did not meet the minimum criteria established by the government. Joining the programme thus implied the dearticulation of the approach to education that had developed during the war, which was based on critical pedagogy, solidarity, and liberation theology. Similarly, in Guatemala, community-based management allowed the government to meet demands from indigenous communities for more autonomy and the ability to hire teachers who spoke the local language, while at the same time avoiding the creation of a separate institutional apparatus that would have implied relinquishing any real control.

These programmes (in El Salvador and Guatemala)[3] likewise sought to weaken teachers' unions, which were often allies of rebel groups and which represented obstacles to reducing state budgets by preventing layoffs, contesting salary cuts, and pushing for more funding to education. The weakening was a result of the fact that teachers in these programmes worked on one-year contracts (renewable at the discretion of school management committees rather than the central government) and were ineligible to join teachers' unions. From the perspective of the dialectic, what stands out is that such reforms – beyond simply aligning with multiple agendas – diluted the power of oppositional forces that contested the legitimacy of the reforms proposed by the state together with international organizations operating in the service of global capital.

System stability through strategic action, embedded logics, and clientelism

There are also other dynamics at play of which one should be aware in order to understand how education reform contributes to system stability. One of these is individual strategic action. Although frequently overlooked, it should not go unacknowledged that certain individuals, in the right place at the right time and with the right political orientation, are able to benefit immensely in a professional sense by strategically championing those reforms that align with the dominant political-economic interests. As was noted in Chapter 3, in Guatemala, the first director of the office that ran the community-based management programme, who was previously a prominent economist with the Center for National Economic Research, would herself go on to become Minister of Education in 2004. Likewise, a key champion of the parallel programme in El Salvador would become Minister of Education in El Salvador in that same year. These are only two of many possible examples of individuals who capitalized on the cachet and experience of working with these prominent education reforms. Many individuals who passed through these programmes would later serve in diplomatic positions, as high-level administrators and leaders within the government, and as consultants with international organizations. While this point was made in Chapter 3, the extension emphasized here is that this is one way in which the system reproduces itself and maintains stability: strategic actors who are willing to serve the interests of the state and international organizations are enabled to ascend to leadership positions. In this way, there is no tension, at least not within these institutions.

Chapters 4 and 13 of this volume argue that embedded logics are a further avenue for system stability. In the first of these, about Honduras' efforts at administrative decentralization, the authors highlight the 'tropicalization' or 'Honduranization' of reform. They show how tensions are resolved by absorbing them within the state: the first step is to hand over power to the minimum extent necessary to still give the appearance of having implemented the reform; then, the second step is to ritualize the actions taken by the functionaries who inhabit the new structures (that is, to empty the actions of any real meaning by making them primarily performative in nature). The takeaway, then, is that it is 'the very nature of the distribution of power in Honduras that blocks any decentralization' (Morales-Ulloa and Moschetti, Chapter 4, this volume). Certainly, Honduras is not alone in this tendency.

The third and final example also connects to embedded logics, but does so in relation to clientelism. This phenomenon was shown to play out in two different ways in Chapter 11, which compared privatization trends in Honduras and the Dominican Republic. As was argued in the case of Honduras (and all postcolonial states), the state does not invest sufficiently in public education to legitimate the promise of capitalism, but rather distributes benefits via clientelistic practices (for example, related to the ways in which teachers' positions are assigned, schools are built, and contracts for educational resources are awarded). Not only do these practices have implications for default or de facto privatization of education in the sense that they incentivize the emergence of private schools for families at all income levels, but it also helps us to understand why, in large part, there is no tension to resolve. As Caravaca et al (Chapter 13, this volume) write:

> With part of the middle class invested in the status quo – that is, in maintaining and deriving benefit from the mediocre status of the Honduran education system through their employment by this system (as teachers, administrators, etc.) – and another part not necessarily employed

by the state but opting for private education, there is little incentive on the part of the government to dedicate itself to improving public education; in other words, there is no great tension for the state to resolve.

More deeply, the study on privatization in Honduras explains clientelistic practices as being a natural outgrowth of the colonial (extractive) and capitalist (profit-oriented) foundations of the modern state apparatus in postcolonial contexts. They use the phrase 'the ethos of privatization' to label the spirit that permeates and animates the state in such contexts (though they are also careful to acknowledge that states in the Global North are not exempt from this ethos). This ethos refers to the way in which individuals within or connected with the state (for example, through personal or professional networks) seek to derive private benefit from their positions rather than serving the 'public good'. The effect in practice is that, perhaps counterintuitively, private schools help to maintain the stability of the system. As Caravaca et al (Chapter 13, this volume) note:

> [T]he ethos of privatization militates not only against the improvement of the public education system but also against the monitoring and regulation of the private school system. When the state knows that it is not providing sufficient educational access for its student population, what sense does it make to persecute those private actors who are filling in for its deficiencies? LFPSs in Honduras are doing the state a favour.

With this ethos guiding the system, the tension that states typically seek to ameliorate through the provision (or rhetoric) of a quality education largely disappears. Chapter 3 also emphasized this point in relation to Honduras:

> [T]here there is a political advantage to a dysfunctional state that does not work well or in the interests of its citizens. Rather than striving to develop well-functioning and modern systems and processes, public sector leaders prefer to retain some degree of flexibility within the state so that politicians and their networks can benefit ... Furthermore, as a perpetual work in progress, the state remains a candidate for international assistance, from which key actors derive value (by bringing in funding, giving the appearance of doing something to address deficiencies, financing pet projects, providing contracts to contacts in their personal networks, etc.). In this way, the aid dance continues, played out on the cultural battlefield of education policy, where the dialectic between the political and economic is facilitated. (Edwards, this volume)

In the Dominican Republic, a similar, self-serving dynamic has played out, but has manifested itself differently: the increase in spending on education (a result of sustained pressure and mobilization from civil society) has opened up an opportunity for increased spending. This increased spending has, in turn, created opportunities for the government to bolster support for itself (for example, through extended school days, the construction of new schools, hiring more teachers, curricular reform, teacher training, and professional development), while also opening up opportunities for private sector involvement in education reform. Private sector actors who benefit from global capitalism now regularly and closely collaborate with the government through their philanthropies and consulting companies to evaluate reform options, to steer the reform agenda, and even to implement reform programmes (for example, teacher professional development). In this way, we again see the dialectic at work. The tension that arose from insufficient funding to education has been resolved through increased spending on education, but this increased spending is being used in ways that do not address the long-term causes of crises that threaten the legitimacy of the state (poverty and inequality, insufficient jobs, meaningful work, etc.). Rather, the increased funding in the 2010s, as was discussed in Chapter 13, was used in ways that follow embedded logics and serve vested interests.

Moreover, when it comes to the dialectic, it can be seen that those private sector actors who are intimately involved in these reform processes use these processes to further enrich themselves, as when their philanthropic arm steers business to their consulting company, which then uses its proceeds to extend its reach to other countries in the region. Thus, the same companies that have historically profited from global capitalism continue to benefit from the predicament of the state. While capitalism incentivizes an underinvestment in education, business philanthropies, through their technocratic approach to policy, help to legitimate the education reform path chosen by the state, all the while further benefiting themselves by preserving the legitimacy of the capitalism system from which they profit.

Global-local dynamics, technology, and policy enactment

Four of the cases in this volume connect with the intersection of global-local dynamics, learning technologies, and policy enactment. These cases focus on Guatemala, Panama, Costa Rica, and El Salvador. These will be discussed in turn.

Personal connections, international assemblages, and the uptake of open educational resources

Chapter 8 focused on open digital education resources (open in the sense of being free for all to access via the internet). What this case showed was that initiatives move beyond global level promotion, are taken up, and affect practice when assemblages and networks, first, align with the dominant interests and structures that shape the global education field and, second, when they address a real need. When there is alignment in this way, initiatives can continue to evolve and even receive support from other actors in strategic positions where they are able to leverage resources. When alignment does not coalesce, new initiatives die.

In the case of the open access website studied in Chapter 8 – through which teachers had access to Guatemala's national curriculum as well as a range of planning tools and teaching resources – it was seen that this project achieved success, at least initially, because of the kind of alignment just described did in fact materialize. Moreover, it was shown that this alignment was, in turn, facilitated not only by the fact that the developer was a Guatemalan citizen but also by the fact that he was a development professional with the right network and the right professional capital, having worked in and with international development organizations for decades. It was not simply good fortune and the presence of generous individuals in these different organizations, but rather this constellation (alignment) of factors that was a key underlying reason why the website in question was able to find success (in the sense of being widely used).

Unsurprisingly, the aforementioned factors complement the lack of governmental resources that has been highlighted previously as common to the CALC region. It was only after seeing that the Ministry of Education could neither afford to offer trainings nor to print manuals for the curriculum that teachers were required to follow that the development professional described in Chapter 8 took it upon himself to digitize the curriculum, put it online, and create a website where content could be added by users (teaching support materials, resources for classroom implementation, planning guides and tools, etc.). This initiative additionally proved useful for teachers both within and beyond Guatemala once the COVID-19 pandemic pushed education online and made it difficult for teachers to work or plan together face to face.

However, it is important to note that alignment and previous connections with international development organizations are necessary but insufficient (on their own) conditions for the success of such an initiative. Just above, the language of 'dominant interests and structures' was used. These include, it should be emphasized, not only the support that was secured for a time from the United States Agency for International Development, but also the multiple national and local-level counterparts who provided key approvals and technical resources, including the Ministry of Education, Guatemalan universities, and a local foundation. When funding from the United States Agency for International Development was lost, stability was ensured through the creation of a US-based nonprofit organization (the Online Learning Initiative) that would have an international advisory board and that would help to institutionalize the initiative so that it would not depend solely on its creator. This form of international or 'global' support for education in the Global South is not commonly studied and thus represents an interesting avenue for future research.

As a final point on this example, while the case of open education resources in Guatemala once again shows how the limitations of the state serve as an opening for international actors, it also demonstrates that judgements about what is 'good' or 'bad' from the Global North should be made carefully. Consider, as Aruch et al (Chapter 8, this volume) write, that:

> The technical aspect of cnbGuatemala presents another layer of global–local interactions. Mediawiki (the software) was devised in the Global North as a tool for a generative encyclopaedia (Wikipedia). However, the software has now expanded to a variety of applications, including the Guatemalan curriculum. The software is free and open-source with the expressed intent of democratizing access to information. In this case, software from the Global North was adopted and adapted for use in the Global South by someone from the Global South living in the Global North.

Additionally, in connecting back to the dialectic of interest in the present chapter, what stands out in the case of open education resources is that this example is able to serve other ends (unrelated, for example, to profit generation, privatization, or the reproduction of inequality) because it sidesteps the logic of capitalism: it is free and open to be used by anyone. This aspect of the case should not be taken lightly.

Mobile technology and the political economy of connectivity

Chapter 10 examined two mobile technology programs implemented in Panama in the context of the COVID-19 pandemic. They show how such programs operate at the intersection of the global, national, and local levels, and they speak to the political economy of connectivity.

The first program was a WhatsApp Remote Reading Recover Project. It sent grade-appropriate digital stories to students in grades 2–6 through their teachers and caretakers. The program was the product of collaboration among three local nonstate actors: a public-private research centre, a nonprofit dedicated to teacher education, and a private university with expertise in online delivery. The program was also supported by the Ministry of Education, which contributed 60 teachers to the initiative and made the program a focus of an official teacher training programme.

The second program was known as Escribo Play Panama. It was a gamified early literacy and mathematics initiative. It was developed and then translated to Spanish by an edtech start-up in Brazil. In addition to acquiring approval for the project from Ministry of Education, the organization also partnered with a private Panamanian university (the same one from the WhatsApp project) to offer free access to kindergarteners and first graders.

However, despite the promising nature of these programs, the political economy of connectivity affected uptake. As the chapter authors note, access to internet connectivity and the necessary technology is characterized by 'stark inequalities':

> those outside of the urban areas are typically at a notable disadvantage, and those in the indigenous areas are often severely isolated from all ICT connections. While the games were free to play, users still needed to have a device where they could download and play the games, as well as periodic access to the internet. These requirements proved to be too restrictive in certain areas of the country, limiting participation among children who could have benefited most from this intervention. (Svenson and Leon, Chapter 10, this volume)

Nevertheless, as was discussed in Chapter 10, companies from the Global North are trying to make headway in countries of the Global South, including in the CALC region. The technologies they promote are not necessarily proven to be 'better', that is, to lead to better learning outcomes. In any event, as noted by Svenson and León (this volume), while the challenges facing low- and middle-income countries are distinct, networks and coalitions of ed tech actors are working together with governments and other actors (for example, universities, as in the case of Panama) to advance the use of various technologies for learning (and profit-making) purposes.

Presently, however, there is no dialectical tension because of insufficient mobile coverage for the poor. More affluent families are sure to look for their own solutions in times of crisis, made possible by their increased access to financial resources. Yet, the future does hold out the possibility of witnessing more of a tension stemming from mobile technology, that is, more pressure on governments to pursue this avenue, to the extent that socioeconomically disadvantaged families significantly increase their connectivity and mobile coverage. The case of Costa Rica likewise connects with this theme.

Capitalist pressures, social-democratic tendencies, and technological responses: continual reform

Chapter 9, discussing Costa Rica, recounts how in the 2010s, corporations and technology companies pushed for curriculum reform that would prepare the human capital they needed for their businesses. However, this effort generated tension in a country with social-democratic tendencies (for example, in the form a welfare regime based on egalitarian principles), where inclusion and meeting the needs of the disadvantaged are political priorities. The response of the government was to create the Tecno@prender programme, an initiative located at the intersection of these tensions. The language of the curriculum reform within which Tecno@prender was embedded addressed the imperatives of both social inclusion and technological preparation for productive employment. It did so by drawing on the notion of the United Nations Educational, Scientific and Cultural Organization (UNESCO) of planetary citizenship, which emphasizes, among other things, appreciation for cultural diversity and sustainable development, and then combining it with the notion of 21st-century skills, which includes a focus on the use of digital technology. The resulting curricular reform – with the title 'Educating for a New Citizenship' – thus accommodated both agendas. This was so in the sense that it sought to provide technological skills for capitalist development while also emphasizing technology access and technology use for planetary citizenship. By virtue of the fact that the language of reform accommodates both agendas, it hides the tensions between them – for example, between capitalist growth and sustainable development.

The curricular reform endorsed by the government was then translated into practice through various programmes. One of them was the aforementioned Tecno@prender, whose task was 'help implement the country's new curriculum by providing digital technology and promoting its inclusion in the more vulnerable zones of the country' (Pietras, this volume). However, in the end, the experience of Costa Rica is similar to that of Panama in the sense that, in practice, the Tecno@prender programme has faced serious challenges when it comes, first, to reaching disadvantaged groups and, second, to providing teachers with the training and resources that they need. In other words, there were challenges not only in ensuring connectivity and providing physical technology access in vulnerable zones, but also related to transportation obstacles for teachers, the resistance of teachers to training, and teacher abilities with technology. Thus, although Tecno@prender began with a concentration on providing technology access to students, it has evolved to focus on strategies for teaching technology, since educators do not have the ability to implement it proficiently in the classroom.

Stepping back, it can be argued that larger dialectical tensions are not controversial when the focus is on the details of how to successfully implement the reform that was previously approved to address those tensions. This is true in many cases and contexts, both within and beyond CALC. Preoccupation with the implementation of technical and technological fixes diverts attention away from the structural constraints and underlying tensions that condition the education system.

Pandemic technology and locally driven innovation: the importance of community organization

Chapter 5 on the intersection of digital technology, the COVID-19 pandemic, and early grade literacy in El Salvador underscores the importance of socioaffective approaches to learning, locally driven innovation, and community organization. As such, it is an example that runs counter to the previous two cases.

The community of teachers studied in this case went against the dominant trend (in the context of the pandemic) of filling out worksheets and infrequent contact with teachers through the WhatsApp messaging service (using a smartphone). This approach was seen as undesirable because the relationship between teachers and students was weakened, because it made it difficult to monitor learning, and because it led to forms of interaction and learning that were perceived as neither meaningful nor engaging for students. Instead, and as alluded to earlier, these teachers rooted themselves in socioaffective approach to learning, meaning making, and text production in literacy development. As Rosekrans et al (Chapter 5, this volume) explain, the teachers in the study, all of whom were working in rural areas:

> created their own learning materials and lessons for students instead of waiting for student learner guides to arrive from the Ministry of Education, Science and Technology (MINEDUCYT). During the first three months of school closings, when teachers lacked MINEDUCYT training and support to transition to remote learning, they shared solutions to technological and teaching challenges and created virtual peer-learning, enabling them to build a community for professional and socioemotional support in the face of uncertainty. Using a socioaffective and communicative approach to literacy development, they engaged their students in learning activities that wove self-expression and social interaction into writing and maths. Reading activities, poems, and letters were exchanged through audio and video formats, and were circulated with the support of parents and community leaders so that students could continue learning. Instead of being based on the traditional view of what the teacher lacks, these teachers drew on each other's knowledge and resources to innovate and shape literacy development and text production to the local context. Their engagement in peer-learning and innovative teaching helped foster resilience among teachers, families, and students.

In addition to calling attention to the distinct features of this approach, it is essential to grasp factors that made such an approach possible. Two stand out. One is support from both a local nongovernmental organization

(NGO) and a nontypical international donor organization. The second is the history of community organization, self-government, and militancy that has characterized for decades the region being studied. On this first factor, in the words of Rosekrans et al (this volume): 'Teachers' efforts were supported by a nonprofit civil society organization, ConTextos, that receives funding and technical support from a Swiss donor, Pestalozzi Children's Foundation (PCF). PCF aims to ensure inclusive, equitable, and quality education, especially to vulnerable and excluded groups, using child-centred pedagogy based on social interaction, communication, and meaningful learning.'[4]

Moreover, it not only stands out that PCF's first office was established in El Salvador following the civil war, but also that this donor's explicit goal was to improve education access, retention, and quality for the most vulnerable children and youth in the former conflict zones of the country. The teachers in this study, who were located in the country department of Morazán, were thus fortunate to have the support of two organizations who shared their orientation to learning and whose priority was to invest in communities and youth who had been affected by the war. At the same time, and with regard to the second factor noted earlier, the support offered by these organizations would not have been nearly as successful without the leadership and organizing capacity that have resulted from decades of experience with community mobilization, activism, and militancy.

The chapter usefully elaborates a number of recommendations for teacher training and teaching literacy. These include rooting literacy development in meaningful learning, expression through text, social interaction, and socioemotional learning rather than prioritizing students' reading speed (the latter of which is the primary focus of dominant approaches to literacy), as well as revising the model of teacher professional development so that, rather than being centralized and uniform, it turns towards learning communities, study groups, peer observation, mentoring, and accompaniment based on dialogue to build knowledge for transforming teaching and learning practices.

However, the question remains how to steer governments and mainstream international organizations away from their typical approaches, particularly given the challenges highlighted in previous sections relating to strategic action, embedded logics, and clientelism. There are no easy answers to this question. However, a first step is to work with allies (such as equity-minded organizations) while also taking the slow but necessary road of building community capacity and leadership. This can then be further complemented by fostering formal and informal international collaborations (both North-South and South-South in nature) built on the principle of solidarity. Such efforts will then feed back into the learning approach advocated by this chapter, wherein local history and contextual knowledge are leveraged as a key resource for education.

Gangs, education, and internationally supported responses: the political economy of the status quo

The example of public safety programmes in El Salvador, in response to the tremendous presence and influence of gangs, is unfortunately an excellent counterexample to that of the locally driven response discussed previously. As explained in Chapter 7, there have been at least three gang-prevention programmes. The first one, known as the Safe School Plan, consists of preventative patrolling and police presence at schools when students enter and leave the premises. In the second programme – the Police Athletic League – police officers 'organize sports and artistic activities with students from communities with high levels of crime and gang presence, and emphasize the importance of team values and skills' (Savenije, Chapter 7, this volume). Lastly, in the Gang Resistance Education and Training programme, police officers provide students with information about crime, violence, drug abuse, and gangs, and then discuss with them the role and responsibilities of students in different contexts (in the family, school, and community).

These programmes constitute a nexus that connects international, national, and local actors. The first programme is a long-standing initiative to government; the other two are more recent and receive support from the United States Agency for International Development as well the United States Bureau of International Narcotics and Law Enforcement. However, within this nexus, the local level loses out. This is so in the sense that these prevention programmes do not address the root causes of the gangs and thus have not been able to alter the reality of gangs at the community level. Notably, the Ministry of Education has shown little interest in gang-related problems, while local and central-level authorities lack comprehensive prevention-oriented policies. The implication is that the government is not particularly concerned with how gangs affect education. The priority is law and order more generally: as long as there is sufficient peace to conduct business, then the most pressing tension felt by the state (to ensure that the economy functions well for those who stand to benefit from it) is relieved. Family, community, and school perspectives and experiences with gangs are not taken seriously. In any event, until recently, no government was able to control the gangs – not until the state of exception enacted by the current president of El Salvador in 2022, through which he has been able to pursue a suppression strategy that would otherwise be unconstitutional because it violates civil rights (for example, locking up suspected gang members without evidence or due process).

The simplistic and insufficient nature of these programmes stands out when one recalls that the gangs have emerged out of geopolitical intervention, international deportation, and the effects of the liberalization of the economy since the 1990s (see Chapter 2). Yet the chapter offers a conclusion about the importance of teachers that resonates with other research on El Salvador (discussed both earlier and later on) and the CALC region generally:

> The international models cited in this chapter and the national prevention programmes based on them ignore the importance of local relationships in and between school, family, and community as fundamental components in violence and gang prevention efforts ... By emphasizing the students' choices and responsibilities, they overlook teachers and schools as key players. (Savenije, Chapter 7, this volume)

More will be said about the centrality of teachers in the next section. For now, what can be highlighted is that neither these feel-good programmes nor the 'Mano Dura' (strong hand) approaches that focus on the suppression and jailing of (presumed) gang members address the social and economic incentives to join gangs, incentives which, it should not be overlooked, have their roots in the social upheaval, military conflict, and economic crisis of the 1980s and 1990s (and before), all of which led (and continue to lead) to the mass exodus of Salvadorans from their home country in search of economic opportunities elsewhere. While many do find jobs elsewhere, particularly in the US, this kind of immigration leads to family separation, weakened communities, and the deterioration of social ties that gangs fill. However, in order to address the root causes and the factors that continue to encourage gang participation, the government and international organizations would have to pursue strategies that go against the historical modus operandi and approach to public policy (again, see Chapter 2). However, this is unlikely, since it would imply, for example, changes to social and economic policy in El Salvador and deportation policy in the US. The alternative is to further pursue the authoritarian tendencies represented by the state of exception, itself a dangerous proposition for democracy given its unconstitutional nature and the fact that it centralizes power in the president without any checks and balances (*El Faro*, 2023; Martínez et al, 2023), although it does open up opportunities for self-enrichment and corruption thanks to the fact that, under the state of exception, the government is not required to adhere to the Law of Acquisitions and Procurement of the Public Administration (WOLA, 2022).

The currency of convivencia*: deriving legitimacy, delivering complacency*

Convivencia is a Spanish term that refers to learning to live together. It has been promoted by UNESCO and is part of the same stream of (global) discourse as child-friendly schools and addressing gender-based violence. In El Salvador, the idea of *convivencia* has been translated into multiple programmes and policies, three of which are analysed in Chapter 6 of this volume. As will be discussed, these programmes certainly represent attempts to build towards a world that is more democratic and less discriminatory. In practice, however, there are multiple shortcomings. The programmes ultimately play the role of providing legitimacy to the educational and cultural systems of El Salvador while also breeding complacency.

The programmes examined by Martin in Chapter 6 deal with student governments, peer bullying, and sexual violence prevention. They have been facilitated by international NGOs and international donors (which provide technical and financial support and help to develop programme materials) in addition to being encouraged by international conferences (focused, for example, on women's rights). They are also grounded in support at the national level in the form of guidelines and legal frameworks.

The programme for student governments at the school level seeks to be a model for a more democratic society. However, as Martin (Chapter 6, this volume) writes: 'However, the key school-level actor is the principal, who leads the process and provides guidelines on how to organize the student governments. Rather than empowering students in democratic skills, the findings point out that the process is adult-centred – that is, activities are planned by adults, including events relating to fundraising for school infrastructure needs.'

The second case examines national guidelines and policies relating to living harmoniously and peer bullying, the latter of which is a broad problem for schools, both among students and teachers. However, the documents which are meant to guide school-level action around bullying either take a non-educational approach (being based instead in a child protection approach) or else fail to address bullying directly or to provide strategies to counteract it (as in the case of the policy for living harmoniously). Moreover, understandings of policy vary widely and depend on teacher beliefs and prior socialization, that is, what they understand 'living harmoniously together' to mean. For many, it is simply the absence of physical violence, a very shallow understanding of bullying or living harmoniously.

Gender equity and sexual violence – the focus of the third case – have been the subject of multiple policies since the 1990s and have culminated in the National Gender Equality and Equity Policy of 2016. This policy integrates a variety of topics such as equality, equity, prevention and treatment of sexual violence, gender violence, early pregnancy, sexually transmitted diseases, and human trafficking. In education, this policy addresses asymmetric gender relationships and focuses on 'de-constructing ideas, beliefs and cultural customs that foster gender discrimination' (Ministerio de Educación, 2016, p 62). However, despite a seemingly strong national policy framework, findings highlight:

the complex, male-centered cultural imaginary that differentiates and asymmetrically values masculine and feminine traits, which then excuses and justifies violence against female students and women. Deep cultural beliefs – often military and religion-based – prevail and link masculine traits with power, force, and domination. As a result, shared ideas around what constitutes sexual harassment and abuse (or does not) generate complicity among men and help to avoid punishment while also transferring guilt to women for their subordination and passivity in the face of harassment and abuse, in addition to directing judgment at the mothers who raised these men. (Martin, Chapter 6, this volume)

All three cases thus attempt to address entrenched hierarchies that serve to benefit adults, men, and the purveyors or enablers of bullying. All three cases likewise underscore the difficulty of transforming ingrained relationships and cultural norms. The challenges are summed up in this way:

individual actors within institutions may veer from the official posture based on their ideas and personal beliefs. Key local actors for enactment, such as parents and community members, are often ignored at the institutional agenda-setting table, and teachers are expected to implement something they have not been a part of creating, for which they have not received training, and about which they do not have shared understandings. In the absence of an effective meso policy level, the distance between macro-level institutional decision-making and micro-level policy enactment interferes with how the actual ideas around the policy are communicated and understood at all levels. (Martin, Chapter 6, this volume)

The validity of these findings and assertions is not in question. But an additional question, from a structural standpoint, is how to interpret the purpose of these programmes. From the perspective of the dialectic, all three policies in this chapter help to legitimate the system, while at the same the government actors involved do not have sufficient motivation for really putting them into practice, since they would threaten the status quo, wherein patriarchy and limited democratic participation are seen as desirable and profitable for those in power while student wellbeing is treated as an afterthought.

Patriarchy, austerity, and neocolonialism: gender equity in perpetual tension

Chapter 14 on Puerto Rico complements the insights from Martin on El Salvador by showing how gender-equity policies are plagued by constant tension at the policy-making level. Moreover, it makes the important connection between gender-equity politics, economic austerity, and the neocolonial position in which Puerto Rico finds itself.

Gender-equity policies in Puerto Rico have a long history. They date to at least to the 1970s and have benefited from pro-gender conventions and discourse of the United Nations and transnational feminist movements. The policies examined by Martínez Ramos (Chapter 14, this volume) are more recent in nature and relate to teaching about gender, giving students choice in terms of the clothing they wear, and protection against discrimination based on gender. Despite their more contemporary nature, these examples, and other like them across Latin America, have not been exempt from intense pushback at the national and international levels from the Catholic Church, military representatives, conservative politicians, special interest groups, and networks that seek to preserve 'traditional family values'. Rather than acknowledging a spectrum of possible gender identities, oppositional groups have sought to 'maintain the naturalization of sex, the man–woman binary, and ascription to rigid gender characteristics and traditional gender roles' (Martínez Ramos, Chapter 14, this volume). In Puerto Rico, the divergent worldviews on gender held by different political parties and politicians 'results in policies that oscillate back and forth in the extent they reflect gender perspectives, recognize sexual diversity, are transversal (meaning that they attempt to embed a gender perspective across different issues and policies), and focus on human rights' (Martínez Ramos, Chapter 14, this volume).

While these tensions around gender policy in Puerto Rico play out, there is a larger dialectic at play. To be specific, the link between the dire economic situation of Puerto Rico and the plight of women (let alone the LGBTQI+ community) is made more clear by its neocolonial relationship with the US. In the words of Martínez Ramos (Chapter 14, this volume) gender inequities:

> are shaped by the country's colonial/territorial situation. In 2016, the US Congress imposed the Financial Oversight and Management Board as part of the Puerto Rico Oversight, Management, and Economic Stability Act (US Congress, 2016). Under the pretext of paying off an unpayable debt of $74 billion in bonds, extreme austerity measures subjected the population to uncertain healthcare, education, and housing conditions and dramatic increases in the cost of living. The Fiscal Supervisory Board has absolute power over Puerto Rico's budget. It controls all laws and regulations of the Puerto Rican government that affect the budget despite no democratic representation of Puerto Rico's constituents in the US Congress, disproportionately impacting poor, vulnerable populations. Women across all possible intersections, albeit in different forms, carry the weight of this imposition.

When it is said that women 'carry the weight' of austerity, this is not only meant in the sense of physical, domestic, or psychological violence from their partners. There are additional dimensions to gender discrimination that are structural in nature and that connect to the state-capital dialectic. Citing Contreras Capó (2021), Martínez Ramos (Chapter 14, this volume) reminds us that:

> To talk about gender violence is not only to talk about the 'Ley 54' [Law for the Prevention and Intervention with Domestic Violence]. We also need to talk about cuts in TANF [Temporary Assistance for Needy Families] benefits because they mainly affect female-headed households; we need to talk about the closing of schools because more than 75% of teachers are women; we need to talk about layoffs in the public sector because most of them are women. (2021, p 168)

While women are disproportionately affected by austerity policies, Puerto Rico as a whole suffers from its geopolitically and economically subordinate position vis-à-vis the US. Just as it has for centuries, Puerto Rico remains a colony that serves the economic interests of foreign capital, as when, in the process resolving the most recent economic crisis (described earlier) the debts owed to corporate bond holders in the US are prioritized over claims for debts owed made by current and former public servants such teachers (Casanova-Burgess, 2021).

Managing legitimacy amid geopolitical constraints

Like Puerto Rico, Cuba is in a very difficult position both economically and politically, particularly since 1991, when the country entered an economic downturn precipitated by the collapse of the Soviet Union, its primary partner in trade and other forms of support. These developments were exacerbated by the embargo imposed by the US since 1958 which results in sanctions being issued against corporations for trading with Cuba – an embargo that continues to the present day. Within this context, Chapter 12 shows how the Cuban government has sought to manage threats to its legitimacy, including through education.

In the 1990s, the Cuban government responded to the economic crisis by veering away from state control of the economy. It did so by 'opening up certain sectors of national industry to foreign investments, expanding the tourism industry, legalizing private employment in 150 occupations, liberating the circulation of US dollars, creating farmers' markets, and developing agriculture cooperatives' (Lee, Chapter 12, this volume). Of course, changes to the economy had significant implications for the labour market. Teachers, despite earning salaries on a par with other professionals in Cuba, flocked to other sectors, particularly tourism.

Various strategies were pursued to mitigate the effects (and threats to legitimacy) of the shifts described previously. Under Fidel Castro, these included increasing teachers' salaries by 30 per cent (though this still did not stem the outflow), establishing a network of emergency training schools at the upper-secondary level (intended to prepare individuals to meet the needs of society relating, for example, to social work, primary teaching, and nursing, and how to use information technology), hiring more primary-level teachers to reduce class sizes, and expanding access to higher education (for example, by offering classes via TV and introducing higher education centres in all municipalities). Outside of education, the government sought to address youth apathy and indifference to socialism by guaranteeing well-paid employment in tasks with a high social value and by launching an ideological offensive to stimulate support for the country's political system.

Once Raul Castro came to power in 2008, the approach of the government changed, but the reforms were still meant to address threats to its legitimacy. Rather than spending and extending access, the new leader focused on efficiency, cost savings, and further opening up of the economy in order to generate employment and encourage economic growth. Some of the programmes introduced previously were scaled back or closed. Resources were also diverted towards technical vocational programmes. In order to address the teacher shortage, pedagogical schools were opened in order to more quickly prepare new teachers for pre-primary, primary, and special education.

While the reforms of the Castro brothers may have helped to preserve the legitimacy of the country's political and economic system, they have not been sufficient when it comes to resolving the teacher shortage. In addition to opportunities in new industries, teachers' salaries over the past 20 years have plateaued and, since 2014, are lower at the entry level than other state professions. Thus, as Lee (Chapter 12, this volume) concludes:

It is likely that the problem of teacher recruitment and retention will continue when considering the plight of teachers in relation to the economic and political forces elaborated earlier. Prevailing political and economic conditions will negatively influence teachers' occupational decision making and will likely serve as reasons for departure. Teachers will leave as long as market economy measures are in place ... Moreover, teachers will leave due to education policies that burden teachers with additional hours (including after retirement), continuously underpay them relative to other professions, and reduce their social status by lowering the entry bar and accepting instructors without qualifications, which ultimately undermines the overall professionalism of the teaching force.

Although the situation around teachers represents a major tension that must be managed by the government – especially since the provision of a high-quality education has been one of the great successes of the Cuban Revolution – the options available for resolving this tension are limited, given the restricted economic position of the country. For the foreseeable future, the Cuban government will, presumably, do its best to address threats to legitimacy while trying to survive in the context of severe geopolitical constraints.

Stepping out of the state-capital dialectic: indigenous approaches

The difficulty of operating a socialist economy within a global capitalist economic system is demonstrated by the case of Cuba. The final chapter discussed here – on indigenous educational initiatives – offers two examples from Guatemala that take a different approach to stepping outside of the state-capital dialectic. Chapter 11 acknowledges tensions between capitalism and modern schooling, on the one hand, and indigenous ways of life and seeing the world, on the other hand. Importantly, the chapter delineates how 'the Western development paradigm, which so profoundly shapes the epistemological framework of the modern-day capitalist and globalized civilization, proscribes Western-raised and educated people from understanding, valuing, and respecting the alternative epistemologies of indigenous people and communities' (Roberts, Chapter 11, this volume).

As Roberts spells out, this paradigm prioritizes the individual over the community and advances a capitalist economic system characterized by 'unrelenting growth' (Roberts, Chapter 11, this volume). Yet, what often goes unquestioned is the fact that these systems are premised on a fundamentally violent worldview. Drawing on a publication from the United Nations at the beginning of the 'international development' era, Roberts (Chapter 11, this volume) reminds the reader that, from the Western development perspective: 'Ancient philosophies have to be scrapped, old social institutions have to disintegrate; bonds of caste, creed, and race have to burst; and large numbers of persons who cannot keep up with progress have to have their expectations of a comfortable life frustrated' (United Nations Department of Social and Economic Affairs, 1951, p 19). What goes unstated here, but what is nevertheless understood, is that the scrapping of ancient philosophies should be followed by the adoption of a worldview rooted in modern science and Western rationality (wherein the distinction between self and other, subject and object, and individual and nature become naturalized).

Even less frequently acknowledged is that the modern development paradigm effectively implies the replacement of one religious philosophy with another. While the modern world may be nominally secular, it has emerged out of a Christian ontology. For example, Enlightenment thinking – with its assumptions about the ability of science and positivism to produce laws and findings that are applicable regardless of context – would not have been possible without the dominance in Europe in the preceding centuries of the Christian ontology, wherein there is one all-knowing, all-seeing God who has created the world and who controls it according to his commands (Grosfoguel, 2013). For our purposes, a key point is that this history is the invisible context out of which technical and technicist approaches to development and modern administration have emerged. Furthermore, an essential implication is that the Western approach to development is simply one among many worldviews, all of which have their roots in religious traditions – and all of which presuppose different kinds of relationships with oneself (or the lack of a self), with each other, and with the natural world. The myth of secular reason obscures this fact.

Chapter 11 presents two examples of initiatives created by the Maya Ixil people of the western Guatemalan highlands that operate according to different philosophies. They are intended to combat the inherently racist, colonialist, and capitalist nature of Western development and the ontology on which it is based. These initiatives are likewise intended to reverse the outflow of youth from their communities, an outflow that is encouraged by a modern education which not only depreciates non-Western ways of being and knowing but which is also geared towards preparing students for jobs in the modern economy – jobs which do not exist in the communities from which these students come. The examples are premised on a relationship with the natural world and with surrounding communities that takes into account the biophysical limitations of the places, territories, and ecosystems where individuals and communities live. Only brief details of these fascinating examples will be recounted here; for more, see Roberts (this volume).

The first example is the Ixil University. In the words of Roberts (Chapter 11, this volume):

The Ixil University was founded in 2011 after a group of elders, traditional authorities, and young people began to question why the values and ethics of 'Tiichajil' were entirely excluded from the official education system ... [T]he founders of the Ixil University rightly began to question the basic tenets and promises of the official education system. Whereas many young people ask 'Where are the promised rewards and the pathway to prosperity and progress that we were assured?', the Ixil University questioned why the values, ethics, and practical livelihoods associated with Tiichajil were abandoned in the first place.

From this starting point, the initiative had to address some key challenges, including the fact that young people no longer had 'an intimate, experiential knowledge regarding the basic tenets of Tiichajil' because '[t]he sacred transmission of knowledge between generations had been severed' (Roberts, Chapter 11, this volume).

In order to transmit their way of knowing and being to students, the Ixil University employs the following strategies:

- Classes held in natural settings (for example, where food is produced, near rivers, in sacred locations).
- Teachers are those who are repositories of traditional knowledge (for example, midwives, spiritual guides, ancestral authorities, leading farmers, and the 'Alcaldía Indígena' – a group that administers and oversees traditional justice).
- Experiential learning in order to reintroduce young people to the lands from which they come (including spending hours hiking through forests and mountains to discover their communities' boundaries and water sources and to learn about the flora and fauna).
- Cross-cutting themes that are essential to the harmonious functioning of the community (resource management, traditional spirituality, gender issues, traditional justice patterns, collective governance of communal management of forests and pasturelands, Mayan calendars and sense of time, etc.).
- Community participation to learn a different way of being and relating to each other (for example, sitting in on the sessions of the 'Alcaldía Indígena' to see how conflicts are resolved traditionally without relying on the police or Guatemalan court system, or involvement in the communal labour of cleaning freshwater springs, protecting communal forests, and cultivating agriculture).

These strategies for learning are then complemented by a non–Western form of knowledge production. After two years of classes based on the strategies mentioned earlier, students spend their third year reflecting on community challenges and needs in order to identify a problem. The final year is then dedicated to developing a potential response that is presented in the form of an oral dissertation (that may also take a written form) that is presented to and defended before the community, including traditional authorities of the Ixil people, and outside academics.

The second initiative complements the Ixil University. It is known as the Utz Kaslimaal Collective and its purpose is to work with outside communities and organizations in order to share the wisdom and way of life of the Mayan Ixil with students from Western universities. Importantly, the orientation of this initiative is not that the Mayan Ixil need to be studied, helped, or pitied, but rather that visitors are invited to learn from them and, in so doing, to reflect on their own assumptions and ways of being. As part of the programme, visitors are exposed to contemporary governance challenges (for example, the contamination of Lake Atitlan) as well as diverse perspectives on how to respond to them (based, for example, on both Western rational-technical approaches and holistic indigenous thinking).

More than the other cases in this volume, Roberts' chapter brings to the fore many issues and layers that are often left invisible, including in the dialectical analysis offered throughout this chapter – a fact which highlights the need for neo-Marxist perspectives to further evolve and to decolonize (see, for example, Fúnez-Flores, 2022; Fúnez-Flores et al, 2022). This point, and the layers of analysis highlighted by Roberts, will be revisited in the conclusions (Chapter 16) when reflecting on the ways forward for scholarship and action that are suggested by the analysis presented throughout this volume and particularly the present chapter.

Notes

[1] For more on how states have adapted their role in the context of New Public Management, see Hibou (2004).

[2] For more on the acceptability of certain sources of research, see Verger et al (2016).

[3] The community-based management programme of Honduras also fits here (see Gainimian, 2016). However, this is not addressed in the text because the chapters did not take this programme as a focus of their analysis. The case of Nicaragua does not fit here, since school-based management there was not seen as a means of undermining the teacher's union; for more on this, see Chapter 3.

[4] Child-centred pedagogy is defined in the chapter as the adaptation of teacher strategies to the particular needs and interests of each student in order to make learning a meaningful and social experience for each child (McCombs and Whistler, 1997).

References

Casanova-Burgess, A. (Host) (2021). The Bankruptcy Letters (No. 6). Audio podcast episode. *La Brega*, Futuro Media Group and WNYC Studios, , 23 February. https://www.wnycstudios.org/podcasts/la-brega/articles/bankruptcy-letters

Contreras Capó, V. (2021). Debt and structural gender violence. *Critical Times*, 4(1), 167–169. https://read.dukeupress.edu/critical-times/issue/4/1

Dale, R. (1989). *The State and Education Policy*. Open University Press.

Edwards Jr., D. B. (2023). *Rethinking World Bank Influence: Governance Reforms and the Ritual Aid Dance in Indonesia*. Routledge.

El Faro (2023). No gangs, but no more democracy. https://elfaro.net/en/202302/opinion/26697/No-Gangs-but-No-More-Democracy.htm?fbclid=IwAR3Jk-Ou6R0tT-NpHPdfMXS3vxifEQvUaBnx-lPmL4HpbQRNLJkRWXQEIAA

Fúnez-Flores, J. (2022). Toward decolonial globalisation studies. *Globalisation, Societies and Education*, 21(2), 166–186. DOI: 10.1080/14767724.2022.2048796

Fúnez-Flores, J., Díaz Beltrán, A., and Jupp, J. (2022). Decolonial discourses and practices: geopolitical contexts, intellectual genealogies, and situated pedagogies. *Educational Studies*. Online ahead of print. DOI: 10.1080/00131946.2022.2132393

Ganimian, A. J. (2016). Why do some school-based management reforms survive while others are reversed? The cases of Honduras and Guatemala. *International Journal of Educational Development*, 47, 33–46.

Grosfoguel, R. (2013). The structure of knowledge in Westernized universities: epistemic racism/sexism and the four genocides/epistemicides of the long 16th century. *Human Architecture*, 11(1), 73–90.

Hibou, B. (2004). *Privatizing the State*. Columbia University Press.

La Brega (2021). *The Bankruptcy Letters*. https://www.wnycstudios.org/podcasts/la-brega/articles/bankruptcy-letters

McCombs, B. L., and Whisler, J. (1997). *The Learner-centered Classroom and School: Strategies for Increasing Student Motivation and Achievement*. San Francisco, CA: Jossey-Bass, pp 63–101.

Martínez, C., Lemus, E., and Martínez, Ó. (2023). Régimen de Bukele desarticula a las pandillas en El Salvador. *El Faro*, 3 February. https://elfaro.net/es/202302/el_salvador/26691/R%C3%A9gimen-de-Bukele-desarticula-a-las-pandillas-en-El-Salvador.htm?fbclid=IwAR0j5vqfVpQQVkKEueBZsPz5VS9NBzMsGKLFRWPKsKi8NUuB8AVFVnDvmSs

Ministerio de Educación (2016). *Política de Equidad e Igualdad de Género. Plan de Implementación del Ministerio de Educación El Salvador*. Ministerio de Educación. https://www.transparencia.gob.sv/institutions/mined/documents/265940/download

United Nations Department of Social and Economic Affairs (1951). *Measures for the Economic Development of Under-Developed Countries*. United Nations Digital Library System. https://digitallibrary.un.org/record/708544

US Congress. Puerto Rico Oversight, Management, and Economic Stability Act (PROMESA), Pub. L. No. 114–187, 130 Stat. 549 (2016).

Verger, A., Lubienski, C., and Steiner-Khamsi, G. (2016). The emergence and structuring of the global education industry: towards an analytical framework. In A. Verger, C. Lubienski, and G. Steiner-Khamsi (eds.), *World Yearbook of Education 2016: The Global Education Industry* (pp 3–24). Routledge.

WOLA (2022). *Corruption under the State of Emergency in El Salvador: A Democracy without Oxygen*. WOLA. https://www.wola.org/2022/09/corruption-state-of-emergency-el-salvador/

16

Whither Education and Development in Central America and the Latin Caribbean? Dialectical Reflections, Decolonial Options

D. Brent Edwards Jr.

Introduction

This brief concluding chapter has two purposes. The first is to reflect on possible paths forward for education and development in Central America and the Latin Caribbean (CALC). Having interpreted each case in the present volume through an international political economy lens, the task at hand is to reflect on the implications for the region. The second purpose is to point to future directions for research and action. The suggestions offered pick up on issues mentioned in this volume about what more can and should be said as stakeholders grapple with how to respond to the tensions that affect the region. As will be seen, this section of the chapter takes a decolonial orientation. The last section of the chapter then offers concluding commentary on contributions of the present volume as well as the new gaps that have become evident in process of filling old ones.

Within and beyond the dialectic of global capitalism

The CALC region is a hotbed of education reform. This is not surprising as education in this region (and all world regions) is one of the key avenues available to governments for managing threats to its legitimacy and the legitimacy of the systems on which it is based. The chapters of this volume draw attention to a wide spectrum of education policies, ranging from school- and community-based management, administrative decentralization to standardized testing, various forms of digital technology, *convivencia* programmes, gender-equity initiatives, gang prevention programmes, and teacher retention schemes. There is no reason to believe that these programmes have not had at least some positive outcomes. However, as the analysis and discussion in Chapters 2 and 15 has emphasized, both education and the state are situated within, and are permeated by, various structures and logics that prevent the aforementioned initiatives from functioning as hoped or as stated in policy. Chief among these structures and logics is capitalism. This section reflects on the implications of, and possible responses to, this system, both generally and in the realm of education. The reason for focusing on capitalism – and the state's relationship to it – in this final chapter is because the state-capital dynamic is, as discussed in the previous chapter, central to what drives 'development' and, within that, education policy.

A first consideration is that the structure of the economy and the state's relationship to it has not changed drastically since the economies of the region were liberalized. CALC countries remain primarily dependent on agricultural and textile (that is, maquiladora) exports. The middle and upper classes are small, as is the proportion of well-paying jobs. A report of the International Monetary Fund from 2008 stated that 50 per cent of the families in this region (with the exception of Costa Rica) live in poverty (Desuelle and Schipke, 2008). Many families thus rely on remittances from relatives who have left the country in search of better opportunities.

One consequence of this is that the public education system does not (and cannot) lead to upward mobility for the majority of the population. Another consequence, at times, is that international organizations themselves encourage the countries of the region to increase social spending in order to improve the quality of life for the average citizen and to preserve the stability of the system (Desuelle and Schipke, 2008). However, these reforms depend on the political dynamics found within each country. The concentration of wealth at the top of the income pyramid does not bode well for the passage of redistributive economic policies or for the collection of additional tax revenue to fund social programmes. Inaction or inconsequential action is more likely to prevail.

To this end, as long as the state remains trapped by the global capitalist economy (see Chapter 2), the lives of the majority of citizens in the CALC region will at best be characterized by precarity. By this, I not only mean economic insecurity, in the sense of there being too few jobs, unstable employment, subsistence livelihoods, and markets that are dependent on the whims of the global economy, but also social insecurity, in the sense of too few and inadequate social services (healthcare, education, housing, food assistance, social workers, fire fighters, etc.) (Azmanova, 2020). In other words, precarity can be defined as 'that politically induced condition in which certain populations suffer from failing social and economic networks of support and become differentially exposed to injury, violence, and death' (Butler, 2009, p ii). Exposure to these threats is both a direct and indirect consequence of precarity – direct because the absence of the kinds of social services mentioned earlier makes many forms of employment more dangerous, and indirect because the nature of the economic opportunities available drives many to embark on treacherous migration journeys to the US or other countries in search of better opportunities. These are only two of many possible examples.

However, not everyone in Central America finds themselves in an equally precarious position. Indeed, across this region, there has emerged a transnational elite class that has benefited and emerged from the economic restructuring of the 1980s and 1990s and who identify more with the global economy than they do with the success of any nation-state. Moreover, the success of this transnational class goes hand in hand with processes of marginalization that lead to the kinds of precarity described earlier. Robinson writes:

> To the extent that transformative processes generate a mass of under- and unemployed that hold down the general wage level and that provide a ready pool of reserve labour for transnational capital to tap, or similarly, to the extent that these processes result in a bloated informal sector that transfers the responsibility for social reproduction from the state and from private capital to the marginalised groups themselves, then we can say that these processes – under the conditions of the global capitalist economy – are quite 'modernising' even as they result in marginalisation and immiseration. (2002, p 247)

The point that this quote emphasizes is that, for many people, the process of 'development' and 'modernization', where these mean joining the global capitalist economy, is actually violent and discriminatory in its nature, despite the tendency of governments and private capital to portray it otherwise. And the ill effects are only likely to continue, especially since 'countries across the region have shown a premature drop in their levels of industrialization' due to technological developments, automation, and the reduction of labour (that is, employment) that these imply (Cadena et al, 2019).

The question going forward is how, if at all, governments in the region will respond to create economic opportunities and to put in place the social services (including education) needed to provide the region's population with a minimum quality of life. Many of the chapters in this volume provide a response to this question. Another question is how the aforementioned comments connect back to education and what education can offer when it comes to moving forward. Despite the seemingly bleak picture painted earlier, there is much that can and should be done. However, as Robinson (2002) notes, the solution is not a policy problem, since the problem is the system. And, in any event, since public policies are passed by the state, the implication is that the necessary response is not likely to come from the government, not when the government is captive to the system or at least cannot be expected to change the status quo without significant pressure from civil society (see Chapter 15 for examples). The task thus falls to, among others, individuals, networks, so-inclined organizations, and social movements: (a) to educate themselves and others about the limitations of the current system; (b) to work together to experiment with alternatives; and (c) to pressure political and economic actors to take actions that will benefit those most adversely affected by the present state of affairs.

At face value, these suggestions imply that what is needed are modifications to the current system, for example, modifications that redistribute resources both economically and educationally and that shift power politically. Economically, these modifications might mean providing a universal minimum income, pushing for price controls or subsidies for basic needs, pursuing tax reform to raise funds for social services, providing incentives for economic cooperatives, or stimulating initiatives that are environmentally responsible and sustainable. Politically, modifications might entail experimenting with deliberative democracy, participatory budgeting, cooperatives, collaboration with social movements, or deeper and broader forms of community participation that go beyond school- and community-based management (see Chapter 3) and that encourage civil society to hold the government (rather than poor communities) accountable for the provision of quality public services.

Educationally, the kind of activism suggested here might have as its goal well-equipped schools, equitably distributed resources, highly trained teachers, regular professional development, training and teaching rooted in local context and culture, anti-discrimination policies, salary increases for teachers, or more appropriate uses of testing and evaluation (for example, accompanied by ongoing support from the Ministry of Education to address deficiencies). When it comes to students, schools should, at a minimum, be well equipped in terms of materials and infrastructure. But it is also possible to think more broadly. For example, the provision of education could be coordinated with the provision of other kinds of social services. Schools could offer or could facilitate wraparound services such as school psychologists, counsellors, social workers, and visits to health professionals.

What should not be missed in these suggestions is that they imply a notion of education quality that has nothing to do with test scores. As was noted in Chapter 3, the idea of education quality has evolved over time and has reflected the trends in thinking about international development. Having critiqued (see also Chapter 3) the approach of New Public Management and its implications for education, the suggestions given previously depart from a different orientation, one that envisions more leadership and support from the state and from ministries of education at all levels. As opposed to seeing the state as a 'manager' that engages in sector governance through market principles and practices borrowed from the business world, the assumption embedded in the comments in the previous paragraph is that the state should be a caretaker of its citizens, that it should beef up its investment in, and support to, the education sector, and that it should seek to integrate the provision of social services. In doing these things, the assumption is that education quality will improve, in the sense that teachers and schools would be in a better position to help meet the basic needs of students (and their families) in environments that are safe and that possess the resources necessary to learn values and skills for individuals to flourish, for communities to thrive, and for the planet to be preserved.

Through these recommendations, it may be the case that test scores go up, but this is not seen as what is most important. Academic achievement on standardized assessments does not mean anything in the abstract. Rather, what is essential – and what must be the subject of debate and dialogue – are the ideas, behaviours, and worldviews that schools impart to students. This assertion is, of course, normative. While schools in multicultural societies are not likely to satisfy the preferences of all students and their families, this does not mean, from a critical perspective concerned with social justice, that progress cannot be made. Such a perspective not only calls for better equipped schools and better trained teachers, for example, but also for the pursuit of policies, practices, and investments that would benefit those who are – and who have historically been – marginalized. However, the major limitation of the suggestions made previously is that the state is not likely to pursue such policies, at least not in a meaningful way, without significant pressure from civil society. The discussion in Chapter 15 of the way in which education is conditioned by the dialectic between the state and capitalism makes this abundantly clear.

Decolonial possibilities

The recommendations offered here are only first steps. While they would address some limitations of the current political, economic, and educational systems, they would not directly address the foundations (discussed later on) of those systems and the ways in which those foundations permeate the work and logics that characterize the institutions that have been constructed to enable the systems' functioning. As such, the recommendations represent 'liberal' as opposed to 'progressive' measures (Edwards and Klees, 2015). But, more importantly, the point here is that future directions for education should go beyond a focus on resources and training to also engage in a critique of the current economic system and, furthermore, the broader foundations of thought that have guided the development of – and the belief in – the systems of Western rationality, modern states, neoclassical economics, global governance, and education. In other words, what should be explored is a decolonial approach to unpacking the features of modernity, for it is these foundations of thought out of which those discriminatory practices have grown that continue to affect the peoples of the CALC region, both generally and through education (Dussel, 2000; Quijano, 2000; Grosfoguel, 2013). The idea behind a decolonial approach is to understand the 'logic, metaphysics, ontology, and matrix of power' that have resulted from colonization (Maldonado-Torres, 2016, p 10). To be able to see these foundations, which often remain invisible, the following issues should be taken seriously:

(a) the racist and patriarchal nature (and legacy) of colonialism;
(b) the exclusionary and violent nature of Christianity (in the sense that a central focus of Christianity is the conversion of peoples from other religions because, according to it, there is only one true God);
(c) the ontological foundations of modernity (meaning the ideals of positivism and the individualized self that were spread by the Enlightenment);
(d) the ways in which capitalism creates, reproduces, and exacerbates inequality and environmental destruction on a global scale (for example, in the sense that it always seeks out more land, labour, and resources without knowing any limits);
(e) the limited vision embedded at the heart of modern states (which only ever had individual and social, as opposed to economic or worldview, rights as a focus of their preoccupation); and
(f) the ways in which each of the aforementioned dimensions serve as the conceptual horizons and reproducing tendencies for both modern education systems and the system of global education governance that has been constructed through the cooperation of modern states (for example, in the form of multilateral organizations such as the World Bank and the United Nations).

Only by wrestling with these foundations and seeking to move beyond them is there a chance of progressing towards a world that is not satisfied with addressing the consequences of the currently dominant economic and political systems, and so makes its mission an exploration of the possibilities inherent to alternative ways of being, knowing, and organizing society, with the ultimate goal of advancing beyond economic and social justice to achieve cognitive justice, by which we mean a system that recognizes and enables the flourishing of indigenous and non-Western peoples whose ways of being, knowing, and social organizing do not align with the colonial, capitalist, positivist, Christian, and state-centric tendencies described earlier (de Sousa Santos, 2007).

The concluding chapter of the present book is not the appropriate place to offer a further excavation of the dimensions/issues delineated previously as warranting attention going forward. For now, it will have to be sufficient to gesture in these directions. Those who are interested in a further discussion of the layers of the state and the way in which the modern state has been constructed on the basis of practices, relationships, and logics that are colonialist and capitalist in nature can refer to the references cited in the previous section, to Roberts (this volume), or to the recent book by Edwards et al (2023) entitled *Globalization, Privatization, and the State: Contemporary Reform in Post-colonial Contexts*. While this book focuses on the case of Honduras, its insights are relevant to the CALC region more broadly. Additionally, it can be mentioned that a companion book project – *The State and Education in Latin America: Foundations, Fault Lines, and Alternatives* – is under way which continues to move in the directions suggested earlier (Edwards et al, forthcoming).

Contributions and conclusions – or filling some gaps, only to see new ones

As this discussion has indicated, the process of producing the present volume has highlighted issues that warrant additional attention. However, in concluding, it is important to keep in mind the contributions that have been made. Throughout this volume, the chapters have, first, examined various global forces together with local responses and the role that national actors play as they are caught in the middle. Second, the chapters have sought to explicate how the current political, economic, social, and cultural systems work, and with what consequences for education. Chapter 1 showed that analyses of this nature are uncommon in relation to education policy in the CALC region.

In the end, the CALC region is caught in a very difficult position. The present volume has highlighted that it has been, and continues to be, subject to:

- the pressures of the globalized and liberalized global economy;
- geopolitical intervention and subordination, including relationships of neocolonialism;
- authoritarian tendencies, including the repression of constitutional rights and social movements;
- the activism of private philanthropies, corporations, and companies that seek to make inroads into, and to profit from, education;

- outmigration incentivized by economic policies and the lack of decent employment, which, in turn has devastating consequences for communities, families, schools, and students;
- governing logics and relationships of extraction and clientelism; and
- a modern development paradigm premised on ecological exploitation, individual enrichment, and the elimination of alternative (that is, noncapitalist, non-Western) ways of being and knowing.

While there are no easy answers, scholarship can and should contribute by addressing how the region has arrived at this point and what possibly can be done in the future. The work ahead includes not only thinking about how to contest unjust political, social, and economic formations, but also how to address the epistemological and ontological issues and injustices that undergird these more visible structures – for, while they are uncommonly acknowledged, they are intimately intertwined with any and all efforts relating to education and development.

References

Azmanova, A. (2020). *Capitalism on Edge: How Fighting Precarity Can Achieve Radical Change without Crisis or Utopia*. Columbia University Press.

Butler, J. (2009). Performativity, precarity and sexual politics. *Revista de Antropología Iberoamericana*, 4(3), i–xiii. http://www.aibr.org/antropolo gia/04v03/ criticos/040301b.pdf

Cadena, A., Giraut, J., Grosman, N., and Oliveira, O. (2019). *Unlocking the Economic Potential of Central America and the Caribbean*. McKinsey & Company.

Desuelle, D., and Schipke, A. (eds.) (2008). *Central America: Economic Progress and Reforms*. International Monetary Fund.

De Sousa Santos, B. (2007). *Another Knowledge Is Possible: Beyond Northern Epistemologies*. Verso.

Dussel, E. (2000). Europe, modernity, and Eurocentrism. *Nepantla*, 1(3), 465–478.

Edwards Jr., D. B., and Klees, S. (2015). Unpacking participation in development and education governance: a framework of perspectives and practices. *Prospects*, 45(4), 483–499.

Edwards Jr., D. B., Moschetti, M. and Caravaca, A. (2023). *Globalization, Privatization, and the State: Contemporary Reform in Post-colonial Contexts*. Routledge.

Edwards Jr., D. B., Moschetti, M., and Díaz Ríos, C. (eds.) (forthcoming). *The State and Education in Latin America: Foundations, Fault Lines, and Alternatives*. Brill-Sense.

Grosfoguel, R. (2013). The structure of knowledge in Westernized universities: epistemic racism/sexism and the four genocides/epistemicides of the long 16th century. *Human Architecture*, 11(1), 73–90.

Maldonado-Torres, N. (2016). Outline of ten theses on coloniality and decoloniality. *Fondation Frantz Fanon*. http://frantzfanonfoundation-fonda tionfrantzfanon.com/article2360.html

Quijano, A. (2000). Coloniality of power, Eurocentrism, and Latin America. *Nepantla: Views from South*, 1(3), 533–580.

Robinson, W. (2002). Globalisation as a macro-structural-historical framework of analysis: the case of Central America, *New Political Economy*, 7(2), 221–250.

Index